# Contents

| | | |
|---|---|---|
| *Acknowledgements* | | iv |
| *Notes on contributors* | | v |
| *Abbreviations* | | vii |
| | The origins of the First World War | 1 |
| | *Professor Sir F. H. Hinsley* OBE, MA, FBA | |
| 1 | Austria-Hungary | 9 |
| | *Fritz Fellner* | |
| 2 | Germany | 27 |
| | *John C. G. Röhl* | |
| 3 | Serbia | 55 |
| | *Mark Cornwall* | |
| 4 | Russia | 97 |
| | *Keith Neilson* | |
| 5 | France | 121 |
| | *John. F. V. Keiger* | |
| 6 | Belgium | 151 |
| | *Jean Stengers* | |
| 7 | Britain | 175 |
| | *Keith Wilson* | |
| 8 | Japan | 209 |
| | *Ian Nish* | |
| 9 | Ottoman Empire | 229 |
| | *F. A. K. Yasamee* | |
| | *Index* | 269 |

# Acknowledgements

Leeds & Holbeck Building Society was the chief sponsor of the Conference in connection with which the contributions to this volume were produced. I would like to thank Arthur E. Stone, Director and Chief Executive of the Leeds & Holbeck, for his generosity, without which I would not have been able to invite the speakers who came from Europe and North America. The other sponsors were the Royal Historical Society, the Defence Studies Dining Club of the University of Leeds and the School of History. I owe a particular debt to Colonel Alan Roberts, Pro-Chancellor of the University of Leeds, for being so facilitative in this and other respects.

The sessions of the conference were chaired by Professors F. R. Bridge, J. Gooch and P. M. Thody of the University of Leeds, and Dr K. Lerman of the University of North London. I am most grateful to all of them for their participation and expertise. Professor Sir F. H. Hinsley kindly agreed to deliver the keynote address at the conference, and to allow this to become, in effect, the introduction to this book.

Mrs Christine Cascarino worked well beyond the call of duty in preparation of the final text. Finally, it has been a pleasure to work with UCL Press in general, and Steven Gerrard, their commissioning editor, in particular.

# Notes on contributors

*Mark Cornwall* is Lecturer in European History at the University of Dundee. He is the editor of *The last years of Austria-Hungary, 1908–18* and has written articles on twentieth-century nationality problems in Eastern Europe. He is currently completing a study of the collapse of the Habsburg Empire in the First World War.

*Fritz Fellner* is Emeritus Professor of Modern and Contemporary History at the University of Salzburg. Amongst his many publications are *Der Dreibund*; *Schicksaljahre Österreichs: das politische Tagebuch Josef Redlich, 1908–14*; and the forthcoming *Vom Dreibund zum Volkerbund: Studien zur Geschichte der internationalen Beziehungen, 1882–1919*.

*F. H. Hinsley* is former Professor of the History of International Relations at the University of Cambridge. His publications include *Power and the pursuit of peace*; *British foreign policy under Sir Edward Grey* and *British intelligence in the Second World War, volumes 1–4*.

*John F. V. Keiger* is Reader in French History and Politics at the University of Salford. He is the author of *France and the origins of the First World War* and co-editor of 35 volumes of *Europe, 1848–1914* in the series *British documents on foreign affairs*. He is currently completing a biography of Raymond Poincaré.

*Keith Neilson* is Head of Department at the Royal Military College of Canada. He has written many articles and is the author of *Strategy and supply: the Anglo-Russian alliance, 1914–17* and the forthcoming *Britain and the last Tsar: British policy and Russia, 1894–1917*.

*Ian Nish* is Emeritus Professor of International History in the University of London. He has served as President of the British Association for Japanese Studies and the European Association for Japanese Studies. His publications include *Alliance in decline; Japanese foreign policy, 1869–1942* and *The origins of the Russo-Japanese war.*

*John C. G. Röhl* is Professor of European History at the University of Sussex. His many publications include *Germany without Bismarck; 1914: delusion or design?* and *Who ruled in Berlin? The Kaiser and his court and the governance of Germany.* An English translation is in preparation of the first volume of his three volume biography of Wilhelm II.

*Jean Stengers* is Emeritus Professor of Contemporary History at the University of Brussels and a member of the Belgian Royal Academy. He has written extensively on Belgian history and international relations. His books include *Leopold III et le gouvernement: les deus politiques belges de 1940* and *L'action du Roi en Belgique depuis 1831: pouvoir et influence.*

*Keith Wilson* is Reader in International History at the University of Leeds. His publications include *The policy of the Entente; Empire and continent; A study in the history and politics of the Morning Post 1905 + 1926* and *Channel Tunnel visions 1850–1945: the British establishment and the channel tunnel project.*

*Feroz A. K. Yasamee* is Lecturer in the department of Middle Eastern Studies at the University of Manchester. He is the author of several studies on later Ottoman and Balkan history and of a forthcoming book on the subject of Ottoman foreign policy in the late nineteenth century.

# *Abbreviations*

AEB   Brussels, Archives du Ministère des Affaires Etrangères

BD   *British documents on the origins of the war, 1898–1914* (London, 1926–38)

BDOFA   *British documents on foreign affairs* (Bethesda, Maryland, 1989)

BN   Bibliothèque nationale

DD   *Die deutschen Dokumente zum Kriegsausbruch*, (Berlin, 1919)

DDI   *I documenti diplomatici italiani. Quarta seris, 1908–1914* (Rome, 1964)

DDF   *Documents diplomatiques français, 1871–1914 (Paris, 1929–62)*

DDNB   *Diplomaticheski dokumenti po nameseta na Bălgariya v Evropeyskata voyna* (Sofia, 1920)

DSP   *Dokumenti o spolnoj politici Kraljevine Srbije* (Belgrade, 1980)

GD   *Outbreak of the World War: German documents collected by Karl Kautsky* (New York, Oxford, 1924)

IBZI   *Die internationalen Beziehungen im Zeitalter des Imperialismus (Dokumente aus den Archiven der Zarischen und der Provisorischen Regierung)* (Berlin, 1931–36)

MAE   Ministère des Affaires Etrangères

NGBT   *Nihon Gaiko Bunsho* (Tokyo, 1966)

ÖUA   *Österreich-Ungarns Aussenpolitik von der bosnischen Krise 1908 bis zum Kriegsausbruch 1914* (Vienna, 1930)

# European frontiers in 1914

# Changes in Balkan frontiers, 1912 and 1913

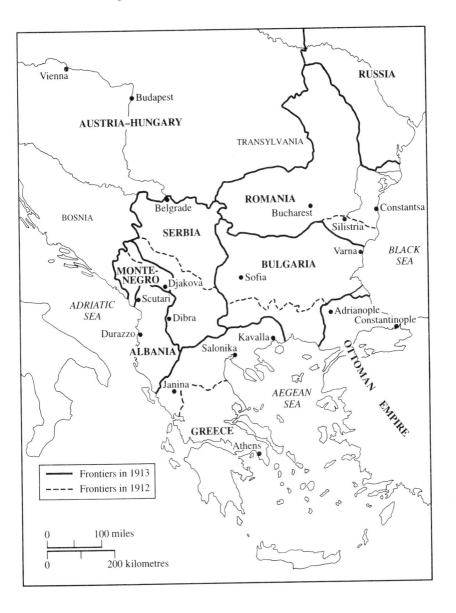

Introduction

# The origins
# of the First World War

Professor Sir F. H. Hinsley, OBE, MA, FBA

In one important respect, if not in all, the First World War is far from being unique among the wars of modern history. Some ten or eleven wars since 1494 have involved all or most of the leading states in the international system. We call it the First World War, rather than the ninth or tenth general war of modern times, only because it coincided with, and helped to complete, processes that were making the international system co-extensive with the physical world.

This alignment was coincidental. The same can hardly be said of the fact that, like every general war since 1494, the war of 1914 broke out when the international system was undergoing a massive shift in the sources and the distribution of international power, and became general on that account. Not all the wars that have taken place in such periods of transition have been general wars; were that the case, and since these periods are normally protracted, it would be impossible to accommodate the many limited wars of the past 500 years – some 200 in number. But there has been no general war outside these transition periods, and all the evidence suggests that the converse is also true. No fundamental change in the configuration of international power has as yet been completed without a major war.

Far more than with limited wars, historians studying the origins of a general war are accordingly confronted with a problem which, though it attends on all or most historical enquiry, especially complicates analysis of the causes of war. They have to try to disentangle impersonal from personal contributions to the outcome and assess their relative weight. This distinction is not identical with some

1

others that are commonly invoked – with the difference between long-term and immediate causes, or between underlying and proximate causes. Both long-term or underlying, and immediate or proximate, causes may also be either impersonal in character or the exercise of choice and will, as may be those other causes that are designated necessary or sufficient. The distinction which demands attention is that between the given conditions with which governments necessarily live and, on the other hand, the effect of the policies they pursue and the actions on which they decide. In the jargon of social scientists it has been dignified as the distinction between the structural or functional and, on the other hand, the intentionalist contribution to developments.

The profusion of terminology for the causes of war tells us that this distinction is difficult to make. So does the tendency of social scientists to be either rigidly structuralist or rigidly intentionalist in their views: this is one way of reducing the difficulty. It may be added that even if an exclusively structuralist or an exclusively intentionalist conclusion were satisfactory for the outbreak of some of history's great wars, it might not be so for others. The given conditions might be different, and the social, cultural and intellectual assumptions underlying the conduct of governments will certainly be changed from one age to another.

Herbert Butterfield, who was perceptive about the changes in historical judgement that come with the passage of time, appealed to them – that is, to historiography – in support of a structuralist approach to the causes of all wars. He used to argue that historians start with a heroic version, seeing only the sins of the enemy and ignoring what he called the structural dilemmas which provoke international clashes, but that, with time, historiography enters the academic phase and they then see that it was the situation which contained the causes of conflict, irrespective of what he called any special wickedness. Perspective teaches historians to sympathize with all the parties; tragedy supplants melodrama. It cannot be said that revisionism in this particular form has yet made much progress for the origins of the Second World War despite – or perhaps because of – A. J. P. Taylor's crude attempt to advance it. As for the origins of the First World War, every conceivable judgement has been put forward, and in that sense revisionism has been actively pursued. But it has still not brought historians out into the clear air in which they obtain the unclouded vista and the uncontested conclusion which Butterfield believed perspective would provide. It has still not persuaded them, in particular, that they should abandon the effort to establish who was responsible.

This is not something to be deplored. Butterfield held that historians should refrain from being judgemental, by which he meant, as is indicated by his emphasis on sin and wickedness, that they should eschew moralizing and self-righteous accusations. We can agree with that. But historical judgement permits, indeed it requires, that we should be concerned to see whether responsibility can properly be established, even if it also calls for the understanding which can distinguish between attaching it to error, visiting it with blame and attributing it to evil. If judgements about the causes of the First World War continue to be less than wholly convincing, this is not because historians still seek to allocate and apportion responsibility for it, but for another reason. It is because they bring an intentionalist approach to the final crisis, and to what they regard as the immediate causes, while viewing the underlying causes in largely structuralist terms, as having been impersonal historical forces or given conditions that lay beyond the control of governments.

The genesis of this approach can be traced back to the Versailles settlement, which set historians to work to uphold or discredit the unprecedented war-guilt clauses. It was perpetuated as governments, with much the same motives, released documents about the final crisis on a unprecedented scale: historians who had lost interest in attacking or defending the war-guilt clauses sifted the growing mass of evidence in the belief that an impartial examination of it must yield an objective and unambiguous conclusion to the debate as to who had been responsible for the outbreak of war. And that this belief has not yet lost its hold is illustrated by James Joll's tolerably recent book, *The origins of the First World War* (1984). He distinguishes between the decisions taken in the final crisis and, on the other hand, general forces which might explain the decisions as part of a broader and inevitable historical process. He fears that the problem of relating this broader process to the decisions is a problem of historiographical and philosophical proportions which may be insoluble. And he suggests that we are therefore driven either to confine ourselves to a study of the short-term reasons for the final decisions, or to resign ourselves to a two-tier account in which we study separately the broader forces that led inevitably to armed conflict, such as industrialization and long-term contradictions in capitalist societies, and, on the other hand, the individual decisions in the final crisis that can alone explain why a particular war broke out in 1914, and alone establish who was responsible for it.

This conclusion echoes an ancient dictum, reiterated most recently by Martin Wight: war is inevitable, though particular wars can be avoided. As a general axiom, this is of dubious value. Applied narrowly to the First World War, it is useful for emphasizing an important point. If the Sarajevo crisis had not precipitated a particular great war, some other crisis would have precipitated a great war at no distant date. This other war would have been essentially the same war as that which in fact broke out, and this other crisis would have been only the occasion for it, as the Sarajevo crisis was only the occasion for the outbreak of war in 1914. Because it was only the occasion, the decisions taken during the crisis reveal how it ended in war, but they do not establish who was responsible for the outcome. They cannot establish this because they were taken when the governments had been overwhelmed by the international situation in which the crisis arose.

This is not to say, however, that the governments had lost control of their decisions. It is sometimes said – and it may sometimes have been true – that states go to war not from rational calculation of their vital interests and their relative war capacity, but from the misperception and paranoia which, accompanying the breakdown of communications and the loss of nerve, carry them into war by accident through an escalating spiral of threat and bluff. This was not the case in 1914. Those who took the decisions did not underestimate the risk of a general war, and they were anxious not solely as to whether war would bring victory or defeat, but also as to what it might portend for the established order, even for civilization. They were not on that account deflected or deterred. But their forebodings ensured that every decision was a deliberate decision, reached after debate and even against opposition.

It is this feature of the crisis that has fuelled the debate as to whether Austria, Germany, Russia, France or Serbia was most culpable, or whether that unenviable distinction should be accorded to more than one of the states, or whether all must share the responsibility. Each decision by one state of course led to the next decisions taken by the others. It may therefore seem reasonable to assume that if one or other of the states had decided otherwise, the outcome would have been different. On this assumption, verdicts as to responsibility will conflict according to whether this, that or another stage of the crisis is seen to have been most fateful. But the assumption is founded on an illusion. The Sarajevo crisis could not be the occasion for a repetition of the Bosnian crisis, or for only a third Balkan war, or for a repetition of the Congress of Berlin, but only for a general war. Before Austria declared war on Serbia, Grey accepted that this step would make a great war inevitable. Bethmann Hollweg later lamented that once the dice had been set rolling, nothing could stop them. They were not regretting that the governments would have, or had had, no choice as to what to decide. They were recognizing that the states would have, or had had, to choose to decide as they did – that at last the chips were down.

But if we would be wise to share their fatalism as to the management of the crisis, we should not adopt it when considering the grounds on which it was based. It was based on the fact that relations between the Great Powers had deteriorated beyond repair by the time the crisis erupted, and the reasons for this deterioration, which constitute the underlying causes of the war, are not illuminated by a deterministic approach. It is true that they sprang from structures and forces that were impersonal in the sense that they were not to be moved or prevented or reversed by human policy or design. But the structures and the forces were not themselves the causes of the international breakdown that produced the war. They were the given conditions which created the problems governments were faced with, constituting a challenge to their statesmanship.

It is easier in some directions than in others to demonstrate the truth of this proposition. Take the belief, less widespread now than it used to be, that the war was the inevitable consequence of the existence of sovereign states. Even Salisbury, the astute 3rd Marquess, once opined that Europe would avoid another great war only if it became a federation. But that was in a moment of foreboding after a particularly disturbing exchange with the Kaiser. He knew, as we know, that unless it were universal in scope, a federation would only replace several states by one state in a continuing system of states; and that there would be no logic in a programme that sought to better the international system by abolishing it. Take the argument, which still has its adherents, that the war was the inevitable result of modern capitalism in its imperialist phase. War was far more frequent and imperialism no less prevalent among pre-capitalist societies than they have been since capitalism was fully developed. The war of 1914 was a war between capitalist societies because the societies were capitalist societies. It was not because they were capitalist societies that there was a war.

It is more difficult to dismiss other structural factors or historical forces as having been no more than part of the context which gave rise to the problems that governments had to deal with. They were more destabilizing, and the problems they created were such that it may seem unrealistic to claim that they were any more soluble by governments than the given conditions associated with them were preventable or reversible. This is particularly the case with the massive change in the criteria and distribution of power that was brought about from the 1870s, and especially after 1890, by the uneven development, as between the different states, of industrialization based increasingly on technology and science.

By 1890 this phenomenal change had shifted the states of western and central Europe decisively away from the rough equality of strength that had prevailed among them since the defeat of Napoleon. From that date the spread of industry and the increase of wealth and population were producing modern states in Russia, the United States and Japan, and promising the end of Europe's insulation from a wider balance of power. On these foundations, at a time when the European structure was beginning to be incorporated into a wider structure but had not yet been wholly incorporated, and when new criteria of state power were establishing themselves to different extents in the leading European states, Germany approached a degree of material primacy in Europe which no power had possessed since 1814 – but did so when her power beyond Europe was negligible and her prospects of enlarging it were rapidly diminishing. It requires no great stretch of the imagination to see that these developments, exerting a powerful impact on the policies of all European powers, generated the mounting international tensions that preceded the outbreak of war. It requires so little imagination, indeed, as to make it tempting to conclude that the developments were themselves the sufficient causes of war.

Did they not make it inevitable that Germany, in its geographical position and with its new-found leading strength, would seem to be contemplating the domination of the continent of Europe, the more so as the decline of the Ottoman Empire was accelerating and the Habsburg Empire was threatened by disorder in the Balkans? Did it not necessarily follow that the other states would seek to defend the balance of power by contracting alliances, and that this would convince Germany that it was being encircled? Should it cause surprise that competing alliances led to arms races and produced that poisoned atmosphere in which people spoke of being in a state of "dry war" or occasionally, even then, of "cold war"? These are persuasive arguments – and all the more so since no comparable shift in international relative power has yet been completed without the resort to war. But they are inadequate because they take no account of the elements of will and design in the choice of policy.

Governments could not prevent nor control the forces which produced the shift. They had to adjust to them. As a means of adjusting to them they no doubt had little choice but to rely on the balance of power, alliances and military build-up – the devices associated with power politics. But far from invariably leading to war, these devices can avert war if used prudentially. What caused the First World War was the fact that the resort to them by other states met with, was indeed precipitated by, wilfulness amounting to paranoia on the part of the men who governed Germany. Self-assertive on account of Germany's power, they resented any check to their assertiveness as a hostile act. Insecure in spite of Germany's power, their suspicion blinded them to the threat they posed to the security of others. And instead of learning from experience as these attitudes led to setbacks, they became more assertive and felt more insecure after every disappointment, and thus were always raising the tests for what would give them satisfaction.

It may well be that they deserve from historians what the governments they confronted could not extend to them: sympathy for their predicament. But sympathy should not exonerate them from responsibility; they were the authors of their predicament, not the victims. Perhaps the best defence of them is to suggest that their conduct in no way differed from that of their predecessors in the use of force to turn leading strength into domination. Their bid was indeed less blatant, and more hesitant, in reflection of the fact that it was made a century after the consolidation of a system of co-operation between

# Chapter One
# *Austria-Hungary*

## Fritz Fellner

In the summer of 1974, in a conference held on the occasion of the 50th anniversary of the outbreak of the First World War, I spoke about the responsibility of the Austrian government for unleashing the war, and explained, in analysing the so-called "Hoyos mission", how readily people in Vienna and Budapest seized on the assassination of the Archduke Franz Ferdinand as a welcome opportunity to set in motion the long-discussed necessity of settling accounts with Serbia. I started by pointing out "that the fact that the controversy in Germany over Fritz Fischer's theses necessitates a critical assessment, at least, of Austro-German co-operation in preparing the war against Serbia, has had no impact on the historically-conscious public in Austria".[1]

Twenty years later this statement is still true. Individual professional researchers in Austria have accepted my arguments about the deliberate unleashing of war against Serbia in full knowledge of the risk that this might start a European war, but the question of responsibility for the crisis of July 1914 has never been the subject of an academic debate in Austria, nor has it been taken up in the public press or been articulated and debated as a problem of Austrian historical consciousness.[2] Since the Anglo-Saxons discovered in the Viennese *fin de siècle* the birthplace of the Modern World,[3] people in Austria have been basking in the rôle of protagonists of progressive art and thought; they are so delighted by Anglo-Saxon interest in Mahler, Wittgenstein, Klimt, Schnitzler and Schönberg that they pass over the fact that the Anglo-Saxons are also aware of other, less "modern" elements in the history of the Habsburg Monarchy in the first decade of the twentieth century, and that the *fin d'empire* is equally well known, investigated and open to question.

Professional historians know the works of Samuel Williamson,[4] James Joll,[5] Zara Steiner,[6] and Norman Stone,[7] but the results of their research have not made an impact on the wider public and the general historical consciousness. All the same, we are greatly indebted to Anglo-Saxon research for insights into the problems of Austro-Hungarian foreign policy and the outbreak of the war; and it was, above all, a British historian, John Leslie, whose work was so tragically ended by his death in 1993, who provided us with the documentation on the ideological and intellectual background to policy in 1914 which reveals to us the political and ideological attitudes from which the fateful decisions of those days emerged.[8] In a contribution to the Festschrift for Othmar Baron von Aretin, Leslie published a memorandum by the Austrian diplomat Leopold Baron von Andrian[9] which, in addition to the memoranda by Count Hoyos that I have edited, must be regarded as a key document for the investigation of the responsibility for the outbreak of the First World War. In his last work, "The antecedents of Austria-Hungary's war aims", published only a few weeks before his death, Leslie assigned a central importance to further extremely informative source materials which provide definitive evidence on "policies and policy-makers in Vienna and Budapest before and during 1914".[10] Over the years Leslie investigated archive materials and private papers with such thoroughness that it can be said that there are few documents he did not know about. Nobody who wishes today to write a history of Austro-Hungarian policy can really say much more than Leslie has produced in his research. Leslie's last work appeared in a series Wiener Beiträge, and has probably not yet received its due appreciation in the Anglo-Saxon world. But any new work on Austria-Hungary's rôle in the crisis of July 1914 must take as its starting point the results of Leslie's new research.

If, in what follows, I paraphrase and present the conclusions of a good deal of Leslie's last two works, this must be seen in the light of what I have just said. I should also like this presentation of the results of Leslie's research to be seen as a tribute to a scholar whose work was cut short all too soon, whose broad concept of an account of Austro-Hungarian war aims and the history of the Polish question in the First World War was not completed, but who, in the fragments he has left behind, and in the many suggestions he made in innumerable private and public historical discussions, has made such a rich contribution to our knowledge of the history of these years. We are all most deeply indebted to him for all that he achieved – even when he was stricken by serious illness – and I should like, in presenting here the results of his research, to offer homage and thanks to John Leslie.

When I investigated the Hoyos mission of 5 July 1914, I pointed out that the unleashing of the war could be attributed in no small part to the activities of younger diplomats in the Viennese foreign office.[11] The cast of mind of the younger generation of diplomats who in July 1914 formulated the anti-Serbian policy of Austria-Hungary – people such as János Count Forgách, Alexander Baron von Musulin and Alexander Count Hoyos – was marked by the dynamic-imperialist principles of the former Imperial and Royal foreign minister, Alois Count Lexa von Aehrenthal. The members of this group, who came from different social (and, above all, national) backgrounds, were held together – and here Leslie takes my suggestion further – by their pious memory of that minister (who had died in February 1912) and by their belief in the necessity of pursuing his long-term programme of Habsburg domination, direct or indirect, of the Balkans. They all belonged to the same generation, they had all joined the diplomatic service around the turn of the century, and after 1906 they had all participated in the formation of Aehrenthal's expansionist Balkan policy, which culminated in the annexation crisis of October 1908. This group included Alexander Baron von Musulin (b. 1869), Alexander Count Hoyos (b. 1875), János Count Forgách, former minister in Belgrade (b. 1875), Friedrich Count Szápary, formerly Aehrenthal's *chef de cabinet* and in the summer of 1914 ambassador in St Petersburg (b. 1869), Otto Count Czernin (b. 1875), Leopold Baron von Andrian-Werburg (b. 1875), Georg Baron von Franckenstein (b. 1878) and Emanuel Urbas (b. 1878). Their mentor Aehrenthal had taught them – so Leslie argues convincingly – that an active foreign policy directed towards expansion was the best cure for the internal stagnation that they all criticized, and would provide that unifying force with which the growing signs of social and national decomposition could be overcome. Now, under Aehrenthal's successor, Leopold Count Berchtold, this "fronde of diplomatic cadets", as Urbas called them in his memoirs,[12] played a much more important rôle than in Aehrenthal's time: at that time, this group had been the executive organ of a programme thought out by their admired mentor; now, under Berchtold, they constituted a kind of "collective decision-making body" which was consulted more and more. During the crisis of July 1914, according to Macchio,[13] this group of leading officials would meet the foreign minister late in the evenings, "when the events of the day would be discussed, the texts of dispatches finalised, and the *mot d'ordre* laid down for the following day . . . The evening conferences were always supposed to provide the final clarifications". Macchio calls Forgách the initiator of Vienna's policy in those days after Sarajevo, and as Forgách certainly had personal animosities against Serbian politicians dating back to his own unhappy time in Belgrade in the critical years before and after the annexation crisis (1907–11), his influence meant a decisive shift in Austro-Hungarian policy from dynamic intention to ruthlessly aggressive action. In his memoirs, Macchio lists, along with Forgách, above all Musulin and Hoyos as the driving forces in the Ballhausplatz,[14] a judgement which is confirmed in Count Lützow's notes and in the unpublished diaries of Josef Maria Baernreither and of Archive-Director Schlitter.[15] In the light of the sources published by Leslie and myself one can define the rôles of these three diplomats in the crisis of July 1914 as follows: Forgách was the planner and theorist of the anti-Serbian policy; Hoyos the instrument for securing the endorsement of the anti-Serbian policy by the German Empire; and Musulin the draftsman who drew up the decisive documents that put the plan and the political conviction into action, namely the ultimatum and the declaration of war.

But the pupils and admirers of Aehrenthal, who were so fascinated by the dynamism of his foreign policy, and above all his Balkan policy, had in their enthusiasm for an active policy of expansion failed to recognize one important characteristic of these: Aehrenthal wanted expansion, but not war; he was ready to go to the brink of war, but he was not willing to plunge into the abyss. In the annexation crisis of 1908 he carried out a *fait accompli* which transferred the decision over war and peace to his opponents; but after this he was prepared to sit down at the negotiating table, at which his acquisition was conceded. His pupils and less able successors in July 1914 were not masters of this deftness of touch in imperialist policy. It was fateful for the Great Power position of Austria-Hungary that the statesman who had initiated the dynamic Balkan policy in 1908 should die of leukaemia in February 1912, because under his successor Berchtold the setting of active aims recommended by Aehrenthal turned into aggressive policy. Moreover, Serbia's successes in the Balkan Wars had strengthened Austrian politicians in their conviction that the monarchy was threatened by this little state, and most diplomats, politicians and publicists of those days were convinced that only the overthrow of Serbia could resolve the tensions and remove the threat.

Certainly, Pan-Serbian propaganda was a threat to the consolidation of the south Slav areas of the Habsburg Monarchy, and Serbia's dynamic foreign policy in the era of the collapse of the Ottoman Empire made this small state a tiresome rival for the expansionist policy of the Ballhausplatz; but it is indeed a testimony to a lack of confidence in the monarchy's own capacity for a constructive internal policy or a coherent foreign policy that the statesmen and diplomats of the great Habsburg state should not be able to conceive of any other counter to the Serbian "danger" than a warlike action aiming at the total annihilation of this small state. Those who did not believe a peaceful solution to Austro-Hungarian–Serbian rivalries to be possible represented the assassination at Sarajevo as proof of the correctness of their attitude, and they believed it to be so. Even before it was certain which circles were behind the deed, people in Vienna were already convinced "that the moment has come to solve the Serbian question".[16] On 30 June the German ambassador, Heinrich von Tschirschky und Bögendorff, had reported to Berlin: "Here I often hear even serious people expressing the wish that Serbia can be sorted out once and for all . . ."[17] And only three days after the assassination, on 1 July 1914, the Hungarian prime minister, Count Istvan Tisza, expressed his anxiety to the Emperor, because he had heard from Count Berchtold of that minister's intention to make the crime of Sarajevo the occasion for a settling of accounts with Serbia.[18] The common finance minister, Ritter von Bilinksi, declared in a conversation he had in March 1917 with the journalist Heinrich Kanner: "We decided on war quite early, that was right at the start".[19] The notes that Leopold Baron von Andrian-Werburg made in December 1918 and early 1919 about the outbreak of the war, and which John Leslie published in the Festschrift for Aretin, confirm yet again the will to war on the part of the Austrian statesmen and military. Andrian's notes start: "*We* started the war, not the Germans and even less the Entente – that I know."[20] "I have the distinct impression", he later adds, "that the war was decided on by that circle of younger talented diplomats who formed Berchtold's political council, who influenced him strongly and who, if they were – as they were in this case – in agreement, decided things. Musulin, the impetuous chatterbox, who, when the prospects were good in the war, used to call himself 'the man who caused the war', Alec Hoyos, Fritz Szápary . . . they made the war. I myself was in lively agreement with the basic idea that only a war could save Austria. As the world situation was then, I am also quite sure that, two or three years later, war for Austria's existence would have been forced on us by Serbia, Romania and Russia, and under conditions which would make a successful defence far more difficult than at that time . . . When the existence of his fatherland is at stake, every patriotic statesman, indeed, every patriot, must go to war."[21]

It is this fateful conviction that a war was inevitable, that a preemptive strike, a *Flucht nach Vorne,* offered the only chance of securing the continued existence of the state, that forms the context that makes the decision for war, for war against Serbia, intelligible and explicable. The conviction was widespread – it was also prevalent in the Anglo-Saxon world *vis-à-vis* colonial peoples – that the superiority of one's own culture and civilization provides not only a moral justification, but also a political obligation, to subdue lesser peoples – here the colonial peoples, there the Balkan peoples. And this belief in a moral right to rule was combined in the younger, cultivated generation – of both educated people and aristocrats – with the peculiarly German interpretation of Social Darwinism, an interpretation which saw in the testing and refining of the nation in the fire of war the criterion for the survival of a people. There was a fear that any yielding, any preparedness to accept a peaceful solution of a conflict, would be regarded as weakness; a belief that one must be "strong" and prove oneself in war. The common council of ministers of 7 July 1914 was full of expressions of these beliefs: Berchtold, the foreign minister, demanded a "radical solution"; Count Stürgkh, the Austrian minister-president, described the situation as "demanding a military conflict with Serbia as an absolute necessity"; the common finance minister Bilinksi declared that "the Serb responds only to

14

force, a diplomatic success would make no impression in Bosnia and would be damaging rather than anything else". Finally, all participants were agreed that the concrete demands on Serbia must be so formulated as to compel their rejection and thereby to "prepare the way for a radical solution by military means".[22] When the Austro-Hungarian minister in Belgrade, Vladimir Baron von Giesl, returning to his post on 7 July after a vacation in France, reported to Berchtold for instructions, he came away with the very decisive order: "However the Serbs react to the ultimatum, you must break off relations and it must come to war."[23] In other words, by 7 July war against Serbia had been decided on in Vienna, and all discussions and further diplomatic steps until the declaration of war on 28 July were merely concerned with the implementation of this decision – consistently with regard to the rejection of the slightest indications of preparedness for a pacific solution, inconsistently with regard to military preparations and the transforming of a will to war into military action.

On 14 July the decisive meeting was held in Vienna, in which procedure against Serbia was finally agreed. A discussion between Count Berchtold and the two minister-presidents, Count Istvan Tisza and Count Stürgkh, fixed the details of the ultimatum, and even though the decision was still kept secret, the reports in the newspapers nevertheless gave rise to misgivings abroad. From 18 July onwards the reports of the British and Russian ambassadors in Vienna reveal anxiety that Austria-Hungary had decided on an action against Serbia that would go beyond the diplomatic-juridical character that had originally been expected. Rather, people in Vienna were discussing solely – as the German ambassador von Tschirschky reported as early as 10 July – "what demands could be made that will make it completely impossible for Serbia to accept".[24] In the council of ministers of 19 July the last obstacles were removed and on 20 July the text of the ultimatum was sent to the Austro-Hungarian minister in Belgrade.

Many and varied reasons have been given – both at the time, in the discussions over the action against Serbia, and subsequently in public debate and in discussions among historians about Austro-Hungarian policy in July 1914 – as to why the Austro-Hungarian government postponed repeatedly the start of the action against Serbia that it had decided on at the beginning of July: the need to avoid upsetting the bringing in of the harvest by mobilization was put forward as a well considered argument; the desire to wait until the French president, who was on a state visit to St Petersburg, had left Russia, in order to hinder any co-ordination of French and Russian policy, may well have been a consideration, but can hardly have been decisive. The weightiest factor was surely that the chief of staff, Franz Conrad von Hoetzendorf, after years of demanding a preventive war against Serbia, now, when he was confronted with the reality of military action (which he was also demanding most decisively at this moment too), had to admit that he was unprepared, and had indeed to beg for at least three weeks' grace in order to take the necessary mobilization measures. It is – if one ignores the resulting tragic consequences – indeed grotesque, how little the state of military preparedness and planning accorded with the warlike howl with which people had been demanding an annihilating blow against Serbia since 30 June. The letter with which Berchtold put the draft declaration of war to the Emperor for signature on 27 July stated explicitly that he, Berchtold, regarded it as "not impossible that the Triple Entente Powers might yet try to achieve a peaceful solution of the conflict unless a clear situation is created by a declaration of war",[25] and the chief of the general staff on the same day declared himself to be in no position to start the war he had been demanding and which had been decided on and planned three weeks previously, for a further fortnight.

The words with which the Austro-Hungarian foreign minister justified the necessity for war to his sovereign are so monstrous as to merit a textual repetition: "not impossible that the Triple Entente Powers might yet try to achieve a peaceful solution of the conflict unless a clear situation is created by a declaration of war". This justification, with which Berchtold presented the declaration of war for signature, should have been sufficient to silence from the start all historical and, indeed, all political, debate about the question of responsibility for the unleashing of the war. However dangerous subversive activity in the South Slav provinces of the Habsburg Monarchy might have been, however hostile Russian politicians might have been towards Austria-Hungary, until July 1914 the will to make war was present only in Austro-Hungarian government circles – the will to make war against Serbia, the desire for a local military action to serve the interests of Austria-Hungary's predominant position (*Vor-*

*rangstellung*) in the Balkans, whether in a defensive sense as a protection against a feared Serbian–Russian threat or, secretly, in an expansionist sense as a first step to the conquest of the Balkans, as Count Forgách stated in private letters and as Count Hoyos hinted in Berlin on 5 July.[26] The will to this third Balkan War dominated the thoughts and actions of Austrian politicians and military men.

But, determined as people were on war with Serbia, they did not want to take the decisive step until they were sure that Germany would grant them military cover. Throughout the discussions of the policy to be adopted towards Serbia in July 1914 the anxiety kept breaking through that Russia might come to the aid of Serbia and that the Habsburg Monarchy – if Germany stood aside – would face a superior enemy in the north, which would jeopardize the planned action in the Balkans. To make sure of this cover from the German Empire was indeed the chief aim of the journey which Count Hoyos made on 5 July to Potsdam. People in Vienna had received reports from journalist circles that the German government expected Austria-Hungary to resolve the Serbian question by war. In a conversation with the German publicist, Viktor Naumann, on 1 July, Hoyos emphasized that "it would be very valuable to us to be assured that we could in the event count on Germany's covering us in the rear",[27] and three days later Forgách noted that "the correspondent of the *Frankfurter Zeitung*, who is known to be a confidant of the German embassy, came to the Press department [and] stated that Herr von Tschirschky received him today and declared emphatically and repeatedly – obviously in the intention that he should repeat his words in the Foreign Ministry – that Germany would support the Monarchy through thick and thin, whatever the latter decided to do against Serbia."[28] Count Hoyos' mission of 5 July brought just this declaration of support. In all the documents concerning the various conversations held on that day by the German Emperor and German statesmen and military men with the Austro-Hungarian ambassador, Count Szögyény-Marich, and with Count Hoyos, one sentence recurs time and again: "The Emperor Franz Joseph can rely on His Majesty's standing loyally at the side of Austria-Hungary in accordance with his alliance obligations and his old friendship."[29] Clearest of all is the information which the Oberquartermaster in the German general staff, Count Bertrab, sent from Berlin on 6 July to Count Moltke, chief of the German general staff: "At His Majesty's command, I report the following to Your Excellency: 'The Austro-Hungarian ambassador has . . . handed in . . . a memorandum and has added that the Emperor of Austria is determined to invade Serbia. His Majesty approved this decision in agreement with the Foreign Office and the War Ministry and has declared himself prepared to give Austria cover if Russia should intervene'."[30]

This document from the German soldier seems to be so important because it destroys the argument that the promises given by the Germans in the conversations were exaggerated by Szögyény or Hoyos. When Szögyény reported on 6 July that in the Emperor Wilhelm's view, "there should be no delay about any action against Serbia, and Russia's attitude will be hostile in any case . . . and should it come to a war between Austria-Hungary and Russia, we could be sure that Germany would stand at our side with her usual alliance loyalty",[31] this representation of the assurances given to Austria-Hungary is fully confirmed by the internal German documents just cited. Two things were clearly stated: Germany had promised it cover for any Austro-Hungarian action against Serbia; and Germany regarded the earliest possible moment as the most opportune. The "blank cheque", as these promises were later termed, had indeed been made out.

In the following days, events in Vienna and Berlin took separate courses, but were apparently co-ordinated by various cross-links. They have so far only been investigated and represented in the literature as leading with a certain inevitability to world war. Certainly, people in Vienna had calculated from the beginning that it might not be possible to localize the war against Serbia; indeed, that if Russia could not be prevented from intervening, a European war might develop – even, some said, a world war. People in Vienna took this risk upon themselves with a certain fatalism; but, on the other hand, given the accumulated assurances of German alliance loyalty and military cover they felt confident in directing their preparations exclusively towards the war against Serbia. Political and, above all, military–strategic attention in Vienna remained focused on the problem of Serbia, even though people in the highest military quarters (not, of course, in the foreign office and other political circles) knew that German strategic planning envisaged no possibility of supporting Austria-Hungary in the event of the expansion of the war, but, on the contrary, envisaged Austro-Hungarian military cover against

Russia.[32] While people in Vienna were preparing – with unintelligible dilatoriness and lack of consistency – to wage the "third Balkan War" to subdue Serbia, people in Berlin were not only thinking about a great war, but also, from the very start, carrying out a well-deliberated and well-prepared concept.

In all the publications about the outbreak of the First World War it has never been brought out clearly that the decision for a great European war must have been taken by the Germans at the very same time as they assured Austria-Hungary that they would, as loyal allies, not only stiffen it, but also guarantee its security. The promise given by the German leaders to Austro-Hungarian statesmen meant that the German leaders should have made use of all diplomatic and dynastic channels at least to delay, if not to prevent, the expansion of the war. The attitudes and policy of Great Britain and of Russia between 14 July (the day on which the decision to send the ultimatum was taken in Vienna) and 31 July (the reference to German aggression on France in the Kaiser's telegram of that day) were directed towards mediation or, to put it more cautiously, towards delay. If the German Empire had wished to protect and support Austria-Hungary's interests, it should have taken up these approaches and dragged them out by skilful tactics, until the Austro-Hungarian armies had had time to carry out the local campaign against Serbia. Admittedly, the Austro-Hungarian leadership proved incapable of making use of the time offered; the period of time that was available to it even after the declaration of war against Serbia. But the fact that a European war occurred instead of the planned local Balkan war was not the fault of the Austrian leadership, and was not attributable to its inability to end the crisis by *faits accomplis* before other powers intervened, thus giving rise to a general European conflagration. This escalation was exclusively the consequence and result of a determined German policy, which did not start to operate only in the last days of July. It has not so far been possible to prove from the documents available just how and when the decision was taken to use the Serbian crisis as the occasion for a preventive war against France and Russia. But it must be the case that immediately after the German Emperor had given the Austro-Hungarian envoys the assurances of his support for the military action against Serbia, the machinery was set in motion in the German Empire that – without regard for the interests of its own ally – was to start this preventive war against the other great powers. Remarkably enough, in the literature about the outbreak of the First World War no attention is paid to the fact that it was a precondition for the efficient – and so often admired – implementation of the offensive military operations against Luxemburg, Belgium and France after 1 August, that the decisions – more than this, the relevant orders for carrying them out – must have been taken at least two weeks beforehand. In other words, while people in Vienna were discussing the sending of the ultimatum, and while, trusting in German cover, they were taking as the basis of their action a mobilization plan that directed the military forces of the monarchy primarily to the Balkans, decisions had already been taken in Berlin based on the assumption that Austria-Hungary would send armies to the Russian front to protect Germany's westward-orientated strategic plans. Instead of the cover, so ceremoniously promised, against a feared Russian intervention in support of Serbia, there appeared a German demand that the Austro-Hungarian monarchy provide Germany with cover against Russia, to enable the German military to undertake the preventive strike against France on which the whole of German strategic planning was based.

As German military planning made no allowance for the politicians but, to a certain degree, forced them to fight the First World War with all its consequences, developments acquired a momentum of their own and in the end went completely out of control. So argues Manfried Rauchensteiner in his latest book, which then continues: "Therein really lies the tragic role of the German Empire in the July crisis: not that it promised Austria-Hungary support and signalled unconditional co-operation, but that, in a parallel action, it at once endowed the threatening war with the dimensions of a world war. What was thought and prepared in Berlin was also essentially different from that localized – and limited – view that was taken in Vienna."[33] However, while he quite rightly recognizes that people in Berlin used the occasion for quite different ends from those that had been imagined in Vienna, Rauchensteiner starts from the German assumption (contemporary but also modern) that the Austro-Hungarian war against Serbia was bound to lead to a great war, and that therefore the German leadership had no choice but to start this great war preventively. But this assumption does not follow inevitably from the course of events. Russia, Great Britain and France did not want war at that time, and were prepared to make concessions to

Austria-Hungary's anti-Serbian policy; the war could have been localized if the German Empire had not deliberately organized its escalation. But it was this very policy that conflicted with Austria-Hungary's interests, and was fundamentally a betrayal of the ally who had been promised support, but from whom, at the very moment when the war became reality, support was withdrawn – indeed, from whom unconditional support for Germany's plans was now demanded. Certainly, people in Vienna had been afraid that the war against Serbia could escalate to a European war, and they were prepared – all the private documents prove this – to take the risk of a world war in almost fatalistic fashion. At the same time, however, they had turned to the German Empire for support precisely in order to keep this risk under control. The German Empire was supposed to prevent the escalation of the war; by its declaration of support it was supposed to deter Russia from coming to the support of Serbia. But the actions of German statesmen and military men, German policy and German military activity, were directly in conflict with the declaration of support that had been given.

The discussion of German policy in the July crisis will have to consider what caused the leaders of Germany to take the Serbian crisis as the occasion for launching a European war: as far as Austria-Hungary's rôle is concerned, it will suffice to confirm that all the decisions taken in Berlin from about the middle of July were taken without regard for the interests of Austria-Hungary, and represented a complete abandonment of the declaration of support that had been given. Germany's decisions were not determined by Austria-Hungary's interest in settling the Serbian question once and for all by force of arms, but by strategic planning for a European war. The Germans made no attempt at all to discuss the compromise proposals offered by Great Britain – and by Russia – but deliberately planned a European war and took the decisions necessary for the implementation of this plan days before the Serbian war had even become a certainty.

The telegram of 31 July in which Wilhelm II informed Franz Joseph of Germany's mobilization is a shocking documentation of disregard for the interests of an ally who had been promised loyal friendship and protection – and it is, moreover, based on completely false premises: "I am prepared, in fulfilment of my alliance obligations, to go to war against Russia and France immediately."[34] For there were no alliance obligations demanding such an action. The alliance stated that in the event of a war between Austria-Hungary and Russia, Germany was to go to the assistance of its alliance partner, but not that war with Russia had to start because Germany's partner had decided to fight a local war; and war with France was not included in the alliance obligations at all. Nevertheless, Wilhelm II's telegram goes even further and makes monstrous demands on Austria-Hungary:

> In this hard struggle it is of the greatest importance that Austria directs her chief force against Russia and does not split it up by a simultaneous offensive against Serbia. This is all the more important as a great part of my army will be tied down by France. In this gigantic struggle on which we are embarking shoulder to shoulder, Serbia plays a quite subordinate role, which demands only the most absolutely necessary defensive measures.

I do not understand why in the discussion about the outbreak of the First World War so little weight has been attached to this document, so monstrous in its wording, in its total disregard for the interests of the alliance partner, and in its complete misrepresentation of the situation. Just consider: the Habsburg Monarchy felt threatened by the small Balkan state; it was decided to make the assassination of the heir the occasion for destroying this threat once and for all; war against Serbia was decided upon, the alliance partner was asked to support this action and to provide cover against Russia to prevent its intervention in favour of the Balkan state – by this, all that was intended essentially was that Germany was to deter Russia from intervening in the Balkan conflict by announcing its support for the Habsburg Monarchy. On 5 July the German leaders gave the Austro-Hungarian envoys this assurance and while people in Vienna were setting in motion – slowly and cautiously – this action against Serbia, relying on German cover, people in Berlin, from the middle of July, were starting preparations for a European war at a moment when the conditions that would make such measures necessary did not exist. And when the preparations were complete and the preventive blow was about to be struck, at the very last moment – for throughout July the Austrian ally had not been informed of the steps

Germany was taking (another fact that has still not been brought out in the history of the July crisis), the Germans turned to the alliance partner and commanded – for a command is what the wording of the German Emperor's telegram amounts to – that Austria-Hungary should abandon that very action.

Consider once more the wording of the German Emperor's telegram: "In this gigantic struggle on which we are embarking shoulder to shoulder, Serbia plays a quite subordinate rôle." Betrayal of an ally's interests has never been more crassly formulated than in this telegram.

The frivolity and arrogance with which Austro-Hungarian statesmen, politicians, military men, publicists and diplomats wished for and decided on war against their small neighbour made them guilty of providing the opportunity that the German military were seeking to wage the preventive war they had been recommending for years. Austria-Hungary bears the responsibility for planning a local third Balkan War against Serbia – the responsibility for the escalation of the conflict into a European war does not lie with Austria-Hungary, it lies in Berlin.

## Notes

1. Fritz Fellner, "Die 'Mission Hoyos'", in *Recueil des travaux aux assises scientifiques internationales: Les grandes puissances et la Serbie à la veille de la première guerre mondiale*, V. Cubrilovic (ed.) (Belgrade, 1976). This original publication of my paper is full of misleading printing mistakes since I was never given the opportunity to proof-read it. Therefore this article is better quoted according to a reprint published under the same title in: *Deutschlands Sonderung von Europa 1862–1945*, Wilhelm Alf (ed.) (Frankfurt-am-Main, 1984), pp. 283–316; here p. 283.
2. Most recently, Manfried Rauchensteiner, *Der Tod des Doppeladlers, Österreich-Ungarn und der Erste Weltkrieg* (Graz, 1993).
3. Carl Schorske, *Fin de siècle Vienna, politics and culture* (New York, 1980).
4. Samuel R. Williamson, *Austria–Hungary and the origins of the First World War* (New York, 1991).
5. James Joll, *The origins of the First World War* (New York, 1984).
6. Zara S. Steiner, *Britain and the origins of the First World War* (London, 1977).

7. Norman Stone, "Moltke-Conrad: relations between the Austro-Hungarian and German General Staff 1909–1914", *Historical Journal* IX, 1966; "Hungary and the crisis of July 1914", *Journal of Contemporary History* I, 1966.

8. John Leslie, "Österreich-Ungarn vor dem Kriegsausbruch. Der Ballhausplatz in Wien im Juli 1914 aus der Sicht eines österreichischen Diplomaten", in *Deutschland und Europa in der Neuzeit. Festschrift für Karl Otmar v. Aretin*, Ralph Melville (ed.) (Stuttgart, 1988) vol. II, pp. 661–84; "The antecedents of Austria-Hungary's war aims. Policies and policy-makers in Vienna and Budapest before and during 1914", *Wiener Beiträge zur Geschichte der Neuzeit* 20, pp. 307–94.

9. Leslie, "Österreich-Ungarn vor dem Kriegsausbruch", pp. 675, 684.

10. Leslie, "The antecedents", *passim*.

11. Fellner, "Die 'Mission Hoyos'", p. 285.

12. Ernest U. Cormons [i.e. Emanuel Urbas], *Schicksale und Schatten. Eine österreichische Autobiographie* (Salzburg, 1951).

13. Karl von Macchio, "Momentbilder aus der Julikrise 1914", *Berliner Monatshefte* 14, pp. 763–88, 1936.

14. Ibid.

15. Heinrich Graf von Lützow, *Im diplomatischen Dienst der k.u.k. Monarchie*, Peter Hohenbalken (ed.) (Munich, 1971), p. 218; Fellner, "Der Krieg in Tagebüchern und Briefen", in *Österreich und der Grosse Krieg 1914–1918*, Klaus Amann (ed.) (Vienna, 1988), pp. 208–9.

16. Franz Conrad von Hötzendorf, *Aus meiner Dienstzeit*, 5 vols (Leipzig, 1921–5), here vol. IV, pp. 33ff.

17. Der dt. Botschafter Tschirschky to Bethmann Hollweg, Vienna, 30 June 1914, quoted in Imanuel Geiss (ed.), *Die Julikrise und der Kriegsausbruch 1914* (Hanover, 1963), vol. I, p. 59.

18. Ibid.

19. Interview by the journalist, Heinrich Kanner. The notes of this interview are kept at the Hoover Institution on War, Revolution and Peace at Stanford, Calif. They were partly published by Robert Kann, *Kaiser Franz Joseph und der Ausbruch des Ersten Weltkriegs* (Vienna, 1971). The quoted statement is given on p. 16.

20. Leslie, "Österreich-Ungarn vor dem Kriesgausbruch", p. 675.

21. Ibid., pp. 680–81.

22. *Österreich-Ungarns Aussenpolitik von der bosnischen Krise 1908 bis zum Kriegsausbruch 1914. Diplomatische Aktenstücke des österreich-isch-ungarischen Ministeriums des Ausseren* (cited below as ÖUA) (Vienna, 1930) vol. VIII. p. 447.

23. Kriegsarchiv Wien Nachlass b/61 (Hubka) Nr. 25. Wenn Kriegsgefahr droht, quoted in Rauchensteiner, *Tod des Doppeladlers* p. 75.

24. Tschirschky to Jagow, 10 July 1914, quoted in Geiss, *Julikrise*, vol. I, p. 144.
25. ÖUA, vol. VIII, no. 10855, p. 811.
26. Fellner, "Die 'Mission Hoyos'", *passim*.
27. ÖUA, vol. VIII, no. 9966, pp. 235–6.
28. ÖUA, vol. VIII, no. 10038, p. 295.
29. Geiss, *Julikrise*, vol. I, nos 27, 28, 31.
30. Ibid., no. 33.
31. Ibid., no. 27.
32. Stone, "Moltke-Conrad".
33. Rauchensteiner, *Tod des Doppeladlers*, p. 80.
34. ÖUA, vol. VIII, no. 11125, pp. 944–5.

## Chapter Two

# Germany

### John C. G. Röhl

*In diesem Kriege, den ich vorbereitet und eingeleitet habe, zur Untätigkeit verdammt zu sein, ist grausam* [It is dreadful to be condemned to inactivity in this war which I prepared and initiated].

> Helmuth von Moltke to Field Marshal Colmar
> Freiherr von der Goltz, 14 June 1915.

Whatever the intentions which underlay it, German policy in the crisis of July 1914 must rank as one of the great disasters of world history. The leaders of arguably the most successful country in Europe, a country bursting with energy, boasting a young and dynamic population and an economy second to none, a country whose army, whose administration, whose scientific and artistic achievements were the envy of the world, took decisions which plunged it and the other powers into a ghastly war in which almost ten million men lost their lives, the old internal and international order was for ever destroyed, and popular hatreds were released which were to poison public life for generations to come.

Given the scale of the disaster, it is hardly surprising that those few men who held power in Berlin in 1914 should afterwards deny responsibility and seek to shift the blame, at least in public, particularly when the punitive peace terms imposed at Versailles were predicated on the guilt of Germany and its allies, and there existed a real possibility of extradition to face trial before an international tribunal. In private, however, we know that some of Germany's "men of

27

1914" were haunted by the realization of what they had done. Theobald von Bethmann Hollweg, the Reich Chancellor, admitted in February 1915 to the editor of the democratic *Berliner Tageblatt*, Theodor Wolff, that Germany bore a share of the responsibility for the outbreak of war, and he went on to confess: "If I were to say that this thought oppressed me, that would be saying too little – the thought does not simply oppress me, I live in it."[1] And Gottlieb von Jagow, Germany's foreign secretary in the crisis, once sat up for much of the night with a woman friend confessing that he was no longer able to sleep because Germany had indeed "wanted the war [*den Krieg gewollt*]" that had gone so disastrously wrong.[2]

Whatever the government might officially claim, and whatever the heavily censored press might write and the public be tricked into believing, any German with inside information on how the war had really begun knew that the responsibility for the catastrophe lay principally not with France, or Russia, or Britain, but with a small handful of men in Vienna and Berlin.[3] Throughout the war and after it, men such as Theodor Wolff, Walther Rathenau and Prince Karl Max von Lichnowsky bitterly accused their own leaders of having caused a war which they held to be "the most complete madness",[4] and in December 1914 the Hamburg shipping magnate, Albert Ballin, told Chancellor von Bethmann Hollweg to his face: "I have spent my entire life building up something which has been of immense value to the German Reich, and then you come along with a couple of others and destroy it all." Ballin rejected all Bethmann's protestations and excuses as fairy tales which he should be ashamed to tell.[5] On the first anniversary of the July crisis, Ballin told Jagow that he, the foreign secretary, "must carry the terrible responsibility for the stage-management [*Inscenierung*] of this war which is costing Germany generations of splendid people and throwing it back 100 years",[6] and in 1916 he refused to meet Jagow on the grounds that he "wanted to have nothing further to do with a man who bore the responsibility for this whole dreadful disaster and for the deaths of so many hundreds of thousands of men".[7]

No one was more appalled by German policy in 1914 than Bethmann Hollweg's predecessor as Chancellor, Bernhard Prince von Bülow. In countless conversations, letters and notes, and later in his memoirs, Bülow recorded his conviction that in July 1914 the fate of Germany and Europe had been in the hands of "a group of four men": Bethmann Hollweg, Jagow, Zimmermann and Wilhelm von Stumm.[8] "Is it not terrible", he exclaimed, "to have to admit that everything that led to the ruination of millions of lives, to such dreadful sacrifice of life and limb, to such unending suffering and the undermining of the well-being of Germany and Europe for so many years to come, was decided by two or three men?"[9] Bülow refused to believe that the Kaiser, the Crown Prince or Moltke had been in favour of war, or that there had been a "military party" at work in Berlin in 1914.[10] In putting the blame on the Chancellor and his two or three leading advisers in the Foreign Office in this way, Bülow was transparently seeking to contrast his own diplomatic *savoir faire* with the lumbering incompetence of his successors, initially perhaps even in the hope of being recalled to the Chancellorship. But it would be wrong to discount his judgement simply on such grounds. For one thing, he made such statements not just to others but also held fast to the view that "we ourselves brought about [this war] through the ultimatum to Serbia (which we either permitted or inspired)" in notebooks intended solely for his personal use.[11] And for another, he continued to insist long after the collapse of the Reich in 1918, when even his hopes of a return to office had evaporated, that it was "through the ineptitude and stupidity of Bethmann and Jagow" that Germany had "blundered into war [*in den Krieg taumelten*]".[12] Even in his memoirs, which he insisted should not be published until after his death, Bülow declared that "the Auswärtiges Amt of 1914 was the incubator in which the monstrous egg of the ultimatum to Serbia was hatched. This is where almost all the terrible mistakes were made through which we came to be involved in war".[13]

From 1914 to his death in 1929, Bülow listed consistently the "errors" he felt the "honest schoolmaster" Bethmann and the "petty-minded Junker", the "third-rate diplomat" Jagow[14] had made in July 1914, as follows:

First, he said, the German leaders should never have issued the Austrians with a blank cheque. If he (Bülow) had been summoned to the Wilhelmstrasse in July 1914, he would have said to Bethmann and Jagow: "You have given [the Austrians] *carte blanche* – do you realize what you have done? If the late Prince Bismarck could appear here before you, his first words would be: 'How could you do such a thing, how could you transform a Germany that was the rider into a Germany that is now being ridden by Austria?'" The more Bülow learned of the promises of support made by Germany to Austria on 5 July 1914, the more incomprehensible, the more terrible he found them. "That fifth of July was a bad day for Germany . . . a day of misfortune. How could Bethmann do such a thing!"

Secondly, Berlin should in Bülow's view have insisted absolutely on seeing the Austrian ultimatum in advance and then, on realizing that the Serbians would not be able to accept it, have insisted on the removal of the unacceptable clause or halted the entire Austrian action. No country, not even the Republic of San Marino, Bülow said, could have accepted the critical clause in the Austrian ultimatum. He failed completely to understand how Bethmann could have risked the lives and well-being of 67 million Germans, how he could have gambled the future of the German Reich, by playing this one unseen card.

Thirdly, Berlin should not have allowed the Austrians to declare the Serbian reply to be unacceptable to them, to break off diplomatic relations and to begin military action; the few points over which Serbia had hesitated should have been submitted for international arbitration to the Hague tribunal, where a compromise could easily have been reached.

Fourthly, Bülow found it incomprehensible that the men in the Wilhelmstrasse should have believed that the Austro-Serbian war could be localized, that they could have imagined that Russia would be able to tolerate an Austrian invasion of Serbia. If the Tsar had attempted to stay out of such a conflict, Bülow declared, he would have risked having his throat cut. Only someone totally inexperienced in the affairs of the world could have believed otherwise. To expect the Tsar to stay neutral in such a conflict was analogous to expecting the Pope to hang a portrait of Martin Luther over his writing desk, Bülow believed.

Fifthly, Berlin should have accepted the proposal for a conference of those powers not immediately involved in the Balkan conflict. "Why did Jagow not want the four powers Germany, Italy, France and England to meet and look for a way out?", Bülow asked in exasperation.

Sixthly, it was idiotic of Germany to be the one to declare war on Russia and France, so placing both Italy and Romania *ex nexu foederis*, rather than allowing France and Russia to put themselves in the wrong. "That was a serious and stupid mistake on the part of Bethmann and Jagow", Bülow declared, and one which no one was able to understand.

Seventhly, Bülow stated, Germany should not have violated Belgian neutrality until Germany's enemies had made themselves guilty of that violation. Bethmann's "scrap of paper" speech had been calamitous and would tarnish Germany's name for ever.

Finally, Bethmann, Jagow and Stumm should never have believed that England would be able to stay neutral in a war between Germany and Austria, and Russia and France. Bethmann's "infamous" conversation of 29 July with Sir Edward Goschen, in which the Chancellor had sought to buy England's neutrality by offering to restore (but not respect) the territorial integrity (but not the sovereignty) of metropolitan (but not colonial) France after the war had displayed "a complete ignorance of diplomatic practice", and had done Germany untold harm. "But they did not want to listen", Bülow declared, "and this nice fellow Bethmann, who has no inkling of the world out there, this miserable Jagow who tries to get by on malicious little tricks and has never even seen France, or Russia, or England, or the Orient, and this Stumm, who is insane, or at least half-mad, they were the ones who brought about this catastrophe."[15]

We shall return to Bülow's catalogue of errors in a moment, but before we explore his eight points any further it is important to note that, though his views were shared by several others, there was a significant group of well-informed observers in Germany who construed the actions of the "men of 1914" in fundamentally different terms. Whereas Bülow, whatever suspicions he might have harboured secretly from time to time, emphasized that Germany's leaders in the crisis had been a bunch of incompetents whose *mistakes* had cumulatively led to world war, the other group was convinced that German statesmen had not miscalculated at all during the crisis. It believed that the provocation of a continental war in what were deemed to be exceptionally favourable circumstances guaranteeing a quick German victory had in fact been the secret *intention* behind German policy. In its view, in other words, the Berlin leaders were guilty less of incompetent management of an international crisis – though they too saw their errors clearly enough – and more of would-be Machiavellian cunning.

Among the most prominent and persistent of these critics who came to believe that the war had been "willed" by Bethmann, Jagow, Stumm and others was the Berlin newspaper editor, Theodor Wolff, on whose fascinating diaries, which were published in two volumes in 1984, I have largely based the foregoing account. In the first months of the war, Wolff thought, as did Bülow, that the Wilhelm-strasse had "slithered into the war without having wanted the war".[16] But by the spring of 1915 he felt sure that Jagow and Stumm in particular had "wanted" and actually "made" the war, at least – as he rather strangely put it – "subconsciously".[17]

Three factors brought the astute newspaperman to this new view. First, he was made suspicious by his own experiences and observations during the July crisis itself. He thought it revealing that Jagow and Stumm should have asked him as early as 20 July to return from holiday to assist the Foreign Office in handling the impending Austro-Serbian crisis, for example; and he also suspected that the "curious" and "highly unpleasant" street demonstrations in Berlin on 25 and 26 July 1914 in favour of an Austrian attack on Serbia had been organized from above.[18]

Secondly, he learned a good deal about German actions in July 1914 from informed critical observers such as Albert Ballin and the diplomats Lichnowsky, Hatzfeldt, Wedel, Hans von Flotow and others, who convinced him not only that there had been a desire on the part of Bethmann, Jagow and Stumm for war, but also that the Kaiser, the Crown Prince and especially Moltke and some other generals had played a significant behind-the-scenes part in German decision-making during that fateful summer.[19] Thus in April 1915 the former ambassador to Italy, Hans von Flotow, informed Wolff that Jagow had reckoned throughout the crisis that war would be the most likely outcome of Germany's "action" in 1914. The military had completely misjudged the ability of France to defend itself, he said, as they had misjudged everything else, and the Auswärtiges Amt had conducted its policy in the ridiculous conviction that the French would not even be able to mobilize their army.[20] And Lichnowsky declared, in answer to a question from Wolff, that "of course" Berlin had pressured the Austrians into adopting a sharp stance towards Serbia. Tschirschky had rushed about Vienna saying that if Austria were to accept the murder of the Archduke without taking dramatic action, it would cease to be a great power. Moltke, Lichnowsky insisted, had certainly wanted war, and so in all probability had war minister von Falkenhayn. Moltke had argued that it would be better to have the war now than in two years' time, and had convinced Bethmann Hollweg of this view.[21] This interpretation was strongly supported in February 1916 by Albert Ballin, who was convinced that the Crown Prince and the other generals similarly had pressed for war. Ballin was even able to report – accurately, as documents were later to reveal – that Tschirschky had advised the Austrians initially to desist from too hostile a policy towards Serbia, but that he had then egged them on after receiving instructions to this effect from Jagow. It was Jagow, too, Ballin asserted, who had prevented Austria from accepting the British proposal for an international conference.[22]

But above all it was the direct admission of responsibility he received from the "men of 1914" themselves that persuaded Wolff that German policy in the July crisis had been motivated by a deliberate will to war against France and Russia. Thus, in February 1915, Wilhelm von Stumm, who was widely regarded as a "pathological evil genius" with a hypnotic hold over Jagow,[23] openly admitted to Wolff that "we were not bluffing" in July 1914. "We were reconciled to the fact that we would have war with Russia . . . If the war had not come now, we would have had it in two years' time under worse conditions . . . No one could have foreseen that militarily not everything would work out as one had believed."[24] More than a year later, when the two men met again, Stumm repeated: "It is not at all true that our policy at that time was mistaken . . . If we had not attacked then [*wenn wir damals nicht losgegangen wären*], Russia would have attacked us two years later, and then it would have been much better armed and would have had the railway lines in Poland – half of Prussia would have been devastated."[25]

A few days after this conversation with Stumm, Wolff had the chance to discuss the intentions behind German policy in July 1914 with Bethmann Hollweg's personal assistant Kurt Riezler, whose pre-war diaries could have told us so much about Bethmann's thinking in the years before 1914 had they not been destroyed, apparently at the height of the Fischer controversy in the 1960s.[26] Riezler too, far from claiming that war had broken out by mistake, justified German policy in the July crisis. Everything that was done then had "had to happen", he told Wolff. Germany could not have refused to support Austria in the Serbia business, otherwise it would have lost its only ally. One did not know with any certainty at the time that Russia and England would fight, he claimed. "Besides, the General Staff declared that the war against France would be over in 40 days. All

33

this played its part. Bethmann calculated the risk very carefully" and from all possible angles, Riezler recalled, and was not pushed or manipulated by others. The only mistake that had been made was that the Austrians had not occupied Belgrade in good time so as to create a *fait accompli*, he argued.[27] In a letter Riezler wrote to Wolff many years after the war, he too admitted that Germany had been motivated in July 1914 largely by fear of Russia's future military development. As events were to show, Germany's generals had underestimated Russia's existing military strength, and over-estimated their own, but German policy in 1914 had nevertheless been based upon those calculations.[28]

One of the most profound insights into the thinking of the Wilhelmstrasse in 1914 was provided by Count Botho von Wedel, who was a *Vortragender Rat* in the Foreign Office from 1910 until his appointment as Tschirschky's successor to the embassy in Vienna in 1916. After discussing the origins of the war with Count Paul von Metternich, Germany's ambassador to England from 1901 to 1912, Wedel told Theodor Wolff in October 1916 that there had been a genuine wish on England's part for an understanding with Germany until the failure of the Haldane mission in February 1912, but that thereafter London had been determined to stand by France and Russia as the only way to prevent Germany from achieving its goal of "*Weltherrschaft*" – world domination. From this moment on, Wedel explained, it was clear to Berlin that Germany's position was bound to deteriorate unless Germany took drastic action to alter the world constellation in its favour, and that there existed only two methods by means of which Germany could effect such a transformation: an alliance with England, or continental war. The first would have entailed a complete revolution, not just in the international system, but in German domestic politics as well, involving above all the abandonment of the "Tirpitz System". Such a revolutionary change was, however, unattainable in practice given the Kaiser's unwavering support for Tirpitz and the readiness of both men to mobilize public opinion behind their chauvinistic course. A Bismarck might have been able to effect such a revolution in German policy, Wedel said; Bethmann did not have that kind of power. This had left only the second method, which was war. In this sense, Wedel argued, the view of those who had claimed, "in July 1914 *and earlier*", that war with Russia was bound to come in any case, and that it would be better for

34

it to come now than in two years' time, when Russia would have completed its strategic railways, had gained increasing support and had even had a certain justification.[29] Wedel's interpretation is particularly interesting, not only because it highlights the Kaiser's and Tirpitz's longer-term responsibility and the rôle of nationalistic opinion in determining the policy that led to war, but also because it raised the question – to which I shall return in a moment – of when the German "decision for war" was taken, since such military and geopolitical considerations obviously had little or nothing to do with Sarajevo.

The more historians have examined the – albeit woefully incomplete – documentary record on the motives of German leaders in July 1914, the clearer it has become that this second group of observers was more correct than was Bülow when it emphasized the intentionality behind German policy. It is now apparent that the "men of 1914" in Berlin were working to an elaborate and cunning scenario, a secret plot designed either to split the Triple Entente wide open in order to effect a massive diplomatic revolution, which would have given Germany control of the European continent and much of the world beyond, or – a better method in the eyes of many to achieve the same goal – to provoke a continental war against France and Russia in what appeared to be exceptionally favourable circumstances. If that war could be brought about through a Balkan crisis, rather than through some incident in western Europe, they calculated, three highly desirable advantages would accrue to the Reich: Austria-Hungary would be in the front line and would not be able to wriggle out of its alliance commitments to Germany; the German population could be manipulated into believing that Germany was being attacked by "barbarous" Russia and so would rally to the defence of the Fatherland; and Britain might be persuaded to stay out of the war, at least for the first crucial six weeks during which France would be defeated by means of a lightning attack through Belgium. As Riezler summarized Bethmann Hollweg's calculations in his much-quoted diary entry for 8 July 1914: "If the war comes from the East, so that we are marching to Austria-Hungary's aid instead of Austria-Hungary to ours, then we have a chance of winning it. If war does not come, if the Tsar does not want it or France, dismayed, counsels peace, then we still [sic] have a chance of manoeuvring the Entente apart over this action."[30]

Exactly when this policy was decided on is still a matter of considerable controversy, though it does seem clear that its main outlines were in place from the very earliest days of the July crisis, if not before.[31] The German publicist, Victor Naumann, left Berlin for Vienna on 26 June 1914 after first visiting the Auswärtiges Amt, where he had a lengthy talk with Wilhelm von Stumm. In a conversation in the Austrian Foreign Ministry with Alexander Count Hoyos on 1 July, Naumann reported that in Berlin, "not only in army and navy circles but also in the Auswärtiges Amt the idea of a preventive war against Russia was regarded with less disfavour than a year ago". The recent improvement in Anglo-German relations had produced a "certainty" in Berlin "that England would not intervene in a European war". France, Naumann argued, "would probably be obliged by financial embarrassments to urge Russia not to go to war, but if a European war should come after all, the Triple Alliance was now strong enough". If the Kaiser, still outraged at the Sarajevo murders, were to be "spoken to in the right way", Naumann continued, "he will give us [Austrians] all assurances and this time go to the length of war . . . The Auswärtiges Amt will do nothing to oppose this state of mind because they regard this as the favourable moment for bringing about the great decision".[32]

There can be no doubt that these views, relayed by Naumann to Vienna on 1 July 1914, reflected accurately the thinking in the Wilhelmstrasse throughout the crisis. As Jagow put it in a private letter to Lichnowsky on 18 July, "Russia is not ready to strike at present [jetzt nicht schlagfertig]. Nor will France or England be anxious for war at the present time. According to all competent observation, Russia will be prepared to fight in a few years. Then she will crush us by the number of her soldiers; then she will have built her Baltic Sea fleet and her strategic railways. Our group, in the meantime, will become ever weaker . . . If we cannot attain localisation [of the Austro-Serbian conflict] and Russia attacks Austria, a casus foederis will then arise; we cannot then abandon Austria . . . I do not desire a preventive war, but if the fight does present itself, we must not run away [dürfen wir nicht kneifen]."[33]

Wolff, too, in his conversations in July 1914 with Jagow and Stumm, was able to observe the almost nonchalant attitude of Germany's statesmen to the prospect of a major European war. Jagow told him openly that "the diplomatic situation was very favourable.

Neither Russia, nor France, nor England wanted war. And if it had to be," he said, smiling, "war was bound to come some day if we let things take their course, and in two years' time Russia would be stronger than she was now".[34] Stumm was even more recklessly care-free in his admissions to Wolff: "Like Jagow, he says that war is un-avoidable in two years' time unless we free ourselves from this situation now . . . But Russia would think twice before it attacked [ehe es losschläge]. In a war with Russia astonishing things would happen: revolution in Finland and in Poland – and we would see that everything had been stolen, even the gunlocks on the rifles, and that they had no ammunition. As far as France was concerned – the rev-elations of Senator Humbert were worth their weight in gold. France could not possibly want war. Such a favourable situation would never again present itself. All we need to do is to keep our nerve and our firm resolve!"[35] Bülow heard later that Stumm had boasted in July 1914, while playing cards: "I will bring the Russians to their knees in three days."[36] And Under Secretary Zimmermann told Count Hoyos during the latter's visit to the Auswärtiges Amt on 5 July 1914 that in his judgement there was a "90 per cent probability of a European war if you take action against Serbia".[37]

Chancellor von Bethmann Hollweg, who admitted to Theodor Wolff on leaving office that he had been convinced of the unavoid-ability of a war against Russia and France ever since January 1914,[38] wholly shared the views of his three top Foreign Office advisers. On 17 July 1914, he found himself having to reprimand the Crown Prince for endangering his very carefully calculated strategy through his public declarations of support for the warmongering Pan-German Colonel Frobenius and the Bismarckian historian Dr Buchholz. In a letter which he sealed in two envelopes, and which has remained undiscovered to this day, Bethmann darkly warned the hotheaded heir to the Hohenzollern throne that his actions in favour of war might well bring about the opposite of what he intended. The Reich Chancellor wrote:

> The international situation, which is at present especially tense by virtue of the Austrian–Serbian antagonism, de-mands an attitude on Germany's part which is both decisive and carefully considered. Even though the further develop-ment of the situation might not be evident today, we never-

theless do have at the present moment an absolute interest, while firmly seconding Austria, in not appearing to the outside world as the ones who, through the whipping up of national passions, are working towards a European conflagration . . . A unified and purposeful policy can only be pursued if it is sure of being free from all interference. In view of the peculiarities of the diplomatic game it is not only possible but even likely that an attempt at interference undertaken without knowledge of the circumstances will unintentionally not only help our opponents, but also help to bring about the very opposite of what it was intended to achieve.[39]

There was little difference between these motives of the leaders in the Wilhelmstrasse and those of the military; so little indeed, that it is tempting to speak of the militarization of German diplomacy. The letters of the head of the Kaiser's Military Cabinet, Moritz Freiherr von Lyncker, who accompanied Wilhelm II on his stage-managed North Sea cruise in July 1914, have just been rediscovered. On 21 July he wrote to his wife: "We – i.e. a small circle of the initiated – are certainly in a state of some excitement about how things will develop. What will Russia's attitude be if now – as is very probable – war breaks out between Austria and Serbia? Our own role has been predetermined."[40] Four days later, on 25 July, Lyncker informed his wife that the Kaiser had at last decided to return to Berlin, and he then continued: "Perhaps this journey home will be for us too the first step towards war. In that case we intend to pass the test with honour. The army is in good shape, at least that is what we believe, and will do its duty. Of course it will be a hard fight with 2 fronts, such as we have never before had on such a scale."[41] And on his return to Berlin, the head of the Navy Cabinet, Admiral von Müller, who belonged to the same small circle of the initiated around the Kaiser, defined German policy on 27 July in much the same terms. The "tendency of our policy", he noted in his diary, was "to keep quiet, letting Russia put itself in the wrong, but then not shying away from war".[42] By this stage in the crisis, as a penetrating new biography of Erich von Falkenhayn makes clear, the Prussian War Minister and the Chief of the General Staff had virtually taken over the determination of German policy from the civilians.[43] How well the generals felt their stratagem had succeeded becomes clear from the diary of the Bavarian General von Wenninger. When he visited the Prussian War Ministry on 31 July, just after the news of Russia's mobilization had arrived, he recorded: "Everywhere beaming faces, people shaking hands in the corridors, congratulating one another on having cleared the ditch." The only fear was that France, which was behaving like a petrified rabbit, might yet find a way of slipping out of the trap.[44]

Most of Bülow's criticisms of the "errors" made by Bethmann Hollweg, Jagow and Stumm would therefore seem to have missed the point.

- Far from giving the Austrians control over German policy by means of the notorious blank cheque, the German leaders were concerned throughout the crisis only that Austria's action against Serbia might not be harsh enough.[45]
- Far from failing to insist on seeing the ultimatum in advance, and ensuring that it would be acceptable to Serbia, the Wilhelmstrasse knew of the salient points of the ultimatum almost as soon as it was drafted on 12 July in Vienna, that is to say, nearly two weeks before it was presented, and it also knew, of course, that it was intended to be unacceptable.[46]
- Far from being willing to accept British proposals for international mediation in the looming conflict, Bethmann Hollweg and Jagow advised the Austrians strongly against accepting them, while at the same time explaining – in the most revealing way – that they were compelled to pass on the British proposals to Vienna lest London (and for that matter the German people) should question Berlin's sincerity in wishing to avoid war. As Bethmann Hollweg tellingly informed his ambassador in Vienna on 27 July 1914: "If we rejected every mediation proposal the whole world would hold us responsible for the conflagration and we would be represented as the ones really driving towards war. That would also make our own position at home an impossible one, where we must *appear as the ones being forced into war*".[47] Only a few days later, on 1 August 1914, Admiral von Müller was able to record triumphantly in his diary: "The mood is brilliant. The government has succeeded very well in making us *appear as the attacked*."[48]

Luigi Albertini, Fritz Fischer and Imanuel Geiss have demonstrated with great clarity and an overwhelming wealth of primary evidence that such were the calculations which underlay German policy in the July crisis, and there is little need for me to go over this well-trodden ground again.[49] What still needs to be investigated is the crucial question of when the decision to go to war was taken. The exciting hypothesis is gaining ground, as previously hidden sources come to light, that the decision was taken not in response to the Sarajevo assassination, but some time before that event took place, as a result of a long process which began in earnest with Germany's perceived humiliation in the Second Morocco Crisis. I cannot develop this theme in any detail here, but perhaps I may conclude with a few brief scenes from a longer play – a sort of *son et lumière*, as it were – which I hope will shed some light on the still obscure process by which Germany's leaders decided for war.

*Scene One*   In a top secret memorandum of 1 April 1912, Admiral von Tirpitz formulated the question which seems to have informed all military–political thinking in Germany from Agadir to Sarajevo. Under the heading *Die Herbeiführung des Kriegsausbruchs* – "Bringing about the outbreak of war" – Tirpitz asked: "Should we speed up [the outbreak of war] or attempt to delay it?"[50]

*Scene Two*   Some eight months later, at the so-called "war council" of 8 December 1912, Kaiser Wilhelm II, as is now well known, demanded that Austria deal forcefully with the Serbs, since Austria would otherwise lose control over the Slavs within the Habsburg Monarchy. If Russia then supported the Serbs, which Russia evidently did, the Kaiser stated, "then war would be unavoidable for us too". But in such a constellation, in which Russia had been provoked into a war with Austria, Germany would be free "to fight the war with full fury against France". The German Fleet, the Kaiser said, "must naturally prepare itself for the war against England". There must be submarine warfare against English ships attempting to land troops in Belgium or France, and mine warfare in the Thames. The Chief of the General Staff von Moltke declared that a European war was indeed unavoidable and the sooner it came the better, but he nevertheless suggested some delay in order "to do more through the press to prepare the popularity of a war against Russia". It was at this point in the deliberations that Tirpitz, answering his own question of the previous April, made the observation "that the Navy would prefer to see the postponement of the great fight for one-and-a-half years", until the Kiel Canal had been widened to accommodate dreadnoughts, and the U-boat installations on Heligoland had been completed.[51]

*Scene Three*  Kaiser Wilhelm II, we learn from the report of the Bavarian military plenipotentiary, "agreed to a postponement [of the war against France, Russia and England] only reluctantly".[52] Two days after the so-called "war council", the monarch spoke in a state of great excitement to the Swiss ambassador, of the unavoidable "racial war, the war of Slavdom against Germandom" in which, it was now clear, the "Anglo-Saxons with whom we are related by common ancestry, religion and civilisatory striving, [would] allow themselves to be used as tools of the Slavs". To prevent a Russian or Slav victory, Wilhelm declared, Austria and Germany would have to prevent the creation of a strong Serbian state. Repeatedly he stated that "if this question . . . cannot be solved by diplomacy, then it will have to be decided by armed force. The solution can be postponed", said the Kaiser, "but the question will arise again in 1 or 2 years. The racial struggle cannot be avoided – perhaps it will not take place now, but it will probably take place in one or two years."[53]

*Scene Four*  The issues discussed at the famous "war council" of 8 December 1912 naturally continued to preoccupy the major participants in the weeks and months thereafter. On 25 January 1913 the Austro-Hungarian naval attaché in Berlin, Hieronymus Count Colloredo-Mannsfeld, had a lengthy conversation with Prince Heinrich, the Kaiser's brother, who as a naval man took a deeply pessimistic view of Germany's immediate prospects and emphasized

> that a war would be extremely unwelcome to Germany at the present moment [*daß Deutschland ein Krieg im gegenwärtigen Augenblicke außerordentlich unerwünscht wäre*]. Although in England there was the same declared dislike of a war, England would, according to the statements it had made to the German government, unconditionally stand by Russia and France and actively intervene if the Triple Alliance as such displayed warlike intentions. The German fleet found itself in a very difficult position with regard to the English fleet. The problem of uniting the German Baltic and

North Sea squadrons prior to the completion of the [Kiel] Canal had been studied most thoroughly ... and one could say that the chances of success were no more than even. The English had at their disposal such superior naval forces which they would all use to defeat the German Fleet in the North Sea that it was really very difficult to say what the German Fleet could do. The Prince's remarks sounded very pessimistic compared to the views one otherwise hears in German Navy circles.[54]

At the same time, however, the Austrian military attaché in Berlin, Freiherr von Bienerth, could report that the Kaiser himself was rather more ambiguous than his brother, and that the General Staff was distinctly against a "postponement" of the war for much longer. Kaiser Wilhelm II was seeking to keep the peace, Bienerth reported in February 1913, but had recently stated that if the Habsburg Monarchy "were to become embroiled in a war, he would unconditionally take part with the force of the entire Reich. His Majesty was [however] of the opinion that it would be difficult to explain the necessity of a war to the German people, for the question of 'Durazzo' would not be understood by them. He thought that one should not go to extreme lengths for the sake of couple of Albanian towns." The military attaché had the feeling that the Kaiser's relatively cautious tone on this occasion was influenced by his wish "to spend the year of his 25th anniversary on the throne [1913] in peace, and then also by his fear of England", especially as long as the Kiel Canal was not ready to take dreadnoughts and the Heligoland fortifications had not been completed. "In the General Staff, on the other hand," Bienerth went on, "it is again being stressed that if there is a further postponement of the great decision [*bei einem weiteren Hinausschieben der grossen Entscheidung*], both France and Russia would be able catch up with equipping their field armies with heavy artillery and high-angle guns."[55]

*Scene Five*   On the very same day when the Kaiser had his agitated and revealing conversation with the Swiss ambassador, 10 December 1912, the Chancellor discussed Germany's future with Field Marshal Baron Colmar von der Goltz, who had recently returned from Turkey and who had submitted a lengthy memorandum to the Kaiser on "the political situation of Europe after the collapse of Turkish rule" in the Balkans. In both the memorandum and in his conversation with Bethmann Hollweg, Goltz emphasized the deteriorating position of Germany in view of the rising Slav tide. "The whole trend of the past few years . . . demonstrates the steady advance of Slav power to the Near Orient" and, Goltz asserted, "the Slavic Balkan nations are the vanguard of Russia". Bethmann thereupon brought the conversation round to the huge Army Bill which he, under pressure from the Kaiser, Moltke and Ludendorff, was thinking of bringing before the Reichstag. The House, he said, would approve any military demand the government chose to put before it. General von der Goltz retorted: "Well in that case let us make our demands." Bethmann: "Yes, but if we make such large demands, we must have the firm intention of striking soon [*dann müßten wir doch die bestimmte Absicht haben, bald zu schlagen*]." Goltz: "Yes of course, then we would be pursuing a proper policy!" Bethmann: "But even Bismarck avoided a preventive war in the year [18]75." To which the Field Marshal replied: "That's right! He could do that after fighting 3 preventive wars for the benefit of the Fatherland!"[56] Bethmann, as we know, decided shortly thereafter to introduce his immense Army Bill in the following spring – evidently in clear realization of the consequences.

*Scene Six*  Other astute observers were not slow to realize the implications of this quantum leap in the arms race in such a tense international situation. On 7 April 1913, Britain's ambassador in St Petersburg, George Buchanan, wrote to the King's private secretary Lord Stamfordham: "I trust that when we get over the Balkan Crisis, we shall not be confronted with a European one; but I confess that I feel very nervous about Franco-German relations. I do not believe that either France or Germany will be able to tolerate the strain of their increased armaments for long: and Delcassé is convinced that Germany intends to precipitate a war whenever she thinks that the chances are in her favour. I only hope that he is mistaken."[57] He was not mistaken.

*Scene Seven*  When King George V visited Berlin in May 1913 to attend the wedding of the German Crown Prince, Kaiser Wilhelm II told Lord Stamfordham that a "racial" war was imminent. "The

43

Slavs have now become unrestful and will want to attack Austria. Germany is bound to stand by her ally – Russia and France will join in and then England . . . I am a man of peace – but now I have to arm my Country so that whoever falls on me I can crush – and crush them I will."[58]

*Scene Eight*   In June 1913 the Austro-Hungarian military attaché in Stockholm and Copenhagen sent a secret report to the Austrian Chief of General Staff, Franz Freiherr Conrad von Hötzendorff, on a revealing conversation he had just had with the German ambassador in Copenhagen, Ulrich Count von Brockdorff-Rantzau. Brockdorff-Rantzau told him that when he had arrived at his post the previous year he had said to the Danish Foreign Minister: "If it comes to a conflict between Germany and England, which I neither expect nor wish for, one of two things will happen, either Germany will win or England . . . If in this conflict Denmark has not been absolutely and actively neutral, using all its strength, then if we win you are finished, of that I can assure you. But if Germany is beaten, and that could only really happen at sea, then we will indemnify ourselves at your and France's expense." As the Austrian military attaché commented in reporting this conversation to Vienna, it certainly demonstrated that the ambassador had received "remarkably clear instructions" from Berlin.[59]

*Scene Nine*   When King Albert of the Belgians visited Potsdam on 6 November 1913, the Kaiser told him that war with France was now "inevitable and imminent", that Germany, given its overwhelming military superiority, was certain of victory, and that in the circumstances Albert would do well to remember his ties with the Hohenzollerns. After dinner Moltke, too, spoke to the hapless Belgian king with undisguised menace. War with France was very close, he warned, and went on: "Nothing will be able to resist the force of the *furor teutonicus* once it has been unleashed. The smaller states would be well advised to side with us, for the consequences of the war will be severe for those that are against us."[60]

*Scene Ten*   In a vitally important – and only recently discovered – memorandum dated 18 May 1914, the Quartermaster-General in the German General Staff, Count von Waldersee, analyzed Germany's longer-term military situation in the most pessimistic terms, despite the successful completion of the massive Army Bill of 1913. In this crucial document, far from believing that Germany was in imminent danger of being attacked, he freely admitted that "for the moment we do not have to entertain the possibility that Germany's enemies will begin a war". However, there were clear signs that the Entente powers were constantly arming themselves and would at some point in the future – "at a time which is probably still several years away" – attack Germany from all sides. "It cannot be said that this year of all years will seem inviting to Germany's enemies to mount an attack on the Triple Alliance," Waldersee argued. "Quite the reverse, for the time being none of the main participants can have an interest in beginning an armed conflict." He recognized that France's army was in turmoil, and had only just begun to acquire heavy artillery. Russia's reorganization of its army, he said, would take "several years" to become fully effective, as would the building of its strategic railways. The Irish question and a number of other domestic troubles would ensure that England had for the time being "absolutely no inclination to participate in a war". Waldersee therefore concluded that "Germany has no reason to expect to be attacked in the near future, but that, on the other hand, it not only has *no* reason whatever to *avoid* a conflict, but also, *more than that*, the chances of achieving a speedy victory in a major European war are *today* still very favourable for Germany and for the Triple Alliance as well. Soon, however, this will no longer be the case." Just as Germany's enemies were gaining in strength, so its allies were weakening. "The German Reich would do well to face this situation with a steady gaze and a clear head, unless it wants to buy peace at any price," Waldersee asserted. "With a speedy offensive we will be able to defeat France, but it will cost time. So long as we can count on an Austrian campaign of a certain strength against Russia, the troops which we can spare for the eastern front would suffice in order to keep Russia's armies out of our country until we can free troops in the West. But the Russian army is getting larger year by year." Though the memorandum stops short of overtly demanding war while victory was certain, and argues instead for yet another increase in the size of the German army, the logic of Waldersee's argument is only too clear: his premise led inexorably to the conclusion that Germany must launch a lightning attack on France and Russia in the very near future, before they became too strong and Austria-Hungary too weak.[61]

*Scene Eleven*  Shortly after Waldersee's memorandum reached Helmuth von Moltke, the Chief of the General Staff – who had been pressing for war for months[62] – asked to speak to Gottlieb von Jagow. On either 19 May or 3 June 1914, the two men travelled back together from Potsdam, where they had attended a dinner to celebrate either the Tsar's or George V's birthday (Jagow was unsure which). Moltke told Jagow that "the prospects of the future oppressed him heavily. In two or three years Russia would have completed its armaments. The military superiority of our enemies would then be so great that he did not know how he could overcome them. Today we would still be a match for them. In his opinion there was no alternative to making preventive war in order to defeat the enemy while we still had a chance of victory. The Chief of the General Staff therefore proposed [the Foreign Secretary recalled] that I should conduct a policy with the aim of provoking a war in the near future."[63]

*Scene Twelve*  On 16 June 1914, twelve days before the assassination of the archducal couple at Sarajevo, Quartermaster-General von Waldersee requested the military plenipotentiaries of the German states to cease all reporting in writing to their respective War Ministries until further notice. The General Staff, he said, would in the next few days send special emissaries to explain this extraordinary step orally to the war ministers in question.[64] Waldersee thereby took the first step in a cover-up which to the present day has confused historians over German intentions in the crisis of July 1914.

And if we fail to understand the true purpose behind German policy, which lies at the very heart of that crisis, we shall fail to understand the behaviour of the other governments who were all, in one way or another, responding to the German challenge.

# Notes

1. Bernd Sösemann (ed.), *Theodor Wolff, Tagebücher 1914–1919. Der Erste Weltkrieg und die Entstehung der Weimarer Republik in Tagebüchern, Leitartikeln und Briefen des Chefredakteurs am "Berliner Tageblatt" und Mitbegründers der "Deutschen Demokratischen Partei"*, 2 vols (Boppard-am-Rhein, 1984), I, no. 88, 9 February 1915, p. 156. Cf. the comments made by Wolff and Bülow on 11 May 1916 about Bethmann Hollweg's feelings of guilt, ibid., I, no. 357, p. 379.
2. Ibid., II, no. 819, 27 November 1918, p. 665.
3. When Theodor Wolff, discussing the origins of the war with the colonial secretary Wilhelm Solf, the playwright Frank Wedekind, and a number of officers and politicians in April 1916, asserted with heavy irony that Germany had been the victim of a treacherous attack in 1914, everyone laughed at the joke. Wolff, *Tagebücher*, I, no. 340, 17 April 1916, p. 370. None of the three German ambassadors accredited to the three Entente capitals believed that those in power there had desired the war. On Lichnowsky, see Prince Lichnowsky, *Heading for the abyss: reminiscences* (London, 1928); Edward F. Willis, *Prince Lichnowsky, ambassador of peace* (Berkeley and Los Angeles, 1942); Harry F. Young, *Prince Lichnowsky and the Great War* (1977); John C. G. Röhl, *1914: delusion or design? The testimony of two German diplomats* (London, 1973). Richard von Kühlmann, Lichnowsky's deputy, confirmed that there was no thought at the London embassy that war might be imminent. Wolff, *Tagebücher*, I, no. 435, 27 September 1916, p. 433. Friedrich Graf von Pourtalès, Imperial Germany's last ambassador to Russia, spoke of the existence of a "war party" in St Petersburg but denied that the Tsar or the Foreign Minister, Sergei Sazonov, had belonged to it; he also denied rumours that the Russian army had begun to mobilize in June 1914, ibid., I, no. 76, 8 January 1915, pp. 147ff., and no. 141, 24 April 1915, p. 209. Pourtalès was said to have warned Berlin in good time against the consequences of its policy and at no time to have believed that Russia would be able to accept the Austrian ultimatum to Serbia, ibid., I, no. 650, 27 November 1917, p. 564. Wilhelm von Schoen, the German ambassador to Paris, wrote an anonymous article to demonstrate France's "innocence" in July 1914, ibid., I, no. 78, 16 January 1915, p. 149. Schoen told Wolff that in the critical days of July 1914, there had been no one present in Paris with whom he could negotiate. Poincaré and Viviani were not yet back from St Petersburg, and the under-secretary of state, Abel Ferry, was full of the best intentions but lacking in experience. He, Schoen, had told Viviani on his return to Paris that "the French were not militarily aggressive, but in all these years they had been politically aggressive, and a

country like Germany could not in the long run tolerate a situation such as the one which had been created for it by France, England and Russia", ibid., I, no. 5, 10 August 1914, pp. 70ff.

4. See Wolff, *Tagebücher*, I, nos 37 and 38, 16 and 17 October 1914, pp. 109ff. and *passim*.

5. Ibid., no. 59, 3 December 1914, p. 128.

6. Albert Ballin to Gottlieb von Jagow, 3 July 1915, quoted in Wolff, *Tagebücher*, I, p. 343.

7. Ibid., no. 297, 31 January 1916, p. 343.

8. Ibid., no. 170, 12 June 1915, p. 234.

9. Ibid., no. 170, 12 June 1915, p. 235; no. 297, 31 January 1916, p. 341; no. 310, 16 February 1916; no. 357, 11 May 1916, p. 380; no. 442, 9 October 1916, p. 442.

10. Ibid., no. 170, 12 June 1915, p. 235; no. 297, 31 January 1916, p. 341; no. 310, 16 February 1916; no. 357, 11 May 1916, p. 380; no. 442, 9 October 1916, p. 442.

11. Gerd Fesser, "Bernhard v. Bülow und der Ausbruch des Ersten Weltkrieges", in *Militärgeschichtliche Mitteilungen* 51(2), pp. 317–24, 1992. The quotation is from Bülow's Merkbuch G for the year 1916, ibid., p. 322.

12. Bernhard Fürst von Bülow to Theodor Wolff, 30 April 1925, Wolff, *Tagebücher*, II, letter no. 42, p. 946. See Bülow's comments of December 1914 to Wolff: *"Böswilligkeit lag . . . nicht vor, es fehlte also wohl an der Geschicklichkeit"*, ibid., I, no. 65, 11 December 1914, p. 134.

13. Bernhard Fürst von Bülow, *Denkwürdigkeiten*, 4 vols (Berlin, 1930–31), I, p. 13. See also ibid., p. 240, where Bülow speaks of the "black high summer of 1914" in which the assassination of the Archduke Franz Ferdinand was "forcibly made the starting point for the most absurd and most dangerous measures".

14. Wolff, *Tagebücher*, I, no. 66, 15 December 1914, pp. 139–41. See also ibid., no. 170, 12 June 1915, pp. 233ff.

15. These eight points bring together the criticisms Bülow made in the following conversations with Theodor Wolff: 11 and 15 December 1914, ibid., I, nos 65 and 66; 12 June 1915, ibid., no.170; 31 January 1916, ibid., no. 297; 9 October 1916, ibid., no. 442. See also Bülow's letter to Wolff of 7 February 1925, ibid., II, pp. 937–9.

16. Ibid., no. 44, 29 October 1914, pp. 114ff. and ibid., no. 59, 3 December 1914, p. 128.

17. Ibid., I, no. 164, 30 May 1915; ibid., no. 170, 12 June 1915, pp. 233ff.; no. 357, 11 May 1916, p. 380; II, no. 891, 10 June 1919, p. 731.

18. Ibid., I, nos 1, 2, 3 and 4, 23–6 July 1914, pp. 61–6. Similarly, Wolff later learnt that the German government had ordered the authorities of

the city of Berlin even before the delivery of the Austrian ultimatum to make preparations for the emergency feeding of the population, ibid., no. 87, 4 February 1915, p. 153.

19. See the conversation of 29 October 1914 between Wolff and Count von Wedel on the respective roles of the military and the "state leadership" in July 1914, ibid., no. 44, pp. 114ff. In July 1917 the Austrian politician Josef Redlich told Wolff that in his view "the two General Staffs had made the war, the governments were then sucked in", ibid., no. 580 26 July 1917, p. 524.

20. Ibid., I, no. 126, 5 April 1915, p. 196.

21. Ibid., I, no. 213, 10 September 1915, pp. 283ff. Lichnowsky informed Wolff some months earlier that, as a matter of certainty, Moltke had been one of the agitators for war, ibid., no. 113, 16 March 1915, p. 181.

22. See ibid., I, no. 310, 16 February 1916, pp. 350ff.

23. See ibid., I, no. 14, 20 August 1914, p. 86; no. 37, 16 October 1914, p. 109; no. 65, 11 December 1914, p. 133.

24. Ibid., I, no. 95, 17 February 1915, pp. 166ff.

25. Ibid., I, no. 354, 7 May 1916, p. 376.

26. See Karl Dietrich Erdmann (ed.), *Kurt Riezler, Tagebücher, Aufsätze und Dokumente* (Göttingen, 1972), pp. 7ff. The controversy over Erdmann's edition of the Riezler diaries culminated in 1983 in a comprehensive critique by Bernd Sösemann in the prestigious *Historische Zeitschrift*. See Bernd Sösemann, "Die Tagebücher Kurt Riezlers. Untersuchungen zu ihrer Echtheit und Edition", *Historische Zeitschrift*, 236, pp. 327–69, 1983; and Erdmann's reply, ibid., pp. 371–402. Important additional information on Riezler and his circle is contained in Fritz Fischer, *Juli 1914: Wir sind nicht hineingeschlittert. Das Staatsgeheimnis um die Riezler-Tagebücher* (Frankfurt, 1983). See also Bernd F. Schulte, *Die Verfälschung der Riezler Tagebücher. Ein Beitrag zur Wissenschaftsgeschichte der 50er und 60er Jahre* (Frankfurt, Berne, New York, 1985). See also Karl-Heinz Janssen's extensive report on the controversy in *Die Zeit*, no. 24, 10 June 1983, pp. 9–11.

27. Wolff, *Tagebücher*, I, no. 365, 24 May 1916, pp. 384ff.

28. Kurt Riezler to Theodor Wolff, 21 March 1930, ibid., II, pp. 950ff.

29. Ibid., I, no. 447, 16 October 1916, p. 446 (my italics).

30. Riezler, *Tagebücher*, p. 184. It should be noted that all the entries in Riezler's diary for the July crisis were subsequently reworked by him, so that no one can be certain how authentic this passage really is. See note 26 above.

31. When Lichnowsky passed through Berlin on his way from his estates in Silesia to his post in London on 5 July, under-secretary of state Arthur Zimmermann told him that the Austrians had decided to take "ener-

getic action" against Serbia, to which Lichnowsky immediately replied that in that case world war was inevitable. The ambassador wished afterwards that he had stayed in Berlin to try to avert the catastrophe. Wolff, *Tagebücher*, I, no. 14, 20 August 1914, pp. 86ff.; and ibid., I, no. 48, 10 November 1914, p. 118.

32. Hoyos' conversation with Victor Naumann, 1 July 1914, Imanuel Geiss (ed.), *Die Julikrise und Kriegsausbruch 1914*, 2 vols (Hanover, 1963–4), I, no. 6.
33. Jagow to Lichnowsky, 18 July 1914, ibid., I, no. 135.
34. Wolff, *Tagebücher*, I, no. 3, 25 July 1914, p. 64.
35. Ibid., no. 3, 25 July 1914, pp. 64ff. Cf. Wolff's conversation with Stumm on 30 August 1914, ibid., no. 24, p. 102.
36. Ibid., no. 357, 11 May 1916, p. 379.
37. Quoted in Adolf Gasser, *Preussischer Militärgeist und Kriegsentfesselung 1914. Drei Studien zum Ausbruch des Ersten Weltkrieges* (Basel, Frankfurt, 1985), p. 112.
38. Wolff, *Tagebücher*, I, no. 578, 19 July 1917, p. 521.
39. "*Die durch den österreichisch–serbischen Gegensatz momentan besonders gespannte auswärtige Situation erfordert ein ebenso bestimmtes wie überlegtes Verhalten Deutschlands. Mag auch die weitere Entwicklung heute noch nicht erkennbar sein, so haben wir doch im gegenwärtigen Augenblick ein absolutes Interesse daran, bei entschiedener Sekundierung Österreichs nach aussen nicht als diejenigen zu erscheinen, die ihrerseits durch Aufpeitschung der nationalen Leidenschaften auf eine europäische Konflagration losarbeiten . . . Eine einheitliche und zielbewusste Politik kann nur geführt werden, wenn sie vor jeder Durchkreuzung sicher ist. Es ist bei der Eigenart des diplomatischen Spiels nicht nur möglich sondern wahrscheinlich, dass eine ohne Kenntnis des Zusammenhangs unternommene Durchkreuzung unabsichtlich nicht nur dem Gegner nützt sondern auch das Gegenteil dessen, was mit ihr beabsichtigt war, fördern hilft.*" Bethmann Hollweg to Crown Prince, 17 July 1914, expedited on 19 July 1914, Geheimes Staatsarchiv Berlin, BPH Rep. 54 Nr. 10/3.
40. Moritz Freiherr von Lyncker to his wife, 21 July 1914, Bundesarchiv-Militärarchiv Freiburg, Lyncker Papers, MSg1/3251.
41. Lyncker to his wife, 25 July 1914, ibid.
42. Müller, diary entry for 27 July 1914, quoted in John C. G. Röhl, "Admiral von Müller and the approach of war, 1911–1914", *Historical Journal*, XII(4), p. 669, 1969. Cf. Walter Görlitz (ed.), *Regierte der Kaiser? Kriegstagebücher, Aufzeichnungen und Briefe des Chefs des Marine-Kabinetts Admiral Georg Alexander von Müller* (Göttingen, 1959), pp. 35ff., where this passage is printed in an amended form.
43. See Holger Afflerbach, *Falkenhayn. Politisches Denken und Handeln im*

*Kaiserreich.* Beiträge zur Militärgeschichte, 42 (Munich, 1994), pp. 147–71. Among several new sources, Afflerbach was able to use extracts from the diaries of War Minister von Falkenhayn covering the final days of the July Crisis.

44. Wenninger's diary entry for 31 July 1914, printed in Bernd-Felix Schulte, "Neue Dokumente zu Kriegsausbruch und Kriegsverlauf 1914", *Militärgeschichtliche Mitteilungen* 25, 1979, p. 140.

45. Franz Freiherr von Haymerle, secretary of legation at the Austro-Hungarian embassy in Berlin, who had accompanied Count Hoyos on his visit to the Auswärtiges Amt on 5 July, wrote to the latter three days later: "Everyone here in the Auswärtiges Amt pressed us to engage in an action. The mood towards us is magnificent so long as we do go to war [*losgehen*], otherwise they will give us up as hopeless, I am almost tempted to say." Quoted in Manfried Rauchensteiner, *Der Tod des Doppeladlers. Österreich-Ungarn und der Erste Weltkrieg* (Graz, Vienna, Cologne, 1993), p. 75.

46. The Austrian envoy, Wladimir Freiherr von Giesl, was in Vienna at the time of the Council of Ministers of 7 July 1914, and was instructed by the Austro-Hungarian foreign minister, Count Berchtold, on that same day: "However the Serbs react – you must break off relations and leave [Belgrade]; this must lead to war." Quoted in Rauchensteiner, *Tod des Doppeladlers*, p. 75.

47. Szögyény to Berchtold, 27 July 1914, Geiss, *Julikrise und Kriegsausbruch*, II, no. 479; Bethmann Hollweg to Tschirschky, 27 July 1914, ibid., no. 503 (the italics are mine).

48. Müller, diary entry for 1 August 1914, quoted in Röhl, "Admiral von Müller", p. 670 (my italics). See Görlitz, *Regierte der Kaiser?*, p. 38, where this passage has been altered to read: "In both speeches the completely justified claim is made that we are the attacked." See also Hartmut Pogge von Strandmann, "Warum die Deutschen den Krieg wollten", in *Die Zeit*, no. 10, 4 March 1988, p. 40.

49. See Luigi Albertini, *The origins of the war of 1914*, 3 vols (London, 1952–7). The clearest account by Fischer of German policy in July 1914 is to be found in his *Krieg der Illusionen. Die deutsche Politik von 1911 bis 1914* (Düsseldorf, 1969), pp. 682–738. Fischer bases his chapter largely on the outstanding two-volume documentation *Julikrise und Kriegsausbruch 1914* prepared by Imanuel Geiss.

50. "Die Herbeiführung des Kriegsausbruchs. Sollen wir ihn beschleunigt herbeiführen oder zu verzögern suchen?" Tirpitz, memorandum of 1 April 1912, "Ganz geheim. Von Hand zu Hand", draft by Capelle, BA-MA RM5/v 1608, folio 47.

51. Admiral von Müller, diary entry for 8 December 1912, quoted in Röhl, "Admiral von Müller", pp. 661f. The latest evidence on the so-called

"war council" is discussed at some length in John C. G. Röhl, *The Kaiser and his court. Wilhelm II and the government of Germany* (Cambridge, 1994), pp. 162–89. The question of the completion of the widening of the Kiel Canal has not received the attention that it perhaps deserves. As early as October 1911, Bethmann Hollweg asked Tirpitz "as a matter of the greatest urgency . . . how far our chances in such a war [against England] would be dependent on the completion of the Canal and the installations on Heligoland". Bethmann Hollweg to Tirpitz, 4 October 1911, Bundesarchiv-Militärarchiv Freiburg, RM3/v9. Tirpitz replied that the navy was certainly not yet ready for war with England, and that although its chances would indeed be somewhat improved by the completion of the Kiel Canal and the Heligoland installations, this would not be to any significant degree. The key factor was and would remain the respective number of ships in each fleet; the importance of the canal and of Heligoland should not, he said, be overestimated. Tirpitz to Bethmann Hollweg, 7 October 1911, BA-MA RM3/v9. The Chancellor received very much the same advice from the Admiralty Staff. See Heeringen to Bethmann Hollweg, 7 October 1911, ibid. Admiral von Holtzendorff, however, placed greater emphasis on the importance of completing the widening of the Kiel Canal, though he too saw Germany's main weakness *vis-à-vis* England in the respective sizes of the two fleets. In a memorandum of 25 October 1911 he stressed the need for Germany to avoid war with England, whatever domestic or foreign policy factors might speak in favour of such a war, until it was ready to confront England at sea. "We must not accept the consequences of a provocation until such time as the Fleet is . . . fully ready for war and qualitatively the equal of the enemy." Such a time would not come until the German High Seas Fleet consisted entirely of modern ships-of-the-line and cruisers, and until the Kiel Canal was ready for such ships. Since the introduction of a large new Navy Bill would probably lead to war with England, Germany should wait with such a step at least until it was ready to accept a war knowing that its Navy would be able to inflict serious damage on the enemy Fleet. Holtzendorff argued that "the autumn of 1914 should be regarded as the right time" to introduce a new large Navy Bill and accept whatever consequences ensued, since Germany's Navy would then be on a better footing and the Kiel Canal would have been completed. Holtzendorff to Bethmann Hollweg, 25 October 1911, BA-MA RM3/v9. The widening works were indeed completed in the summer of 1914. On 3 July 1914 the head of the Admiralty Staff asked whether the Kiel Canal was now ready to take dreadnought class ships, and when the first such sailing was to take place. On 9 July 1914 Admiral von Capelle wrote to the State Secretary of the Interior informing him that "from the military point of view it was of the utmost importance for a ship of the dreadnought class to sail through the Kaiser Wilhelm Canal forthwith", and on 25 July 1914 HMS *Kaiserin* passed through the Canal. Admiralty Staff to Reich Navy Office, 3 July 1914; Capelle to Delbrück, 9 July 1914; der Marinekommissar für den Kaiser-Wilhelm-Kanal, memorandum of 25 July 1914, BA-MA RM5.

52. Wenninger's report of 15 December 1912, quoted in Röhl, "Admiral von Müller", p. 663.

53. Alfred de Claparède, report of 10 December 1912, quoted in Terence F. Cole, "German decision-making on the eve of the First World War. The records of the Swiss embassy in Berlin", in *Der Ort Kaiser Wilhelms II. in der deutschen Geschichte,* John C. G. Röhl (ed.), (Munich, 1991), pp. 62f.

54. Captain Hieronymus Count Colloredo-Mannsfeld to Conrad von Hötzendorff, 26 January 1913, Kriegsarchiv Vienna.

55. Bienerth to Conrad von Hötzendorff, 20 (?) February 1913, Kriegsarchiv Vienna.

56. Memorandum of a conversation between Bethmann Hollweg and Field Marshal Baron Colmar von der Goltz, 10 December 1912, printed in Bernd-Felix Schulte, *Vor dem Kriegsausbruch 1914. Deutschland, die Türkei und der Balkan* (Düsseldorf, 1980), p. 156. See Röhl, *Kaiser and his court,* pp. 188f.

57. George W. Buchanan to Lord Stamfordham, 7 April 1913, Royal Archives Windsor, Geo V P284A/8.

58. Record of a conversation between the German Emperor and Lord Stamfordham at Berlin, 25 May 1913, Royal Archives Windsor, Geo V M450/18.

59. Austro-Hungarian Military Attaché in Stockholm and Copenhagen to Conrad von Hötzendorff, 14 June 1913, Kriegsarchiv Vienna.

60. Jean Stengers, "Guillaume II et le Roi Albert à Postdam en novembre 1913", *Bulletin de la Classe des Lettres et des Sciences Morales et Politiques,* 7(12), pp. 234ff., 1993.

61. Count Georg von Waldersee, Denkschrift über Deutschlands militärische Lage Mai 1914, Bundesarchiv-Militärisches Zwischenarchiv Potsdam, Kriegsgeschichtliche Forschungsanstalt des Heeres, W10/50279, No. 94. My sincere thanks are due to my doctoral student Annika Mombauer, who discovered the memorandum in Potsdam shortly before it was moved to the Bundesarchiv-Militärarchiv in Freiburg. Ms Mombauer is working on a history of the German General Staff based on the files of the Kriegsgeschichtliche Forschungsanstalt, which were among the 40 tons of German military records returned to the GDR by the Soviet Union in 1988.

62. The Bavarian envoy to Berlin, Count Lerchenfeld, reported on 31 July

1914 that "several months ago the Chief of the General Staff Herr von Moltke expressed the view that the time [for war] was now as favourable as it would ever be in the foreseeable future." He gave as his reasons the superiority of German heavy artillery and the absence of howitzers in the Russian and French armies, together with the chaos in the French army resulting from the introduction of three-year military service. Lerchenfeld, reports of 31 July 1914, Geiss, *Julikrise und Kriegsausbruch*, II, nos. 916 and 918.

63. Quoted in Egmont Zechlin, "Motive und Taktik der Reichsleitung 1914", *Der Monat*, vol. 209, February 1966.
64. General von Wenninger to War Minister of Bavaria, 16 June 1914, Bayer. Hauptstaatsarchiv München, Abt. 4, MKr. 41.

Chapter Three
# *Serbia*

## Mark Cornwall

Although the Archduke Franz Ferdinand and his wife were dead by 11.30am on 28 June 1914, news of the murders at Sarajevo did not reach Belgrade until the late afternoon. For many Serbians, accustomed to commemorating *Vidovdan* as the date when their medieval Empire had been crushed by the Turks at the battle of Kosovo, the day in 1914 was for the first time one of unusual celebration in view of Serbia's "recovery" the previous year of extensive territory to the south, including the region of Kosovo. *Pijemont*, the extreme nationalist organ of the underground society *Ujedinjenje ili Smrt* (Union or Death), rejoiced on 28 June with an ominous prediction: "Serbia celebrates *Vidovdan* today as the victory of Serb national consciousness which has preserved the memory of Kosovo and which in the future must conquer in Bosnia just as it conquered in Macedonia."[1]

In Belgrade the day had begun with a solemn mass, at which the Serbian Orthodox Metropolitan Dimitrije officiated, and continued with patriotic processions through the city. In the rest of Serbia, swelled in numbers by visitors from as far away as Dalmatia, special festivities were organized for this new "Serbian Easter",[2] most notably on Kosovo plain itself where a series of horse races were attended by some members of the government. Into this atmosphere came the news from Sarajevo. General Panta Draškić, adjutant to Crown Prince Alexander, confided to his diary: "the most joyous *Vidovdan* in the morning was transformed into the most unpleasant in the afternoon".[3] While the general public in Belgrade were greatly surprised but otherwise rather indifferent to the murders, most members of the government – notwithstanding their comments made in hindsight – grasped at the time at least the possibly dangerous repercussions of the event.[4] They only felt calmer on learning that the assassins were Serbs from Bosnia and citizens of Austria-Hungary: it seemed possible, as Dušan Stefanović, Minister of War, assured an anxious Stojan Protić, Minister of the Interior, that the murders would be treated as a domestic incident within the Habsburg Empire and were certainly not the excuse for a war with Serbia.[5]

This may have been the initial reaction also of Nikola Pašić, Serbia's Prime Minister and Foreign Minister, who on the afternoon of *Vidovdan* was on a train bound for Kosovo. Although he learnt something of the murders at Lapovo near Kragujevac, he remained customarily calm and continued his journey southwards to complete engagements linked to the Kosovo festivities. On 29 June he appears to have made a speech in Skopje in which he warned that certain political circles might try to use the "regrettable incident" of the murders against Serbia, but that the country would know how to defend itself.[6]

In order to understand Pašić's attitude during the July crisis (a task made easier by the publication of the official Serbian documents in 1980)[7] it is necessary to set his behaviour in some context. First, Pašić was shocked but also embarrassed by the Sarajevo murders. In early June he had already learnt that two students, bearing arms and travelling from Belgrade to Sarajevo, had been assisted in crossing into Bosnia by Serbian frontier officials. Pašić undoubtedly was ignorant of the students' exact purpose, but was not unaware of rumours that the Archduke's life might be in danger.[8] Therefore, after discussing the matter with colleagues, he and Protić acted to investigate the incident and prevent its recurrence.[9]

These facts have been confirmed through meticulous research by Vladimir Dedijer. In the expanded Serbo-Croat edition of his work on Sarajevo (1978), Dedijer published a new letter from Protić to Pašić of 15 June. In it Protić warned that although arms smuggling had been proceeding without the Cabinet's approval, it was they who would bear all responsibility if the activity became public knowledge; Pašić agreed, minuting on this letter that such "crossings" ought to be prevented "for they are very dangerous for us".[10] Since it was also clear that the Serbian frontier officials were acting on instructions from Colonel Dragutin Dimitrijević ("Apis"), either in his rôle as head of Serbian Military Intelligence or as leader of *Ujedinjenje ili Smrt* (also known as *Crna Ruka* – The Black Hand), Pašić sometime in late June ordered the Minister of War to open an investigation into Apis's activities.[11] Thus, before 28 June Serbia had already begun its own minor inquiry into some of the threads which led to the Sarajevo crime. Pašić and perhaps Protić in particular, were well aware before Sarajevo that Apis's revolutionary agitation in Bosnia "could provoke a war between Serbia and Austria-Hungary, which in the present circumstances would be very dangerous with logical [*neophodnih*] consequences".[12] The reality of Sarajevo naturally left both ministers in an unenviable position: they entered the July crisis fully conscious from events in the preceding weeks that "official Serbia" was somehow implicated in the murders.

The second, broader context for Pašić's behaviour is Serbia's general domestic and foreign situation. Pašić in June 1914 had just emerged, relatively unscathed, from a major domestic crisis.[13] This involved not simply a political power struggle through which the parliamentary opposition, by exploiting Pašić's small majority in the *Skupština*, obstructed parliamentary business with a view to bringing down the government. It was also the climax of a battle, pursued since the accession of King Petar Karadjordjević in 1903, over the degree of military influence within the Serbian state. A group of officers, loosely headed by Apis, surfaced from the Balkan Wars of 1912–13 with a new confidence in Serbia's "Yugoslav" mission and in the army's vital rôle in policy-making. By April 1914 civilian–military horns were locked over the issue of who would control Serbia's new territories (the "Priority Question") and Apis by May was discussing with some of the political opposition the idea of a mini-*putsch* to topple Pašić. This came to nothing, partly because Apis's radical society *Crna Ruka* was actually far weaker and more unco-ordinated than the publicity surrounding it would suggest. It was also the case that Pašić retained support for his policies of consolidation at home and caution abroad from vital quarters: in particular from the Russian minister, Nikolai Hartwig, who in May and June 1914 used his influence to keep Pašić in office; but also from Crown Prince Alexander, who was now inclining to side with Pašić against Apis's mysterious network of contacts. As for King Petar – old, ill and rarely seen in public – his gratitude to the regicides of 1903 (including Apis) was undoubtedly tempered by his experiences of the civilian–military struggle in 1914; when he sent his good friend Živojin Balugðić (the Serbian minister in Athens) to mediate between Pašić and *Crna Ruka*, one of the latter's officers struck and abused Balugðić while another told him that the King's head would roll through the streets of Belgrade before any such reconciliation came about.[14] On 24 June it was suddenly announced that King Petar was temporarily retiring from state affairs for reasons of "ill-health" and handing over his powers to Crown Prince Alexander as Regent. At the same time, new elections were scheduled for 14 August. For Pašić, therefore, the July crisis was to take place during a crucial electoral campaign; while he might hope as a result of it to eliminate Apis and other rivals, he was also bound to play the nationalist card when electioneering and could never afford to have his own patriotism called into question. It was a stance at home which could easily fall out of step with the conciliatory language he would use towards Austria-Hungary.

Pašić at the time of Sarajevo had been cultivating good relations with the Habsburg Empire. Most observers agreed that such a policy was bearing fruit. They witnessed, for example, how officials from Vienna were now present in Belgrade conducting negotiations to transfer control of Serbia's railways to the Serbians.[15] The interruption of these carefully nurtured talks by the Sarajevo murders was a matter of despair for Jovan Jovanović, the level-headed Serbian minister in Vienna; despite his alleged links to *Crna Ruka*, Jovanović undoubtedly agreed with Pašić that Serbia needed a period of reconciliation with Austria-Hungary.[16] For although both Jovanović and Pašić shared the Yugoslav aspirations of men such as Apis, they differed from him in tactics. The lesson which Pašić drew from the Balkan Wars was that Serbia needed a long period of peace – perhaps a generation or more – in order to consolidate its territorial gains before completing the process of Yugoslav unification. Although he himself continued to cultivate southern Slav contacts in Croatia and Bosnia, he persistently advised patience for the moment.[17] The fact was that Serbia had bought its expansion at a heavy cost of a tenth of its mobilized forces and, in the words of one Serbian historian, "the whole nation was in mourning". The wars had not only swallowed up 370 million dinars (three times the budget for 1912), but had also left the army in a wretched state, with guns in disrepair, uniforms worn-out and a huge shortage of ammunition.[18] Although Russia had promised military aid during Pašić's visit to St Petersburg in February 1914, by June nothing had arrived and only on 18 June had the *Skupština* voted an extraordinary credit of 123 million dinars to re-equip the army. Dušan Stefanović, the Minister of War, envisaged a ten-year programme as being necessary to rebuild the armed forces.[19]

In this situation Pašić was bound to act cautiously towards Austria-Hungary. In case of conflict with the latter he could only really expect that Romania or his Greek ally might act if Bulgaria or Turkey moved to violate the Bucharest settlement of August 1913. As for Montenegro, despite secret talks from January 1914 between Belgrade and Cetinje over a projected union of the two kingdoms, Pašić knew that King Nikita remained a thoroughly duplicitous associate, far more interested in securing northern Albania than in advancing south Slav unity.[20] And even Russia, in view of its military weaknesses at that time and past behaviour in 1909 and 1913, could not be wholly relied upon to lend armed support to Serbia in case of an Austrian attack. It is difficult to share the view of Pašić's most recent Serbian biographer, that from February 1914 he was firmly convinced of Russian help in such an eventuality; on the contrary, he and some of his Serbian diplomats seem to have sensed Russian hesitancy, an uncertainty which was reinforced by the absence of Russian military supplies and which was not, in fact, resolved until after 25 July.[21]

It could be argued that however Serbia behaved in the three weeks after Sarajevo, it could not have avoided the Austrian ultimatum of 23 July. Since Vienna was convinced immediately of Belgrade's involvement in the conspiracy, only by pre-empting Austrian demands and opening itself fully to a meticulous Austrian inquiry in the first days of the crisis, might Serbia have extracted itself from a more serious confrontation. Not surprisingly, Pašić could never follow such a path of subservience, a violation of Serbia's sovereignty. It would call forth a strong nationalist reaction (from the army if not the weakened *Crna Ruka*) and show immediately that "official Serbia" was indeed already compromised by Apis's activities. Pašić could, it is true, quickly have launched his own inquiry into Serbia's "possible involvement". On 30 June, Zimmermann hinted as much to the Serbian *chargé d'affaires* in Berlin (who did not inform Pašić);[22] and, as we shall see, the same day the Austrian *chargé* in Belgrade made a more direct suggestion at the Serbian foreign ministry. Pašić's failure to follow this up on any major scale – a particular criticism by Luigi Albertini[23] – is more understandable if we accept, first, that an official secret inquiry into Apis was already proceeding; and secondly, that "official Serbia" from the start of the crisis was trying to preserve a detached stance, treating Sarajevo primarily as a domestic problem of Austria-Hungary.

For example, on the evening of 28 June Belgrade duly showed the correct respect. Protić abruptly curtailed the *Vidovdan* festivities at 10 pm, court mourning was ordered for a week, and a flood of official condolences were despatched to Vienna.[24] The official government line was then set out in the newspaper *Samouprava* the next morning: the leading article expressed its sympathy and horror at the murders committed by some "mentally unbalanced youths" who had not realized the crime's significance. But the article also hinted that Belgrade was anxious as to the possible repercussions for Serbia and Austro-Serbian relations at a time when they had seemed to be improving.[25] Pašić and Protić clearly hoped in the weeks after Sarajevo that, through a conciliatory yet not wholly submissive stance, they could ward off an Austro-Serbian confrontation.

This policy may have received the blessing of Hartwig who, like Pašić, was conscious of Serbia's military weakness.[26] However, it is worth emphasizing, particularly when considering Serbia's relationship to Russia, that there is no evidence that Pašić needed Hartwig's approval for his policy after Sarajevo. The myth (believed, for example, by the Emperor Franz Joseph as well as the ill-informed French minister in Belgrade, and encouraged by Hartwig himself) that the latter was "master at Belgrade and Pašić does nothing without consulting him", was always at variance with the reality of obstinate Serbian independence.[27] Hartwig was indeed Serbia's "incomparable friend", as was to be shown in the unique funeral he was accorded on 14 July.[28] But Austria and its minister Baron Wladimir Giesl misinterpreted this in 1914 and during the July crisis, as total Serbian subservience to Russia. In fact, although Pašić returned to Belgrade around 30 June, he did not turn to St Petersburg for advice until 3 July. Miroslav Spalajković, the Serbian minister on the Neva, replied on the 4th that Sazonov did not feel that Serbia should worry too much about Austrian accusations (which would not be believed in the rest of Europe), but it should restrain itself from any hasty step which might exacerbate tensions.[29] It was advice repeated by Sazonov via Hartwig a few days later, but it only confirmed for Pašić a course which had been adopted automatically a week earlier.[30]

Nevertheless, the words were comforting. They were backed up by Spalajković's assurances that the Russian public generally sided with Serbia and even felt pleased at the death of Franz Ferdinand.[31] This in turn corroborated reports which Pašić received in the first fortnight of the crisis (until the death of Hartwig on 10 July) from his ministers elsewhere in Europe: he could, despite the harsh words from Vienna, always be cautiously optimistic that Sarajevo would not escalate into an Austro-Serbian confrontation. He knew of a consensus in most European capitals that the Archduke's death was not regretted and he received friendly advice from most potential allies. Both Italy and France seemed to be relieved at the Archduke's removal, and both (like Romania) counselled moderation upon Belgrade, René Viviani for example advising Serbia on 1 July to keep "cool and dignified" and not play into the hands of Vienna.[32] Bulgaria, it is true, seemed to be revelling in Serbia's misfortune.[33] But the news from Constantinople was reassuring. Not only did the Turks appear sympathetic,[34] but the general consensus in the diplomatic corps there seemed to be summed up in the unguarded language of the British ambassador: that Franz Ferdinand was a "stupid clerical . . . and a real danger to European peace".[35] While this was hardly the view of the influential Austrian ambassador, Count Pallavicini, who the day after the murders described the Archduke as a "real gentleman" in a conversation with the Serbian minister Milan Djordjević, Pallavicini's general remarks must have pleased Belgrade. He assured Djordjević that while Vienna was now carrying out the "strictest investigation" into the murders, it was not linking the assassination to Serbia; indeed, Count Berchtold was alleged to be satisfied with Belgrade's behaviour and wanted to retain friendly relations.[36] Pašić was never to receive such a favourable impression of Berchtold's views from Jovan Jovanović, but he at least knew from Jovanović that Austria-Hungary's outrage at the crime might not be wholly sincere; for while the demonstrations and press attacks in Vienna seemed, according to Jovanović, to be fomented by a small clerical clique, the general view in public and official circles was apparently one of relief at the elimination of a "short-tempered and basically cruel pair of people".[37]

For Belgrade, however, all these optimistic signs could not outweigh the potential threats of the situation. To be precise, Pašić's policy of treating Sarajevo simply as a criminal act, and not as a pan-Serb plot in which Serbia might be implicated or even interested, was destined to be wrecked almost as soon as it had begun. If it was bound to fail in any case because of Vienna's plans, it was also compromised in the first days of the crisis by Serbian indiscretions which Vienna pounced upon: first, by the uncontrolled language of Belgrade's opposition press, and secondly, by the behaviour of certain Serbian ministers. Both factors need to be examined, for they could only harden Austria-Hungary's attitude in the days before the crucial meeting of the Joint Ministerial Council (7 July). Indeed, the significance of both factors is shown by their inclusion, as points one and nine, in the Austrian ultimatum.

On the morning of 29 June radical newspapers in Belgrade had far exceeded *Samouprava*'s measured tones by praising Gavrilo Princip as a martyr and blaming the murders on Habsburg oppression in Bosnia and the Archduke's stupidity in visiting Sarajevo on *Vidovdan*.[38] The Serbian authorities took swift measures: a Cabinet meeting under the Regent resolved to warn the press about provoking Austria-Hungary.[39] But by that time the government knew that the Austrians were inclining towards treating the murders as part of a huge Serb conspiracy organized in Belgrade. Apart from rumours to this effect stemming from the assassins' initial confessions (especially about the origin of their weapons), there was also news of the destruction of Serb property in Sarajevo and the arrest of prominent Bosnian Serb politicians such as Gligorije Jeftanović. Finally, there were signs that the Viennese press was emphasizing the Sarajevo–Belgrade connection, something confirmed by Jovanović by the evening of the 29th.[40] Jovanović in the next fortnight warned Pašić on several occasions about the Belgrade press.[41] Articles from it were certainly being extracted and translated to whip up excitement in Vienna and Berlin, and its tone remained a regular and useful source of complaint to the Austro-Hungarian and German leaders (Tisza and Jagow among others).[42] In response to Jovanović's concern, Pašić asked the head of the Serbian press bureau to caution Belgrade journalists.[43] But he singled out the Viennese press as the real culprit. On 1 July, in his first instructions to Serbian legations abroad, he emphasized Serbia's correct behaviour with its condemnation of a crime over which it had no control and could not desire; Serbia was currently acting against "anarchist elements" and seeking to calm excitement within the country, but it could not allow the Viennese press to "seduce European public opinion" and blame all Serbdom for the murders.[44] A fortnight later, when the press feud had not abated, Pašić set out his position in blunter terms. He maintained that the Austrian press bureau had been deliberately misinterpreting the tone of Belgrade newspapers by citing only the "gutter press" which (Pašić dubiously asserted) represented no political parties and which "nobody in Belgrade reads". He added that Serbia did not have the constitutional or legal means to censor a free press, and was unlikely to do so, since the papers were often only responding to Austrian press provocations.[45] Although there was a lot of truth in this,[46] Pašić's rather strident argument was unlikely to cut much ice in Vienna or Berlin. There it could be viewed as an impudent response. But it was wholly consistent with his policy of trying to distance "official Serbia" from any responsibility for the crisis.

Before discussing the behaviour of Serbia's ministers at home and abroad, we need to assess more fully the nature of Pašić's own conduct in the first weeks of the crisis. Was he, in Albertini's words, doing "little or nothing to avert the Austrian *démarche*"? Or was he, as the volatile Prince Djordje asserts in his memoirs, acting too submissively: "kissing the hand which will strike us"?[46] The answer is probably a mixture of the two: a difficult balance of reserve and co-operation. Pašić would not act in a way which might imply that "official Serbia" was implicated in the murders; there were, after all, some optimistic signs that the crisis might die down and Serbia would not be called to account by Vienna. Here Pašić might be accused of complacency, but perhaps was, in fact, being characteristically calm in view of the options available to him. He could only surmise Austria-Hungary's intentions. He knew from the start that Vienna was likely to make demands of Belgrade.[49] By 7 July he envisaged that after the Sarajevo inquiry into the murders, Vienna might demand a similar Austrian inquiry in Belgrade. This – it is important to note – he already considered as wholly unacceptable for Serbia: "a *casus belli*", as he told the Italian *chargé*.[50] By 10 July he knew from Jovanović that after the Sarajevo inquiry Vienna would adopt one of two courses: either, as Pašić desired, to treat Sarajevo as a criminal act and ask for Serbian co-operation, or – the more likely course – to create out of the murders a pan-Serb plot.[51]

If the latter course was adopted, Pašić was clearly prepared to resist in some way (as Jovanović also recommended). In the meantime he was consistently trying to present the "first course" to Vienna as the logical path to take: Serbia in turn would adopt a co-operative stance and do nothing to provoke the Austrians. This would be far from easy. When the Austrian *chargé d'affaires*, von Storck, told Pašić on 3 July that Berchtold was anxious about the presence in Serbia of some potentially dangerous students (formerly of the Pakrac theological college), Pašić willingly agreed to investigate the matter and did so.[52] But his assurances were to carry little weight in Vienna, for Storck had that same day already approached Serb officials on this matter and been given false information; he concluded that Austria could expect no support from the Serbian police.[53] Again, when Pašić at a requiem for Franz Ferdinand tried to comfort Storck, saying "we will take care of this as if we were dealing with our own ruler", Storck interpreted this for the Ballhausplatz as another example of "Serbian sloppiness", if not a "ghastly irony".[54] And on 8 July, when Pašić stressed to the German minister in Belgrade that, within constitutional limits, Serbia was already acting against nationalist propaganda and organizations, his statements received short shrift from the German Kaiser.[55] All Pašić's gestures were indeed designed to appease Austria-Hungary, but all excluded any pan-Serbian interpretation of the Sarajevo crime: therefore the gestures were limited and wholly unsatisfactory for Vienna.

The attempt to be co-operative but reserved was also immediately under threat, both because of the Austro-Serbian press feud and because of the behaviour of some Serbian ministers. In many cases they exceeded Pašić's cautious stance, or their language was misinterpreted. On 30 June, when Storck had visited Slavko Gruić, secretary-general at the Serbian foreign ministry, Gruić had adopted a tone which, while consistent with official Serbia's line, was hardly tactful. Storck asked him whether the Serbian police were taking measures to investigate the Sarajevo–Belgrade connection. Gruić answered negatively and asked in return if this was supposed to be a formal request for an "inquiry". Thereupon Storck lost his temper and exclaimed that an official *démarche* should not be necessary before the Serbian police acted.[56] The outcome in this case was that on the same day Protić ordered Vasil Lazarević, the Belgrade chief of police, to investigate the assassins' links with the city; a week later Lazarević concluded triumphantly that the Sarajevo crime had no connection with Belgrade.[57] It was not the sort of limited inquiry or response which Vienna had envisaged, but, as we have noted, Pašić was not prepared to go any further.

In Vienna, meanwhile, the language used by Jovan Jovanović was also likely to irritate the Austrians even if, as usual, it was a mutual process. Jovanović, who was on notoriously bad terms with Berchtold, appears to have visited the Ballhausplatz only twice in the weeks after Sarajevo, and both times spoke to the First Section chief, Baron Macchio. On the first occasion, when offering condolences,[58] he correctly pre-empted Pašić's instructions by stating that Belgrade would willingly bring any accomplices of the assassins to justice if they were discovered on Serbian soil; but he could not resist adding that Serbia had in fact been trying to keep healthy relations with Vienna despite a range of obstacles set up by Austrian diplomacy in 1913.[59] On the second occasion (3 July), Jovanović was clearly suppressing his irritation at the Viennese press's accusations and the series of small anti-Serbian demonstrations occurring regularly outside his legation.[60] When Macchio, excited by reports from Storck, exclaimed that the Belgrade press was "wild" [raspuštena], Jovanović – again pre-empting Pašić's arguments – sprang to its defence and went on to condemn the Viennese press for its lack of respect towards Serbia.[61]

While this language was tactless yet understandable, it was the newspaper interviews provided by some Serbian ministers after Sarajevo which gave Vienna the most ammunition. The interviews compromised Pašić by criticizing Austrian behaviour in Bosnia and emphasizing publicly, at this sensitive moment, Belgrade's pan-Serbian interests. Admittedly, Pašić himself was at fault for not keeping the legations more reliably instructed. But it was also the case that some Serbian diplomats did not possess the foreign minister's careful discipline and could not conceal their "Yugoslav" sympathies. This was possibly true of Milutin Jovanović, Serbian chargé d'affaires at Berlin, who was also Pašić's nephew and another alleged member of Crna Ruka. When on 1 July the newspaper Le Figaro in Paris suggested that a Serb–Montenegrin union was to have been announced on Vidovdan, Jovanović told the German press that the idea was "thoroughly unbelievable". But he went on to portray Serbia and Montenegro as "sisters" who would naturally seek closer unity in the future. This fairly harmless remark was seized upon by the Austrians and given a significance which wholly distorted Jovanović's otherwise conciliatory statements at this time.[62] Sazonov, on learning of Jovanović's indiscretion, labelled him a "fool" and swiftly urged Pašić to suspend all Serb–Montenegrin talks so as not to provoke Vienna.[63] In fact, unknown to Sazonov, the talks had been in abeyance for some months, but however Belgrade now acted Jovanović had unwittingly done considerable damage.[64]

Even more serious were the statements of Miroslav Spalajković in St Petersburg. Spalajković was not only renowned for his volatile personality (even Sazonov termed him "unbalanced"),[65] but also for his keen public interest in Bosnia's fate, all the more so because in 1906 he had married the daughter of one of Sarajevo's most influential politicians, Gligorije Jeftanović.[66] When on 29 June Spalajković learnt of Jeftanović's alleged arrest, he made statements to the Russian press, justifying Bosnian agitation against Vienna and condemning the current Austrian excesses in the province.[67] He went on to embarrass Belgrade further by asserting that Jovan Jovanović had warned Vienna in advance about the possible dangers that might await the Archduke in Sarajevo. This was a rumour being circulated elsewhere immediately after the murders and Pašić, after consulting Jovanović and discovering its veracity, wisely decided to deny it in an interview with the Hungarian newspaper *Az Est*.[68] The truth about Jovanović's "warning" is now clear.[69] For our purposes, what is important is to note that Spalajković's tactless language embroiled "official Serbia" deeper in the Sarajevo plot and its consequences, at a time when Pašić was trying to be conciliatory but reserved. There is no evidence that Pašić reprimanded Spalajković for his behaviour, nor for his later press statements which again implied Serbian obstinacy in the face of Vienna.[70] Only later in the crisis would Pašić think of reproaching one of his envoys – Milan Djordjević – when he publicly made very provocative statements.[71] But the earlier *faux pas* were the most damaging. The Austro-Hungarian leaders, meeting on 7 July, certainly weighed up the language of Spalajković and Milutin Jovanović when discussing the demands to be presented to Serbia; point nine of the final ultimatum referred to the "unjustifiable utterances of high Serbian officials both in Serbia and abroad" after the Sarajevo outrage.[72]

Pašić said later that in the weeks after Sarajevo Serbia had fully cooperated with Austria-Hungary's only official request: to investigate the "Pakrac students". This was true. There had also been a short inquiry by the chief of police in Belgrade and it could be argued that some measures were being planned and taken to reduce nationalist propaganda. This, however, was the limit of Serbia's co-operation. Privately, Pašić was already determined in the first week of the crisis never to permit an Austrian inquiry on Serbian soil. Nor was he prepared to pre-empt Vienna's demands and announce a proper Serbian inquiry since this could imply (and would reveal) Serbia's involvement. Yet he was deluding himself if he thought that he could keep "official Serbia" detached in this way. Vienna, after all, was starting from the premise that the Serbian government was involved in Sarajevo, and would not accept the distinction which Pašić was trying to make between "official" and "unofficial" Serbia: it had the evidence of the Belgrade press, of statements from Serbian ministers, and was also interpreting Pašić's own behaviour in a negative light.

Pašić's interview for *Az Est*, for example, drew the attention of Tisza and was therefore closely scrutinized by Storck. He noted that Pašić's description of the assassins as "fanatical children" described accurately most people in Serbia; while Pašić's usual claim that Serbia would react to an Austrian *démarche* "like any other civilized state" was made only because "the old fox smells a rat" and feared that Serbia might indeed be called to account.[73] On 12 July Pašić gave another interview, to the *Leipziger Neueste Nachrichten* (published on the 17th). In it he denied the involvement of the Serbian government or people in the murders, mentioned Austrian oppression of the Serbs and hinted that if a Great Power attacked Serbia, other small states would come to its aid.[74] It was an article which he soon claimed to have been an informal conversation that had been misinterpreted. Baron Giesl, however, seized on it as "insolence" and both Berchtold and Jagow viewed it as a further black mark against "Serbdom".[75] Meanwhile, they could already deduce further Serb impudence from the show of unity displayed in Belgrade after the death of Hartwig. The unfortunate circumstances of Hartwig's death – while visiting Giesl at the Austrian legation – were enough to arouse fantastic rumours of Giesl and his Croat wife as "modern Borgias" who used "abominable medieval" methods.[76] Giesl then made the excitement worse by warning Pašić, on flimsy evidence, of an impending massacre of Austrian citizens in Belgrade. But it was the decision of the Serbian government to give Hartwig a state funeral which was the most siginificant. Although Pašić, on Russian advice, took precautions to prevent anti-Austrian demonstrations, the enormous ceremony attended by "all Serbdom" on 14 July could only confirm Giesl in his prejudices: Pašić was to be found making a funeral oration in which he praised Hartwig's services to pan-Slavism and eulogized the Russian Tsar as the mighty protector of all Slavs.[77] The distinction between "official" and "unofficial" Serbia was thoroughly blurred.

Both Albertini and Giesl felt that the Russian minister's death dramatically altered the course of Serbian policy in July 1914. Albertini wrote that "the Serbian Government appeared to have lost all sense of direction" and that Hartwig would not have "let Pašić sit with folded hands" in the week before the ultimatum.[78] In fact, the Serbian documents do not support either of these statements. Pašić did not alter his (admittedly rather passive) course after 10 July, nor was he to be inactive in the face of the mounting Austrian threat. On the other hand, Giesl's idea that, if Hartwig had lived, he would have persuaded Pašić to accept all Austrian demands does not ring true either:[79] we have seen that Pašić, before Hartwig's death, was already privately resistant to the idea of an Austrian inquiry on Serbian soil. Moreover, both writers are, of course, making their hypotheses on the assumption that Hartwig was shaping Pašić's policy decisively after Sarajevo; the evidence, again, does not substantiate this, even if Pašić may have closely consulted Hartwig and clearly valued the Russian connection above all others.

But the excitement surrounding Hartwig's death interrupted what was otherwise a lull in the crisis for Belgrade. Although Pašić remained exasperated by the Viennese press and took steps immediately to quell false rumours about violence and disorder at Hartwig's funeral,[80] he possessed little evidence of Vienna's intentions apart from the two possible courses outlined by Jovan Jovanović. He may have heard rumours about the Ministerial Council of 7 July, but was comforted by Tisza's temperate remarks in the Hungarian Parliament;[81] from Berlin too it sounded as though Jagow, just back from his honeymoon, did not view the situation as being particularly serious.[82] On 14 July, the day of Hartwig's funeral, Pašić told Strandtmann, the Russian *chargé d'affaires*, that while Serbia expected new Austrian requests at the end of the Sarajevo judicial inquiry, all was otherwise quiet on the subject of the murders; in fact there were hopeful signs, since the Austrians had agreed to resume railway negotiations in Belgrade.[83]

Within three days this slight optimism was fast disappearing. It could be argued that Vienna had been partially successful in lulling Belgrade into a false sense of security. In mid-July, Jovanović made no haste to pass on to Pašić some useful details about Vienna's possible intentions.[84] But the fact was that Jovanović had little new information to give: his approaches to the Ballhausplatz seem to have been rebuffed with the standard argument that all would be settled after the judicial inquiry had ended.[85] Nevertheless, by 18 July Pašić had clear evidence that a severe Austrian *démarche* was likely in the near future. On the 17th he had received from the Serbian minister in London a warning, stemming from a "well-informed source", "not to believe the calculated peace-loving statements from Austro-Hungarian circles, for they are planning momentous pressure on Serbia which could lead to an armed attack".[86] From Berlin too there was news that Vienna was preparing a strong note and had not ruled out conflict.[87] But the crucial evidence for Pašić came not from any German indiscretion, as Samuel Williamson suggests, but from Tisza's speech on 15 July in the Hungarian Parliament and the comments on this by the Italian ambassador in Vienna. In a widely-publicized speech, Tisza suggested that war against Serbia might be a sad last resort; Count Avarna, according to the Serbian *chargé* in Rome, concluded from this that an Austrian move was unavoidable, with a danger of armed conflict if Serbia did not give satisfaction.[88]

This was perhaps a critical moment for Belgrade. Pašić up to this point, though expecting an Austrian *démarche* eventually, had hoped against hope that it would be "reasonable" so that Serbia could somehow extract itself from the crisis; with this in mind he had vainly tried to keep Serbia calm so as not to provoke more severe demands from Vienna.[89] But the spectre now loomed more clearly of a strict *démarche*, backed up by military threats; along with Tisza's speech, Pašić also had evidence of Austrian troop movements on the border.[90] At midnight on 18/19 July he despatched an urgent telegram to all Serbian legations apart from Vienna. In it he compared Serbia's "correct behaviour" since Sarajevo with Austria's apparent desire (especially its press) to exploit fully the situation; the evidence now suggested that Vienna was planning a *démarche* of some kind "which might provoke unfortunate consequences for the neigh-bourly relations of Serbia and Austria-Hungary" since it would ac-cuse Serbia and pan-Serbianism of the murders. While Serbia would agree to any Austrian requests to bring accomplices of the assassins to justice, "she could not accede to demands unacceptable to any state which guards its independence and dignity". This was to be emphasized to the foreign governments with the request that they might "act in a spirit of reconciliation when a suitable opportunity or necessity arose".[91]

Should Pašić at this point have done more in practical terms to pre-empt the Austrian *démarche*? Advice of this kind was not lack-ing. On 18 July the British *chargé d'affaires*, taking up a proposal by Henry Wickham Steed, the foreign editor of *The Times*, suggested at the foreign ministry that Serbia should voluntarily begin its own in-quiry into the conspiracy on Serbian soil; Gruić, however, still toed the official line, replying that "the Serbian Government had no ma-terial on which such an inquiry could be based" and would wait until Austria-Hungary's own investigation.[92] A similar damper was put on advice from Italy. By the 16th Pašić knew of a proposal by San Giuliano that Serbia should dissolve pan-Serbian societies and thereby pre-empt one of Vienna's probable demands; yet at a Ser-bian Cabinet meeting on 19 July this idea too was rejected on the grounds that it would provoke a "popular revolution".[93] Belgrade's attitude certainly owed something to domestic factors. The election campaign was by then in full swing – Pašić departed on 20 July to campaign in north-east Serbia – and the government had to keep one eye on the electorate. But it is also clear that Pašić still hoped that Austria's demands would be within reasonable limits; if they were not, as seemed possible, he had warned the Powers in his circular that Serbia would not agree to "unacceptable demands" and would expect them to exercise a moderating influence in Vienna.

That they would do so appeared, on 19 July, quite probable. France, Romania and Turkey seemed fully sympathetic to the Ser-bian point of view.[94] More importantly, Spalajković telegraphed from St Petersburg on the 18th that Sazonov did not believe that Vi-enna would do anything; this, coming in the wake of Russian prom-ises to deliver some rifles and ammunition, must have boosted Belgrade's confidence that, in Gruić's words, "Russia would not stand by and see Serbia wantonly attacked".[95] The messages from other Powers could also be interpreted in this way. While Henry Wickham Steed had been urging Serbia to turn to the Powers when Austria-Hungary pounced,[96] the Italians already seemed actively to be counselling moderation in Vienna and Berlin.[97] And even Germany's attitude, despite Jagow's known sympathy for Vienna, was not deemed to be wholly negative; on the 18th Gruić still felt, for some reason, that in a crisis "restraint would be exercised on Austria from Berlin".[98]

As for Serbia itself trying to influence the Austrians directly, all approaches at this time were met with a rebuff. Pašić, it is true, sent no queries or instructions to Jovan Jovanović about the silence from the Ballhausplatz; but, as we have seen, Jovanović could not have provided many answers. Instead, Pašić made it quite clear to Baron Giesl that, when requested by Vienna, Serbia would certainly take any measures "compatible with the dignity and independence of a state".[99] Therefore, when Pašić left Belgrade for Negotin on the morning of 20 July, he could feel that he had set out Serbia's position clearly for all the Powers; he was not complacent in the face of the Austrian *démarche*.[100] But he was certainly rather presumptuous in thinking that if the *démarche* proved to be unacceptable to Serbia, the Great Powers would be able or willing to act and defuse the crisis.

In the days prior to the ultimatum, the likelihood of some Austro-Serbian confrontation became more obvious, but Belgrade received rather vague and mixed messages about how the other Powers might respond. What seemed increasingly clear, from Jovan Jovanović's telegrams and various leaks in the press, was that a severe *démarche* was indeed imminent, that it might include a time limit of 48 hours for Serbian acceptance and that Vienna was hoping to localize any potential conflict.[101] Jovanović – ignorant of Pašić's circular – urged Belgrade early on the 20th to find out the views of St Petersburg;[102] but the Serbian foreign ministry, having despatched the circular, now made no further moves and seems also to have been quite slow in keeping Pašić informed of developments. The replies to the circular should have sounded some alarm bells. Firstly, Berlin's position was now clearer. Jagow on 20 July largely ignored Serbia's request to advise the Austrians, proposing instead that Serbia should approach them directly and be fully co-operative in the face of Vienna's "moderate demands"; it was a reply which Count Berchtold found very satisfactory.[103] Secondly, Italy's response (received in Belgrade very early on the 23rd) was rather disturbing. Although San Giuliano seemed eager to aid Serbia by all diplomatic means, he warned that if this diplomacy failed and Austria attacked, Serbia should not expect Russia to become involved in an armed conflict.[104] The logic of this statement (which the Serbian *chargé* did not pass on to Belgrade)[105] was that Serbia should make every effort to concede Austria-Hungary's demands, for otherwise it might be left to face Vienna alone. By 23 July, it is important to note, Belgrade had had no absolute assurances from St Petersburg that Russia would stand by Serbia in any crisis. On 21 July Spalajković had anxiously submitted Pašić's circular and pressed for "Russian protection"; but Sazonov had been too occupied with President Poincaré's visit to give a response.[106] The only really auspicious sign came from Poincaré himself: when Spalajković was presented to him in the Winter Palace on the 22nd and remarked on Serbia's predicament, Poincaré answered, "we will help you to make it better".[107]

It was perhaps the ambiguity of the evidence possessed by Belgrade which explains Pašić's behaviour at this time. It is clear that late on the 22nd he returned from Negotin to the capital, but after reviewing the situation he still pushed for Lazar Paču, the corpulent Minister of Finance, to be appointed as acting Prime Minister while he himself departed early on the 23rd by boat for Radujevac and another electioneering tour in southern Serbia.[108] Despite the danger signs from abroad, the Austrians were continuing up to the 23rd to make conciliatory noises which undoubtedly misled some members of the Serbian government and explains their shock when they received the ultimatum;[109] the Serbians may also have expected news that the Sarajevo inquiry had ended before Vienna made a *démarche*. As for Pašić, preoccupied with election business, he was prepared to deal with any new foreign development when it arose. But he expected – as shown by his circular and also by his otherwise surprising refusal to return to Belgrade on the afternoon of the 23rd and receive Baron Giesl personally – that if a crisis arose because of Vienna's demands, other Great Powers would act to defuse it in some way over a period of time.[110]

At 6pm on 23 July, Giesl presented a chain-smoking Lazar Paču with the Austro-Hungarian note. He specified that its terms were to be answered and accepted in 48 hours; otherwise he had orders to leave Belgrade and break off diplomatic relations. Paču and the other five members of the government who were not electioneering outside Belgrade were immediately alarmed by the severity of the note, but above all they seem to have agreed that its terms could never be accepted unconditionally by Serbia. This point must be emphasized, for Belgrade's resistance to any Austrian violation of Serbian sovereignty runs like a red ribbon through Serbia's behaviour throughout the July crisis, including the period of 23–5 July. Luigi Albertini, relying primarily on hearsay evidence collected by the Italian journalist Luciano Magrini, asserted that Belgrade from 23 July was ready to accept all Austria's terms and was only stiffened to offer resistance after receiving a clear message of Russian support on the 25th.[111] In fact, the exact opposite seems to be the truth. Serbia was prepared to resist from the start, but in the following two days, faced with insufficient support from the Great Powers, was forced to be more accommodating in its reply.

On the evening of the 23rd, however, the Serbs exhibited a resistance that was not sheer bravado and that immediately implied the need for Great Power support.[112] Paču at once contacted the Russian *chargé d'affaires*, showed him the note and "begged [Strandtmann] that Russia would help us". He then visited the Palace and echoed for Regent Alexander the view of his fellow ministers that "this is European war".[113] No Cabinet meeting appears to have been held that evening.[114] Instead, Alexander agreed that Pašić be recalled to Belgrade before any decisions were made, while Paču despatched a telegram to all legations abroad, informing them of the ultimatum "whose demands are such that no Serbian Government could accept them in full".[115] Alexander's own determination on these lines is clear from his private talks that night both with Strandtmann and with his maverick brother, Prince Djordje. Having consulted King Petar, Alexander told both of them that Serbia could never accept all Austria's demands. Via Strandtmann, he requested help from the Tsar, "whose command alone could save Serbia".[116] To Djordje he confessed, late in the night, that until the ultimatum he had hoped that the other Powers would moderate Vienna's attitude. By then, Serbia was still ready to yield somewhat to Vienna, but would never accept demands which violated its sovereignty; it could, the Regent felt, rely on both Russia and France for support, and if Austria-Hungary was set on war "this time she will encounter an iron fist".[117]

In both conversations Alexander displayed defiance but also anxiety, since he was well aware of Serbia's military weakness. This notwithstanding, military preparations were begun by Serbia late on 23 July – further proof that Belgrade from the start did not think of accepting all Austria's demands.[118] Dušan Stefanović, as Minister of War, realized immediately the need for some preliminary moves towards mobilization, not only because of Serbia's deficient transport network but also in view of the current location of the armed forces: 80 per cent of them were keeping order in the newly annexed southern territories, while new recruits from there (possibly unreliable Albanians or Macedonians) formed most of the five regiments in "old Serbia". In early July, Stefanović, "foreseeing possible difficulties", had taken steps to alleviate this situation. On 23 July, after learning of the ultimatum and consulting Alexander, he launched Serbia on what he later termed a course of "pre-war fever": the Chief of Staff and his deputy were recalled from abroad, all divisional commanders were called up, the railway authorities were alerted, and the five regiments in the north were instructed to prepare assembly points for impending mobilization. If these might be considered provocative moves by Vienna, they were sensible precautions if the Serbian army, still in the south, was to have any chance of meeting an Austrian attack.

When Pašić returned to Belgrade at 5am on 24 July, one of the critical novelties of the situation now facing him was the time limit that Vienna had attached to the ultimatum. He and the rest of the Cabinet, when they met at 10am, were resolved to reject many points of the Austrian note (including, for example, the dissolution of pan-Serbian societies).[119] Therefore it was vital that they extend the deadline and secure a moderation of the demands by pressure from "friendly Powers" in Vienna, or at least that possible allies give definite assurances of military support before the deadline expired. On the morning of the 24th it was not clear that any of this could be achieved; hence Pašić's words to Strandtmann that, although Serbia would ask the Powers to protect its independence, "if war is unavoidable, we will fight".[120] The attitude of "friendly Powers" seemed no clearer than when Pašić had left Belgrade 24 hours earlier. Indeed, the Serbian ministers in both Paris and London – Vesnić and Bošković – had been singularly lax about acting on Pašić's circular of 18 July and reporting back to Belgrade. Vesnić, who *vis-à-vis* Pašić was as independently minded as Spalajković or Jovan Jovanović, was not providing Belgrade with a clear picture of the Quai d'Orsay's views.[121] But perhaps Pašić was sufficiently reassured by Poincaré's promise to Spalajković and this, as well as the fact that France had no representative in Serbia until the 25th,[122] may have deterred him from making any special approach to the French. Britain, in contrast, was more of an unknown quantity, and had been since the Sarajevo murders. Only on the evening of 23 July did Bošković (new to his London post) visit the Foreign Office to report, in line with Pašić's circular, that Serbia was "most anxious and disquieted". Admittedly, Sir Arthur Nicolson's reply – hoping that Serbia "would endeavour to meet the Austrian requests in a conciliatory and moderate spirit" – was hardly encouraging.[123] But since Bošković delayed in reporting this to Belgrade, Pašić knew nothing of London's attitude.[124] Hence, before midday on the 24th, he thought it worth asking Crackanthorpe, the British *chargé d'affaires*, if London could influence the Austrians to moderate their demands; Crackanthorpe duly passed this on, but he failed to mention to Sir Edward Grey the warnings for the future with which Pašić had accompanied his request.[125]

More promising in any case for Pašić was, in view of their recent statements, the possibility of action by Rome, and especially St Petersburg. The Cabinet on the afternoon of 24 July agreed to what may have been Alexander's own suggestion,[126] that he despatch (at 5 pm) a personal telegram to his uncle, the King of Italy, urging him as an ally of Austria-Hungary to persuade Vienna to prolong the time limit and moderate its demands.[127] But prior to this, in the morning, a similar but more elaborate telegram had been sent by the Regent to Tsar Nicholas II. The fact that both Alexander and Pašić set great store by Russian support is evident from their exaggerated, almost sycophantic, language to Strandtmann earlier in the day.[128] But Pašić in particular was unsure of how Russia might react. In view of Russian behaviour towards Serbia in 1909 and 1913, it is not surprising that during the July crisis several Serbian diplomats are on record as questioning whether Russia would, in fact, stand by Serbia in an Austro-Serbian conflict.[129] Hence Alexander's telegram to the Tsar appealed emotionally to his rôle as protector of the Slavs and laboured the idea of a defenceless Serbia which was about to be attacked. While describing the Austrian note as "humiliating" and "imperious", Alexander stressed that Serbia might agree to demands consistent with its sovereignty as well as any which the Tsar might advise it to accept.[130]

With these appeals despatched to Russia, Italy and Britain, Serbia could do nothing but wait for the replies. By the evening of 24 July the general situation looked even bleaker. Jovan Jovanović had been asked by Paču to sound out Vienna about its possible intentions (presumably any such approach to Giesl had been rebuffed); he answered that Berchtold expected a "satisfactory reply" before the given deadline, barring which hostilities seemed very likely.[131] Moreover, if they occurred, Serbia at this point had no firm backing from any of the other Balkan states. Even Montenegrin support seemed slightly suspect. At 11am, when Pašić had told Lazar Mijušković, the Montenegrin minister, about the unacceptable ultimatum, Mijušković had promised solidarity.[132] Yet his word was not binding; King Nikita's flirtation with the Austrians during July had exasperated Belgrade and still seemed to be a possible danger.[133] As for the attitude of Romania and Greece, Pašić could at least feel confident that if Bulgaria sought to exploit the crisis and attack Serbia, these two would move to prevent a violation of the Treaty of Bucharest; Greece was bound to this by its alliance with Serbia, while Romania might feel morally bound, since the Serbians only a few days earlier had warned Sofia that they would intervene in any Romanian–Bulgarian conflict.[134] However, in the case of a localized Austro-Serbian war, Romanian or Greek support was far more doubtful. On 24 July, Romania seemed to be suggesting that Serbia would have "to rely on her own strength", while the Greek minister in Belgrade gave Pašić little hope of altering their alliance to cover an Austrian attack. At 7.30pm, therefore, Pašić telegraphed to the legations in Romania, Greece and Montenegro, ordering them to report immediately on these states' intentions in case of an Austro-Serbian conflict.[135]

Since the outlook was so uncertain, Serbia had during the day also been stepping up its military preparations; in Giesl's words, "the swarm of bees was fully active".[136] Stefanović gave orders for the mining of bridges over the Sava river, and for a military take-over of the railways. The scale of activity at this time seemed to some observers already to be tantamount to mobilization. In fact, Stefanović was trying to prepare Serbia for the order for full mobilization. This included calling up the first levy of reserve troops, many of whom were still gathering in the harvest. It also meant arranging to evacuate Belgrade and move the government to Niš.[137] That the Cabinet had decided on this so quickly shows not only its low estimation of Serbian military preparedness, but also its firm belief that Austrian troops – rumoured to be massing on the border – would attack as soon as the ultimatum expired.

For the Cabinet, in session into the night, the lack of international support was of course a prime consideration in these decisions. How far in their discussions they began to weaken from opposing so many of Austria's demands is difficult to say in the absence of any Serbian Cabinet minutes for 1914. Serbian sources suggest that a first draft of the reply, written largely by Pašić and Protić, was ready on 24 July and a final draft by 11am on the 25th.[138] Therefore, already by the 24th the Cabinet had yielded somewhat from its initial obstinacy. For example, on two points at first anathema to Alexander: they agreed, after reservations, to dissolve the propaganda society *Narodna Odbrana* (point 2); and further agreed to remove officials guilty of propaganda against Austria-Hungary (point 4), with the reserve that this must be proved by the Sarajevo judicial inquiry. As is evident from these two points, the Serbians still made reservations in most of the concessions in their reply, usually tying them to proof being supplied by the Austrians. Nor, it seems, were they ever prepared to concede fully on points 5 and 6 (allowing Austrian officials into Serbia), since these would violate Serbian sovereignty, which Pašić had sworn to uphold from the beginning of the crisis. Indeed, the reply being drafted was consistent with Pašić's stance over the previous weeks: it would try to resist "extreme demands" but yield to a certain degree on others, particularly if there was no sign of international support or mediation.

According to Albertini, Serbia by 25 July was ready to concede Austrian demands almost entirely, but was encouraged to change its mind by a telegram arriving from Russia at midday. In fact, as we will see, the opposite may be true. Pašić was probably disappointed at the degree of Russian support on the 25th and there is no evidence that Russian advice substantially altered the terms of Serbia's reply. First, however, it is necessary to discuss the extent to which on 25 July Serbia could rely on other countries for support or mediation; how far did Pašić's appeals on the 24th bring a favourable response? Of the Balkan states only Montenegro could be relied on. Early on 25 July

Mijušković confirmed for Pašić that his government was resolved to go "through good and bad in soldarity with Serbia", but added that Serbia should now act according to Russian and French advice.[139] From Romania and Greece, however, the response for Pašić remained thoroughly vague and unsatisfactory, exacerbated by the delay in convoking a Romanian Cabinet meeting and by the fact that Venizelos, the Greek Prime Minister, had to be contacted in Munich. Both states seemed concerned above all to keep an Austro-Serbian conflict localized rather than offer support to Serbia; their bland advice in any case failed to reach Belgrade before the ultimatum expired.[140]

More importantly, the news from Britain, Italy and even France seemed now to be equally disheartening. None of these Powers appeared to be doing anything definite to influence Vienna; all of them wanted Serbia's reply to be as conciliatory as possible, with a view to keeping the peace and then arranging some compromise. For Belgrade, the British attitude was still the most unsatisfactory. On 25 July, Pašić knew only of Bošković's visit to Nicolson (on the 23rd) which had failed to provide any clear picture of British views; he also knew of Grey's shock at the ultimatum, and of the "general opinion in London" that all now depended on Russia to stop Austria-Hungary.[141] Pašić had no reply of any kind to his special request that Grey himself should put pressure on Vienna. Bošković delayed until the afternoon of the 25th before again visiting the Foreign Office and reminding them of Pašić's hope of support.[142] But Grey in any case would not have been forthcoming. His instructions to Crackanthorpe (on the evening of the 24th) made no mention of Pašić's request. And since Crackanthorpe himself decided not to pass on even Grey's advice (to give "fullest satisfaction" in their reply), Pašić could feel that little was to be expected from the British: he would not consider it worth approaching them again.[143]

Similarly, the Regent's appeal to Italy seemed to have fallen on deaf ears. The Italians simply continued to advise Belgrade to concede as much as possible since, they argued, the Austrian demands in practice could be altered. The Serbian *chargé d'affaires* concluded that while Italy might mediate in the conflict, "we cannot count on actual help . . . here they feel that the focal point of the serious situation lies in the behaviour of Russia".[144] Russia indeed seemed now to be Serbia's only possible support before the ultimatum expired. For by the 25th, the French too appeared to be taking Italy's line: the Quai d'Orsay now emphasized that by being as conciliatory as possible in its reply, Serbia would gain time, enabling the Great Powers to step in and arbitrate.[145] Pašić naturally would have preferred some signs of French or Italian mediation, for he undoubtedly expected that any conditional reply by Serbia could result in an immediate Austrian attack, with no further chance of international arbitration.[146]

Into this gloomy scenario the advice which Serbia received from Russia on the morning of 25 July certainly brought some light. But the Serbian documents now show that Russia's attitude was neither as encouraging nor as clear as Belgrade would have liked. As we have seen, the Serbian Cabinet – contrary to Albertini's account – had at first been very resistant to Austria's demands; then during their long session on the 24th they had, possibly under Pašić's influence, softened a little, but were probably still resolved to resist the crucial points 5 and 6 of the ultimatum and were taking military precautions accordingly. It was highly unlikely, except under extreme pressure, that they would concede these two points, all the more so since no "friendly state" (except perhaps Italy) seemed to be advising unconditional surrender and the violation of Serbian sovereignty. Only Russian pressure, added to that of the other Powers, might extract the utmost concessions.

Years later, Miroslav Spalajković always denied the existence of "missing telegrams", sent by him to Belgrade on 25 July, in which Russia had allegedly pressed Serbia to withstand Austrian demands.[147] The current evidence supports this denial. On learning of the ultimatum on the 24th, Spalajković had hurried back to St Petersburg from his summer villa in Finland. At 6pm he had been received by Sazonov and, in a meeting lasting an hour, they had perused the ultimatum together. During the night Spalajković seems to have sent only three telegrams to Pašić, all of which arrived on the morning of 25 July. One of these was of little importance except in confirming that Germany was determined to localize the conflict.[148] The most significant was a telegram sent in two parts, discussing Sazonov's conversation with Spalajković.[149] In the first part, despatched at midnight and arriving at 4.17am, there were hopeful signs. Sazonov "condemned the Austrian ultimatum with disgust" since it contained demands which no sovereign state could accept;

he added that Russia had been taking "energetic steps" in Vienna and Berlin and that Serbia could certainly rely on Russian help. However, as Spalajković himself noted, Sazonov did not specify what form this help would take, since the Tsar and France had to be consulted. Rather, he proposed that if Serbia was unable to defend itself, it should make a declaration to all countries that it was innocent of the Sarajevo crime and had been behaving correctly towards Austria-Hungary.

Some of Sazonov's words were encouraging to Belgrade: it is important to note that in the telegram Spalajković did not mention Sazonov's hope that Serbia would accommodate Austria as much as possible in its reply.[150] Yet Sazonov's language in the telegram was also too vague to be wholly satisfactory for Pašić. Although Pašić seems to have inferred that "energetic steps" meant efforts to extend the time limit of the ultimatum,[151] there was no clear sign of military support and the implication therefore was that Serbian concessions were necessary. This was reinforced when the second part of the telegram arrived at 10am. In it Sazonov passed on the advice, agreed by the Russian Ministerial Council on 24 July, that if the Serbians could not defend themselves they should not resist an Austrian invasion but simply withdraw southwards and appeal to the Powers; when Spalajković had queried this, Sazonov had replied that "Serbia's decision had to depend on her capability for defence". Again the implication was that, although Russia was working on Serbia's behalf, for the present the latter would be alone in its conflict with the Austrians. Only in Spalajković's third telegram, received at 11.30 am, was there a slight hint of something better: it mentioned that Russia might even mobilize and that an official communiqué was to be issued in which Russia would act to protect Serbia.[152]

Pašić was certainly pleased to some extent with Russia's attitude: he minuted on the second telegram that he had read it "with gratitude". But these messages from St Petersburg by midday on 25 July were still imprecise. Far from advising the Serbians to stand firm and resist (in their reply or militarily), Sazonov appeared to be suggesting that they should concede and withdraw for the present. Admittedly the third telegram – perhaps to be identified as the crucial "midday telegram" – gave a hint of military support. But it seems highly unlikely that, knowing of this vague prospect, Pašić was suddenly moved to stiffen the terms of the Serbian reply. The idea that this occurred stems largely from unsubstantiated rumours or from Austrian sources, including Baron Giesl, who by his own admission was from 23 to 25 July kept informed of events chiefly by journalists.[153] Moreover, none of the Serbian participants in the events of this time acknowledge that Russian support was crucial in strengthening Serbia's note. Indeed, there is reliable evidence that this was unnecessary. On the morning of the 25th Pašić was still planning to accept some demands of the ultimatum but to reject others, probably points 5 and 6, which had always been the real stumbling block.[154] Serbia, in other words, was still not prepared to concede all of Austria's demands. Only a few witnesses – particularly the British *chargé* whose reports are not wholly reliable – seemed to think that Serbia would do so; in fact, when Crackanthorpe asked Gruić about the Serbian note he was given the standard answer: that the note was to be "most conciliatory", meeting Austrian demands "in as large a measure as possible" – a euphemism for the rejection of points which violated Serbian sovereignty.[155]

It is therefore quite probable, as Jovan Jovanović wrote later, that Russian advice had little effect on the framing of Serbia's note.[156] It may even, when coupled with the advice from France and Italy on the morning of the 25th, have weakened Serbia's resolve still further, encouraging it in the final draft to concede point 5 of the ultimatum (with a reservation) and reject only point 6. The final note, which Pašić presented to Giesl at 6pm, was certainly more submissive because Serbia had few signs of international support for its cause. The Italian *chargé d'affaires* noted that the number of concessions had been due to Serbia's fear at the last moment of international isolation.[157] Two days later, Pašić himself would reflect that if he had known on 25 July that Serbia was later to gain such international support, he would never have conceded so much.[158]

When Pašić gave Giesl a note which, though conciliatory, was in fact still full of reservations, he knew that this could be a decision for war with Austria-Hungary; but it was only on receiving Giesl's reply, severing diplomatic relations, that this seemed to be a reality. Pašić was very shaken: he had clearly not expected such an abrupt reaction and now, according to information from Jovan Jovanović, faced an immediate Austrian attack.[159] In anticipation of this risk it had already been decided to transfer the government and the diplomatic corps to the fortified city of Niš. While this was beginning on the evening of the 25th, Alexander signed the order for general mobilization. Throughout the day Belgrade had been on a war footing, with the beating of drums outside the cafés to call up the conscripted.[160] It was undoubtedly this which caused Giesl to err in telling Vienna that the Serbs had mobilized at 3pm – a step which Berchtold seized upon as a "hostile act" – when in fact the official announcement was only made late that night.[161]

The Serbian government now expected an Austrian declaration of war. When it did not materialize in the following 48 hours, their hopes were slightly raised that the Powers might indeed be arranging some international arbitration. As we have seen, Russia, France and Italy had all advised or hinted to Belgrade that the Powers could mediate in the crisis; with this in mind, and possibly following suggestions from the French and Spalajković respectively,[162] Serbia's note had ended with an appeal that the dispute be placed before either the International Court at The Hague, or those Great Powers that had drawn up Serbia's declaration to Austria-Hungary in March 1909. Serbia therefore now left a solution of the crisis in the hands of the Powers (and they were to lose valuable time because they did not receive a text of the Serbian note until 27 July). Serbia itself took no diplomatic initiative of any importance after 25 July. It did not envisage going further and accepting Austria's ultimatum unconditionally since, as Lazar Paču remarked, the Serbian note was a satisfactory basis for a compromise.[163] Yet it was unconditional acceptance that Berchtold still hoped for, and which the Italians continued to advise. Despite Austrian mobilization on 26 July, the only sign that Serbia might yield further came not from the Serbian government but from the Serbian *chargé d'affaires* in Rome. Acting on his own initiative, Mihajlović told the Italians that Serbia might indeed accept Austria's demands in full if requested to do so by the other Powers. It was an idea that San Giuliano by the 28th had eagerly communicated to Britain and Germany, but both immediately rejected it.[164]

It was in any case highly doubtful that the Serbian government would now concede further without extreme pressure from all the Powers. For on 27 July the international situation had improved dramatically for Pašić: it became clear at last that Vienna and Berlin would not be able to localize an Austro-Serbian conflict and might be forced by the other Powers to bring the dispute to the conference table. Whether this happened or not, Serbia knew on 27 July that it possessed the international support that had been so uncertain or absent two days before. For example, when Pašić arrived in Niš during the night of 26/7 July he received a far clearer picture of Russia's attitude. In a range of telegrams, Spalajković ecstatically reported the Russians' partial mobilization and their determination to launch a "most energetic offensive" as soon as Austria-Hungary attacked Serbia: "here in all circles without exception, from the Tsar right down to the least individual, there is the greatest enthusiasm for Serbia and an indescribable belligerency."[165] Knowing this, Pašić and the Cabinet decided early in the morning to reject a proposal by Sazonov (only at this stage communicated by Strandtmann) that Serbia should turn and ask Britain for mediation. This did not seem a promising move in view of Britain's silence when appealed to on 24 July; and Pašić felt that it might even encourage the British to continue what he still viewed as a vague and detached stance.[166] Only later in the day did he learn of Grey's own initiative for a "Four Power" conference, an optimistic sign to Pašić that Serbia might still emerge "favourably" from the crisis.[167] He was also by then particularly satisfied at the attitude of Italy: its declaration that it would stay neutral if Austria attacked Serbia seemed likely, with the prospect of a general war, to force Berlin and Vienna to back down.[168] This new auspicious atmosphere stiffened Pašić's resolve to wait on events. As he minuted on the evening of 27 July: "we have made our last concession – further we will not go, nor will we seek mediation, for that would suggest that we are ready to yield even more. Russia is resolute. Italy neutral."[169] Admittedly, Pašić remained somewhat anxious, not least about Bulgaria's behaviour in the event of a conflict.[170] But whether the crisis ended in war or peace, the Serbians were now fully confident of international support.

For Serbia, most of the uncertainty of the crisis ended when Austria-Hungary declared war on 28 July. The evidence suggests that during the previous month Serbia was far more independent and obstinate than historians have previously imagined. In the wake of the Sarajevo murders, Nikola Pašić hoped to extract Serbia from potential dangers by making a few conciliatory gestures and relying on the Powers to negotiate a diplomatic settlement if necessary. But this dependence on "friendly Powers" never meant total obedience to their wishes. Above all, Serbia throughout July 1914 was prepared to refuse Austrian demands incompatible with its status as a sovereign and "civilized" state and, like the Great Powers, it would even risk war at this time to defend its status. This obstinacy stemmed partly from Serbia's new confidence after its expansion in the Balkan Wars; and partly from the government's need to pander to Serbian patriotism in the midst of an electoral campaign and after months of tension with the Serbian military. Naturally, few in Belgrade wanted to provoke war with Austria-Hungary, but Serbian prodding of the tiger still continued in the weeks after Sarajevo and even Pašić himself (albeit unwittingly) could not avoid indulging in it. When by 18 July a severe Austrian *démarche* seemed a real possibility, Pašić was quick to appeal to the Powers to place the dispute on an international footing. This proved to be impossible before the expiry of the Austrian ultimatum on 25 July. Serbia, suddenly faced with a tight deadline for meeting Austrian demands, remained almost isolated during the crucial 48 hours and lacked sufficient backing even from the Russians. As a result the government produced (from its own point of view) a very conciliatory reply, but one still hedged with reservations and still resistant over the vital points: despite Serbia's military weaknesses and near-isolation diplomatically, the kingdom was prepared on 25 July to run the risk of a localized war with Austria-Hungary. The prospect of meaningful Russian aid, diplomatically or militarily, remained uncertain on the 25th and therefore probably had little influence on Serbia's reply; indeed, Pašić perhaps did not even fully accept the limited advice received from Sazonov at this time. Only in the next few days did Pašić receive firm assurances of Russian military support, including a letter of "*cordiale sympathie*" from the Tsar.[171] The uncertainty about Russia was then removed. As Spalajković telegraphed excitedly, the Russians had resolved to carry out their "historic task", providing Serbia at last with a marvellous opportunity to complete its unification. By the end of July 1914 Pašić knew that if Greater Serbia materialized, it would be out of the fires of a full European war. Serbia itself had helped to create this war because during the July crisis it was not prepared to return to the status of an Austro-Hungarian satellite.[172]

# Notes

1. Quoted in Ministère des Affaires Etrangères, *Documents diplomatiques français (1871–1914) 3e série (1911–1914)* [hereafter *DDF*], X, no. 469, p. 673.
2. Jovan M. Jovanović, *Borba za narodno ujedinjenje 1914–1918* (Belgrade, 1935), p. 19.
3. Savo Skoko, *Vojvoda Radomir Putnik*, II (Belgrade, 1985), p. 27.
4. See, for example, the memoirs of the Minister of Education, Ljuba Jovanović, published in *Krv Slovenstva* (Belgrade, 1924) and translated as *The murder of Sarajevo* (Chatham House, 1935), p. 4; the memoirs of the Trade Minister, Velizar Janković, published in *Politika*, 10 July 1931; and the reminiscences of one official in the Finance Ministry: Milan Stojadinović, *Ni rat ni pakt. Jugoslavija izmedju dva rata* (Rijeka, 1970), pp. 64–5.
5. Stefanović memoirs (*Politika*, 13 August 1931), translated in Alfred Wegerer, "Der ehemalige serbische Kriegsminister über den Ausbruch des Weltkrieges", *Berliner Monatshefte*, October 1931, pp. 992–4.
6. L. Bittner & H. Übersberger (eds), *Österreich-Ungarns Aussenpolitik von der bosnischen Krise 1908 bis zum Kriegsausbruch 1914*, VIII (Vienna, 1930) [hereafter *ÖUA*], no. 9973. It is difficult to give credence to a thirdhand account, according to which Pašić on learning the news (supposedly in Belgrade) mumbled, "It is very bad. It will mean war." (Hamilton Fish Armstrong, "Three days in Belgrade, July 1914", *Foreign Affairs*, January 1937, p. 267).
7. Vladimir Dedijer & Života Anić (eds), *Dokumenti o spolnoj politici Kraljevine Srbije*, VII/2 (Belgrade, 1980) [hereafter *DSP*].
8. See, for example, the anonymous letter dated 11 [possibly 24?] June 1914, found during the war in Pašić's private archive by the Austrians (Austrian State Archives, Kriegsarchiv, Evidenzbüro 1917, Faszikel 5697/10404): the author, writing from the spa of Koviljača Banja, speculated that Austria might arrange to have "that foolish Ferdinand" assassinated during the current manoeuvres in Bosnia as an excuse to attack Serbia; he warned of how defenceless and isolated Serbia would then be.
9. This story was first revealed in 1924 by Ljuba Jovanović (*The murder of Sarajevo*, p. 3) and resulted in a two-year polemic with Pašić who always denied that he knew of a specific plot to murder the Archduke Franz Ferdinand.
10. Vladimir Dedijer, *Sarajevo 1914*, II (Belgrade, 1978), pp. 117–19.
11. Dedijer implies (ibid., p. 115) that the investigation was in progress during the July crisis, but the documents concerning it have never been discovered (p. 121).

12. Ibid., p. 119: draft letter from the Ministry of Interior to the Ministry of War, 24 June 1914.

13. The following is based largely on Vojislav J. Vučković, "Unutrašnje krize Srbije i prvi svetski rat", *Istorijski Časopis* XIV–XV, pp. 182ff, (1963–65). For other accounts, see Vladimir Dedijer, *The road to Sarajevo* (London, 1967), ch. 17; and David MacKenzie, *Apis: the congenial conspirator. The life of Colonel Dragutin T. Dimitrijević* (New York, 1989), pp. 108–22.

14. Vučković, "Unutrašnje krize", p. 189: the officer who assaulted Balugðić was Major Vojin Tankosić, who supplied the Sarajevo assassins with their arms and whose violent methods or threats are well documented (see Dedijer, *The road to Sarajevo*, pp. 380, 382, 388); Tankosić was to be named in point 7 of the Austrian ultimatum to Serbia.

15. Wladimir Giesl, *Zwei Jahrzehnte im nahen Orient* (Berlin, 1927), p. 254; Otto Hoetzsch (ed.), *Die internationalen Beziehungen im Zeitalter des Imperialismus (Dokumente aus den Archiven der Zarischen und der Provisorischen Regierung)*, I (Berlin, 1931–6) [hereafter *IBZI*], IV, no. 51, Hartwig to Sazonov, 1 July 1914.

16. G. P. Gooch & H. W. V. Temperley (eds), *British documents on the origins of the war 1898–1914*, XI (London, 1938) [hereafter *BD*] nos 28, 29; Dedijer, *Sarajevo 1914*, II, p. 137; Jovanović, *Borba*, p. 13: "vital interests prescribed peace with Austria".

17. Djordje D. Stanković, *Nikola Pašić i Jugoslovensko pitanje*, I (Belgrade, 1985), pp. 136–43.

18. Skoko, *Vojvoda Radomir Putnik*, II, pp. 19–20: Skoko now estimates the number of Serbian dead in the wars at 37,500.

19. Stefanović memoirs (*Berliner Monatshefte*), pp. 991–2.

20. See Mark Cornwall, "Between two wars. King Nikola of Montenegro and the Great Powers, 1913–1914: 1. The union with Serbia", *The South Slav Journal*, IX(1–2), 1986; and "2. The Albanian border", *The South Slav Journal*, IX(3–4), 1986.

21. See the two-volume study of Pašić by Vasa Kazimirović, *Nikola Pašić i njegova doba 1845–1926*, II (Belgrade, 1990), p. 291; unfortunately this massive work does not properly examine the issue of Pašić's behaviour during the July crisis. For one Serbian diplomat's uncertainty about Russia, see the comments of Milenko Vesnić: *I documenti diplomatici italiani. Quarta serie: 1908–1914*, XII (Rome, 1964) [hereafter *DDI*], no. 85.

22. Max Monteglas & Walter Schüking (eds), *Outbreak of the World War: German documents collected by Karl Kautsky* (New York, Oxford, 1924) [hereafter *GD*], supplement IV, no. 1. There is no evidence that the Serbian *chargé*, Milutin Jovanović, informed Pašić of this meeting;

nor did the Russian ambassador in Berlin inform Sazonov that Zimmermann had suggested that Russia advise this in Belgrade (*IBZI*, IV, no. 62).

23. Luigi Albertini, *The origins of the war of 1914*, II (Oxford, 1953), p. 273.

24. *IBZI*, IV, no. 35, Hartwig to Sazonov, 30 June; *DDF*, X, no. 469, Descos to Viviani, 1 July 1914.

25. *Samouprava*, 29 June 1914: translated in *DDF*, X, no. 469, pp. 677–8.

26. As Hartwig mentioned during his last conversation with Giesl: Giesl, *Zwei Jahrzehnte*, p. 260.

27. *GD*, no. 9; *DDF*, X, no. 451. See the valuable comments of Barbara Jelavich in "When diplomats fail: Austrian and Russian reporting from Belgrade, 1914", occasional paper no. 20, East European Program, Wilson Center, Washington DC (n.d.), p. 17.

28. The words of the Serbian minister in Paris, Milenko Vesnić: *DSP*, no. 383, Vesnić to Pašić, 10 July 1914.

29. *DSP*, no. 332, Spalajković to Pašić (tel[egram]), 4 July 1914. (The version in no. 338 is the abbreviated form, published in the Serbian Blue Book in late 1914.)

30. *IBZI*, IV, nos 112, 148: these telegrams (on 7 and 9 July respectively) indicate the gap in communications between Sazonov and Hartwig with regard to Pašić's behaviour in the first weeks of the crisis.

31. *DSP*, no. 376, Spalajković to Pašić (tel), 9 July 1914.

32. *DSP*, no. 337, Vesnić to Pašić, 4 July; no. 309, Mihajlović (Rome) to Pašić, 1 July; *DDI*, nos 90, 101 (the Italian *chargé d'affaires* spoke to Pašić on 7 July); *DSP*, no. 346, Stanojević (Bucharest) to Pašić (tel), 6 July 1914.

33. *DSP*, no. 310, Čolak-Antić (Sofia) to Pašić, 1 July 1914. Čolak-Antić subsequently confirmed that through a German loan to the Bulgarians, they were being tied closer to the camp of the Triple Alliance.

34. See, for example, the words of an official at the Turkish foreign ministry: *DSP*, no. 370, Djordjević to Pašić, 9 July 1914.

35. Britain's attitude otherwise did not appear too favourable at first: see *DSP*, no. 292, Bošković (London) to Pašić (tel), 30 June 1914, describing English press reports which were using Austrian sources; but the attitude of *The Times* later seemed more promising (no. 337).

36. *DSP*, no. 293, Djordjević to Pašić, 30 June 1914.

37. *DSP*, no. 349, Jovanović to Pašić, 6 July; no. 359, 7 July; no. 423, 14 July 1914.

38. See *DDF*, X, no. 469 for the articles in *Pijemont* and *Odjek*; *DDI*, no. 40, for the views of the perceptive (if pro-Serbian) Italian *chargé d'affaires*, Giuliano Cora.

39. Djordje Karadjordjević, *Istina o mome životu* (Belgrade, 1969), p. 309.

40. *DSP*, no. 286, Jovanović to Pašić (tel), 29 June; no. 287 (tel), 29 June 1914.
41. *DSP*, no. 286, Jovanović to Pašić (tel), 29 June; no. 344 (tel), 6 July; no. 379 (tel), 10 July; no. 380 (tel), 10 July 1914.
42. See Tisza's remarks in *GD* no. 79, and at the Joint Ministerial Council of 7 July: Miklos Komjáthy (ed.), *Protokolle des gemeinsamen Ministerrates der österreichisch-ungarischen Monarchie 1914–1918* (Budapest, 1966), p. 142; and Jagow's comments: *DSP*, no. 410, Milutin Jovanović to Pašić (tel), 14 July, and *GD*, nos 33 and 72. See also Milutin Jovanović's report from Berlin (*DSP*, no. 390) in which the editor of the *Berliner Tagblatt* openly admitted misusing extracts from the Serbian press.
43. *DSP*, no. 344, Jovanović to Pašić (tel), 6 July: minute by Slavko Gruić, 6 July; *Neue Freie Presse*, no. 17913 (Abendblatt), 9 July 1914.
44. *DSP*, no. 299, Pašić to all Serbian legations (tel), 1 July 1914.
45. *DSP*, no. 415, Pašić to all Serbian legations, 14 July 1914; the passage about the nature of the "gutter press" (one of which was *Odjek*, the organ of the Young Radicals) was omitted from this letter in the Serbian Blue Book of 1914.
46. Even Baron Giesl admitted Pašić's impotence in the face of the Serbian press: Wladimir Giesl, "Konnte die Annahme der serbischen Antwortnote den Ausbruch des Weltkrieges verhindern?", *Berliner Monatshefte*, 5, May 1933, p. 463.
47. Albertini, *Origins*, II, p. 275.
48. Karadjordjević, *Istina*, pp. 312–13.
49. Initially Jovanović wrote that this would happen after the Archduke's funeral: *DSP* no. 303, Jovanović to Pašić (tel), 1 July 1914.
50. *DDI*, no. 101, Cora to San Giuliano (tel), 7 July; no. 148 (tel), 11 July; *DDF*, X, no. 488, Descos to Viviani, 9 July 1914.
51. *DSP*, no. 355, Jovanović to Pašić, 7 July 1914.
52. For Pašić's action on this matter see, for example, *DSP*, nos 401, 436; *ÖUA*, no. 10527, enclosing Serbian *aide-mémoire* of 22 July 1914.
53. *ÖUA*, no. 10002, Storck to Berchtold (tel), 3 July 1914.
54. *ÖUA*, no. 10000, Storck to Berchtold (tel), 3 July; no. 10004, 3 July 1914.
55. *GD*, no. 32, Griesinger to Bethmann Hollweg, 8 July 1914.
56. *ÖUA*, no. 9950, Storck to Berchtold (tel), 30 June; *DDI*, no. 40, Cora to San Giuliano, 1 July 1914.
57. *Neue Freie Presse*, no. 17911 (Morgenblatt), 7 July 1914.
58. There are two accounts of this meeting which seems to have taken place on 30 June: *DSP*, no. 296, Jovanović to Pašić, 30 June; no. 317, 2 July 1914.
59. Notably Austrian hostility to an independent Albania and Serbian ac-

cess to the Adriatic, and its ultimatum in October 1913.

60. Jovanović played down the demonstrations to Pašić, judging that they were not spontaneous but organized by a few clerical fanatics such as Hermenegild Wagner, the Bulgarophile journalist of the *Reichspost*: see, for example, *DSP*, no. 419, Jovanović to Pašić, 14 July 1914.

61. There are again two versions by Jovanović of this conversation, one more moderate than the other: *DSP*, no. 327, Jovanović to Pašić, 3 July; no. 329, 3 July 1914. For Macchio's less explicit account: *ÖUA*, no. 9981.

62. *Frankfurter Zeitung*, no. 181, 2 July; *Pester Lloyd*, no. 151 (Abendblatt), 6 July 1914.

63. *ÖUA*, no. 10086; *IBZI*, IV, no. 112, Sazonov to Hartwig (tel), 7 July; no. 148, Hartwig to Sazonov (tel), 9 July 1914.

64. Hartwig naturally assured Sazonov that Pašić had halted the talks "precisely on Sazonov's suggestion"; in fact the talks, because of King Nikita's reluctance, had not been "active" since May at least (see Cornwall, "The union with Serbia", pp. 68–70; and Novica Rakočević, *Politički odnosi Crne Gore i Srbije 1903–1918* (Cetinje, 1981), pp. 210–14).

65. *ÖUA*, no. 10461.

66. In 1899, Spalajković had published a propaganda brochure in Paris entitled *La Bosnie et l'Herzégovine*. See the discussion of Spalajković and his "South Slav temperament" by Alfred Rappaport in *Berliner Monatshefte*, no. 7, July 1935, pp. 555ff.

67. *ÖUA*, nos 10016, 10017. Spalajković's "anonymous statements" appeared in *Vecherneye Vremya* on 29 June and *Novoye Vremya* on 1 July; in the latter he denied that the murders could be attributed to all Serbs, and expressed surprise at the arrest of Jeftanović, the "most popular and most beloved" personality in Bosnia. He later asked Sazonov to enquire as to Jeftanović's fate and was soon assured that he had not even been arrested (*IBZI*, IV, nos 66, 89).

68. *DSP* no. 331, Pašić to Jovanović (tel), 4 July; no. 334, Jovanović to Pašić (tel), 4 July 1914. The rumour was circulated by Djordjević in Constantinople (*DSP*, no. 293), but Spalajković and Vesnić clearly knew it as a fact (Albertini, *Origins*, II, p. 98; *DDF*, X, no. 466). It was also publicized in the Belgrade *Štampa* on 30 June.

69. From documents discovered by Vladimir Dedijer in 1977, it has been proven that Jovan Jovanović gave the Ballhausplatz a vague warning in early June about possible dangers if the Archduke visited Sarajevo, but that Pašić did not instruct Jovanović to act in this way. The documents confirm that both Jovanović and Pašić spoke truthfully about the incident in the 1920s and that Albertini's discussion is inaccurate (see Dedijer, *Sarajevo 1914*, II, pp. 136–7, and p. 341 note 156;

Albertini, *Origins*, II, ch. 3; and, for example, the letters of Jovanović to R. W. Seton-Watson in 1924–5: *R. W. Seton-Watson and the Yugoslavs. Correspondence 1906–1941*, II (London & Zagreb, 1976), nos 119, 135)

70. In early July some newspapers in St Petersburg had reported that Spalajković, on meeting Sazonov, had stressed that Serbia could never permit Austrian officials to launch an inquiry in Belgrade: *DDI*, no. 145, Carlotti to San Giuliano, 10 July 1914.

71. See *Neue Freie Presse*, no. 17920 (Abendblatt), 16 July; and *ÖUA*, no. 10414. Djordjević's interview with the Rome newpspaper *Tribuna* may have provoked his transfer from Constantinople; it certainly irritated Jovan Jovanović: see *DSP*, no. 395, Jovanović to Pašić (tel), 13 July 1914.

72. *ÖUA*, no. 10146; Albertini, *Origins*, II, p. 171. A further example of tactless language was the Serbian *chargé d'affaires* in Rome speaking of "barbarism in Bosnia" to Italian journalists: *DSP*, no. 309, Mihajlović to Pašić, 1 July 1914.

73. *ÖUA*, no. 10152, Storck to Berchtold, 9 July 1914.

74. See *DDF*, X, no. 548; and for criticism by the Serbian press bureau: *Neue Freie Presse*, no. 17925 (Morgenblatt), 21 July 1914.

75. *ÖUA* no. 10437, Giesl to Berchtold, 21 July; *GD*, nos 72, 87, 137; *IBZI*, IV, no. 332.

76. See Giesl, *Zwei Jahrzehnte*, pp. 257ff; *DDF*, X, no. 499, Descos to Viviani, 11 July; *IBZI*, IV, no. 223, Strandtmann to Sazonov, 14 July 1914.

77. *IBZI*, IV nos 222, 223; *ÖUA*, no. 10256; *DSP*, no. 435, Jovanović to Pašić, 15 July: showing Vienna's irritation; *DDF*, X, nos 511, 512; *DDI*, no. 196; Ljuba Jovanović, *The murder of Sarajevo*, p. 9: Jovanović asserts that he acted as a bodyguard for Giesl during the funeral procession. See also Jagow's comment on 21 July about Pašić's oration: *IBZI*, IV, no. 332.

78. Albertini, *Origins*, II, pp. 276, 279.

79. Giesl, *Zwei Jahrzehnte*, p. 260. It is also the case that, had he lived, Hartwig was planning to go on extended leave from 12 July.

80. *DSP*, no. 396, Pašić to Jovanović, [14 July]; no. 416, Pašić to all Serbian legations (tel), 14 July 1914.

81. *DSP*, no. 433, Jovanović to Pašić, 15 July 1914. Tisza had warned parliament on 8 July not to identify all Serbs with the Bosnian conspirators and asked them to await the results of the judicial inquiry. On rumours of the meeting of 7 July, Ljuba Jovanović alleges his anxiety at the time: *The murder of Sarajevo*, p. 10.

82. *DSP*, no. 386, Milutin Jovanović to Pašić (tel), 10 July 1914.

83. *IBZI*, IV, no. 238, Strandtmann to Sazonov, 15 July; in fact, by 19 July

agreement over the railways seemed far from certain.

84. For example, *DSP*, no. 433, Jovanović to Pašić, 15 July: this paid some attention to the Ministerial Council of 7 July and Tisza's speeches, but was only received in Belgrade on 21 July. There is no evidence of him telegraphing Pašić on 15 July: cf. Albertini, *Origins*, II, p. 280.

85. *BD*, no. 56. In Belgrade too, Giesl gave nothing away: *DDF*, X, no. 499.

86. *DSP*, no. 449, Bošković to Pašić (tel), 16 July 1914. (The version of this telegram published in the Serbian Blue Book and used by Albertini was abridged and altered.)

87. *DSP*, no. 457, Milutin Jovanović to Pašić (tel), 18 July 1914.

88. *DSP*, no. 451, Mihajlović to Pašić (tel), 17 July 1914. Tisza's speech: *IBZI*, IV, no. 249. Cf. Samuel R. Williamson Jr, *Austria-Hungary and the origins of the First World War* (London, 1991), pp. 201–2.

89. See Ljuba Jovanović, *The murder of Sarajevo*, p. 8.

90. *IBZI*, IV, no. 286, Strandtmann to Sazonov (tel), 19 July 1914.

91. *DSP*, no. 462, Pašić to all Serbian legations except Vienna (tel), 18 July 1914.

92. *BD*, no. 61, Crackanthorpe to Grey (tel), 19 July 1914.

93. *DDI*, no. 363, Cora to San Giuliano (tel), 20 July 1914; see also *DDI*, nos 201 and 285.

94. *DSP*, no. 413, Djordjević to Pašić (tel), 14 July; no. 445, Stanojević to Pašić (tel), 16 July; no. 412, Djordjević to Pašić (tel), 14 July 1914; *DDI*, no. 238.

95. *DSP*, no. 455, Spalajković to Pašić (tel), 18 July; *IBZI*, IV nos 74, 274; *BD* no. 61.

96. *DSP*, no. 449, Bošković to Pašić (tel), 16 July 1914: according to this report, Steed assumed that Serbia was already conducting its own investigation into the murders.

97. *DSP*, no. 427, Mihajlović to Pašić, 14 July 1914. (It is not, in fact, clear when this report reached Belgrade.)

98. *BD*, no. 61. For Jagow's views (and his "ignorance" of the Austrian note), see *DSP*, no. 410, Milutin Jovanović to Pašić (tel), 14 July; no. 457 (tel), 18 July 1914. Milutin Jovanović seems to have felt at times that Germany was trying to moderate the views of the Vienna press (see, for example, *DSP*, no. 390) but Gruić may simply have been misled by Jagow's reserve.

99. *BD*, no. 53, Crackanthorpe to Grey (tel), 17 July 1914.

100. Cf. Albertini, *Origins*, II, p. 281: "Pašić made not the slightest move to forestall Austrian designs."

101. *DSP*, no. 463, Jovanović to Pašić (tel), 20 July; no. 473 (tel), 21 July; no. 476 (tel), 22 July; *ÖUA*, no. 10476, Giesl to Berchtold (tel), 22 July 1914.

102. *DSP*, no. 463.

103. *DSP*, no. 464, Milutin Jovanović to Pašić (tel), 20 July; cf. *GD*, no. 91, Jagow to Tschirschky (tel), 20 July, giving a less conciliatory version of the conversation with the Serbian *chargé*; *GD*, no. 95; *BD*, no. 77.

104. *DSP*, no. 483, Mihajlović to Pašić (tel), 22 July 1914.

105. Compare San Giuliano's version of the conversation: *DDI*, no. 424.

106. *DSP*, no. 474, Spalajković to the Russian government, 21 July; no. 477, Spalajković to Pašić (tel), 22 July 1914.

107. *DSP*, no. 484, Spalajković to Pašić (tel), 22 July. The newspaper *Russkiya Vedomosti*, no. 159, 25 July, remarked on the special attention which Poincaré had paid to Spalajković.

108. Slavko Gruić's memoirs (published in *Politika*, 22–5 July 1936), translated in *Berliner Monatshefte*, 7, July 1935: pp. 586–7. According to Gruić, Pašić had speaking engagements and electoral difficulties to resolve in Radujevac, Zaječar and Knjaževac before proceeding to Niš. Late on 22 July, Pašić may have spoken with the Italian *chargé* in Belgrade: *DDI*, no. 432.

109. See *ÖUA*, no. 10476.

110. Gruić memoirs, p. 587. According to Gruić, Pašić had already reached Niš and given his speech there when Paču telephoned his assistant Dr Šajinović to report Giesl's intended visit. It seems unlikely, as Gruić suggests, that Paču specifically said that Giesl would deliver a note. Pašić in any case was by then exhausted and planning to take a few days' rest in Salonika (*Neue Freie Presse*, no. 17927 (Abendblatt), 23 July 1914).

111. See Albertini, *Origins*, II, p. 352 (based on Luciano Magrini, *Il dramma di Sarajevo. Origini e responsibilità della guerra europea*, Milan, 1929). One of Magrini's "witnesses" was Colonel Živko Pavlović, deputy chief of staff, who was in fact abroad at this time and not present at any alleged Cabinet meeting on the evening of 23 July.

112. Cf. Albertini, *Origins*, II, p. 350.

113. Ljuba Jovanović, *The murder of Sarajevo*, pp. 14–15; *IBZI*, V, no. 10, Strandtmann to Sazonov (tel), 23 July. Gruić's at times unreliable memoirs state that the Austrian note was dictated by him to Strandtmann and Crackanthorpe, the British *chargé*, but it is clear that Crackanthorpe first learnt of the note from Cora (*BD*, no. 89).

114. The ministers (apart from Protić, who was incapacitated at home) visited the palace separately. Although some of them had met in the late afternoon there is no substantiated evidence for a Cabinet meeting in the evening (cf. Albertini, *Origins*, II, p. 352).

115. *DSP*, no. 498 (and note), Paču to all Serbian legations (tel), 24 July 1914. Paču's telegram, published in the Serbian Blue Book (1914), has not been found in the Serbian archives. In a second telegram to the legations (after midnight) he sent the full text of the ultimatum.

116. *IBZI*, V, no. 75, Strandtmann to Sazonov (tel), 25 July 1914.

117. Karadjordjević, *Istina o mome životu*, pp. 315–21.

118. The following is based largely on Stefanović's memoirs in *Vreme*, no. 2723, 26 July 1929, discussed by Rudolf Kiszling in "Die serbische Mobilmachung im Juli 1914", *Berliner Monatshefte*, 7, July 1932, pp. 674–9.

119. *DDI*, no. 463, Cora to San Giuliano (tel), 24 July 1914.

120. *DSP*, no. 501, Pašić to Spalajković (tel), 24 July; *IBZI*, V, no. 35, Strandtmann to Sazonov (tel), 24 July 1914.

121. See, for example, *DSP* no. 490, Vesnić to Pašić, 23 July 1914.

122. Leon Coulard-Descos, the French minister, had had a nervous breakdown (see *ÖUA*, no. 10294 for his bizarre behaviour) and his successor, Jules Boppe, left Paris for Belgrade on the evening of 23 July. This whole situation, together with the state of the Quai d'Orsay, seriously weakened Franco-Serbian contacts in July 1914.

123. *BD*, no. 87, "communication by the Servian minister", 23 July 1914.

124. Not only did Bošković not report Nicolson's words accurately; his telegram did not reach Belgrade until 25 July: *DSP*, no. 536, Bošković to Pašić (tel), 24 July 1914.

125. *DSP*, no. 502, Pašić to Bošković (tel), 24 July; *BD*, no. 92, Crackanthorpe to Grey (tel), 24 July 1914.

126. It is not clear whether this idea originated with Alexander or Strandtmann: see *IBZI*, V, no. 75, 25 July 1914.

127. *DDI*, no. 473, Cora to San Giuliano (tel) 24 July 1914.

128. See Strandtmann's later comments: *IBZI*, V, Beilage 8.

129. Mihajlović: *DDI*, no. 424; Balugðić: *DDI*, no. 466; and even Jovan Jovanović: *DDF*, XI, no. 55.

130. *DSP*, no. 505, Regent Alexander to Tsar Nicholas II (tel), 24 July 1914; *IBZI*, V, no. 37.

131. *DSP*, no. 499, Paču to Jovanović (tel), 24 July; no. 511, Jovanović to Pašić (tel), 24 July 1914.

132. *ÖUA*, no. 10578, Giesl to Berchtold (tel), 24 July; *DSP*, no. 516, Gavrilović (Cetinje) to Pašić (tel), 24 July 1914; Rakočević, *Politički odnosi*, p. 229.

133. *DDI*, no. 274; *DSP*, no. 512, Gavrilović to Pašić (tel), 24 July 1914. For Nikita's behaviour, see John Treadway, *The falcon and the eagle. Montenegro and Austria-Hungary 1908–1914* (West Fayette, Indiana, 1983), ch. 10.

134. *DSP*, no. 472, Stanojević to Pašić (tel), 21 July 1914; *DDF*, X, nos 545, 560.

135. *DSP*, no. 510, Stanojević to Pašić (tel), 24 July; *ÖUA*, no. 10578; *DSP*, no. 500, Pašić to legations at Cetinje, Athens, Bucharest (tel), 24 July 1914.

136. Giesl, "Konnte die Annahme", p. 464.
137. Kiszling, "Die serbische Mobilmachung", pp. 680–81; *IBZI*, V, no. 36, Strandtmann to Sazonov (tel), 24 July; *GD* no. 158, Griesinger to Jagow (tel), 24 July 1914.
138. Jovanović, *Borba za narodno ujedinjenje*, p. 26; Gruić memoirs (*Berliner Monatshefte*), p. 590.
139. Novica Rakočević, "Odnosi Crne Gore i Srbije u periodu 1912–1914. godine", in *Velike Sile i Srbija pred prvi svetski rat*, Vasa Čubrilović (ed.) (Belgrade 1976), p. 585; *DSP*, no. 532, Gavrilović to Pašić (tel), 24 July 1914.
140. See *DSP*, no. 518, Stanojević to Pašić (tel), 24 July; no. 535 (tel), 25 July; no. 534, Balugðić to Pašić (tel), 25 July: the Greek foreign minister even suggested that if Serbia rejected the ultimatum there would not be serious consequences!
141. *DSP*, no. 536, Bošković to Pašić (tel), 24 July 1914.
142. *BD*, no. 119, "communication by the Servian minister", 25 July 1914.
143. *BD*, no. 102, Grey to Crackanthorpe (tel), 24 July; no. 111, Crackanthorpe to Grey (tel), 25 July 1914.
144. *DSP*, no. 528, Mihajlović to Pašić (tel), 24 July 1914 [received on 25 July at 5.16am]. See Albertini's discussion of Italian behaviour: *Origins*, II, pp. 311ff.
145. *DSP*, no. 529, Vesnić to Pašić (tel), 24 July 1914 [received on 25 July at 5.36am].
146. See Pašić's talk with Baron Squitti (the Italian minister) on the morning of 25 July: *DDI*, no. 520, Squitti to San Giuliano (tel), 25 July 1914.
147. See Alfred von Wegerer, "Eine 'Fabel' deutscher Historiker? Erklärungen des Dr Spalajković zur Kriegsschuldfrage", *Berliner Monatshefte*, May 1934, p. 409. Cf. Albertini, *Origins*, II, pp. 353ff.
148. *DSP*, no. 504, Spalajković to Pašić (tel), 24 July 1914, telling of a meeting with the German ambassador, Pourtalès.
149. *DSP*, no. 527, Spalajković to Pašić (tel), 24/25 July 1914. Dedijer is incorrect in noting that this was Spalajković's only telegram to arrive on 25 July before 6pm.
150. See *IBZI*, V no. 25.
151. See Pašić's remarks to Baron Squitti (*DDI*, no. 520). It is not clear if Sazonov told Strandtmann (and therefore Pašić) on the morning of 25 July more precisely about Russian moves in Vienna but it seems unlikely.
152. *DSP*, no. 503, Spalajković to Pašić (tel), 25 July 1914; this document is incorrectly dated by Dedijer as 24 July.
153. Giesl, "Konnte die Annahme", pp. 464–6; Giesl, *Zwei Jahrzehnte*, pp. 267–8.

154. *DDI*, no. 520.
155. *BD*, no. 114, Crackanthorpe to Grey (tel), 25 July. See also no. 111; and Pašić's language in DSP, no. 537, Pašić to all Serbian legations (tel), 25 July 1914.
156. Jovanović, *Borba za narodno ujedinjenje*, p. 26: "the hope placed in Russia was great, it was justified, but it had no effect on Serbia's reply".
157. *DDI*, no. 547, Cora to San Giuliano (tel), 26 July 1914.
158. *Die Kriegsschuldfrage* (Berlin) 3, March 1928, p. 245: Čaprašikov (Bulgarian minister to Serbia) to Radoslavov, 27 July 1914.
159. *IBZI*, V, Beilage 8, Strandtmann to Sazonov, 6 August 1914.
160. Predrag Marković, "Svakodnevni život Beograda na početku rata 1914. godine", *Istorijski Glasnik* I, p. 95, 1986.
161. Serbian official sources confirm this: see *Veliki rat Srbije za oslobodjenje i ujedinjenje Srba, Hrvata i Slovenaca*, I, (Belgrade, 1924) p. 29; cf. *ÖUA*, no. 10646, and the discussion in Kiszling, "Die serbische Mobilmachung", pp. 684–5. For Berchtold's view: *ÖUA*, nos 10733, 10915.
162. See *DSP*, nos 518, 527.
163. Julius Griesinger, "Die kritischen Tage in Serbien", *Berliner Monatshefte*, September 1930, p. 843.
164. See *DDI*, nos 554, 665; *GD*, nos 249, 357; *BD*, nos 202, 231; Albertini, *Origins*, II, pp. 417ff. Mihajlović had added that Austria would need to give assurances over points 5 and 6, something which Grey did not think was possible.
165. *DSP*, no. 556, Spalajković to Pašić (tel), 26 July; no. 570 (tel), 25 July; no. 578, Mihajlović to Pašić (tel), 27 July 1914.
166. *IBZI*, V, nos 49, 149. Cf. Albertini's criticism: *Origins*, II, p. 310.
167. Griesinger, "Die kritischen Tage", pp. 845–6; *DSP*, no. 600, Pašić to all Serbian legations (tel), 27 July 1914.
168. *DSP*, no. 579, Mihajlović to Pašić (tel), 27 July; and minutes by Pašić on no. 586; *IBZI*, V, no. 151; *DDF*, X, no. 162.
169. Pašić's minute at 6.50pm: *DSP*, no. 588.
170. Pašić on 27 July told Strandtmann (*IBZI*, V, no. 151) of alarming reports from Sofia (*DSP*, no. 542) and the still unsatisfactory attitude of Romania and Greece. Despite Bulgaria's announcement of neutrality, the Serbian minister in Sofia continued to feed Pašić with ideas of Bulgarian insincerity (*DSP*, no. 610); Pašić in turn on 28 July, after Vienna's declaration of war, tried unsuccessfully to persuade Greece that the *casus foederis* had now arisen (see *DSP*, nos 620, 648, 658).
171. *DSP*, no. 604, Tsar Nicholas II to Crown Prince Alexander (tel), 27 July 1914; Pašić on receiving it, on the Regent's behalf, gushed with emotion (*IBZI*, V, no. 120, note 3).

172. *DSP*, no. 598, Spalajković to Pašić (tel), 26 July; and Pašić's general review of the European situation: *DSP*, no. 732, Pašić to the Serbian High Command, 31 July 1914.

# Chapter Four
# *Russia*

## Keith Neilson

The Russian decision to go to war in 1914 was momentous: as a result of the First World War, old Russia was swept away by revolution and civil war. In itself, this was not exceptional, as similar fates befell the Austro-Hungarian, German and Ottoman Empires, but what followed in Russia was exceptional. The coming to power of the Bolsheviks meant that Russia's entry into the war was inextricably linked with the rise of Communism. An unhelpful consequence of this is that the Russian decision to go to war in 1914 is rarely analysed for its own sake.[1] Instead, and especially in the context of Russian and Soviet history, it has been regarded as the preliminary to 1917 and the final manifestation of the inability of the Tsarist regime to manage its affairs. This interpretation of events has been based on the presumption – shared by Marxists and non-Marxists alike – that Russia's entry into the war was irrational, given that Russia lacked the economic, financial and military strength to engage in a conflict with the Central Powers.[2] Such argumentation, a heady mix of hindsight and economic determinism, has meant that arguments about Russia's decision to enter into First World War have centred around such relatively unimportant matters as whether the Russian decision to mobilize on 29–30 July was the proximate cause of the outbreak of the war.[3]

However, such an approach is inadequate and essentially sterile. For, as F. H. Hinsley has argued, it is necessary to distinguish "between what caused the First World War and what occasioned it".[4] Further, again as Hinsley has pointed out, when considering why wars break out it is necessary to take account of two different kinds of force that shape human events: "the impersonal and the man-made". Hinsley's two points have a particular relevance to the Russian case. This results from the fact that, by itself, a consideration of the assassination of the Archduke Francis Ferdinand and the events of July 1914 – generally speaking, what "occasioned" Russia's entry into the war – does not illuminate the Russian decision. Indeed, to take the debate about the Russian determination to go to war in 1914 to the level advocated by Hinsley requires that the July crisis be seen in the context of both the impersonal and the man-made forces that shaped the particular decisions made by Nicholas II and his government. To do so, it is necessary to consider closely several aspects of late Imperial Russian history. Four of these – the Russian economy, the Russian armed forces, Russian foreign policy and the way in which decisions were made in the Russian government – are particularly relevant.

## The Russian economy

The essential starting point for discussions of the Russian economy is the work of Alexander Gerschenkron.[5] In the early 1960s, as part of his general arguments about economic backwardness, Gerschenkron contended that Russia's modernization was achieved by means of state intervention and at the expense of the peasantry. This interpretation has been challenged since the early 1980s by a number of specialist works.[6] These studies have produced a very different picture of the Russian economy in the years before 1914. Perhaps the most significant change to emerge is an upward revision of the annual rate of growth for the Russian economy from 2.75 per cent to 3.25 per cent. This seemingly small alteration has wide-ranging implications. First, while Russian output on a per capita basis lagged behind the major industrial powers, on an aggregate basis the Russian economy was substantial.[8] Secondly, Russia's position relative to the other major economies was improving on this aggregate basis. By 1913, Russia's national income was 97.1 per cent that of Great Britain; 171.5 per cent that of France; 83.5 per cent that of Germany; and 21.1 per cent that of the United States. In fact, Russia's economy from 1885 to 1913 was typical of the rapidly growing economies of the era.[9] In this respect, Russia's continual need for foreign capital, easily regarded as a sign of her economic backwardness, should instead be seen as a sign of economic growth.

Another aspect of the Russian economy that needs to be reconsidered is agriculture. Russian agricultural production was by far the largest in Europe; indeed, Russia's grain production in 1913 was almost exactly equally to that of Britain, France and Germany combined, and 84.2 per cent of that of the United States, the world's largest producer.[10] Per capita output was nearly on a par with that of France, substantially greater than in Britain, and 45.8 per cent of America's. Nor was this achieved at the expense of the peasantry, whose standard of living rose between 1861 and 1914.[11] The major causes of famines in that era appear to have been regional variations in soil types, yearly fluctuations in weather and the unreliability of the national distribution system rather than the oppressive nature of the Russian state.[12] Even prior to 1861 and emancipation, the peasants had more than adequate strategies to deal with the central government and thereby to ensure their own quality of life.[13]

Two other issues concerning the Russian economy are particularly significant. The first concerns whether there existed a native Russian entrepreneurial class; the second deals with the place of foreign businesses in Russia. These are important matters. A lack of a well developed entrepreneurial class would suggest a dependency on foreigners in line with assumptions of economic underdevelopment. And the rôle of foreigners in Russia's economy is significant because it is tied to a number of issues: to what extent did Russia lack the funds, the technology and the skills to undertake modernization on her own; and to what extent could the Russian government control these foreigners?[14] The traditional view, as found in explanations of the so-called "Witte system", is that the Russian government undertook a series of actions – in particular, placing Russia on the gold standard – designed to increase the flow of investment and technology into Russia because the Tsarist state lacked the means to modernize on its own.[15]

Recent research has come to the conclusion that the Russian *kupechestvo* (roughly, "merchantry") played a larger rôle in Russia's economic development than was previously believed.[16] Further, this group had a well-developed corporate sense, until at least 1905 was patriotic, and worked closely with the Russian government towards national goals.[17] However, this should not be taken to mean, in the Marxist sense, that the government was controlled by the *kupechestvo*. Frequently, for reasons of state, the Russian government rejected the lobbying efforts of business, preferring instead *dirigiste* means of influencing the economy.[18] Nor were the *kupechestvo* a united body. Instead, they were divided both by regional loyalties and by the fact that there were a disproportionately large number of Old Believers among the merchant class.[19] Nonetheless, families such as the Guchkovs and the Riabushinskys, each of which had made their fortunes in textiles and become prominent in Russian politics, illustrate the degree to which native Russian entrepreneurs played a major rôle in Russia before 1914.

The question of the influence of foreigners is a complicated one. This is particularly evident with respect to foreign investment in Russia. New research has challenged previous assumptions. Rather than credit the Russian government with attracting foreign capital by artificial means, it is now evident that such inflows instead resulted from the normal search by investors for the best possible return.[20] However, even disregarding this argument, and a similar one about the size of the total of foreign investment in Russia, it is evident that foreign money was important to the Russian economy.[21] The reason for this was that the kind of modernization undertaken in Russia from about 1890 to the outbreak of the First World War was capital-intensive. State-of-the-art technology and economies of scale demanded large sums of money.[22] Thus there is no question that foreign funds flowed into Russia; what remains a matter of debate is whether this foreign investment was essential for Russian modernization, or simply speeded up the process.

This is also difficult to answer. In addition to needing to know the exact amount invested in Russia by foreigners, it is also necessary to know in which industries this money was placed and to determine what impact these industries had on overall growth. Much of the foreign money was placed in the high-growth industries that had a disproportionate influence on growth rates, simply because these industries were most amenable to producing high profits by means of the utilization of imported technology. The textile, oil and metalworking industries in particular benefited substantially from a wholesale importation of leading Western technologies.[23] Unlike the matter of the impact of foreign capital, it is not difficult to assess the effect that this flow of technology had on the Russian economy. By 1914, Russia had a considerable number of large industrial works employing the most modern of equipment.

But did the importance of foreign money and technology mean that foreigners were able to manipulate the Tsarist government? The answer seems to be an unqualified "no". While the French advanced large sums to Russia, this money was never able to influence the Tsarist government into pursuing a foreign policy or taking military decisions in line with French wishes.[24] Only when the interests of the Russian military aligned themselves with those of the French – with respect to the building of strategic railways, for example – were French loans able to be tied to specific projects or to shape Russian foreign policy in any way.[25] Nor did foreign businessmen and financiers have any means to coerce the Russian government.[26] The political independence of the Russian government and its importance in Great Power politics meant that foreigners had little impact on policy. Only through the use of Russian lobbyists, and in a fashion similar to that utilized by Russian firms themselves, could foreigners hope to influence the Tsarist regime. The fact that investment tended to pursue profit over and above political goals is underlined by the fact that British investment in Russia, after the signing of the Convention between the two countries in 1907, grew steadily, but this growth was a result of the high yields that Russian bonds, in particular, offered rather than a reflection of politics.[27]

In sum, it appears that the development of the Russian economy before 1914 does not fall into any neat category devised by economic theorists. Instead, its development followed a path that was, in Clive Trebilcock's phrase, "deeply and peculiarly Russian".[28] A combination of state policy designed to be relatively friendly towards capitalist endeavours (both foreign and native) and state restrictions on such developments resulted in a rapid economic growth. The Russian economy, in aggregate terms, was the world's fourth largest, although it rated far less well on a per capita basis.[29] By 1913, Russia had ceased to have a backward economy, although many individual aspects of that economy remained undeveloped.[30] In particular, Russian agriculture was much more advanced than is usually believed, and Russian industry perhaps less important in contributing to national growth than conventional wisdom would argue. Whether this economy was strong enough to support Russia during the First World War – a war that put unprecedented strains on the economies of all the belligerents – is a moot point; what is clear, however, was that the Russian economy before 1914 was sufficient to support Russia's status as a Great Power.

## The Russian armed forces

In 1905, Russia's armed forces were in tatters.[31] With the Baltic fleet at the bottom of the Straits of Tsushima and both the army and navy mutinous, Russia emerged from the Russo-Japanese conflict in sore need of a complete military overhaul. Further, the country was in the midst of a revolutionary political crisis. Both problems necessitated that strict attention be paid to Russian finances, for the war with Japan had left Russia short of funds and in need of foreign loans to stabilize the regime.[32] A. F. Rediger, the Russian Minister of War, estimated in December 1906 that it would require a lump sum of 2,133 million roubles to bring the military – particularly artillery and engineering – up to fighting capacity, and that subsequent budgets would have to be increased by an annual amount of 145 million roubles.[33] It was evident that if Russia wished to regain her military prestige and to stabilize the regime, then the country needed first to be placed on a firm financial basis.

This goal was achieved more quickly than even the most optimistic might have believed possible.[34] Buoyed by generally excellent harvests before the First World War, the income of the Russian government soared.[35] This money allowed the Tsarist government to pursue an ambitious rebuilding and expansion of the fleet at the same time as refurbishing the army.[36] Expenditure on defence rose from 608.1 million roubles in 1908 to 959.6 million in 1913.[37] And the percentage of government spending on defence rose also, from 23.2 per cent in 1907 to 28.3 per cent in 1913.[38] The fears of the British in 1908 (some months after the signing of the Convention that had eliminated many of the quarrels between the two countries) that the expense of the Russian naval building plans would mean that "any chance of Russia regaining a position in the concert of Europe is at an end for years to come" proved groundless, at least in the narrow financial perspective.[39]

The upswing in defence spending also provided a welcome windfall for Russian heavy industry, which had suffered from the twin blows of the international economic downturn just after the turn of the century and the problems caused by the labour unrest of 1905.[40] From 1908 to 1913, industrial production increased by almost 50 per cent in Russia, with defence-related industries leading the way. The Putilov works in St Petersburg illustrate this trend clearly. Whereas in 1900, 53.3 per cent of Putilov's output was directed towards railway equipment and only 14.6 per cent towards defence, by 1912 the defence sector took 45.8 per cent of production and the railways had fallen to 29.6 per cent. The production of iron and steel reflects the spurt in defence spending. Rolled iron and steel production rose from 163 million puds to 247 million puds in the period from 1909 to 1913; of this, about 50 per cent was consumed by the state, nearly evenly divided between rails and defence.

On a wider front, reform of the Russian army began even while the war with Japan was winding down. In June 1905, the Council for State Defence (*Sovet gosudarstvennoi oborony*), under the leadership of the Grand Duke Nicholas Nicholaevich, was established. It had a mandate both to co-ordinate the activities of the various departments of the Russian government concerned with defence and to serve as a sounding board for the wider issues of defence.[41] While the Council achieved some successes, these were limited. This was due to a number of things: the opposition resulting from the fact that Nicholas Nicholaevich was disliked by many senior military men; the attempts of the Duma's Commission for State Defence (headed, interestingly, by Alexander Guchkov) to gain greater control over the Russian military apparatus; and the divisions between the army and navy within the Council itself. None the less, although the Council was dissolved in 1909, it cleared the decks for subsequent improvements.[42]

Much of the improvement was directed at the army. During his tenure at the War Ministry (1905–09), Rediger moved to correct the problems that had manifested themselves in Manchuria.[43] Under Rediger, a substantial number of senior officers were retired and pay increases for officers were granted in order to attract better candidates. Equally, once the army was able to give up acting in aid of the civil power (which many Russian officers, including Rediger, resented having to do because they felt it distracted them from the pursuit of their own profession), it was able to hold manoeuvres and address some of the combat lessons of the Russo-Japanese War. Rediger worked closely with the Duma Commission for State Defence, a fact that made it easier to get funds, but which eventually contributed to weakening his position with Nicholas II, who believed that the commission was undermining his autocratic prerogatives.[44]

Rediger's successor, General V. A. Sukhomlinov, remained as Minister for War until 1915. Although Sukhomlinov has had a bad press, under his leadership the Russian military carried out a wide range of reforms and underwent a spectacular expansion.[45] Sukhomlinov was more fortunate than Rediger in that the former's time in office was not hampered by the need to divert troops to help maintain internal security, nor were finances the concern that they had been. While Sukhomlinov and Kokovtsov, the Russian Finance Minister, disliked each other, the latter was unable to block the increases that Sukhomlinov's ambitious plans – and the even more grandiose plans of the Russian navy – demanded. Sukhomlinov reformed the reserve system of the Russian army, attempted (although he was blocked from doing so by vested interests) to withdraw forces from the indefensible forward positions in western Russia, and completely re-equipped the Russian artillery with modern weapons of the most advanced type.[46]

The centrepiece of Sukhomlinov's time in office was the so-called "Great Programme" of 1914.[47] By means of increasing the annual draft contingent, the "Great Programme" was designed to increase the standing peacetime Russian army from 1.3 million in 1914 to 1.75 million by 1917. The number of artillery batteries was to be increased from 639 eight-gun batteries to 1,197 six-gun batteries, with the most dramatic increases occurring in the number of heavy guns. Efforts were also made to tackle the shortage of officers and non-commissioned officers in the Russian army, a problem that Sukhomlinov had begun to address earlier, in 1910.[48] Clearly, in the period from 1905 to 1914 the Russian military and naval forces were completely rebuilt, a fact made possible by both the improvement in Russia's finances and the manifest political will of both the autocracy itself, and a substantial proportion of the political public, that Russia remain a Great Power.

What was the result of the "Great Programme" and the various naval building programmes? Was the money spent on armaments and personnel justified by the creation of Russian armed forces worthy of a Great Power? Some figures are useful in attempting to come to grips with these questions. As mentioned above, on the eve of war the Russian standing army was about 1.3 million strong, the German 800,000, the French just over 600,000 and Austria-Hungary's about 425,000.[49] The wartime strength (this before the "Great Programme" could come into effect) of the Powers makes clear the numerical edge enjoyed by Russia. The wartime establishment for Russia was 5.29 million men, for Germany 4.15 million, for France 3.87 million and 2.27 for Austria-Hungary. These figures, while not taking into account such important, but difficult to quantify, matters as relative effectiveness, are nevertheless clear signs that Russia was not abdicating its position as a Great Power.[50]

This was also evident with respect to the Russian navy. While the naval battles of the Russo-Japanese War had been catastrophic for the Russian fleet, the material losses had been less important than a first glance would reveal. The revolution in naval technology brought about by Britain's launching of HMS *Dreadnought* in 1906 meant that the Russian ships that had been lost were at least obsolescent and possibly obsolete.[51] Even before Russian finances had stabilized, in 1908 the Russian government began an ambitious building plan to create a new, modern Russian fleet. This immediately brought about a competition for scarce funding within the Russian government, for the army felt that it should have first call on resources.[52] Despite the fact that there were no plans for the Russian navy to pursue a major rôle in time of war – generally speaking, it was to serve as a coastal or "brown-water" navy – the navy received substantial funding in the period from 1908 to 1914.[53] Through a series of naval plans – the small programme of 1908 and the larger programme of 1912 – the Russian navy was in the process of being thoroughly reconstructed by 1914.

Unfortunately, the building of a modern fleet was expensive, technologically complex, and slow. This resulted in naval building being closely tied to Russian politics. It was the navy that called for a reform of Russian acquisitions policy. The navy wanted to get permission either to build ships abroad or to allow foreign companies to compete for contracts to be placed inside Russia. This, it was believed, would ensure both that the highest possible technological levels were achieved and that this was done at the lowest possible price. The result was that by 1914 the Russians were building a fleet of the most modern type. In the Baltic, Russia had under construction four *Borodino*-class and four *Gangoot*-class battleships; while in the Black Sea, three *Ekaterina II*-class battleships were being built. The last, in particular, were impressive ships, quite comparable technologically to anything afloat.[54]

The production of military matériel also gives a favourable picture of Russian readiness. By the beginning of the First World War, in line with the premise of the "Great Programme" that the war would be one of brief duration, Russia had established substantial reserves of war *matériel*.[55] By the outbreak of war, the Russians had just over seven million artillery shells in total, a number amounting to 1,000 per gun and just slightly in excess of that required by the Russian war plans.[56] These holdings, based on estimates determined by Russia's experience in the Russo-Japanese War, proved to be completely inadequate, but this was a common feature for all the participants in the war. As to the amount of artillery itself, Russia had a total of 7650 light and 253 heavy guns available. While this placed Russia in a position of inferiority with respect to the German artillery, it certainly does not suggest a lack of artillery itself. [57]And, the shortages in 1915 were as much the result of mismanagement as anything else. The insistence of the Russian General Staff on keeping large amounts of both shell and artillery pieces in the fortresses in the exposed Polish salient led to enormous losses when these positions fell in 1915.[58] The loss of some 3,000 guns and two million shells in what Norman Stone refers to as "artillery-museums" was a body blow to the hard-pressed Russian *intendantstvo* (quartermaster service).

But the clear thrust of an examination of the Russian armed forces before 1914 is that they had recovered from the debilitating experiences of the Russo-Japanese War. The Tsarist government's determination to shore up Russia's armed might after 1905, a determination reflected by its willingness to spend prodigious amounts of money on armaments, had yielded impressive results. While the Russian military establishment was not certain that they could achieve a victory against the Central Powers in 1914, the use of force to support Russian diplomacy was no longer precluded by military weakness.[59]

## Russian foreign policy

In 1905, Russian diplomacy, like the Russian armed forces, was in need of a thorough overhaul.[60] The Russians were given a taste of the effect that military defeat and domestic unrest could have on their international standing even before the end of the Russo-Japanese War. In March 1905, the Tangier incident began the first Moroccan crisis, one that was widely seen as a test of the newly created *entente cordiale* between Britain and France. However, in Russia there was a strong feeling that Germany had chosen to challenge the French at a time when Russia, France's closest ally, was otherwise engaged. This, coupled with Germany's refusal to help Russia financially after the war, led to a cooling in Russo-German relations.[61]

In May 1906, Alexander Isvolsky became Russia's new Foreign Minister. Isvolsky immediately began attempts to shore up Russia's diplomatic position. Over the next two years, he restored good relations with Japan, tightened Russia's relations with France, negotiated the Anglo-Russian Convention and attempted to come to an understanding with Germany over the Baltic and with Austria-Hungary in the Balkans.[62] By the end of 1907, Isvolsky could congratulate himself on having improved Russia's standing in the international arena dramatically, and with having reduced the external threats to Russia significantly. Here, the Anglo-Russian Convention, which eliminated the long-standing quarrels between the two states in Central Asia, was perhaps the most important.

However, not everything was satisfactory. By early 1908, Isvolsky's secret attempts to negotiate an agreement with Germany that would have converted the Baltic into a Russo-German lake, at the same time as allowing Russia to fortify the Åland islands, had led to French suspicions of a Russo-German *rapprochement*. Further, Austro-Hungarian railway plans in the Balkans seemed likely to reduce the influence of both Russia and Russia's Balkan ally, Serbia, in that area. Of the two problems, the latter was by far the most significant, for its end result was the Bosnian crisis.[63] This crisis, which ended in March 1909 with Russia having to back down in the face of a German ultimatum, made manifest the linkage between Russia's military weakness and her foreign policy. Being unable to risk war in support of foreign-policy goals meant that Russia was temporarily demoted from the ranks of the Great Powers.

Although he remained in office until mid-1910, the Bosnian crisis effectively ended Isvolsky's tenure as Foreign Minister, and discredited his policies. His successor, Sergei Sazonov, took the Bosnian crisis to indicate that Russia could not pursue a policy that would place her in direct opposition to Germany.[64] Sazonov thus attempted to steer a middle course between Germany and Russia's existing obligations to Britain and France. In November 1910, Nicholas II met with the German Kaiser, Wilhelm II, at Potsdam. The result was a *rapprochement* between the two countries in which Russia dropped her objections to German efforts to secure railway concessions in the Middle East in exchange for German undertakings not to support Austria-Hungary in another Balkan adventure and not to build railways into Persia and the Caucasus.[65]

This policy was a difficult one to manage, as the events of the summer of 1911 demonstrated. The outbreak of the second Moroccan crisis on 1 July made it hard for Sazonov to continue to ride two horses simultaneously.[66] In August, Russian support for France was only lukewarm (possibly in retaliation for France's hesitant support in the Bosnian crisis), creating the impression that Russia was either unwilling or unable to support her alliance partner.[67] Although Russia subsequently threw her weight behind France, it was not immediately evident that the Franco-Russian alliance would stand firm against German pressure.[68] To some extent, Franco-Russian relations were patched up in 1912. The new French Foreign Minister, Raymond Poincaré, travelled to Russia in August and patched up the differences between the two states.[69] But Sazonov's foreign policy underwent another crisis later in the year. When the First Balkan War began in October 1912, Russian public opinion strongly supported Serbia's claim for an Adriatic port, a result that was unacceptable to Austria-Hungary.[70] Sazonov found himself trying to find his way between two unpleasant possibilities: that support for Serbia might lead to a Russian war with Austria-Hungary; and that a failure to support Serbia might seem a repetition of the Bosnian episode and lead to his sharing Isvolsky's fate. Policy was determined on 23 November, when a meeting was held between Nicholas II, his leading ministers and the chief of staff.[71] Sukhomlinov, the War Minister, wished to mobilize against Austria-Hungary, but the pacific advice of Kokovtsov, the chairman of the Council of Ministers, and Sazonov, persuaded the Emperor to cancel any such plans. While the impetus for this decision had been purely Russian, the fact that the German Chancellor, Theodore von Bethmann Hollweg, told the *Reichstag* on 2 December that Germany would support Austria-Hungary in a war against Russia gave the Russian decision the appearance of weakness and raised the ghost of the Bosnian *débâcle*.[72]

Thus, when the July crisis broke in 1914, Russian diplomacy had a decade of failure behind it. Isvolsky's time in office, from 1906 to 1910, for the most part had been a period of *recueillement*, a policy dictated by the results of the Russo-Japanese War. His effort to reverse this trend by means of a diplomatic coup that would give Russia control of the Straits turned into the *débâcle* of the Bosnian crisis, and led to his dismissal. Sazonov's time in office had marked a return to a Russian foreign policy that attempted to keep the Tsarist state on good terms with the Triple Alliance while simultaneously maintaining the Dual Alliance and the Anglo-Russian Convention. The Moroccan crisis in 1911 and the First Balkan War had underscored the fact that Russia was not prepared to resort to war in all circumstances. But these were choices made of necessity and engendered a growing sense of irritation in Russia. The improvements in Russia's economic and military strength meant that the July crisis would be considered differently.

## The nature of the Tsarist state

This brings us to the need to consider the nature of the Tsarist state. Sir Charles Hardinge, the British ambassador to Russia during 1904–5, was in no doubt about the character of the autocracy: "It is an anachronism", he wrote in 1905, "existing now only in semi-civilised & barbarous states, & must inevitably be modified to meet the requirements of the great advance in civilisation made in Russia during the past 20 years."[73] Even after the creation of the Duma in 1905, Hardinge's remarks had force. While the new legislative body had some power, Nicholas II's own authority was largely undiminished, because he was able to dismiss the Duma when he chose, and, if necessary, implement laws by decree.[74] Despite the efforts of Stolypin (discussed below), there was no collective responsibility among Nicholas's ministers for their decisions, and they could be, and were, appointed and dismissed individually. In essence, despite the Duma, Russia remained an autocracy supported by an apolitical bureaucracy.[75]

Within this state, there was clearly a ruling elite, centred around the autocrat, and it is Nicholas II himself who must hold our attention.[76] Nicholas has traditionally been seen as weak and vacillating, overly fond of family life, henpecked by the Empress and under the influence of the most recent person to speak to him. Only part of this picture is correct, and it overlooks certain aspects of Nicholas's character. The first is that Nicholas was quite capable of standing firm whenever he felt that it was necessary, either for the sake of his rôle as autocrat or for what he perceived as the good of Russia. During the negotiations for the peace settlement at the end of the Russo-Japanese War, for example, Nicholas was adamant that Russia should not agree to a humiliating peace.[77] Secondly, Nicholas shared what John Keep has termed the "Romanov military style", that is, a belief in his duty to serve as Russia's military commander, a fact that goes a long way to explain his assumption of command in 1915.[78] Finally, careful analysis suggests that Nicholas made his own decisions on the basis of an intelligent appreciation of his own rôle as autocrat and without being overly influenced by his wife, by Rasputin or by any of his ministers.[79]

However, while it was Nicholas who made the final decisions, the influence of his ministers cannot be dismissed out of hand. After the Russo-Japanese War, there was a growth of what has been termed "united government" in Russia.[80] In it, Stolypin attempted to establish some sort of collective responsibility for Russian foreign policy, in order to prevent unofficial influences from involving Russia in another *débâcle* like that of 1904–5. When Izvolskii attempted, with the connivance of Nicholas II, to play a lone hand in the Bosnian crisis, it was the combined influence of Stolypin and the Minister of Finance, V. N. Kokovtsov, that clipped his wings and imposed a pacific policy on Russia. This state of affairs did not last long after Stolypin's death in 1911, and his replacement as chairman of the Council of Ministers by Kokovtsov.[81] Kokovtsov lacked Stolypin's prestige. Further, he was bitterly opposed by a number of ministers, including Sukhomlinov, who resented the financial restraints that Kokovtsov attempted to impose on military expenditure, and Alexander Krivoshein, the Minister of Agriculture.[82] During the crisis of November 1912, both Sukhomlinov and Krivoshein had advocated using military force on behalf of the Serb claims, and only Kokovtsov's threat of resignation and Sazonov's belated support for the chairman had thwarted them.[83] But Nicholas felt that Kokovtsov's threat was in effect an infringement on the powers of the autocrat, and was determined to reassert his own authority. The culmination of this was what Nicholas termed his *"coup d'état"* in February 1914.[84] Here, the Emperor replaced Kokovtsov with the ageing functionary, I. L. Goremykin, and made P. L. Bark the new Minister of Finance.[85] The driving force behind these changes was Krivoshein, and his voice, along with that of N. A. Maklakov, whom Nicholas had appointed Minister of the Interior in 1913, was the dominant one among the Tsar's ministers. Thus, on the eve of war, Nicholas was surrounded by a very different group of men from those who had steered Russia past the possibility of war in 1909 and 1912.

## Conclusion

When the leading men of the Council of Ministers met on 24 July 1914 to determine Russia's actions in the international crisis in the Balkans, both the "impersonal" and the "man-made" forces that determine events had changed profoundly since 1905.[86] Russia had regained (and even enhanced) her economic and military strength. Diplomatically, thanks to improved relations with Japan and Great Britain, Russia no longer faced threats in the Far East and Central Asia. However, Russian policy in the Balkans had suffered two humiliations, in 1909 and 1912, the cumulative effect of which was to diminish Russia's standing as a Great Power. The ministers most responsible for Russian policy were no longer men such as Stolypin and Kokovtsov, who opposed war unequivocally because of their belief that Russia was not in a position to fight.

In this context, the Russian decision to offer support to Serbia against Austria-Hungary was almost a foregone conclusion. Sazonov argued that Germany was determined to establish a paramount position in Europe; Krivoshein stated that Russia's position had improved since 1905 and that, while war should be avoided if possible, Russia must now take a firmer stand. The two service ministers, Sukhomlinov and I. K. Grigorovich, the Minister of the Marine, refused to promise victory, but asserted that there were no military reasons why Russia should back down. Finally, Bark, although wary about the ability of Russia's finances to support a war, supported the consensus. The following day, Nicholas II chaired a second meeting of the Council, which confirmed the decision of 24 July.

What followed was an anticlimax. When the Russians began their partial mobilization on 26 July, this triggered the military plans of the other Great Powers. For Germany, Russian mobilization meant that Germany either had to abandon her support for Austria-Hungary or begin her own mobilization at once, since the Schlieffen plan was based on the Kaiser's forces obtaining a rapid victory against France while Russia was still unprepared. The German attempt – in the fashion of the Bosnian crisis – to cow Russia into ceasing her military preparations on 29 July failed for the simple reason that Russia was no longer prepared to cave in. While being far from willing war to occur, the Russian government was prepared, in light of the changes that had occurred in the five years since the Bosnian humiliation, to risk a conflict rather than abdicate its position as a Great Power.

## Notes

1. Two exceptions are D. W. Spring, "Russia and the coming of war", in *The coming of the First World War*, R. J. W. Evans & H. Pogge von Strandmann (eds) (Oxford, 1988), pp. 57–86; and D. C. B. Lieven, *Russia and the origins of the First World War* (London, 1983).

2. This is implicit in Paul Kennedy, *The rise and fall of the Great Powers: economic change and military conflict from 1500 to 2000* (New York, 1987), pp. 232–41.

3. Argued by L. C. F. Turner, "The Russian mobilisation in 1914", in *The war plans of the Great Powers 1880–1914*, Paul M. Kennedy (ed.) (London, 1979), pp. 262–6, and rebutted by Lieven, *Russia and the origins*, pp. 148–51.

4. F. H. Hinsley, *Power and the pursuit of peace. Theory and practice in the history of relations between states* (Cambridge, 1963), pp. 289–90. The following discussion is informed by ibid., pp. 289–308.

5. His basic assumptions about the Russian economy can be found in Alexander Gerschenkron, *Economic backwardness in historical perspective* (Cambridge, Mass., 1962), pp. 5–31, 119–51.

6. Paul R. Gregory, *Russian national income, 1895–1913* (Cambridge, 1982); Peter Gatrell, *The Tsarist economy 1850–1917* (London, 1986);

Olga Crisp, *Studies in the Russian economy before 1914* (New York, 1976). The literature on the peasantry is outlined in Ben Eklof, "Ways of seeing: recent Anglo-American studies of the Russian peasant (1861–1914)", *Jahrbücher für Geschichte Osteuropas* 36, 1988, particularly on pp. 68–70. The major revisionist work is Heinz-Dietrich Lowe, *Die Lage der Bauern in Russland 1880–1905* (Sankt Katharinen, 1987).

7. The first figure is that of Raymond Goldsmith, "The economic growth of Tsarist Russia, 1860–1913", *Economic Development and Cultural Change* 9, 1961, pp. 441–75; the latter figure is from Gregory, *Russian national income*, pp. 55–79.

8. The following figures are derived from Gregory, *Russian national income*, pp. 153–65.

9. Ibid., 192–3.

10. All figures are derived from ibid., p. 156.

11. James Y. Simms, Jr, "The crisis in Russian agriculture at the end of the nineteenth century: a different view", *Slavic Review* 36, 1977, pp. 377–98; Lowe, *Die Lage der Bauern*; Robert E. Smith & David Christian, *Bread and salt: a social and economic history of food and drink in Russia* (Cambridge, 1984), pp. 286–7.

12. High infant mortality, often attributed to poor nutrition (and, hence, an inferred low standard of living), may have resulted from disease: see Mary Kilbourne Matossian, "Climate, crops, and natural increase in rural Russia, 1861–1913, *Russian Review* 45, 1986, pp. 457–69.

13. Stephen L. Hoch, "Serfs in imperial Russia: demographic insights", *Journal of Interdisciplinary History* 13, 1982, pp. 221–46; two articles by Rodney D. Bohac, "Peasant inheritance strategies in Russia", *Journal of Interdisciplinary History* 16, 1985, pp. 23–42; and "The mir and the military draft", *Slavic Review* 47, 1988, pp. 652–66.

14. There is a large volume of literature on foreign business in Russia. The essential starting point is John P. McKay, *Pioneers for profit: foreign entrepreneurship and Russian industrialization 1885–1913* (Chicago and London, 1970). Also important are F. V. Carstensen, "Foreign participation in Russian economic life: notes on British enterprise, 1865–1914", in *Entrepreneurship in imperial Russia and the Soviet Union*, G. Guroff & F. V. Carstensen (eds) (Princeton, New Jersey, 1983), pp. 140–58.

15. Theodore H. von Laue, *Sergei Witte and the industrialization of Russia* (New York, 1963).

16. A. J. Rieber, *Merchants and entrepreneurs in imperial Russia* (Chapel Hill, North Carolina, 1982), pp. 415–16.

17. Thomas C. Owen, *Capitalism and politics in Russia: a social history of the Moscow merchants, 1855–1905* (Cambridge, 1981), pp. 206–12;

Jo Ann Ruckman, *The Moscow business elite: a social and cultural portrait of two generations, 1840–1905* (DeKalb, Illinois, 1984), pp. 141–8; James L. West, "The Rjabusinski circle: Russian industrialists in search of a bourgeoisie, 1909–1914", *Jahrbücher für Geschichte Osteuropas* 32, 1984, pp. 358–77.

18. Thomas C. Owen, "The Russian industrial society and Tsarist economic policy, 1867–1905", *Journal of Economic History* 45, 1985, pp. 587–606; Ruth A. Roosa, "Russian industrialists and 'State Socialism'", *Soviet Studies* 23, 1972, pp. 395–417; and Clive Trebilcock, *The industrialization of the continental Powers 1780–1914* (London and New York, 1981), pp. 222–3.

19. James D. White, "Moscow, Petersburg and the Russian industrials", *Soviet Studies*, 24, 1973, pp. 414–20; Owen, *Capitalism and politics*, pp. 1–9; Rieber, *Merchants and entrepreneurs*, pp. 143–7.

20. Malcolm Falkus, "Aspects of foreign investment in Tsarist Russia", *Journal of European Economic History* 8, 1979, pp. 5–39.

21. The debate is outlined in the translators' introduction to P. V. Ol', *Foreign capital in Russia*, trans. Geoffrey Jones & Grigori Gerenstain (New York and London, 1983). A good Soviet discussion is in V. I. Bovykin, *Formirovanie finansovogo kapitala v Rossiia: Konets XIX v.–1908 g.* (Moscow, 1984), ch. 3. Comparative figures can be found in René Girault, *Emprunts russes et investissements français en Russie, 1887–1914* (Paris, 1973), pp. 84–5; and Crisp, *Russian economy*, p. 199. There is a good discussion of the importance of foreign capital in Gatrell, *Tsarist economy*, pp. 222–9.

22. Trebilcock, *Industrialization*, pp. 244–7; and Malcolm Falkus, "Aspects of Russian industrialization before the First World War", *Australian Journal of Politics and History* 12, 1966, p. 338.

23. Trebilcock, *Industrialization*, pp. 223–5; McKay, *Pioneers for profit*, pp. 112–57 and 337–67.

24. See the discussion in Dietrich Geyer, *Russian imperialism: the interaction of domestic and foreign policy, 1860–1914*, trans. Bruce Little (Leamington Spa, 1987), pp. 169–86; and John P. Sontag, "Tsarist debts and Tsarist foreign policy", *Slavic Review* 27, 1968, pp. 529–41. The definitive rebuttal is D. W. Spring, "Russia and the Franco-Russian alliance, 1905–14: dependence or interdependence?", *Slavonic and East European Review* 66, 1988, pp. 564–92.

25. See D. N. Collins, "The Franco-Russian alliance and Russian railways, 1891–1914", *Historical Journal* 16, 1973, pp. 777–8.

26. McKay, *Pioneers for profit*, pp. 274–5, 285; Crisp, *Studies in the Russian economy*, pp. 174–88.

27. For the growth in British investment, see D. C. M. Platt, *Britain's investment overseas on the eve of the First World War* (London, 1986),

pp. 89, 92–3; and notice the high relative interest offered on Russian railway bonds in 1913 and the substantial discount at which they were sold, ibid., p. 43.

28. Trebilcock, *Industrialization*, p. 285.

29. See the figures in Paul Bairoch, "Europe's gross national product: 1800–1975", *Journal of European Economic History* 5(2), 1976, table 6, p. 286; and in Gregory, *Russian national income*, table 7.1, pp. 155–6.

30. This is the conclusion of Gatrell, *Tsarist economy*, pp. 231–4, which I support.

31. For the best detailed account of this, see John Bushnell, *Mutiny amid repression: Russian soldiers in the revolution of 1905–1906* (Bloomington, Indiana, 1985); but see also Michael Perrins, "Russian military policy in the Far East and the 1905 revolution in the Russian army", *European Studies Review* 9, 1979, pp. 331–49. The best look at the period is Bruce W. Menning, *Bayonets before bullets: the imperial Russian army, 1861–1914* (Bloomington, Indiana, 1993), pp. 200–78; also interesting is William C. Fuller, Jr, *Strategy and power in Russia 1600–1914* (New York, 1992), pp. 394–451. As the following reveals, I do not agree with all Fuller's conclusions. On the naval side of things, see J. Dane Hartgrove, "The Kronstadt mutiny of October 1905", in *New aspects of naval history*, Craig L. Symonds (ed.) (Annapolis, Maryland, 1981), pp. 268–77, which also introduces the Soviet literature. The political crisis of 1905 is best seen in Andrew M. Verner, *The crisis of Russian autocracy. Nicholas II and the 1905 revolution* (Princeton, New Jersey, 1990).

32. On the negotiation of the 1906 loan, see Girault, *Emprunts russes*, pp. 435–43. This loan was opposed, both in France and in Russia, by liberals who felt that the money would be used to prop up the Tsarist regime; see James William Long, "Organized protest against the 1906 Russian loan", *Cahiers du monde russe et soviétique* 13, 1972, pp. 24–39; and Olga Crisp, "The Russian liberals and the 1906 Anglo-French loan to Russia", *Slavonic and East European Review* 39, 1961, pp. 497–511.

33. K. F. Shatsillo, *Rossiia pered pervoi mirovoi voinoi (vooruzhennye sily tsarizma v 1905–1914 gg.)* (Moscow, 1974), p. 39.

34. The fundamental examination of this is A. L. Sidorov, *Finansovoe polozhenie Rossii v gody pervoi mirovoi voiny (1914–1917)* (Moscow, 1960), pp. 14–106.

35. See Stone, *Russian front*, p. 18

36. On the fleet, see K. F. Shatsillo, *Russkii imperializm i razvitie flota nakanune pervoi mirovoi voiny (1906–1914)* (Moscow, 1968) and, on the high emphasis placed on spending for the fleet, *idem*, "O dispro-portsii v razvitii vooruzhennyk sil Rossii nakanune pervoi mirovoi

voiny (1906–1914 gg.)", *Istoricheskie zapiski* 83, 1969, pp. 123–36. There is excellent commentary on the ramifications of this naval building programme in Peter Gatrell, "After Tsushima: economic and administrative aspects of Russian naval rearmament, 1905–1913", *Economic History Review*, 2nd series, **43**, 1990, pp. 255–70.

37. See table 4 in Gatrell, "Tsarist economy", p. 105.

38. These figures are derived from table F.1 in Gregory, *Russian national income*, p. 252. Slightly different, but quite comparable figures, can be found in the outstanding Soviet work, A. L. Sidorov, *Finansovoe polozhenie Rossii v gody pervoi mirovoi voiny (1914–1917)* (Moscow, 1960), p. 43. I prefer Gregory's figures because of the increased sophistication of his estimates concerning related government expenditure on defence. Interestingly, despite the fact that this was a time of rising weapons costs, the percentage of the military budget spent on weapons, as opposed to subsistence, remained well within the historical norms for the Russian army; see Walter M. Pintner, "The burden of defense in imperial Russia, 1725–1914", *Russian Review* **43**, 1984, fig. 1, p. 242; and the discussion on pp. 243–5.

39. Although it could be argued that this increased military spending deflected money from more economically useful destinations. The quotation is from Louis Mallet's undated minute (Mallet was the superintending clerk in the department of the British Foreign Office that dealt with Russia) on O'Beirne (British *chargé d'affaires*, St Petersburg) to Grey despatch 213, 2 May 1908, PRO, FO 371/516/16030. I have discussed the British perceptions of Russian military power before 1914 in Keith Neilson, "Watching the 'steamroller': British observers and the Russian army before 1914", *Journal of Strategic Studies* 8, 1985, pp. 199–217.

40. The rest of this paragraph, and the figures used in it, are from Gatrell, "Tsarist economy", unless otherwise noted.

41. My account of the Council for State Defence is based, except where otherwise noted, on Michael Perrins, "The Council for State Defence 1905–1909: a study in Russian bureaucratic politics", *Slavonic and East European Review* 58(3), 1980, pp. 370–98. The wider range of Russian bureaucratic organization for war can be found in I. I. Rostunov, *Russki front pervoi mirovoi voiny* (Moscow, 1976), pp. 26–41.

42. This is Perrins' conclusion: Council for State Defence, p. 396.

43. The following is based on W. T. Wilfong, *Rebuilding the Russian army, 1905–14: the question of a comprehensive plan for national defense* (PhD thesis, Indiana University), pp. 62–97; William C. Fuller, *Civil–military conflict in imperial Russia 1881–1914* (Princeton, New Jersey, 1985), pp. 129–68 and 202–3; and Neilson, "Watching the 'steamroller'".

44. On the relationship between the Duma Commission and Rediger, see J. F. Hutchison, "The Octobrists and the future of imperial Russia as a Great Power", *Slavonic and East European Review* 50, 1972, pp. 227–9.

45. A good, brief summary of Sukhomlinov's time in office that also introduces the literature is Wildman, *End of the Russian imperial army*, pp. 65–74. In addition to Wilfong, "Rebuilding the Russian army", pp. 97–120, John D. Walz, *State defense and Russian politics under the last tsar* (PhD dissertation, Syracuse University, 1967), pp. 98–237 is very good on the Sukhomlinov era. Unless otherwise indicated, my account of Sukhomlinov is based on these two sources.

46. Stone, *Eastern front*, pp. 30–32. See the useful comparison of the artillery armaments of the various belligerents in 1914, found in I. I. Rostunov (ed.) *Istoriia pervoi mirovoi voiny 1914–1918 v dvykh tomakh* (Moscow, 1973), vol. I, p. 105.

47. Well outlined in A. Zhilin, "Bolshaia programma po usileniiu rosskoi armii", *Voenno-istoricheskii zhurnal* 16, 1974, pp. 90–7. The details of the scheme with valuable remarks by a contemporary expert, Colonel A. F. W. Knox (British military attaché, Russia, 1911–18) can be found in his two despatches of 18 March 1914 and 28 March 1915, W[ar] O[ffice] 106/1039, PRO. The following figures are from Zhilin.

48. Neilson, "Watching the 'steamroller'", pp. 209–10.

49. These figures (and those that follow), with the exception of those for Germany, are from 1910 and can be found in British General Staff, War Office, *Report on changes in foreign armies during 1910* (London, 1911), pp. 9–10. The German figure is from Holger H. Herwig, "The dynamics of necessity: German military policy during the First World War", in *Military effectiveness*, vol. I, *The First World War*, Allan R. Millet & Williamson Murray (eds) (London, 1988), p. 83.

50. Certainly this was the belief of the other European Great Powers. For a discussion of their impressions of Russia's growing might, see Risto Ropponen, *Die Kraft Russlands: wie beurteilte die politische und militarische Fuhrung der europaischen Grossmachte in der Zeit von 1905 bis 1914 die Kraft Russlands?* (Helsinki, 1968); for the British, Neilson, "Watching the 'steamroller'".

51. See Shatsillo, "O disproportsii", pp. 127–9. The rest of this paragraph, except where otherwise noted, is based on this article.

52. See Shatsillo, *Russkii imperializm i razvitie flota*, pp. 52–7.

53. Naval plans can be found in N. E. Saul, *Sailors in revolt: the Russian Baltic Fleet in 1917* (Lawrence, Kansas, 1978), pp. 37–44.

54. This positive evaluation of the Russian fleet leaves out any consideration of the personnel that manned the ships. The British naval attaché in Russia, Commander H. G. Grenfell, was extremely critical of the

Russian navy's human, as opposed to its material, resources. He viewed the higher administration as being both corrupt and lazy, the officer corps as incompetent and the men as ill-trained and often mutinous; see Grenfell's despatch of 21 August 1912, FO 371/1470/35876; H. O'Beirne (British *chargé d'affaires*, St Petersburg) to Grey, despatch 194, 25 June 1912, FO 371/1470/27674; Grenfell's report for 1912 included in Buchanan to Grey, despatch 7, 9 January 1913, FO 371/1743/1685 and, particularly, Grenfell to Buchanan, 19 March 1914, *British documents on the origins of the war, 1898–1914 [BD]* (London, 1926–38), vol. X, part 2, pp. 771–2.

55. For pre-war thinking, see Sidorov, *Ekonomicheskoe polozhenie*, pp. 5–18; the figures for shells and artillery pieces are from Rostunov, *Russkii front*, pp. 98 and 97 respectively. The belief that the war would be a short one was shared by all the belligerents, to the detriment of their planning for the consumption of war *matériel*; see L. L. Farrar, Jr, *The short-war illusion* (Santa Barbara, California, 1974); and David French, *British economic and strategic planning 1905–1915* (London, 1982), pp. 51–73.

56. In fact, the goal of 1,000 shells per artillery piece was met only for those in the field and there were noticeable shortfalls of heavy shell.

57. Stone, *Eastern front*, pp. 37–8 argues that the Germans' superiority was not particularly significant, resulting primarily from their large amounts of high-trajectory pieces suitable only for siege work.

58. See Stone, *Eastern front*, pp. 30–2 and 148–9. The figures are from the latter pages and the quotation from p. 149.

59. Cf. William C. Fuller, Jr, "The Russian Empire", in Ernest R. May, *Knowing one's enemies: intelligence assessment before the two world wars* (Princeton, New Jersey, 1984), pp. 98–126; and Menning, *Bayonets before bullets*, p. 246.

60. A. V. Ignatev, *Vneshniaia politika Rossii v 1905–1907 gg.* (Moscow, 1986); B. J. Williams, "The revolution of 1905 and Russian foreign policy", in *Essays in honour of E. H. Carr*, C. Abramsky (ed.) (London, 1974), pp. 101–25.

61. J. Steinberg, "Germany and the Russo-Japanese War", *American Historical Review* 75, 1970, pp. 1965–86; B. F. Oppel, "The waning of a traditional alliance: Russia and Germany after the Portsmouth Peace Conference", *Central European History* 5, 1972, pp. 318–29; I. I. Astafev, *Russo-germanskie diplomaticheskie otnosheniia 1905–1911 gg. (ot portsmutskogo mira do potsdamskogo soglasheniia)* (Moscow, 1972), pp. 10–58.

62. V. A. Marionov, *Rossiia i Iaponiia pered pervoi mirovoi voiny (1905–1914 gody)* (Moscow, 1974), pp. 23–51; J. Long, "Franco-Russian relations during the Russo-Japanese War", *Slavonic and East*

European Review 52, 1974, pp. 213–33; D. W. Spring, "Russia and the Franco-Russian Alliance, 1905–14: dependence or interdependence?", Slavonic and East European Review 66, 1988, pp. 564–92; A. F. Ostaltseva, Anglo-Russkoe soglashenie 1907 goda (Saratov, 1977); P. Luntinen, The Baltic question 1903–1908 (Helsinki, 1975); A. V. Ignatev, "Baltiicheskii vopros vo vneshei politike Rossii 1905–1907 godov", Voprosy istorii 3, 1986, pp. 22–36; F. R. Bridge, "Izvolsky, Aehrenthal, and the end of the Austro-Russian Entente, 1906–8", Mitteilungen des Österreichischen Staatsarchivs 29, 1976, pp. 315–62.

63. Best followed in D. M. McDonald, United government and foreign policy in Russia, 1900–1914 (Cambridge, Mass. and London, 1992), pp. 127–51.

64. Astafev, Russko-germanskie diplomaticheskiia otnosheniia, pp. 219–48, especially pp. 241–2; A. S. Avetian, Russko-germanskie diplomaticheskie otnosheniia nakanune pervoi mirovoi voiny 1910–1914 (Moscow, 1985), pp. 66–82.

65. This latter would have threatened Russian business interests; see Alan Bodger, "Russia and the end of the Ottoman Empire", in The Great Powers and the end of the Ottoman Empire, Marian Kent (ed.) (London, 1984), pp. 76–110.

66. For the crisis, see J-C. Allain, Agadir 1911. Une crise impérialiste en Europe pour la conquête de Maroc (Paris, 1976); and K. A. Hamilton, Bertie of Thame: Edwardian Ambassador (London, 1990), pp. 214–47.

67. Lieven, Russia and the origins, p. 38.

68. L. A. Neiman, "Franko-russkie otnosheniia vo vremia markokkanskogo krizisa 1911 g.", Frantsuzskii ezhegodnik (1969), pp. 65–91; John F. V. Keiger, France and the origins of the First World War (London, 1983), pp. 42 and 88–9.

69. Keiger, France and the origins, pp. 96–7.

70. McDonald, United government, pp. 180–87.

71. In addition to ibid., see also Turner, "Russian mobilization", pp. 252–6.

72. McDonald, United government, p. 189.

73. Hardinge to Knollys (private secretary to King Edward VII), letter, 8 February 1905, Hardinge Papers, vol. 6, University Library, Cambridge University.

74. See "Who ruled in Petersburg?", in Lieven, Russia and the origins, pp. 50–64; and pp. 65–138 on the personalities and influence of the Tsar's entourage.

75. On this, see the essays in Russian officialdom: the bureaucratization of Russian society from the seventeenth to the twentieth century, Walter McKenzie Pintner & Don Karl Rowney (eds) (Chapel Hill, North Carolina, 1980).

76. On the composition of this elite, see the magisterial work of Dominic

Lieven, *Russia's rulers under the old regime* (New Haven, Conn., 1989). The best study of Nicholas is also by Lieven, *Nicholas II: Emperor of all the Russias* (London, 1993); also important are Verner, *Crisis of Russian autocracy*; and McDonald, *United government*. My views are somewhat at variance with those of Verner.

77. Raymond A. Esthus, "Nicholas II and the Russo-Japanese War", *Russian Review* 40, 1981, pp. 396–411.

78. John Keep, "The military style of the Romanov rulers", *War & Society* 1, 1983, pp. 61–84.

79. See David R. Jones, "Nicholas II and the supreme command: an investigation of motives", *Sbornik* 11, 1985, pp. 47–83.

80. The concept is developed in and gives the title to McDonald, *United government*.

81. Ibid., pp. 168–98.

82. Lieven, *Nicholas II*, pp. 183–5.

83. McDonald, *United government*, pp. 184–6.

84. Raymond Pearson, *The Russian moderates and the crisis of Tsarism 1914–1917* (London, 1977), p. 11.

85. Lieven, *Nicholas II*, pp. 184–8.

86. What follows is based on the accounts of July found in Turner, "Russian mobilization", pp. 260–6; and Lieven, *Russia and the origins*, pp. 139–51.

## I

The French state visit to Russia, Sweden, Denmark and Norway had been organized six months previously. The party comprising Raymond Poincaré, President of the Republic, René Viviani, then Premier and Foreign Minister, and Pierre de Margerie, political director of the Quai d'Orsay, set sail from Dunkirk in the early hours of Thursday 16 July, leaving France devoid of its senior political and foreign policy decision-makers. The decision to embark on a voyage timed to last until 31 July was an indication of the extent to which the French at least were blithely unaware of any trouble on the international scene. Back in Paris the Minister of Justice was deputizing at the Quai d'Orsay, while the newly appointed *Sous-secrétaire d'état* for foreign affairs had confessed before his appointment to being ignorant of all things diplomatic.[2] All this was at a time when radio cabling was in its infancy and there was little expectation of being able to keep in constant contact with the presidential party. Should the question of France's responsibility in the outbreak of the First World War still be an issue, in the words of one historian: "It is hard to imagine the leaders of the country indulging in the joys of tourism . . . having plotted the outbreak of a European war."[3] Furthermore, the forceful ultimatum that Austria was preparing to issue to Serbia was only communicated on 23 July, once Berlin and Vienna were sure that Poincaré and his party had set sail from Russia for stage two of the presidential tour. In this way, it was calculated that France and Russia would not be able to co-ordinate a response to the Austrian note. Thus, as a result of a combination of accident and design, on the eve of the First World War French leaders were literally and metaphorically at sea. By the time they finally cut short their trip and returned to Dunkirk on 29 July it was probably too late to stop the outbreak of war. To a large extent, then, France's action could only be reactive, and not preventive. This was well understood by the Bavarian minister in Paris, von Ritter, who on 26 July wrote to the King: "The French government, the French press, and public opinion have been inconceivably surprised by the sending of the Austrian note to the Serb government. After the heated debates on income tax, deputies and senators had turned their backs on the capital and since Paris has become almost dead . . . All the ambassadors, except M. de Schoen, are absent from Paris. The Italian ambassador, M.

Tittoni, is in Iceland. The running of the ministry for Foreign Affairs is in the hands of the Minister of Justice, Bienvenu-Martin, who is unfamiliar with foreign matters."[4]

From the moment the French state party landed on French soil at 8 am on Wednesday 29 July, France's principal decision-maker was the President of the Republic. The crowds which greeted him filled him with a strong sense of mission: "It was no longer to a person that these acclamations were addressed; it was to the representative of France *vis-à-vis* the world." This gave him the confidence he needed to put aside his characteristic self-doubt and to assume the fullest rôle that the constitution of the Third Republic afforded to him. Justifying to himself that Viviani would be "hesitant and pusillanimous", he noted: "I am determined to take over the responsibility for Viviani's action." He ordered Cabinet meetings, which the President of the Republic chaired, to be held every morning.[5] He took firm control of the affairs of state; but he soon came to the conclusion that there was little that he could do to stop the course of events now in train.

Two weeks had passed in which the diplomatic and political masters of France had been absent from the hub of events and, to a large extent, intentionally isolated from that chain of events now known as the July crisis. The German government had even sent instructions to its radio transmission service at Metz to jam all Franco-Russian radio communications as well as those between the presidential cruiser *France* and Paris, as the instructions in the service log for 27 and 28 July show.[6] Poincaré could merely familiarize himself with the communications and news of which he had been deprived since his departure from Russia five days earlier. His reading of those documents gave him the impression that the international situation was far more serious than he had at first believed. Certainly within the next 48 hours, if not immediately, he would come to the conclusion that war was inevitable. For that reason, and because of his long-held belief that France's salvation rested with her unity, his strategy would be to ensure that the country entered the war united. That would be no mean feat; the most cursory glance at back copies of the left-wing press showed a widespread hostility to war which ranged from a reiteration of the CGT trade union's official policy of a general strike in the event of war being declared, to the socialist party's appeal for international action against war. Rhetoric apart there had been a substantial demonstration against war in Paris on 27 July and a host of other protests were organized for the capital and provinces for 30 and 31 July.[7] More independent observers, such as the British ambassador in Paris, Sir Francis Bertie, also believed that French public opinion was against going to war over Serbia.[8] While wishing to avoid war, Poincaré clearly understood that if a decision for war was to be taken it was essential that every precaution should be taken to make sure that France's action should be perceived by her own citizens as well as in the eyes of the world as being defensive. Like many other Republicans, he had not forgotten what was viewed as the disastrous French diplomacy surrounding the outbreak of the Franco-Prussian War of 1870–1, when the French Foreign Minister, the Duc de Gramont, had fallen into the trap laid by Bismarck in the form of the "Ems telegram" to goad France into declaring war on Prussia, thereby forfeiting international support. Henceforth, France's domestic, foreign and defence strategies became one: a marketing strategy to present any French decision for war as being defensive.

An essential element conditioning France's management of the international crisis was Russia. The Alliance limited French freedom of action. This explains why Poincaré was constantly at pains to maintain the fine balance between too great, or too little, a show of support for her ally, either of which could have dire consequences.[9] The question of the rôle of France's ambassador in St Petersburg, Maurice Paléologue, in his dealings with Russia during the crisis has been the subject of even more polemic. However, new evidence about his rôle, which will be discussed below, must lead to a less blameworthy picture of his activities. But whatever Paléologue's attitude in the crisis, Russia continued to give the impression of remaining peaceful, as both the Austrian and German ambassadors in St Petersburg were prepared to state, at least in private. Indeed, Germany continued to believe as late as 29 July that France was "setting all levers in motion at St Petersburg to exercise a moderating influence there".[10] And this was after Austria had declared war on Serbia on 28 July. Even the Socialist leader, Jean Jaurès, at that time believed that French action was peaceful, as his speech to the International Socialist meeting in Brussels on 29 July showed: "We [French Socialists], do not have to impose a policy of peace on our government. It is carrying one out. I who have never hesitated to take head-on the hatred of our chauvinists by my stubborn desire, which will never weaken, for a Franco-German *rapprochement*, I have the right to say that at this moment the French government is the best ally for peace of this admirable English government, which has taken the initiative toward conciliation."[11]

By this time most Powers were in the preparatory stages of mobilization.[12] The French Minister of War, Adolphe Messimy, had recalled French officers from leave and taken steps to protect the railways on 26th as a response to similar German measures in Alsace. A potential problem for decision-makers in Paris was Russian actions during this period of tension. Intemperate moves by her ally risked the undermining of France's strategy of ensuring that any decision for war should be perceived as being defensive by both domestic and foreign opinion. As if France's principal decision-makers had not been obstructed enough by their inability to communicate with other powers during their Baltic cruise, they were now to be faced with inadequate information about the activities of their principal ally. Traditionally, historians have placed the blame for this on the French ambassador in St Petersburg, Maurice Paléologue, who supposedly wished to keep Paris in the dark about the advanced state of Russian war preparations for fear that the decision-makers in France would require Russia to act with more restraint, which was indeed the case. New evidence produced by Jean Stengers relieves Paléologue of much of the blame by showing that the French ambassador was himself handicapped by poor information.[13] As Paléologue's position in the management of the crisis has hitherto been considered to be important, it is necessary to take a new look at his rôle.

Evidence of a less conspiratorial rôle on the part of Paléologue is to be found in the diary of the wife of the French military attaché at the Petersburg embassy, the Marchioness de Laguiche. Just after 10 pm in the evening of 29 July the French military attaché, General Pierre de Laguiche, was told by the Russian military authorities that a general mobilization had been ordered. The Marchioness de Laguiche notes: "Pierre is asked to inform Paris, but not to speak to Paléologue until midnight, his lack of discretion being known!"[14] Despite Russian attempts to keep the news from Paléologue, he learnt of the general mobilization order at 11 pm, not from Laguiche but from Basily, the Deputy Director of the Chancery at the Russian Foreign Ministry.[15] Paléologue immediately ordered the First Secretary at the French embassy, Chambrun, to take a telegram to the Russian Foreign Ministry for despatch to Paris, explaining that the Russian government had decided on two things: first, to order that night the mobilization of 13 army corps for use against Austria; and, secondly, to begin secretly general mobilization. The reason why the telegram was taken to the Pont aux Chantres was because it was feared that the French embassy cipher might not be secure.[16] When Chambrun reached the Russian Foreign Ministry he met Laguiche, who had been summoned there to be informed by the *chef de cabinet*, Schilling, that the Tsar had rescinded the general mobilization order. Schilling then insisted to him that this news should remain secret: "I confide this to you alone in the whole world, not a word to the Embassy staff, neither Basily nor anyone else knows about it."[17] As the Marchioness de Laguiche remarked, this put her husband in an invidious position *vis-à-vis* Paléologue. Laguiche ordered Chambrun to suppress the last sentence of the telegram for despatch to Paris, which stated that the Russian government had decided "secretly to begin general mobilization".[18] According to the Marchioness, the next morning Paléologue was furious with both her husband and Chambrun.[19] Thus it would seem that Paléologue did not intentionally keep Paris in the dark about the short-lived Russian general mobilization order and its abrogation; rather it was he who was obstructed by others.[20] Indeed, Paléologue appeared particularly anxious that news of the Russian general mobilization should reach Paris as soon as possible. At midnight on 29 July, before he had learnt of the Tsar's counter-order, he telegraphed (no. 306) to Paris: "Please collect from the Russian Embassy *as a matter of extreme urgency, my telegram no. 304.*"[21]

As yet, the poor quality of information being sent to Paris had not had a serious effect on the French management of the crisis, which was predicated on the notion of restraining Russia so as not to give a pretext for war to Germany. The French desire to restrain their ally was clear on the night of the 29–30 July following an urgent message conveyed to Viviani by the Russian *chargé d'affaires* in Paris, Sevastopoulo. It was in the form of a telegram from Sazonov to Isvolskii, warning that Russia was about to ignore German threats and begin mobilizing because Austria had already mobilized and that war was imminent. More worrying still, it instructed Isvolskii to thank the French government "for the declaration which has been made to me officially in its name by the French Ambassador that we can entirely count upon the allied support of France. In the present circumstances, this declaration is particularly precious to us."[22] Viviani was so disturbed by this message that he called on the Minister of War and together they hurried to the Elysée to wake the President just before two o'clock in the morning. A telegram was drafted and despatched at 7am on 30 July with Poincaré's approval; it stated quite clearly that Russia "should not immediately proceed to any measure which might offer Germany a pretext for a total or partial mobilization of her forces".[23] Though the telegram arrived in St Petersburg after Russian partial mobilization had been declared, it was a clear sign that Poincaré and Viviani were exercising a restraining influence on Russia, whose forward policy was in danger of undermining their strategy for managing the crisis.[24] That strategy was designed to allow Germany to incur the blame for the conflict in the eyes of French domestic and international public opinion. The initiative for such a policy clearly seemed to come from Poincaré, who, as usual, chaired the Cabinet meeting on the morning of 30 July and whose way of thinking pervaded the business at hand. Abel Ferry, *sous-secrétaire d'état* for foreign affairs, recorded in his notes of that meeting:

> Impressive cabinet. Solemn men.
>
> 1  For the sake of public opinion, let the Germans put themselves in the wrong [*Laisser vis-à-vis de l'opinion les torts du côté allemand*].
>
> 2  Do not stop Russian mobilization
>    Mobilize but do not concentrate
>    Cabinet calm, serious, ordered.[25]

Ferry's second point suggests that the Russian partial mobilization was discussed, with a view to asking the Russians to rescind it for the reasons already made plain earlier that morning. But at that time, because of the inadequate communications from the St Petersburg embassy, the French Cabinet was unaware of how close to general mobilization Russia was, and the decision to do nothing was carried.

Where the question of information from the St Petersburg embassy did have an impact on the French management of the crisis was following the Russian decision to "proceed secretly with the first measures of general mobilization", of which Paléologue informed Paris in his telegram of 30 July at 7.50pm.[26] Paléologue was by then very worried about the safety of the French embassy cipher and the possibility that French communications were being intercepted by Germany. For that reason he had informed the Quai (apparently via the very circuitous Scandinavian route for safety, as the telegram took more than 24 hours) that he was changing the embassy cipher. In the end he felt that even that was insufficient and decided to use the Scandinavian route to inform Paris of the Russian general mobilization, which the Russians were so insistent about keeping secret. This was the route which his Belgian colleague also used that day.[27] This explains the notorious delay with Paléologue's telegram to Paris on 31 July marked "*extrême urgence*" announcing the general mobilization of the Russian army and minuted at 8.30am.[28] His wire took nearly 12 hours to reach the Quai d'Orsay, with another half an hour for deciphering. By then Viviani had left for home, from where he went on to a Cabinet meeting.[29] As a result, French decision-makers were again less well informed than were other powers. At that time they had received neither from Isvolskii nor from Paléologue official notification of Russian general mobilization. This explains Viviani's anxious telegram to Paléologue on the evening of 31 July, minuted at 9pm and 9.20pm, informing him that the German government was insisting that Russia had ordered "*total*" mobilization and that if they did not demobilize Germany would herself mobilize. Viviani was forced to tell von Schoen that he had not been informed of Russian total mobilization. Thus, when asked by the German ambassador what France's attitude would be in the event of a Russo-German conflict, Viviani told Paléologue that he had not replied. He ordered Paléologue rather crisply to tell Sazonov of all this and for Paléologue to inform Viviani urgently of the "so-called" Russian general mobilization. He ended with the remark: "As I have already informed you, I have no doubt that the Imperial government, in the greater interest of peace, will avoid, for its part, anything which could begin the crisis."[30] It is hard, therefore, to disagree with Poincaré: "However useless these instructions, they proved once more not only that France had remained ignorant of Russian mobilization but that she continued to regret this measure and to find it precipitate."[31]

Paléologue replied with a distressed telegram on the morning of 1 August enquiring as to whether Viviani had received his telegram announcing general mobilization.[32] He then drafted a memorandum detailing the reasons for the delay in his telegram reaching the Quai d'Orsay. In the light of the new evidence unearthed by Stengers, suggesting that the French ambassador's rôle was more innocent than has hitherto been suggested, it now seems fair to give more credence to Paléologue's own explanation for the delay in the receipt of his telegram announcing Russian general mobilization, given, in particular, the Russian authorities' desire to keep this a secret.[33]

Paléologue states that he learnt of the Russian general mobilization at 6am on 31 July. He asked his second military attaché to check with the Russian General Staff as to whether the order had been posted up across the Empire. He then discussed the situation with his first secretary. Following the return of the second attaché he wrote telegram 318 (announcing the general mobilization of the Russian army). At 8.30am this was taken urgently to the telegraph office, which was at a distance of three-and-a-half kilometres from the embassy. The bearer of the telegram returned at 9.30am explaining that the telegraph office had been particularly agitated following the military authorities' requisitioning of it. Paléologue then adds that he saw another reason for the delay. As the normal route for telegrams from St Petersburg to Paris via Berlin was no longer secure he had used the route specified by the French and Russian General Staff in the event of war, which he explained to be via the Scandinavian and British wires. But in order to do this, he further explained, it was necessary to inform all the intermediary posts, which he lists as "Helsingfors, New Biggin, Londres et la variante Copenhague, Esbjerg, Calais". This would have amounted to a delay, according to specialists, says Paléologue, of three to four hours. Thus he calculated that his telegram should have reached Paris at about 6pm. He concludes his memorandum by stating that he did not understand why at 9.30pm Viviani should have sent him a telegram stating that he did not know of the Russian general mobilization.[34] Certainly, choosing such a circuitous route was nothing exceptional, as the Belgian ambassador's action proves. On 1 August Paléologue took a similar precaution when he telegraphed to Paris via "Odessa and Fredericia" the news that the German ambassador had informed Sazonov of his country's declaration of war against Russia.[35] Thus it would seem that the French ambassador did not act so conspiratorially in informing Paris of the Russian general mobilization. More importantly, the criticism that Russian general mobilization was approved in Paris appears contrary to evidence, as well as being a contradiction of France's overall strategy for managing the crisis, which was to let Germany make the first aggressive move.

## II

Though France was reacting to events more than creating them, it did appear to have a clear strategy, as described earlier, namely of ensuring that any French decision for war should be seen as defensive at home and abroad; it was not deflected from that aim by problems such as poor communications with its principal ally, Russia. But on the 31 July one event seemed as though it might undermine the whole strategy for a united domestic front. That evening, the Socialist leader, Jean Jaurès, was assassinated by a half-witted fanatic driven to action by the vituperative attacks in the nationalist press against the "pro-German Socialist traitor". Poincaré, who had often crossed swords with Jaurès in Parliament, believed that he was far from being a traitor: "Jaurès had over the last 8 days expiated many faults. He had helped the government in its diplomacy and, if war breaks out, he would have been amongst those who would have known how to do their duty." And he noted emotionally at the end of his diary entry: "*Quel crime abominable et sot!*"[36] Though his outrage at the assassination was heartfelt, it was partly motivated by the fear of a reaction in the labour and trade union movements which could have devastating consequences for national unity as France stood on the brink of war. Former minister Etienne Clémentel's private diary echoes that fear: "It is a stupid crime and could have grave consequences on the eve of mobilization. The crime is all the more absurd as the socialists have an excellent attitude and as Jaurès' articles since the start of the crisis have been irreproachable."[37] The fear that the assassination could have a destabilizing effect was all the more apparent because the trade union movement had stressed repeatedly an implacable opposition to war, with certain elements well known to the police threatening insurrection or a general strike to combat mobilization.[38] To defuse the situation, the otherwise moderate government immediately sought to associate itself with the Socialist Party's mourning. Poincaré wrote messages of condolence to Jean's brother, Admiral Jaurès, and Mme Jaurès, probably with the intention that they be published, in which *L'Humanité* duly obliged. The letter to Jaurès's widow displayed a mixture of genuine sympathy, political expediency and a clear understanding of the press as an instrument of policy. It spoke of "a moment when national union is more necessary than ever" and was intended to head off the possibility of demonstrations of sympathy combining with the strong anti-war feeling on the left to paralyse France at such a critical moment. Hennion, the Prefect of Police, warned the Cabinet that disturbances were very likely. The Cabinet agreed to retain in the capital two regiments of cavalry which had been scheduled to depart for the eastern frontier. A further measure was the immediate posting up across the country of a manifesto associating the government with the mourning and appealing for "union": "In the grave circumstances through which *la Patrie* is passing, the government counts on the patriotism of the working class, of the whole population, to remain calm and not to add to public emotion by agitation which would bring disorder to the capital."[39] Assurances were immediately sought and obtained from the socialists that they would help maintain calm. This was facilitated by the arrest of the murderer that evening. Meanwhile, Poincaré's friend, the nationalist Maurice Barrès, wrote a public letter of condolence, probably at Poincaré's behest, to Mme Jaurès, dissociating the nationalist right from the crime.[40] Even the nationalist press, such as the *Action Française*, which had hitherto pilloried the socialist leader, joined in the chorus of condemnations. By 1 August the labour movement was abandoning opposition to war rapidly, in favour of that old Republican reflex of duty to defend *la patrie en danger*. The headlines in *La Guerre sociale* of 1 August perfectly summarized the transition: "National Defence above all! They have assassinated Jaurès! We will not assassinate France!"[41] The government's skilful handling of the asssassination proved more successful than could have been hoped. Paradoxically, national union was forged around one of the foremost opponents of war; it was only a small step from there to *union sacrée*.

## III

The question of British participation on France's side in the event of war also conditioned France's management of the crisis. Like

Sazonov, many French diplomats were convinced that the preservation of peace lay in Britain's hands. If Britain declared its willingness to come to France's assistance in the event of France being attacked, then there was a chance conflict could be avoided. Poincaré certainly believed this. But despite pressing appeals by the French ambassador, Paul Cambon, to Sir Edward Grey, this was not forthcoming. Tired of Grey's tergiversations, on 31 July, Poincaré, backed by the government, made a direct appeal by letter to King George V. It was, however, to no avail. Nevertheless, Poincaré remained optimistic: "I do not despair; the Foreign Office is very well disposed towards us; Asquith also; the English are slow to decide, methodical, reflective, but they know where they are going."[42] Of course Britain's assistance was not valued in merely military terms. Poincaré would not have disagreed with Clémentel's assessment of a British refusal to come to France's assistance: "It would be a serious complication which would lead to the diminution of moral force by the reduction in confidence."[43]

Despite the gravity of the situation, Poincaré's diaries reveal a remarkable calm. He noted on 1 August that Russia had ordered general mobilization on the grounds that Germany had begun her mobilization; Germany had then immediately called on Russia to suspend those measures; "it is almost inevitable war". And Poincaré revealed his frustration: "Germany clearly does not wish that we negotiate on an equal footing; she claims to agree to talk; but she does not want Russia and us to be able to defend ourselves in the talks."[44]

Poincaré's diaries show that by 1 August he was convinced of the inevitability of war. Without precluding further negotiations for a peaceful settlement, his strategy did not waver from ensuring that France should appear to be the injured party to unite the country in a defensive war and to ensure that she obtained the necessary diplomatic and military support of countries such as Britain and Italy. Indeed, good news on this front had arrived on the evening of 31 July, with Italy announcing that it considered the attack on Serbia to be an act of aggression which released Italy from the conditions of the Triple Alliance and allowed it to declare itself neutral.

In the meantime France had taken certain military precautions whose moderation was specifically designed to convey to domestic and international opinion the fundamentally defensive nature of French action. Following discussions between Poincaré, Viviani,

Messimy, the War Minister, and General Joffre, Chief of the General Staff, in which Poincaré probably played a prominent rôle, it was decided to put to the French Cabinet a set of proposals, which were duly accepted on the morning of 30 July.[45] These stipulated that, without beginning general mobilization, covering troops should be ordered to take up positions along a line from Luxemburg to the Vosges mountains, but on the express condition that they get no closer than ten kilometres to the frontier. This was, as the Cabinet agreed, to avoid giving German patrols a pretext for war and to convince British public opinion of France's reasonableness. Moreover, it would also have a positive effect on French domestic opinion.

The propaganda value of such action to the French can be measured in terms of the military risks that such restraint incurred at a time when France's principal decision-makers believed in the inevitability of war. General Joffre, for one, was not happy with this decision, because he was aware that Germany was proceeding with military preparations. Apart from the fact that the withdrawal formed no part of France's Plan XVII, Joffre had calculated precisely what France was sacrificing. The following day he informed the War Minister and the Cabinet that every 24 hours' delay in mobilizing the eastern army corps was equivalent to a 15- to 20-kilometre loss of French territory.[46] But the Cabinet was convinced of the moral value of such a measure, as the Minister of War subsequently commented: "Nothing made such an impression on British opinion (all accounts are agreed on that point), nothing was better proof of our pacific intentions than this decision to keep troops at a slight distance from the frontier."[47] The immediacy with which the British government was informed of the measures and the degree of sacrifice involved merely confirm the extent to which French decision-making was conditioned by Britain. Though Joffre bowed to his political masters, early the next morning, following news that Germany had begun serious mobilization measures, the Chief of General Staff was threatening the Minister of War with resignation if the mobilization order was not issued. It was calculated on 31 July that France was two days behind German mobilization.[48] Again revealing where decision-making really lay, Messimy marched Joffre off to the Elysée. Poincaré allowed him to appear before the Cabinet. It was agreed that mobilization notices be issued that afternoon, Saturday 1 August, at 4pm, with effect from the following day, but that the ten-kilometre withdrawal from the frontier be maintained.[49] The seriousness with which Poincaré above all wished the demarcation zone to be respected, as well as its motive, were revealed in a telegram from the Minister of War to the High Command:

> The Ministry of War insists again, on behalf of the President of the Republic, and for serious diplomatic reasons, on the necessity of not crossing the demarcation line indicated by the telegram of 30 July and reiterated in a telegram of today. This prohibition applies as much to the cavalry as to other units. No patrol, no reconnaissance, no post, no element whatsoever, must go east of the said line. Whoever crosses it will be liable to court martial and it is only in the event of a full-scale attack that it will be possible to transgress this order, which will be communicated to all troops.[50]

Poincaré revealed the extent to which this was for propaganda purposes. Though in his published record of events he attributed to the Cabinet the initiative for issuing the public proclamation explaining the mobilization measures, its motive and true source were clear from his secret diary: "In order to maintain, to the end, the pacific character of the measures we are taking, I have proposed that a proclamation of the government to the country be posted up throughout France. It seemed to me to be necessary that I sign it myself and have it countersigned by all Ministers." Viviani then pointed out, correctly, according to Poincaré, that two or three ministers had privately criticized the decision to mobilize immediately, in particular the Minister of Work and Social Affairs, Senator Couyba. But Poincaré noted of Viviani: "In truth, he has hesitated more than the others and is not annoyed to be covered by all." That meant that a quarter of the Cabinet had doubts about the decision to mobilize. But the imperative was to hold up the government's unity as an example to the country, as Poincaré wrote in his diary: "the idea that everyone sign is, in any case, a means of proving government solidarity. At my request, Viviani then drew up rapidly in the Cabinet a proposed statement." Poincaré then made alterations, which were adopted.[51] The two-page proclamation was a clear appeal to unity which presaged Poincaré's call for a *union sacrée*. Stating that "mobilization is not war" it ended:

Strong in the ardent desire to reach a pacific solution of the crisis, the government, protected by the necessary precautions, will continue its diplomatic efforts and hopes still to succeed.

It counts on the composure of this noble nation not to allow itself to indulge unjustified emotion. It counts on the patriotism of all Frenchmen and knows that there is not one of them who is not ready to do his duty.

In this hour, there are no parties. There is *la France éternelle*, peaceful and resolute France. There is the *patrie* of right and justice, completely united in calm, vigilance and dignity.

As Poincaré remarked: "The cabinet has itself, therefore, in preparing this statement, given the example of unity which it recommends to the country."[52] He was particularly pleased that when the Minister of the Interior revealed the proclamation to waiting journalists it was greeted with cries of "*Vive la France*".

At seven o'clock on 31 July, the German ambassador had called at the Quai d'Orsay to learn of France's intentions should war break out between Russia and Germany. Would France remain neutral? Poincaré and Viviani had already discussed this problem and had come to the conclusion that a clear reply should be avoided. On getting this response, von Schoen replied that he would return for an answer early the following afternoon. He returned on 1 August at 11 am. But now Berlin was insisting that even if France pledged to remain neutral, she would still have to surrender the principal fortresses along her eastern frontier as a guarantee of her "sincerity". Viviani, having concerted with Poincaré, replied that France would act in accordance with her interests.[53]

Further evidence of the importance to Poincaré of the need to engineer the most propitious circumstances to rally all sections of public opinion to the defence of the nation was revealed in his diary entry for the night of 1–2 August. At 11.30pm he received a visit from Isvolsky, who had come to learn of France's attitude following Germany's declaration of war on Russia earlier that day. Poincaré explained that France would respect the alliance, "but that we had an interest, Russia and us, that mobilization should be taken as far as possible before war was declared. I added that it would be better that we were not obliged to declare it ourselves and that it be declared on us. That was necessary for both military and domestic political reasons: a defensive war would raise the whole country; a declaration of war by us could leave, amongst part of public opinion, some doubts about the alliance." The Russian ambassador, in sombre mood, acquiesced. Poincaré immediately called a Cabinet meeting, which lasted from midnight until four in the morning and at which his replies to Isvolsky were endorsed unanimously. Only one member of the Cabinet was not present, Senator Couyba, the Minister for Work and Social Affairs, who according to Poincaré's published account could not be contacted, but who in the diaries was rumoured to be going around "repeating, that we are leading France into war".[54]

News of the German declaration of war on Russia and of German incursions into France across the eastern borders, about which France formally protested in writing,[55] led General Joffre to request that the ten-kilometre withdrawal be lifted. The Cabinet hesitated, then agreed to lift the order at 2pm. The note which Joffre despatched at 5.30pm to the army commanders, after agreement with Viviani, and doubtless Poincaré, again revealed the French obsession with ensuring that Germany appear the guilty party: "For national reasons of a moral nature and for imperious reasons of a diplomatic kind, it is indispensable that the Germans are left with full responsibility for hostilities. Consequently, and until further notice, covering troops will restrict themselves to expelling across the frontier any assault troops without giving chase any further and without encroaching on opposing territory."[56]

On that Sunday, 2 August, attempts were made to reshuffle the Cabinet to bring in Briand and Delcassé, possibly in an attempt to weed out the waverers. Though the socialists blocked the move, Poincaré still described their mood as "excellent". On the morning of 2 August a meeting of the socialist party in Paris made known its intention to defend France in the event of war. With the question of national unity firmly on his mind, Poincaré noted: "Excellent attitude of the socialists, even of the revolutionaries and of the CGT." It seemed, therefore, that there would be no need to take repressive measures to guard against opposition to war breaking out: "We have not had arrested any of the individuals registered in the Carnet B, apart from a few rare exceptions, when the *Préfets* believed themselves confronted with dangerous anarchists."[57] The decision not to arrest trade unionists, pacifists, anti-militarists and suspected spies named in the black list, compiled by the authorities and known as the "Carnet B", helped rally support to the cause of national defence as the impending struggle came increasingly to be presented by the press and the government as a case of *la patrie en danger*, the great rallying cry of the Republic since the Revolution.[58] The government was helped in this by Germany's invasion of Luxemburg that same day and reports of German violations of the French border. The German declaration of war against Russia on 1 August had confirmed her guilt in Poincaré's eyes: "Thus Germany assumes full responsibility for a horrific war."[59]

The conditions for a *ralliement* of the whole of France were now in place. This was apparent following news from London on 2 August that the British Labour Party was about to organize a public demonstration against British participation in any conflict. Viviani was able to get the influential socialist, Marcel Sembat, to write to Ramsay MacDonald, the British Labour Party leader, to ask for the Party's support in favour of British intervention.[60]

But the need for calm, dignity and patience was still a priority in Poincaré's mind as the French dutifully awaited the British decision. This explains his genuine distress at the anti-German demonstrations which were breaking out in Paris, and which targeted German-owned companies such as Maggi, the food manufacturer. The repressive measures he ordered demonstrated the level of his concern:

> Yesterday Paris gave a sad spectacle which contrasts with the *sang-froid* of these last days and with the *sang-froid* of the whole of France. There were many incidents of pillaging of shops. The dairies of the Maggi company were widely plundered; it is true that the cause of this violence is competition between this company and small milk suppliers. But, on top of this, German and Austrian shops were looted; and the police stood passively by these scenes of disorder: officers even watched them with a certain complicity. I instructed Malvy [Minister of the Interior] to ask Hennion [Prefect of Police] to be merciless and to maintain public order at all costs. The fomenters will appear before a war tribunal.[61]

The calm, order and unity which Poincaré had worked for nationally needed to be reflected in the Cabinet. The Minister of the Navy,

Gauthier, had shown incompetence, even negligence, and was replaced on 3 August on "health grounds". Viviani was a unifying figure for the left in Parliament, but gave the impression of not
understanding foreign affairs. Given his continuing neurasthenic
state, on 3 August he was at last persuaded to relinquish the foreign
affairs portfolio in favour of Gaston Doumergue, much to the relief
of senior diplomats at the Quai d'Orsay, and Poincaré in particular. It
was the confused Viviani who, in Poincaré's words, was "extraordi-
narily ignorant of foreign affairs" and who "was not able, even once,
when reading a telegram from Vienna to speak of the Ballplatz without saying the Boliplatz or the Baloplatz".[62]

Other measures designed to seal national unity had been taken in
the Cabinet on the afternoon of 2 August. These bear Poincaré's im-
print: suspension of the recent decree ordering the closure of various
religious establishments; and an amnesty for revolutionaries condemned for violation of the press laws. Poincaré noted: "No; there
are no more parties." He was particularly gratified by a letter from
Prince Roland Bonaparte, one of the pretenders to the French throne,
offering to serve the government of the Republic. Though this was
forbidden by the law of 1886, the Prince put his home at the country's disposal for use as a hospital.[63] This seemed to symbolize to
Poincaré the degree of national unity that had been achieved in those
few days since his return to France. A few days later he would suggest
to the Cabinet, without success, that the law be repealed, following
further similar offers from other pretenders and their relatives.[64]

What is extraordinary about the days preceding the German declaration of war against France is the extent to which Poincaré was
managing events; and he had every opportunity to do so. Cabinet
meetings, which the President of the Republic chaired, were now
taking place several times a day, on his orders. This was one constitutional prerogative that he used to the full. Although there was no
such thing as Cabinet minutes, it is apparent that the Cabinet was almost in permanent session and taking decisions which, in the British
system, were assumed by individual ministers. Since Poincaré's return to France the decision-making process had given the distinct
impression of being one long *conseil des ministres*. Despite what he
recorded in his published memoirs and his volume on how war came
about, which expressly state that his constitutional rôle precluded
him from taking a lead in decision-making, Poincaré's unpublished

diaries give a quite different picture. However, those diaries show no evidence for the idea that Poincaré either wanted, or was instrumental in bringing about, war. On the contrary, many of the decisions he took or initiated have since been attributed erroneously to people such as Viviani, whose peaceful image was never tarnished. Poincaré never sought to correct that impression because it opened him immediately to the charge of overstepping his constitutional position, about which he was acutely sensitive. Such a charge in the hands of his worst critics after the war, including the Germans, was more than likely to be used to implicate him still further in the war guilt debate. But his diaries do show him attempting to square the circle between bringing to bear on events his considerable organizational skills and sense of perspective, and a lawyer's respect for the constitution.[65]

## IV

It now looked as though the first condition for a French decision for war had been met: national unity. The second was still in doubt: Britain's participation alongside France. All France's efforts were now channelled in that direction.

On Sunday 2 August Poincaré had signed the proclamation of a state of emergency. The constitution now demanded that Parliament be recalled from recess within 48 hours. Once again, the extent to which French policy remained conditioned by Britain's actions was demonstrated by the French Cabinet's decision to delay calling Parliament until the following Tuesday precisely because it was hoped that by then there would be a British response. On the Sunday evening of 2 August the British Cabinet learnt of the German invasion of Luxemburg and the following morning of the German ultimatum demanding free passage through Belgium. The importance to Britain of Belgian neutrality was something Poincaré understood well. In 1912 he had turned down Joffre's request to develop an offensive strategy based on a French violation of that neutrality as a means of countering a German strike before it reached France. Now he reflected on the value of that decision and how its benefits should not be squandered: "We are expecting, of course, a German attack through Belgium, as our High Command has always predicted. We have constantly recommended to General Joffre not to permit any crossing of the Belgian frontier nor over-flying of Belgium until further notice. On that depends the support of England and the attitude of Belgium. When King Albert came to Paris, he promised that Belgium would defend herself against Germany. Let us do nothing which could discourage that good will."[66]

King Albert and the Belgian government rejected the German demand the following morning. Up to that time, the French had heard nothing from the German ambassador in Paris. Poincaré remained cynical about the ambassador's activities in Pari: "He ostentatiously goes to dine at the Palais d'Orsay and appears to be seeking to be insulted so as to provoke an incident." But at 6.30pm on 3 August, on the false pretext that French aeroplanes had bombed Nuremberg, which Poincaré described as *"une audacieuse invention"*, Germany declared war on France. Again, serious precautions were taken to see that the German ambassador was not the subject of demonstrations: "all measures have been taken to ensure that he is not insulted by the crowd. For the last two days we have dreaded demonstrations against him and his embassy." At the Cabinet meeting that evening the whole of Poincaré's strategy, and thus that of the government since his return to France, was spelt out:

> It was for all the members of the Cabinet a relief. Never before had a declaration of war been welcomed with such satisfaction. France having done all that was incumbent upon her to maintain peace and war having nevertheless become inevitable, it was a hundred times better that we should not have been led, even by repeated violation of our frontiers, to declare it ourselves. It was indispensable that Germany, who was entirely responsible for the aggression, should be led into publicly confessing her intentions. If we had had to declare war ourselves, the Russian alliance would have been contested, national unanimity would have been smashed, it would probably have meant Italy would have been forced by the clauses of the Triple Alliance to side against us.[67]

Naturally, such words, innocent as they were, never saw the light of day in the published form of his memoirs. Taken out of context they could have been used with explosive impact by Poincaré's adversaries.

Poincaré's obsession with national unity was also reflected in the sympathy he felt for Sir Edward Grey's attempts to maintain the British Cabinet's unity and carry public opinion. Whereas Viviani continued to fluctuate between blind optimism and telling journalists that England was betraying France, Poincaré more than anyone understood Grey's predicament: "Grey is evidently having some difficulty in obtaining the unanimity of the Cabinet for energetic resolutions. Burns, Morley, Harcourt, are creating difficulties for him; but his tenacity will overcome their resistance." This might explain why the previous day the President's own tenacity had been in evidence when he had announced to the *conseil des ministres* that he would expect the resignation of any ministers unable to maintain secrecy, clearly in the hope of silencing any internal opposition and thus avoiding Grey's problems. The way he spoke about the British question to the new Foreign Minister showed his calm and how he was now seeking to extend his influence over Doumergue: "I demonstrate to him that England always proceeds step by step and promises, in general, less than she gives."[68] An hour after writing those words Poincaré learnt that on the Monday afternoon Grey had spoken in the Commons in favour of British intervention on the side of France.

If British actions had been of the utmost importance in determining Poincaré's moves, and thus France's, Grey's thinking and method of proceeding continued to have a considerable influence on Poincaré. Both men were sharply focused on the necessity of preserving and maintaining the unity of their respective nations, so essential to success. Poincaré described Grey's speech to the House of Commons on Monday 3 August as "of supreme skill . . . English public opinion, quietly led by Grey to where he wished to take it, is now completely in favour of France." It was not only that Grey had carried British opinion in favour of supporting France, but also Grey's ability to unite the House of Commons, and through it the nation, which most impressed Poincaré. Grey's speech provided the model for Poincaré's own famous message to the French Parliament on 4 August. He had already written and read a first version to the *conseil* on 2 August. But that first draft contained a passage which other ministers rightly believed could, and would, have been misconstrued: "I had spoken of the [illegible] of things and added that at last we could release the cry, until now smothered in our breasts: *Vive l'Alsace Lorraine*. Thomson and Augagneur rightly pointed out to me that that it would be better, *vis-à-vis* foreign countries and even *vis-à-vis* part of French public opinion, to say nothing which could detract from the strictly defensive nature of the war. I bowed to their observations."[69] The reference to Alsace and Lorraine was excluded and the speech was redrafted in the light of Grey's performance in the Commons.

Poincaré's famous *union sacrée* speech was never, in fact, spoken by him. Constitutionally the President of the Republic had no right to address the Chambers directly. Thus at three o'clock on the afternoon of 4 August the presidential message was read by the Minister of Justice to the Senate and by the Prime Minister to the Chamber of Deputies. It encapsulated all that Poincaré believed he had worked for since 1912. It emphasized the peacefulness of France for the previous 40 years, and in particular since the Austrian ultimatum, and placed the blame for war squarely on the German Empire, which would have to bear, "before History, the crushing responsibility". Describing the President of the Republic as *"l'interprète de l'unanimité"*, the speech stressed the unity of the nation and its "coolness since the beginning of the crisis". Supported by Russia and Britain, and with the sympathy of the civilized world, it noted that France once more represented liberty, justice and reason and would have Right and its moral strength on its side. It ended by reiterating that elusive quality which throughout his political life Poincaré, and others, had worked to instil in the nation: unity. Most rewarding to him was that his strategy for managing the crisis had paid off and unity had been achieved: "In the Chamber, the reception was enthusiastic and absolutely unanimous. The socialists were as ardent as the others. The ministers returned to the Elysée, totally moved by this grandiose occasion. In the Senate, same unanimity and same patriotic fervour."[70]

On the morning of 4 August 1914, treating their guarantee of Belgian neutrality as a "scrap of paper", German troops crossed into Belgium. A British ultimatum demanding their withdrawal was disregarded and as Big Ben struck midnight Britain became France's ally in the war with Germany.

## V

For the third time in a century France was faced with a German invasion. But unlike in 1815 and 1870, France was not alone. The country which had annexed Alsace and Lorraine and had appeared to threaten France in 1875, 1887, 1905 and 1911 was perceived once more as the aggressor. The *union sacrée* was not, however, the result of a nationalist revival since 1905, with Germany as the focal point. Nor did a majority of Frenchmen believe in the inevitability of war. In August 1914 patriotic feeling was buoyant, but most people did not want war. Opposition to the war was much greater than has often been thought, whether in France or elsewhere, until about a week before it broke out. French decision-makers understood that: hence their desire first and foremost to unite the country. The mystery and rapidity of international events, as well as the disconcerting assassination of Jaurès, managed skilfully by the government, confused people into last-minute patriotism and war. The idea that they were fighting a just war for values common to most Frenchmen, indeed most civilized nations, removed what had always been a cause of anxiety for Poincaré, and produced a united France. This is what had inspired Poincaré's every move since his return to French soil and which he later summarized: "I have always believed, of course, that the French did not want to declare war for Serbia. I even believed that France would not rise up together to keep the promises of the alliance with Russia and that, if we had been led into declaring war, the country would be cruelly divided. But I had never had doubts about France in the event in which she were attacked, even if it was over Serbia."[71] The success of this policy was reflected more objectively by the Bavarian minister in Paris, who on 4 August, before leaving French soil, wrote to the king: "I had until the last moment the impression that the French government wanted to avoid war at any cost."[72]

The Army General Staff had expected that up to 10 per cent of French conscripts might reject the mobilization order. In the event, the national average was 1.5 per cent,[73] a remarkable success given the state of anti-militarism and the opposition to war that had characterized the French labour movement and its political representatives as late as the third week of July. Though Poincaré could not have known it at the time, the *union sacrée* was merely a truce for the duration of hostilities, in order to win the war. In reality there was no abandoning of convictions on either side. The war was all things to all men: the Left were fighting in defence of the Rights of Man and democracy; the Right to defend its own conception of France.

Of course, the *union sacrée* was the more solid for having been conceived at a time when most of Europe believed this would be a short war, over by Christmas at the latest. Thus the *union sacrée* was not a myth created by Poincaré or the government, nor was it the climax of nationalist feeling. Nationalism was not in evidence after mobilization was decreed *revanche* was hardly evoked, Alsace Lorraine even less. Once war began that was another matter. Indeed, it would have been churlish for the French, more so their political leaders, not to have as a war aim the return of the "lost provinces". In that respect, Gambetta's old dictum of "Think of it always; speak of it never" was no longer valid, as Poincaré had shown in drafting his message to Parliament.[74]

France entered the war united behind the man who had been its effective leader from January 1912. Poincaré's diplomatic efforts to strengthen the bonds of the Triple Entente in order to protect against future German aggression survived the final test of fire. During the July crisis Poincaré remained the principal decision-maker. However, because of his isolation from events during the trip to Russia he, more than any other European statesman, was reacting to events more than controlling them. Russia remained a major preoccupation. Speculation has always surrounded his three-day visit to Russia and whether he encouraged the country into intransigence. At the time, the Austrian ultimatum had not been delivered. The Serbian crisis was discussed, as one would expect between major allies. But it seems unlikely, while Poincaré might have encouraged firmness, that he should have made any clear commitment to Russia, come what may. The Russian military did not think so; they were still uncertain of French support. Five days after the visit, the Russian military attaché in Paris even asked General Joffre whether, according to the Franco-Russian agreement, in the event of Germany mobilizing part of her forces against Russia, France would mobilize. Pierre Renouvin has seen this as proof that Poincaré, in his talks in St Petersburg, did not go any further than a simple statement of fidelity to the Alliance.[75]

Poincaré, like Sir Edward Grey, was finally constrained by events into taking his country into war – a defensive war. His freedom to choose a different course of action was severely limited. Failure to honour the Franco-Russian alliance would have condemned Russia to certain defeat, thus ever more gravely jeopardizing France's security. Even if the final decision had not been made for France by Germany's declaration of war, France would have felt compelled to fight alongside Russia. In the end France, like Britain, entered the war for negative reasons – because not to have done so would have been a threat to her national security in both the short and the long term. Thus, just as Britain's decision for war was not in essence to uphold the 1839 treaty of guarantee of Belgian neutrality, but because it feared the consequences of German domination of the continent, so France did not go to war simply to honour the Franco-Russian alliance, but because it was not willing to live again in the shadow of an almighty Germany. These strategic reasons apart, both Grey and Poincaré believed that they were fighting a just war against German aggression. But whereas Grey made plain his hatred of war, and his fear of it, and was for many reasons ill-suited to deal with it,[76] Poincaré, because he acted with firmness, resolve and confidence, gave the impression that he accepted it without regret. This, however, was not true. On 3 August he reflected deeply on the toll in human lives that war would bring.[77] But to a certain extent Poincaré was a victim of his own success. In peacetime he had prepared relentlessly for any eventuality and had worked for national unity. War was now a reality, the nation was united, determined to fight and supported by strong allies. The crisis had been well managed. Critics would not forgive a Lorrainer this coincidence.

## Notes

1. See J. F. V. Keiger, *France and the origins of the First World War* (London, 1983), pp. 145–67.
2. Raymond Poincaré, *Notes journalières*, Bibliothèque nationale (BN) nafr 16027, 18 June 1914.
3. J-J. Becker, *1914 Comment les français sont entrés dans la guerre* (Paris, 1977), p. 140.
4. *Le Temps*, 7 March 1922, in Ministère des Affaires Etrangères (MAE), *Europe 1918–1940*, sous série, Allemagne, vol. 327, Politique intérieure; "Responsabilité de la guerre" Article on Bavarian documents in *Bayerische Dokumenten über den Kriegsausbruch*, edited by Dr Puis Dirr on behalf of the Bavarian Diet.
5. Poincaré, *Notes journalières*, BN nafr 16027, 29 July 1914.
6. See copies in Poincaré, *Comment fut déclarée la guerre de 1914* (Paris, 1939), p. 64.

7. See A. Kriegel & J-J. Becker, *1914: la guerre et le mouvement ouvrier français* (Paris, 1964), pp. 63–85 and 92–3.

8. Lady Algernon Gordon Lennox (ed.), *The diary of Lord Bertie of Thame, 1914–18* (London, 1931), vol. I, pp. 1–4.

9. On Poincaré's attempts to maintain that fine balance from 1912 to the outbreak of war, see Keiger, *France and the origins*, pp. 88–102 and *passim*.

10. Quoted in Albertini, *The origins of the war of 1914* (London, 1965), vol. II, p. 161.

11. *L'Humanité*, 30 July 1914, quoted in Becker and Kriegel, *La guerre et le mouvement*, pp. 88–9.

12. For details of what was happening across Europe see, Keiger, *France and the origins*, pp. 157–62.

13. Jean Stengers, "1914: the safety of ciphers and the outbreak of the First World War", in *Intelligence and International Relations*, C. Andrew & J. Noakes (eds) (Exeter, 1987), pp. 29–48.

14. Quoted in Stengers, "Safety of ciphers", p. 35.

15. See Paléologue's "Récapitulation des faits qui se sont produits du 23 juillet au 4 août 1914", in MAE, *Papiers d'agent*, Paléologue, Correspondance politique, I, 1914, f. 81, confirmed by the Marchioness de Laguiche, in Stengers, "Safety of ciphers", p. 35

16. See Laguiche diary, Chambrun's remark to General Laguiche: "Nous allons le télégraphier au Ministère, le chiffre de l'Ambassade n'étant pas sûr", in Stengers, "Safety of ciphers", p. 36 and fn. 40; also Poincaré, *Comment*, p. 94, who explains that it was Basily who insisted that the Russian cipher be used for greater secrecy. This confirms Russia's desire to keep general mobilization absolutely secret, even by delaying news of it to Paléologue.

17. Quoted in Stengers, "Safety of ciphers", p. 35.

18. Laguiche, ibid., p. 36; see also the original telegram, Paléologue to Paris, 29 July 1914, no. 304 (23h45) with the following marginalia in red ink: "Ce télégramme a été expédié par l'entremise de l'Ambassadeur de Russie à Paris. Suppression au crayon dans le dernier paragraphe de l'indication 1o. et de la phrase: 2o. *à commencer secrètement la mobilisation générale*" (underlined in text), in MAE, *Papiers d'agent*, Paléologue, Correspondance politique, I, 1914, f. 44.

19. Stengers, "Safety of ciphers", p. 36. This corroborates Paléologue's evidence to the Commission for the publication of the *Documents diplomatiques français*, in which he stated that Chambrun took the initiative to suppress the last sentence of the telegram and then informed his ambassador. *DDF*, 3e série, vol. XI (Paris, 1936), no. 283.

20. For further details, see Stengers, "Safety of ciphers", pp. 36–7.

21. Paléologue to Paris, 29 July 1914, no. 306 (24h), MAE, *Papiers d'agent*,

Paléologue, Correspondance politique, I, 1914, f. 46 (underlined in original).

22. Poincaré, *Comment*, p. 88.

23. Quoted in Albertini, *Origins*, vol. II, p. 604; Poincaré, *Comment*, p. 89; Poincaré, Notes journalières, BN nafr 16027, 30 July 1914.

24. In a telegram to Paris that afternoon Paléologue explained that he had told Sazonov not to take any military action that could give Germany a pretext for action. Paléologue added that the Russian Foreign Minister had replied that "dans le cours de la nuit dernière l'Etat-major russe avait précisément fait surseoir à quelques précautions secrètes, dont la divulgation aurait pu alarmer l'Etat-major allemand". Certainly Paléologue could have been more explicit about the fact that those measures were total mobilization. Paléologue to Paris, 30 July 1914, no. 311 (15h50), MAE, *Papiers d'agent*, Paléologue, I, Correspondance politique, 1914, f. 49.

25. Note by Abel Ferry, 30 July 1914, MAE, *Papiers d'agent*, Abel Ferry.

26. Paléologue to Paris, 30 July 1914, no. 315 (19h50), MAE, *Papiers d'agent*, Paléologue, Correspondance politique, I, 1914, f. 51. According to Poincaré, this telegram arrived at the Quai at 11.30pm that same evening, Poincaré, *Comment*, p. 96.

27. Stengers, "Safety of ciphers", p.37; see the excerpt from the hitherto unpublished telegram about the change of cipher, ibid.

28. Paléologue to Paris, 31 July 1914, no.318 (8h30), MAE, *Papiers d'agent*, Paléologue, Correspondance politique, I, 1914, f. 52.

29. Poincaré, *Comment*, p. 119.

30. Viviani to Paléologue, 31 July 1914, nos 483–4 (21h, 21h20), MAE, *Papiers d'agent*, Paléologue, Correspondance politique, I, 1914, f. 56; Poincaré, *Comment*, pp. 118–19.

31. Poincaré, *Comment*, p. 119.

32. Paléologue to Paris, 1 August 1914, no. 324 (9h40), "Réponse à votre télégramme no. 484", MAE, *Papiers d'agent*, Paléologue, Correspondance politique, I, 1914, f. 58.

33. Stengers, "Safety of ciphers", p. 37 and *passim*.

34. "Note rédigée après l'envoi de mon télégramme no. 324", 1 August 1914, MAE, *Papiers d'agent*, Paléologue, Correspondance politique, I, 1914, ff. 59–62.

35. Paléologue to Paris, 1 August 1914, no. 333 (19h30), ibid., f. 68.

36. Poincaré, *Notes journalières*, BN nafr 16027, 31 July 1914.

37. Entry for 31 July 1914 in Guy Rousseau, "Impressions dans la tourmente. Le journal d'Etienne Clémentel dans l'été 1914", *Guerres mondiales*, **156**, 1989, p. 92.

38. See Kriegel & Becker, *La guerre et le mouvement*, pp. 5–7.

39. Quoted ibid., pp. 112–13.

40. See Poincaré, *Comment*, p. 125.
41. Quoted in Kriegel & Becker, *La guerre et le mouvement*, p. 117.
42. Poincaré, *Notes journalières*, 1 August 1914, BN nafr 16027.
43. Diary entry 1 August 1914 in Rousseau, "Journal de Clémentel", p. 92.
44. Poincaré, *Notes journalières*, nafr 16027, 1 August 1914.
45. Poincaré, *Comment*, pp. 105–6; Poincaré, *Notes journalières*, BN nafr 16027, 3 August 1914, p. 142; A. Ferry, note, 30 July 1914, MAE, *Papiers d'agent*, Abel Ferry.
46. Poincaré, *Comment*, pp. 119–20.
47. Quoted ibid., p. 105.
48. "Note rédigéé de la main d'Abel Ferry, 31 July 1914", MAE, *Papiers d'agent*, Abel Ferry, f. 7. The *député*, officer and well-informed *rapporteur* of the Chamber War Ministry budget, Paul Bénazet, informed Clémentel that the delay was about 30 hours. Diary entry 1 August 1914 in Rousseau, "Journal de Clémentel", p. 92.
49. Poincaré, *Comment*, p. 127.
50. Ibid., p. 129.
51. Ibid., pp. 129–30; Poincaré, *Notes journalières*, BN nafr 16027, 1 August 1914.
52. Poincaré, *Comment*, pp. 129–31.
53. Ibid., pp. 116–17 and 126–7.
54. Poincaré, *Notes journalières*, BN nafr 16027, 1 August 1914. There is some confusion in the manuscript of the Poincaré diaries regarding the date of this entry, which appears alternately as 1 and 2 August. The latter is correct.
55. Two German officers were shot on French soil while requisitioning. See Poincaré, *Notes journalières*, BN nafr 16027, 3 August 1914.
56. Poincaré, *Comment*, pp. 139–40.
57. Poincaré, *Notes journalières*, BN nafr 16027, 2 August 1914.
58. See Becker & Kriegel, *La guerre et le mouvement*, pp. 114–33.
59. Poincaré, *Notes journalières*, BN nafr 16027, 2 August 1914.
60. Poincaré, *Comment*, p. 141.
61. Poincaré, *Notes journalières*, BN nafr 16027, 3 August 1914.
62. Ibid., 1 August 1914; ibid, 3 August 1914, quoted in Keiger, *France and the origins*, p. 162.
63. Poincaré, *Comment*, pp. 142–3.
64. Ibid., p. 155.
65. See, for example, ibid., p. 109.
66. Poincaré, *Notes journalières*, BN nafr 16027, 3 August 1914.
67. Ibid., 3 August 1914.
68. Ibid.
69. Ibid., 4 August 1914.
70. Ibid.

71. Poincaré, *Notes journalières*, BN nafr 16029, 8 January 1915.
72. *Le Temps*, 7 March 1922, in MAE, *Europe 1918–1940*, sous-série Allemagne, vol. 327, f. 113.
73. P. J. Flood, *France 1914–18: public opinion and the war effort* (London, 1990), p. 15 and fn. 40.
74. For a full discussion of French public opinion and the *union sacrée*, see Becker, *1914*, pp. 6–9, 99–117, 123–6, 130–31, 190, 249 and 367; on the labour movement, Becker & Kriegel, *La guerre et le mouvement*, pp. 87–105.
75. P. Renouvin, *Le Monde*, 29 July 1964.
76. K. Robbins, *Sir Edward Grey: a biography of Lord Grey of Fallodon* (London, 1971), pp. 298–9; Z. Steiner, *Britain and the origins of the First World War* (London, 1979), pp. 240–41.
77. Poincaré, *Comment*, p. 152.

# Chapter Six
# *Belgium*

## Jean Stengers

### I

Belgium did not decide to go to war: it was invaded. The only question for its government was to decide whether to resist the invasion, and if it did resist, how? Belgian policy, up to the war, was a very simple and determined one: to keep the country out of any European conflict. This implied both a diplomatic and a military stand.

The diplomatic stand consisted in sticking strictly to the principles of neutrality. Neutrality was imposed on Belgium by its treaty obligations, but there are many ways of interpreting international obligations. Belgium's interpretation was a very rigid and scrupulous one.[1] A German specialist was sent to Brussels during the war to ransack the Belgian archives in order to prove Belgium's "guilt", that is, violations of its duties as a neutral. To his great disappointment, he found none.[2]

Belgium, owing to its neutrality, abstained from playing any part in the "*grosse Politik*". One initiative, nevertheless, must be mentioned. In November 1913, when confronted with the Kaiser's assertion that the provocations of France must "inevitably" lead to war, King Albert decided to let the French ambassador in Berlin know about the frame of mind of the German Emperor.[3] His main aim, in such a case, was to try to reduce the tension.

The pre-1914 Belgian neutrality was in one aspect different from the neutral stand Belgium would later choose voluntarily in 1939–40, during the "phoney war". King Leopold III considered in 1939–40 that to be neutral also implied a kind of moral neutrality:

the Belgian press, in particular, should not express any partisan view about the conflict. The government did not fully agree with the King, but considered that any offence against one of the belligerent countries must be avoided.

Moral neutrality, in the pre-1914 years, was regarded as a duty only at government level. The press was free to express its preferences or its critical views; it did so sometimes quite vehemently. The main victims were often the British. The Boer War was an occasion for very violent attacks on Britain. Afterwards, the British were denounced as greedy imperialists trying to evict the Belgians from the soil of Africa (such was the interpretation, at least at the beginning, of the British campaign against the Congo abuses). The Belgian government might express its regrets privately about such outbursts – especially when they included attacks against Queen Victoria – but they were powerless: any press offence could be judged only by a jury, and they knew that a jury would acquit enthusiastically those who expressed vehement but popular views. Generally speaking, the main influence on the Belgian press was that of Paris.[4] The French newspapers sold in Belgium by the thousand.[5] This was a matter of great regret for the German authorities, but they could not devise any practical means for redressing the balance. It is very difficult to find any direct relationship between this and the attitude Belgian public opinion took in 1914, except in one way, and this is an important one: the Belgians reacted as a people accustomed to freedom.

Belgian military policy was dominated by the idea of deterrence. Its main aim, and in fact its sole aim, was to discourage aggressors by showing them clearly the price they would have to pay. This policy was twofold: fortifications and the reinforcement of the army. Fortifications meant the establishment at the end of the nineteenth century of a barrier on the Meuse – with forts at Liège and Namur – and the extension a little later of the defences around Antwerp, where the Belgian army could retreat in case of need. Two important military laws were passed, in 1909 and 1913, which aimed to make the army more efficient and larger. The 1913 law was a major step: it established general compulsory service.

The government's reasoning was expressed succinctly by the head of the Cabinet when speaking in February 1913 before the Chamber of Deputies:

Gentlemen, ignorant people laugh at the idea of 340,000 Belgian soldiers being opposed to the millions of men of our great neighbours. [But let us examine the facts.] At present, what is called the Triple Alliance has at its disposal 53 army corps: 25 German, 16 Austrian, 12 Italian; whereas on the other side, the Triple Entente may count upon 52 army corps: 27 Russian (I speak only of the forces stationed in Europe, not in Asia), 21 French, 4 English. As you see, the difference between the two camps is at present only of one army corps. Believe me, gentlemen, in such circumstances, the addition of 340,000 well armed and well commanded Belgian soldiers is a formidable one; it breaks the equilibrium to the profit of those who respect our neutrality and to the detriment of those who would violate it.[6]

Were the Belgian authorities optimistic about the future? In fact, they harboured neither great illusions nor great pessimism, for they knew very little. The King seems to have known that the French military plan had at one time envisaged the invasion of Belgium.[7] About the German plans they seem to have remained almost completely in the dark: "the designs of the German high command", the Belgian minister in Berlin wrote at the beginning of July 1914, "are inscrutable".[8] A mere glance at the military map, however, obliged them to prepare for the worst.

Nor were the Belgian authorities blind to the dangers of the international situation. In that respect the news they received from the Belgian diplomats in Berlin was somewhat more reassuring than the despatches from Paris. There was a general belief in Belgian diplomatic circles – which were rather pro-German – that Germany wanted peace. "There is no doubt", the Belgian Minister in Berlin wrote in November 1912, "that the Kaiser, the Chancellor and the Foreign Secretary are passionately pacific."[9] The Belgian minister in Paris, on the contrary, repeatedly warned his government of the dangers he saw around him. The *"politique nationaliste, cocardière et chauvine"* of some French political leaders, as he described it in January 1914, seemed to him "a threat for Europe – and for Belgium . . . I see there what is at present the greatest peril for the peace of Europe".[10] Six months later, adding Germany to the picture, he insisted that "Nobody can have any doubts about the spirit of the Kaiser, which is still pacific; but how long can we count upon it in presence of the menacing attitudes of France and Russia, and the reactions they provoke in the chauvinistic and militarist circles of Germany?"[11] The King, speaking in June 1914 to the German military attaché, agreed – at least if we believe the report of the attaché, who may have added a touch of his own to the words of the sovereign – that the French danger was the greatest one. That opinion, the King said (according to the German military attaché) was also that of the Belgian nobility and of the great majority of the Catholic Party.[12]

Preparing for the worst meant, at the diplomatic level, preparing for the event of invasion and, in that case, for the attitude to be taken towards the other powers which would come to the help of Belgium. The latter could not be treated as allies. In that respect, the Foreign Office officials were adamant. The interests of Belgium would at any rate remain different from those of foreign powers, however friendly.

A draft convention with France was drawn up at the Foreign Office to deal with German aggression. It said:

Art. 1   The French armies will co-operate with the Belgian army for the defence of Belgian neutrality and in order to preserve, during and after the present war, the independence of Belgium.

Art. 2   The Belgian army will have to take part in military operations against the German armies only with the aim of expelling the latter from Belgian territory.

Art. 3   Once this aim is reached . . . adequate French forces will remain in Belgium as long as the Belgian Government deem it necessary to avoid a new offensive and a new violation of Belgian neutrality. But it is agreed that Belgian territory will not serve as a basis for strategic operations by the French armies against Germany other than those aiming at the preservation of Belgian neutrality.[13]

The basic idea was that of the necessity of a specific Belgian rôle in the war which had to be agreed upon beforehand by the foreign "helpers". Responsible ministers shared that view.[14] In official declarations or in private, the Belgian authorities, including the King,[15] always declared that Belgium, according to its treaty obligations, would defend its neutrality with arms. Foreign diplomats and observers, however, were often far from taking such declarations at their face value.

There was no suspicion that Belgium had entered into a secret pact with one of its neighbours. When, at the height of the August 1914 crisis, Paul Cambon, in London, interpreted a Belgian despatch as a possible indication of "some secret deal between Germany and Belgium",[16] his reaction was the result of momentary excitement and not of previous and serious thoughts. The honesty of the Belgian neutrality before 1914 was not questioned.

Two things, however, *were* questioned: the military capability of Belgium to defend itself; and its real will to do so, given both the relative powerlessness of the country and its political proclivities. Neither the Germans nor the French had a very high opinion of the Belgian army. The "little capable Belgian troops will be easily dispersed", wrote Moltke in 1911.[17] The French military attaché, Duruy, said in 1909 of the Belgian army that it would be "if not inoffensive, at least of little danger to the invaders".[18] At the beginning of 1912, his opinion had not changed: we can have only "a very limited confidence in the capability of the Belgians to resist a violation of their territory by the Germans".[19] His successor as military attaché, Génie, observed some improvements, but in spite of that he wrote: "the Belgian army is not capable of doing much".[20] He was particularly severe on the officer corps, where he saw much more vanity (*"pour le panache, les galons, les décorations"*) than military value.[21] The nation itself, he felt, lacked the "feelings of abnegation and of sacrifice" which were the necessary bases of a good army.[22]

As regards the possible impact of the political sympathies of the country, the French and Germans held diverging views, according to their particular analysis of the situation. The Germans observed the all-pervading influence of French culture and the great sympathies for France, apparent especially in the Walloon part of the country, and this made them uneasy. The French were still more uneasy, for as good Republicans and often as good anticlericals, they had little confidence in the Catholic Party and the Catholic government, and resented the admiration for Germany and its conservative order which they observed in those circles. The British envoy wrote likewise in 1914: "During the last two years I have on various occasions stated that in official and purely Conservative circles the proclivities were decidedly German."[23] The French representatives in Brussels, when trying to guess what the Belgian government would do in case of war, oscillated between optimism and pessimism – that is, they were not at all sure of what would happen.[24]

What would happen? The great fear of the French, when thinking of a German invasion – and the reverse, the great hope of the Germans – was that Belgium would eventually offer only a symbolic resistance, that the Belgian army would be content with a few cannon salvoes and would avoid a confrontation with a too powerful enemy. On 29 July 1914, the French minister in Brussels, Klobukowski, still assumed that the Belgian government would do little, merely wait until they knew who were the victors, whose camp they would then enter.[25] The German diplomat Kühlmann, when meeting a Belgian colleague, openly advised him to adopt such a reasonable course of action. Belgium, he said, "would fulfil all its obligations as a neutral state by opposing only a token resistance, for instance by aligning its army along the road taken by the German forces, and firing at them a few gunshots. This would be quite sufficient to prove that the Belgian troops have yielded before the crushing superiority in numbers of the imperial forces."[26] Winston Churchill, at the beginning of August 1914, did not believe that the Belgians would do much more.[27]

Still worse, the Belgians could offer no resistance at all, especially if the invasion took place only in the southern part of the country. Duruy thought in 1909 that they would probably only observe events from beyond the Meuse.[28] General Wilson, the Director of Military Operations, wrote to Churchill in August 1911: "As far as my knowledge goes Belgium will remain passive and neutral if she possibly can even if, and when, German armies overrun all her country south of the Meuse and Sambre."[29] In a memorandum of September 1911, Wilson repeated his warning about "the danger that Belgium may allow German troops to cross her southern territories (under verbal protest of course) and confine her energies and defence to the neutrality of her southern provinces".[30] Such fears were not wholly unfounded, because in March 1914, when learning that the German invasion might be limited to a small part of southern Luxemburg, no less a man than the political director of the Foreign Ministry, Gaiffier d'Hestroy, recommended that in such a case the rest of Belgium should remain neutral.[31]

Worst of all, the Belgians could simply and deliberately ally themselves with the strongest party in the war. Such a policy was advocated in 1911 by a serving general of the Belgian army writing under a pseudonym. He was severely disavowed, but as the strongest party, in his reasoning, could evidently be no other than Germany, the incident did not leave a very good impression on the French.[32]

Up to the last moment, at any rate, there were doubts about the Belgian attitude. During the night of 2–3 August 1914, when the proud Belgian answer to the German ultimatum was being drawn up at the Foreign Ministry, Klobukowski, who had no official news, came to the conclusion that the Belgians were yielding to the Germans; he had already minuted a telegram to Paris announcing their acceptance.[33] Thus the attitude of Belgium in case of war could not fully be foreseen – and it was in fact to some extent unforeseeable. It was unforeseeable even for the Belgians themselves, as, apart from some general ideals – preserving to the utmost the neutrality of the country, defending the independence of Belgium – they had no clear conception of what an emergency could be.

## II

The Belgian decision was not preceded by long deliberations: the storm broke too suddenly for that. In the Belgian press, in July 1914, there was no particular sign of alarm. The assassination of Franz Ferdinand at Sarajevo naturally caused great emotion. After that came a lull. One newspaper wrote on 18 July: "We are entering the period of holidays, a period feared by newsmen who for lack of important events are often obliged to be content with second-rate news."[35] A new shock came only with the Austrian ultimatum to Serbia. Comments in the Belgian press mainly followed party lines. The Catholic newspapers showed a strong sympathy for Catholic Austria-Hungary, a feeling of sympathy which was not shared by most liberal newspapers, and still less by the socialists. Even the Austrian ultimatum, and even the declaration of war on Serbia, did not alter this attitude significantly. Most Catholic newspapers defended the rights of Austria-Hungary, even its right to the use of force when its vital interests were at stake.

The government did not receive from its diplomats any important news that was different from what they could read in the press. From Beyens, however, the Belgian envoy in Berlin, they received inside information which was among the most valuable, for the general interpretation of events, to be found in the diplomatic correspondence of the time. In a letter written on 26 July, which he sent by private courier, Beyens reported the conversation he had had the day before with the French ambassador, Jules Cambon. The present moments, Cambon said, were the most cruel he had ever experienced: "Today the fate of France and the conservation of the peace of Europe depend upon a foreign will, that of the Tsar. What will he decide, and upon what advice?" If he decides for war, "France, the victim of her alliance, will follow the destiny of her ally on the battlefields."[36] These remarkable words, however, did not clarify things as regards Belgium itself.

When the crisis became more acute, the government took military precautions. On 27 July, the army was put on the alert. A partial mobilization was ordered on 29 July. General mobilization was decided at the end of the afternoon of 31 July. This was a decision greatly influenced by the King, who presided over the Council of Ministers; some ministers were hesitant.[37] King Albert and his personal rôle here enter the scene. Both the partial and the general mobilization took place in good order, and in great calm.[38] Neither the government nor public opinion considered that mobilization meant war: the best chance for Belgium was to be strong. The interpretation of the German General Staff, in its daily report for 29 July, was the right one: "Belgium wants to oppose an invasion of the French as well as of the Germans."[39]

On 2 August at 7 o'clock in the evening, the German minister delivered at the Belgian Foreign Office the German ultimatum demanding the free passage of the German army through Belgium. The timing of the German ultimatum must be explained by the military disposition of Belgium. It was the relative strength of Belgium that compelled Germany to act swiftly.

The execution of the Schlieffen plan implied the invasion of Belgium. But why not delay the invasion until the full forces of the German army had been mobilized and concentrated for the attack? This delay would not have hampered in any way the development of the manoeuvre on the Western front, as planned by the German High Command. And what a political advantage such a delay would have offered! The chain of events could have been: first a Russian declaration of war, then the response of Germany against Russia, then the entrance of France in the war to support its ally. The figure cut by Germany would have been totally different. Admiral von Tirpitz asked with anger: why did we not wait?[40] The answer consisted of one word: Liège. As Liège was fortified, it was imperative, according to Moltke, to seize it before the Belgians had time to take their defence measures, which would block the advance of the German army.[41] Once war was in sight, Liège must be seized immediately. The explanation of the ultimatum was there.[42]

The military character of the ultimatum was because it was drawn up by the General Staff, and by Moltke personally. In Moltke's text, drawn up on 26 July, he justified the German demands by the plans for a French invasion of Belgium about which, he said, the German government had reliable information. To prevent that enemy attack, Germany had to enter Belgian territory. If Belgium in those circumstances took sides with Germany (*auf die Seite Deutschlands treten*), Germany would not only guarantee the integrity and the independence of the country, but would also be ready to envisage territorial compensations (clearly, at the expense of France). Germany would pay cash for all that would be necessary in Belgium for its troops, and also pay an indemnity for any damage done. But if Belgium adopted a hostile attitude, Germany would treat it as an enemy to which no guarantee at all could be offered. The future would be left "to the decision of arms" (*der Entscheidung der Waffen*).[43]

The draft was transmitted to the Wilhelmstrasse, where it was examined on 29 July by the director of the political section, von Stumm. Von Stumm made a few alterations, two of which were important: instead of demanding that Belgium should "take sides" with Germany, he required "a friendly attitude"; as for the territorial compensations, what was implicit in Moltke's draft was made explicit: it would be "*auf Kosten Frankreichs*". Moreover, the final passage expressing the hopes of the German government was reinforced. If Belgium did not oppose the march of the German troops, the revised text said, "the friendly ties which bind the two neighbouring states will grow stronger and more enduring" (*würden die freundschaftlichen Bande, die beide Nachbarstaaten verbinden, eine weitere und dauernde Festigung erfahren*).[44] This final part of the text, it must be observed, was never published officially in Germany during the war: it would have shown too clearly that Germany had no grievance against Belgium.[45]

The revised text was approved by the Chancellor and sent on the same day to Below-Saleske, the German envoy in Brussels, inside a sealed envelope to be opened by Below only when invited to do so by telegram.[46] That telegram was sent to Below on 2 August at the beginning of the afternoon: the envelope was to be opened and the ultimatum delivered at 8pm precisely (7pm Belgian time).[47] But at the same time, two supplementary modifications of the text were prescribed:

- the semi-promise of territorial compensations was cancelled, the German Foreign Office having come to realize that this would have infuriated Britain still more than the violation of Belgian neutrality itself (the fact that Bethmann Hollweg had not perceived it at first sight does not argue for his political acumen);
- the delay imposed on the Belgian Government for their answer was reduced from 24 to 12 hours. This was expressly asked for by Moltke:[48] the German High Command was in a hurry.[49] [All this may perhaps have caused some surprise at the German Legation in Brussels: it seems as though Below-Saleske, who had only recently taken up his post, had not been let into the secret of the Schlieffen plan.[50]]

The final text of the ultimatum was carefully transcribed on a piece of paper bearing the heading of the *Kaiserliche Deutsche Gesandtschaft in Belgien*.[51] This was the document which Below brought at 7 o'clock on 2 August to Davignon, the Belgian Minister for Foreign Affairs.[52] Things happened very quickly after that. The text of the ultimatum was translated by high officials of the Foreign Office, and at 8 o'clock, the head of the government, de Broqueville, went to the Palace with the document, to see the King.

The decision was in the hands of the King and de Broqueville. The situation could not have been worse for Germany's designs: the King was a model of moral rectitude and resolution, and de Broqueville was the minister who had devoted his best efforts to the reinforcement of the defence of the country, and had, moreover, the character of a proud *"gentilhomme"*.[53] Both of them apparently had no hesitation: the answer would be "no". In this historic hour, it must be stressed, the King of the Belgians had a greater part in the decision than the Tsar of Russia, to whom Jules Cambon had alluded a few days before. The decision to support Serbia, by arms if necessary, was taken in St Petersburg by the Russian Council of Ministers, and submitted to the Tsar for approval.[54] In Brussels, the King was immediately in the first line: this was in conformity with the great tradition of the Kings of the Belgians. At this momentous time, however, de Broqueville was the most important of the two men: he was politically responsible. He could truthfully write, a few days later: "*I took the burden, with the agreement of the Head of State, of the decision.*"[55] In the life of any Belgian Prime Minister, this was probably the finest hour.

The rest followed almost automatically. At 9 o'clock, the Council of Ministers met under the presidency of the King. It was followed immediately by a "Conseil de la Couronne", where the ministers with portfolios were joined by the "ministers of state" (these being ministers with a purely honorary title which was awarded to distinguished statesmen). Resistance was approved unanimously.[56] The answer to the German ultimatum was drawn up during the night at the Ministry of Foreign Affairs. The two key sentences were: "The Belgian Government, if they were to accept the proposals submitted to them, would sacrifice the honour of the nation and betray at the same time their duties towards Europe . . . The Belgian Government are firmly determined to repel, by all the means in their power, every encroachment upon their rights."

The document bore the time of 7am, 3 August – well within the twelve hours fixed by the German ultimatum. It was immediately handed over to Below-Saleske. It was probably not the intention of the government to alert the country; they probably still believed in the virtues of secret diplomatic steps. But the government was short-circuited by the minister of France, Klobukowski, who, when informed, lost no time in passing the information to the correspondent of the Havas agency.[57] The gist of the ultimatum and that of the Belgian answer were thus revealed simultaneously.[58] Belgian newspapers immediately announced them in special editions and the news spread throughout Belgium during the day. It caused an extraordinary outburst of outrage, indignation and patriotism.[59]

This reaction was quite spontaneous. Wrath and the national will to resist literally exploded. As symbols, national flags appeared on façades; the centre of Brussels became deluged with tricolors. There have been few instances where the government, Parliament (which met on 4 August) and public opinion were inseparable. As Henri Pirenne writes, the answer of the King and the government to the

German ultimatum was the answer of the population. "One was proud of it."[60] The King deduced from this spectacle that if the government had not taken a firm stand, it would have been overthrown by the Belgians. "*Si nous avions hésité, on nous aurait le lendemain matin pendus aux réverbères.*"[61] Whether his deduction was right or not, we shall never know.[62] Up to 3 August, ever-present political divisions – Liberals and Socialists versus Catholics – had influenced even the interpretation of the international crisis. Then, party alignments gave way to national unanimity. The excited language of the socialist newspaper *Le Peuple*, from that moment, was the same as that of the rest of the press.[63] Dissenting voices were nowhere to be heard. At the meeting of Parliament on 4 August the representatives of the nation reacted as the nation itself, in perfect unity.[64]

What is striking in this reaction is that it was not an ephemeral phenomenon. For weeks to come (and even years, for many of them) the feelings of the Belgians remained basically the same. On 12 August, the British envoy, Sir Francis Villiers, wrote from Brussels describing "a movement of patriotism and self-sacrifice which spares no effort and shrinks from no cost in the cause of national integrity and independence . . . The energy, discipline, courage, patriotism and self-sacrifice of all classes are beyond all praise."[65]

There were, however, some differences in attitude on 3 August compared to 4 August. On 4 August Belgium was invaded, and the defence of the national territory became then and thereafter the great national cause. On 3 August, before the invasion, the outrage to the national honour was the German ultimatum. National honour was a key word and a key feeling. Germany had offered a deal to Belgium in exchange for a betrayal of its duties. Henri Pirenne, writing as a great historian but also as a keen observer, says: "At that tragic moment, what emerged before everything else was that honour was at stake. One felt insulted by a proposition where one resented injury still more than threat."[66] *Le Peuple* wrote in a vivid way:

> What did the Kaiser and his diplomats demand from us? Not much, except the sacrifice of our neutrality, the abdication of our independence, the betrayal of our international obligations and the abasement of our national dignity . . . In exchange for that, we were promised for our servility the thirty pieces of silver of Judas. [But] we are not yet ready to

sell against German money the honour of our blood, the respect of our pledged word and the treasure of our liberties.[67]

"We have refused to forfeit our honour", King Albert simply said in
his proclamation to the army and to the nation on 5 August.

This shows what a terrible psychological blunder the German ultimatum amounted to. If the Germans had purely and simply invaded
Belgium, without warning – as they did on 2 August in the case of
Luxemburg[68] – and had given afterwards any pretext such as the necessity of pre-empting a French military action, there would have
been a Belgian national resistance but probably much less outrage.
And causing outrage was the inexpiable fault. But the Germans could
not have done anything else. If they wanted to keep Britain out of
the war, the only way to do so was to try to curb the Belgians, and to
curb them they had to offer them a deal. The Germans thought that
if the Belgians were rational people, with a clear understanding of
where their interests lay, they should accept it.

Even after Belgium had decided to resist, many Germans did not
understand such an irrational attitude. "Oh, the poor fools", the
counsellor of the German legation kept repeating, "Oh, the poor
fools! Why don't they get out of the way of the steamroller. We don't
want to hurt them, but if they stand in our way they will be ground
into the dirt. Oh, the poor fools!"[69] German socialists visiting their
Belgian "comrades" in Brussels at the beginning of the German occupation told them: "We do not understand you. Our government offered you not to do any harm and to repay all the damages that
might be caused. And you did not accept it. Why?" "It was a matter
of honour," the Belgian socialists answered. But honour, the Germans replied, "is a form of bourgeois ideology".[70]

The German government, even after the beginning of the war, still
entertained hopes that reason would prevail. On 8 August, they
asked the American minister in Brussels, Brand Whitlock, to trans-
mit a message to the Belgian government. This was just six days after
the ultimatum, and four days after the invasion. The message ran:

> The fortress of Liège has been taken by assault after a brave
> defence. The German Government most deeply regret that
> bloody encounters should have resulted from the attitude of
> the Belgian Government . . . Now that the Belgian army has

upheld the honour of its arms by its heroic resistance to a
very superior force, the German Government beg the King
of the Belgians and the Belgian Government to spare Belgium the further horrors of war . . . Germany once more
gives her solemn assurance that it is not her intention to appropriate Belgian territory to herself and that such an intention is far from her thoughts. Germany is still ready to
evacuate Belgium as soon as the state of war will allow her
to do so.[71]

Brand Whitlock found a pretext for not transmitting the message.[72]
On 9 August the offer was repeated through an intermediary, the
Netherlands. It was immediately rejected.[73]

There was, it must be admitted, an element of irrationality, and of
unexpected irrationality, in the sudden and sovereign price the Belgians did attach to their national honour. Could that rationally be
expected from a population which for decades had lived in peace
and had a most peaceful character, which seemed mainly attached to
its material interests and which, while showing signs of real patriotism, had never been inclined to any chauvinism? The image was that
of a calm, prosperous people, not of a particularly proud people. Individual pride was not a Belgian characteristic, either: duelling, for
instance, which is a rather good indication of what individual attitudes are, was never popular in Belgium.[74]

The most rational prevision was that of Klobukowski, writing in
March 1913. Belgium, he said, "conscious of its lack of strength,
turned more by temperament to the study of economic problems and
to the development of its commerce and of its industry, than to the
realities of war", will have the desire, if a catastrophe occurs, "to keep
clear of the dangers to which it is exposed with the least possible damage".[75] What happened was quite the reverse. If we try to find a psychological explanation to what is, in fact, partly beyond the sphere of
positive explanation, we must turn to what amounted to an inner, yet
completely unostentatious, feeling of self-esteem. Belgium, from an
economic point of view, had achieved great things at home and in the
world; it had helped to build an Empire in Africa and had become its
master; it was renowned as a land of civil liberties and had maintained
for decades its free institutions. These were things to be proud of.
Such a people would not admit the offer of the "silver coins of Judas".

Nor in a country where the internal struggles were so visible, had the strength of Belgian patriotism been assessed accurately. It erupted in August 1914 in its most elementary form. Going back to Julius Caesar, to quote his words about the peoples of Gaul, *horum omnium fortissimi sunt Belgae*, "of all of them, the Belgians are the bravest", was something which in normal times often provoked a slight smile. But nobody smiled when King Albert, in his proclamation of 5 August, solemnly declared: *"César a dit de vos ancêtres: De tous les peuples de la Gaule, les Belges sont les plus braves."* This fully corresponded to the spirit of the time.

A parallel could be drawn, as regards honour, particularly with Britain's reaction to the violation of Belgian neutrality. In his famous speech of 3 August in the House of Commons, where he measured up what such a violation would mean for Britain, Sir Edward Grey insisted on the dictates of both the "interests" of the country and its "honour". In the reaction of public opinion on 4 August, it is evident that the idea of British honour was paramount.

That reaction also had not been foreseen. When the Belgian government, on 4 August, sent an appeal for the military co-operation of Britain (as well as that of France and Russia) for the defence of its independence, there was a real anxiety about what the answer would be: would Britain really intervene?[76] They had not anticipated that the popular reaction in Britain would be similar to that of Belgium. "A House of Commons that had hesitated an hour after the invasion of Belgium said a witness, "would have been swept out of existence by the wrath and indignation of the people."[77]

In many ways 1914 was a drama of the unexpected. Foreign powers did not expect the rage with which Belgium defended itself against German aggression; Belgium did not expect the rage that the aggression would provoke among the British people; and the German army did not expect the strong resistance it met in Belgium[78] – and their disappointment was certainly one of the reasons for the fury with which they reacted, with arson and murder, to the alleged attacks of Belgian *"francs-tireurs"*. The German Emperor did not expect such a resistance, and his personal fury took the form of a repeated demand, in August–September 1914, that parts of Belgian territory should be annexed, and the Belgian population established there expelled in order to make place for German colonists.[79]

The excitement of public opinion in Belgium did not leave the government time to implement what had been prepared in case of war, that is, a convention with the powers which would come to the help of Belgium. The proposal for such a convention was put on the Ministers' table on 4 August, but it found insufficient support: a convention was equivalent to a delay, and it was evident that no delay was possible in announcing publicly the appeal to France and Britain.[80]

This is not the place for a description of the military operations of August 1914, but one remark is necessary: from a military point of view, Belgium had to pay the price for its strict pre-1914 neutrality. This means that no plan existed for a co-ordination of the Belgian forces with those of France and Britain. The King complained about the insufficient help he received. Even after the war his chief military adviser, Galet, wrote with his approval: "It is for us a painful fact: whereas Belgium has done its duty, our guarantors have not done theirs; they could preserve the major part of the country from enemy occupation; they did not bother to do so; they have not guaranteed us."[81] This was rancour, not realism.

### III

Belgium, in 1914, had nothing to hide. The two Belgian Grey Books, however, which were published in 1914 and 1915,[82] were not entirely unexpurgated: the choice of documents was sometimes rather biased. When on 28 July 1914 the Belgian minister in Paris quoted the German ambassador as saying: "Germany is ready to enter into any arrangement which would ensure the preservation of peace", the comment, at the time of the preparation of the Grey Book, was: "*Dangereux, à supprimer*".[83] The whole despatch was omitted. In the telegrams and despatches which were published, a few passages which might have made a bad impression were also left out. This was the case, for instance, as regards the reflections of Jules Cambon about the Tsar and Russia, quoted by Beyens in his letter of 26 July (see above). When Beyens himself wrote similarly two days later: "The issue of the crisis is always contained in the same question: what will Russia do?", the Grey Book also omitted that passage.[84] Still worse, Beyens had written on 1 August: "The price of France's fidelity to its alliance with Russia is that it will probably lose its existence as a great power. The German newspapers are quite certain that the German victory will be brilliant, overwhelming, crushing . . . Did the fathers of the Russian alliance, M. Ribot and de Freycinet, make a cruel mistake, and when they forged that defensive weapon against Germany, did they ever conceive that it could be a two-edged one, and that France would one day be exposed to perish by defending Russia?" This too was struck out.[85]

Foreign countries, either friendly or neutral, must not be offended. About France, Beyens wrote on 24 July: "One does not very well see how France, the France of radicalism, of the Caillaux trial and of the disturbing revelations of M. Charles Humbert about the state of the army, could accept a European war where its existence would be at stake, in order to save Serbia from an unprecedented humiliation": omitted from the Grey Book.[86] About Serbia, Beyens spoke in the same despatch of "the indelible stain impressed on the Serbian nation by the assassinations of Sarajevo": also omitted.[87] About Italy, Beyens on 26 July compared the Austrian ultimatum to Serbia to the Italian ultimatum to Libya, which was also destined to make war inevitable: also omitted.[88] About Romania, the Belgian minister in St Petersburg reported on 31 July that according to his Romanian colleague, his country would choose the camp of those which made in its favour the greatest territorial promises: omitted.[89]

One text at least was expanded to give a better explanation of the chain of events. It is a telegram from the Belgian envoy in London, Lalaing. The case of Lalaing in London is at first sight similar to that of Paléologue, the French ambassador in Russia; they were both rather reticent in their diplomatic correspondence. But the reasons were different: Lalaing was a nonentity, whereas Paléologue chose to keep much to himself.[90] At any rate, both needed amendments when their texts were published. In the case of Paléologue, it was the notorious no. 118 of the French Yellow Book, where to the simple sentence of Paléologue's original telegram, "The general mobilization of the Russian army has been ordered", a long explanation was added – it was a complete fabrication – to justify the decision of Russia. Lalaing was similarly very brief when he wired on 4 August: "England this morning has called on Germany to respect Belgian neutrality. Ultimatum expires midnight." The Grey Book added some lines making the attitude of Britain more explicit.[91] There was, however, a fundamental difference: the Yellow Book's fabrication falsified the facts. The Grey Book's fabrication did not.

# Notes

1. The standard works are those of H. Lademacher, *Die belgische Neutralität als Problem der europäischen Politik, 1830–1914* (Bonn, 1971); J. E. Helmreich, *Belgium and Europe: a study in small power diplomacy* (The Hague, 1976); and D. H. Thomas, *The guarantee of Belgian independence and neutrality in European diplomacy, 1830's–1930's* (Kingston, Rhode Island, 1983).

2. Schwertfeger to Oswald, 16 February 1928, in I. Meseberg-Haubold, *Der Widerstand Kardinal Merciers gegen die deutsche Besetzung Belgiens 1914–1918* (Frankfurt–Bern, 1982), p. 346 n. 33. See other quotations from Schwertfeger's writings in Lademacher, *Die belgische Neutralität*, p. 28. In spite of their date, the books of E. Waxweiler, *La Belgique neutre et loyale* (Paris, 1915); and *Le procès de la neutralité belge* (Paris, 1916); and of A. De Ridder, *La violation de la neutralité belge et ses avocats* (Brussels, 1926) still remain valuable.

3. See J. Stengers, "Guillaume II et le roi Albert à Potsdam en novembre 1913", *Acad. Royale de Belgique. Bull. de la Classe des Lettres et des Sc. morales et politiques*, 6th series, IV, 1993.

4. J. Willequet, "La légation d'Allemagne, la presse et les milieux de presse bruxellois entre 1887 et 1914", *Revue belge de philologie et d'histoire*, XXXVI, 1958.

5. H. Haag, *Le comte Charles de Broqueville, Ministre d'Etat, et les luttes pour le pouvoir (1910–1940)* (Louvain-la-Neuve, 1990) vol. I. p. 180.

6. Speech of Broqueville of 14 February 1913, *Annales parlementaires, Chambre*, 1912–1913, p. 617.

7. That plan has now been changed, the King told the German military attaché in May 1914 (Klüber to Waldersee, 7 May 1914, Auswärtiges Amt, Belgien 60 secr., vol. 7; see *Berliner Monatshefte*, July 1930, p. 796; and L. Albertini, *The origins of the war of 1914*, vol. III (London, 1957), p. 443). This was certainly an echo of the information sent by the Belgian military attaché in Paris, Major Collon (see note of Gaiffier, the political director of the Foreign Ministry, of 2 March 1914); Brussels, Archives du Ministère des Affaires Etrangères (abbrev. henceforth: AEB), Indépendance, Neutralité, Défense militaire de la Belgique; see also Haag, Le comte Charles, vol. I, p. 192). Joffre, in 1911–12, had in fact asked to be granted the right to be the first to enter Belgian territory (see G. Pedroncini, "L'influence de la neutralité belge et luxembourgeoise sur la stratégie française: le plan XVII", *Actes du Colloque international de Téhéran, 1976* (Bucharest, 1978), pp. 299–310). It may have come to the ears of the Belgians.

8. Private letter of Beyens of 6 July 1914: AEB, Correspondence politique. Légations. Allemagne, vol. XVIII. See also Lademacher, *Die belgische*

*Neutralität*, p. 459, who gives, however, a wrong date and prints "dossiers" instead of "desseins"). It seems as though the French were not in a much better position: see J. K. Tanenbaum, "French estimates of Germany's operational war plans", in E. R. May (ed.) *Knowing one's enemies: intelligence assessment before the two World Wars* (Princeton, New Jersey, 1984), pp. 166–7.

9. Beyens to Davignon, 30 November 1912, in B. Schwertfeger (ed.), *Die Belgischen Dokumente zur Vorgeschichte des Weltkrieges 1885–1914*, additional volume, *Belgische Aktenstücke 1905–1914* (Berlin, 1925), p. 265.

10. Guillaume to Davignon, 16 January 1914, ibid., p. 297. On his previous despatches, which were in the same vein, see Stengers, "Guillaume II et le roi Albert à Potsdam", pp. 242–3.

11. Guillaume to Davignon, 24 June 1914, AEB, Correspondance politique. Légations. France.

12. Stengers, "Guillaume II et le roi Albert", p. 245.

13. Haag, *Le comte Charles*, vol. I, p. 175.

14. Ibid., pp. 175–6; R. Devleeshouwer, *Les Belges et le danger de guerre 1910–1914* (Louvain–Paris, 1958), p. 148.

15. He is very firm in that respect, for instance, in his conversation of May 1914 with the German military attaché (see the despatch by Klüber of 7 May 1914, quoted above).

16. Cambon to Viviani, 2 August 1914, in *DDF*, 3rd series, XI, p. 469.

17. G. Ritter, *Der Schlieffenplan. Kritik eines Mythos* (Munich, 1956), p. 179. See, in general, J. Willequet, "Appréciations allemandes sur la valeur de l'armée belge et les perspectives de guerre avant 1914", *Revue internationale d'histoire militaire* XX, 1959.

18. A. Duchesne, "L'armée et la politique militaire belges de 1871 à 1920 jugées par les attachés militaires de France à Bruxelles", *Revue belge de philologie et d'histoire* XXXIX, 1961, p. 1113.

19. Ibid., pp. 1124–5.

20. Report of 27 July 1914, in A. Duchesne, "L'armée et la politique militaire belges", *Revue belge de philologie et d'histoire* XL, 1962, p. 382.

21. Ibid., p. 380.

22. Ibid., p. 379.

23. Villiers to Grey, 12 August 1914, *BD*, vol. XI, p. 350.

24. As Henry Contamine says, speaking of the "inconnue belge": "De papiers pessimistes, les plus nombreux, en papiers optimistes, on n'était jamais arrivé à savoir ce que ferait le gouvernement de Bruxelles" (H. Contamine, *La revanche 1871–1914* (Paris, 1957), p. 213).

25. *DDF*, 3rd series, XI, p. 241.

26. Report of Lalaing, Belgian minister in London, of 15 February 1911,

AEB, Correspondance politique. Légations. Grande-Bretagne; see Helmreich, *Belgium and Europe*, p. 160. Kühlmann (who was six years later to become the German Foreign Secretary) was speaking in 1911 to a member of the Belgian legation in London, de Ramaix. In 1914, he reiterated his views to Lalaing himself: see R. von Kühlmann, *Erinnerungen* (Heidelberg, 1948), p. 394.

27. "Belgium did not count so largely in my sentiments at this stage. I thought it very unlikely that she would resist. I thought, and Lord Kitchener, who lunched with me on the Tuesday [28 July 1914], agreed, that Belgium would make some formal protest and submit. A few shots might be fired outside Liège or Namur, and then this unfortunate State would bow its head before overwhelming might", W. S. Churchill, *The world crisis, 1911–1914* (London, 1923), p. 202.

28. Duchesne, "L'armée et la politique militaire belges", *Revue belge* XXXIX, 1961, p. 1113.

29. K. M. Wilson, "The war office, Churchill and the Belgian option: August to December 1911", *Bulletin of the Institute of Historical Research*, November 1977, p. 219.

30. C. Hazlehurst, *Politicians at war, July 1914 to May 1915* (London, 1971), p. 314; see also especially p. 309.

31. Haag, *Le comte Charles*, vol. I, pp. 174, 193. I cannot agree with Helmreich, who sees in this a "Belgian decision" (*Belgium and Europe*, p. 167; see also pp. 166, 168 and 170). It was only a recommendation from a high official.

32. See Devleeshouwer, *Les Belges*, pp. 135–40; Willequet, Appréciations allemandes, pp. 639–40; A. Duchesne, "L'armée et la politique militaire belges", p. 1124; Stengers, "Guillaume II et le roi Albert à Potsdam", p. 245.

33. Note of Gaiffier d'Hestroy of 3 August 1914, AEB, Correspondence politique. Légations. France. There is naturally no trace of this in Klobukowski's memoirs: A. Klobukowski, *Souvenirs de Belgique 1911–1918* (Brussels, 1928).

34. For a survey of the Belgian press of July 1914, see Devleeshouwer, *Les Belges*, pp. 223ff., and M. Palo, *The diplomacy of Belgian war aims during the First World War*, PhD thesis, University of Illinois, 1977 (Ann Arbor, University Microfilms, 1978), pp. 151ff. For Liège, see R. Demoulin, "La presse quotidienne liègeoise et la France à la veille du premier conflit mondial", *Les relations franco-belges de 1830 à 1934. Actes du Colloque de Metz, 15–16 novembre 1974* (Metz, 1975), pp. 97–111.

35. *Bien Public*, 18 July 1914, quoted by R. Devleeshouwer, *Les Belges*, p. 232.

36. AEB, Correspondance politique. Légations. Allemagne, vol. XVIII. See J.

Stengers, "July 1914: some reflections", *Annuaire de l'Institut de Philologie et d'Histoire orientales et slaves* XVII, 1963–5, p. 120.

37. Cf. General Galet, *S. M. le roi Albert commandant en chef devant l'invasion allemande* (Paris, 1931), pp. 35–6.

38. L. de Lichtervelde, *Avant l'orage, 1911–1914* (Brussels, 1938), pp. 150–51; Haag, *Le comte Charles*, vol. I, p. 197.

39. K. Kautsky (ed.), *Die deutschen Dokumente zum Kriegsausbruch*, (hereafter *DD*) vol. II, p. 93.

40. Grand-Amiral von Tirpitz, *Mémoires* (French trans.) (Paris, 1930), pp. 290–91.

41. G. Ritter, *Der Schlieffenplan*, pp. 148 and 180.

42. On the Liège factor, see G. Ritter, *Staatskunst und Kriegshandwerk*, vol. II (Munich, 1960), pp. 332–3, and the English translation, *The sword and the sceptre: the problem of militarism in Germany*, vol. II (London, 1972), pp. 266–7; G. Ritter, "Der Anteil der Militärs an der Kriegskatastrophe von 1914", *Historische Zeitschrift*, August 1961, pp. 89–91; L. C. F. Turner, "The significance of the Schlieffen plan", in *The war plans of the Great Powers, 1880–1914*, P. M. Kennedy (ed.) (London, 1979), pp. 212–16; S. E. Miller, S. M. Lynn-Jones & S. Van Evera (eds), *Military strategy and the origins of the First World War* (revised edn) (Princeton, NJ, 1991), pp. 75, 78, 94, 125, 219 and 257. As Gerhard Ritter writes so well: "The powerful forces meant for the advance through Belgium had to be assembled as soon as possible in the Aachen–Wesel area. Even so, this meant a lapse of at least eight to ten days until hostilities proper could really commence. A formal declaration of war on France and Belgium could well be postponed that long without doing any military harm. What could not be postponed, however, was the attack Moltke planned on Liège" (*The sword and the sceptre*, vol. II, p. 266).

43. *DD*, II, pp. 98–100, no. 376. See, in general, L. Leclère, "La Belgique et l'Allemagne du 26 juillet au 4 août 1914", *Revue de l'Université de Bruxelles* XXIX, 1923–4.

44. Leclère, "La Belgique et l'Allemagne".

45. A. De Ridder, *La Belgique et la guerre, vol. IV. Histoire diplomatique 1914–1918* (Brussels, 1922), pp. 130–31.

46. *DD*, II, p. 97, no. 375.

47. *DD*, III, pp. 122–3, no. 648.

48. See Moltke to Foreign Office, 2 August 1914, *DD*, III, p. 135.

49. The more so that it received information about the special military preparations being made in and around Liège: see U. Trumpener, "War premeditated? German intelligence operations in July 1914", *Central European History* IX, 1976, p. 80.

50. There is no other plausible explanation for the fact that in the morning

of 2 August he gave an interview at the German legation to a journalist of *Le Soir* and told him: "L'idée a toujours prévalue chez nous [i.e. in Germany] que la neutralité de la Belgique ne serait pas violée . . . Les troupes allemandes ne traverseront pas le territoire belge. Des événements graves vont se dérouler. Peut-être verrez-vous brûler le toit de votre voisin, mais l'incendie épargnera votre demeure" (*Le Soir*, 3 August 1914, edition published on 2 August at 3pm: see Paul Hymans, *Mémoires*, vol. I (Brussels, 1958), p. 83). The last sentence caused a sensation. Below-Saleske's predecessor in Brussels, Flotow, had certainly been "in the know": in a despatch of January 1911, he explicitly refers to "die Pläne unserer Generalstabes" as regards Belgium (Flotow to Bethmann Hollweg, 26 January 1911, Auswärtiges Amt, Belgien 60 secr., vol. 5).

51. Facsimile in De Ridder, *La Belgique*, vol. IV, pp. 128–9. The document was in German, whereas the Austrian ultimatum to Serbia had been drawn up in French (see V. Dedijer & Z. Anic (eds), *Documents sur la politique extérieure du royaume de Serbie*, vol. VII, 2 (Belgrade, 1980), pp. 628–31, no. 494). Luigi Albertini sees this use of the German language as "an extra touch of knavery" in *The origins of the war of 1914*, vol. III, p. 456. This may be a malicious interpretation.

52. Davignon had no German (this is a clear indication of the limits of German influence in Belgium). Below-Saleske informed him of the general significance of the ultimatum (see R. Recouly, "Les heures tragiques d'avant-guerre. IV. A Bruxelles. Récit de M. le Baron de Gaiffier d'Hestroy", in *Revue de France*, 1 September 1921, p. 34, and his book, *Les heures tragiques d'avant-guerre* (Paris, 1922), p. 131).

53. See his biography by Henri Haag, *Le comte Charles*. His title was in 1914 that of "chef du cabinet". The title of "premier ministre" was introduced only after the First World War.

54. See J. Stengers, "1914: the safety of ciphers and the outbreak of the First World War", in *Intelligence and international relations 1900–1945*, C. Andrew and J. Noakes (eds), (Exeter, 1987), pp. 30–31.

55. Haag, *Le Comte Charles*, vol. I, p. 233.

56. M. R. Thielemans & E. Vandewoude, "Les conseils des ministres et de la Couronne du 2 août 1914", in *Histoire et méthode = Acta Historica Bruxellensia*, vol. IV (Brussels, 1981), pp. 417–44; Haag, *Le comte Charles*, vol. I, pp. 206–15.

57. See A. Klobukowski, *Souvenirs*, p. 88.

58. The full text of the two documents was made public only on 4 August, when both were read by de Broqueville in the Chamber.

59. For what follows, see J. Stengers, "La Belgique", in *Les Sociétés européennes et la guerre de 1914–1918*, J. J. Becker & S. Audoin-Rouzeau (eds) (Nanterre, 1990), pp. 75–91.

60. H. Pirenne, *La Belgique et la guerre mondiale* (Paris, 1928), p. 48. See also a striking page in Paul Hymans, *Mémoires*, vol. I, p. 92.

61. Hymans, *Mémoires*, vol. II, p. 827.

62. Klobukowski made a similar reflection on 5 August, when speaking of the appeal of the government to France and England: "Je crois que, s'il eût hésité davantage, une révolution se fût produite", Klobukowski to Doumergue, 5 August 1914, *DDF*, 3rd series, XI, p. 565.

63. Devleeshouwer, *Les Belges*, p. 262.

64. See two vivid descriptions of the sitting of 4 August by two American diplomats, Brand Whitlock in *The letters and journal of Brand Whitlock: the journal*, A. Nevins (ed.), (New York, 1936), pp. 7ff.); and Hugh Gibson, *A journal from our legation in Belgium* (New York, 1917), pp. 12ff.).

65. Villiers to Grey, 12 August 1914; and Villiers to Nicolson, same date, in *BD*, vol. XI, p. 350.

66. Pirenne, *La Belgique*, p. 47.

67. *Le Peuple*, 5 August 1914.

68. See Albertini, *The origins*, vol. III, pp. 202–4.

69. Gibson, *A journal from our legation*, p. 22.

70. E. Vandervelde, *La Belgique* (Paris, 1915), p. 29.

71. A. Nevins (ed), *The letters and journal of Brand Whitlock*, p. 23.

72. Ibid., pp. 24–5.

73. Royaume de Belgique. *Correspondance diplomatique relative à la Guerre de 1914 (24 juillet–29 août)* (Antwerp, 1914) = First Belgian Grey Book, pp. 19–22; E. Waxweiler, *La Belgique neutre et loyale* (Paris, 1915), pp. 112–13; De Ridder, *La Belgique et la guerre*, IV, pp. 159–60.

74. See Don Alfonso de Bourbon et d'Autriche-Este, *Résumé de l'histoire de la création et du développement des Ligues contre le duel et pour la protection de l'honneur dans les différents pays d'Europe* (Vienna, 1908), p. 27; L. Rivet, *La question du duel* (Brussels, 1910), p. 25.

75. Klobukowski to Jonnart, 8 March 1913, *DDF*, 3rd series, V, pp. 654–5.

76. Waxweiler, *La Belgique neutre*, p. 173 (a first-class testimony). It must be remembered that the guarantee of Belgian neutrality did not automatically entail armed intervention in favour of Belgium.

77. Quoted in R. J. W. Evans & H. Pogge von Strandmann (eds), *The coming of the First World War* (Oxford, 1988), p. 161.

78. See Klobukowski to Doumergue, 5 August 1914, *DDF*, 3rd series, XI, p. 565; General de Selliers de Moranville, *Contribution à l'histoire de la guerre mondiale, 1914–1918* (Brussels, 1933), p. 260; F. Van Langenhove, *Comment naît un cycle de légendes. Francs-tireurs et atrocités en Belgique* (Paris, 1916), p. 104.

79. Cf. F. Fischer, *Griff nach der Weltmacht. Die Kriegsziel-politik des*

*kaiserlichen Deutschland 1914–1918* (new edn) (Düsseldorf, 1977), p. 99; W. Basler, *Deutschlands Annexionspolitik in Polen und im Baltikum 1914–1918* (Berlin, 1962), pp. 54–5 and 381–3.

80. Haag, *Le comte Charles*, vol. I, pp. 221–7.

81. General Galet, "S. M. le roi Albert commandant en chef devant l'invasion allemande. VIII. A Anvers", in *Le Soir*, 30 October 1931. For the approval of the text by the King, see Stengers, "Guillaume II et le roi Albert à Potsdam", pp. 233–4. The Minister for Foreign Affairs, Paul Hymans, when he read Galet's article, reacted very swiftly. He told the King that he found "cette condamnation des garants maladroite, dangereuse, inutile . . . Il y aura des protestations du côté de la France, des froissements, des polémiques. Je serais contraint, si l'Ambassadeur de France venait se plaindre, d'exprimer des regrets" (note by Hymans, Archives Générales du Royaume, Papiers Hymans, no. 253). The King acquiesced; the passage was struck out of Galet's book (of the same title as the article in *Le Soir*) which was in print (see the book, p. 192).

82. *Correspondance diplomatique relative à la guerre de 1914 (24 juillet–29 août)* (Antwerp, 1914) = First Grey Book; *Correspondance diplomatique relative à la guerre de 1914–1915*, II (Paris, 1915) = Second Grey Book.

83. Guillaume to Davignon, 28 July 1914, AEB, Correspondance politique. Légations. France.

84. Beyens to Davignon, 28 July 1914, AEB, Corr. pol. Légations. Allemagne; Second Grey Book, no. 12.

85. Beyens to Davignon, 1 August 1914, AEB, Neutralité. Indépendance. Défense militaire de la Beligique; Second Grey Book, no. 20.

86. Beyens to Davignon, 24 July 1914, AEB, Corr. pol. Légations. Allemagne; Second Grey Book, no. 4.

87. Ibid.

88. Beyens to Davignon, 26 July 1914, AEB, Corr. pol. Légations. Allemagne; Second Grey Book, no. 8.

89. Buisseret à Davignon, 31 July 1914, AEB, Corr. pol. Légations. Russie; Second Grey Book, no. 17.

90. See Stengers, "1914: safety of ciphers", where the case of Paléologue is discussed.

91. Lalaing to Davignon, 4 August 1914, AEB, Corr. pol. Légations. Grande-Bretagne; First Grey Book, no. 39.

# Chapter Seven

# *Britain*

## Keith Wilson

### I

The third chapter of Lloyd George's *War memoirs* is a sustained and vitriolic attack on the persona of Sir Edward Grey and on his handling of British foreign policy throughout the crisis which was to develop into what became known as the "Great War". "Grey's mind", according to Lloyd George, "was not made for prompt action . . . He altogether lacked that quality of audacity which makes a great Minister . . . The facts tell their own tale of a pilot whose hand trembled in the palsy of apprehension, unable to grip the levers and manipulate them with a firm and clear purpose." Lloyd George made a series of assertions:

> Had [Grey] warned Germany in time of the point at which Britain would declare war – and wage it with her whole strength – the issue would have been different. I know it is said that he was hampered by the divisions in the Cabinet. On one question, however, there was no difference of opinion – the invasion of Belgium. He could at any stage of the negotiations have secured substantial unanimity amongst his colleagues on that point. At the very worst there would have been only two resignations, and those would have followed our entry into war, whatever the issue upon which it was fought. The assent of all the Opposition leaders was assured, and thus in the name of a united people he could have intimated to the German Government that if they put into

operation their plan of marching through Belgium they would encounter the active hostility of the British Empire. And he could have uttered this warning in sufficient time to leave the German military authorities without any excuse for not changing their dust-laden plans.[1]

Lloyd George's offensive against Grey began long before the publication of his *War memoirs*. It commenced at least as early as 7 October 1914, on which date Ramsay MacDonald, the leader of the Labour Party, lunched with Lloyd George and Edwin Montagu, the Financial Secretary to the Treasury, at Montagu's house. As MacDonald recorded it, "They agreed Grey's Foreign policy responsible for war. Belgium did not determine Grey's attitude".[2] There is some evidence from the same source that, indeed, Belgium did not determine Grey's attitude. On the previous day, MacDonald had lunched with John Morley, one of the ministers who resigned in August 1914, and been told:

> The subordination of Belgium in the causes of the war is proved by the fact that Grey threatened to resign if the Cabinet declared for neutrality on Wednesday 29 July . . . before Belgium was mentioned seriously (if at all) in the Cabinet discussions. That day Grey said: "I am sorry to have brought all this upon you, but if you decide to be neutral I am not the man to be responsible for that policy." The question then was how far we were committed to France and what answers were to be given to M. Cambon . . . Belgium had nothing whatever to do with the Cabinet decisions. Without it there would have been more resignations but there still would have been war.[3]

Morley's lunchtime tale is not thoroughly reliable: there is clear evidence from other sources that the Cabinet *did* discuss the issue of Belgium on Wednesday 29 July. On the other hand, MacDonald recalled being told by another minister that Grey had threatened to resign on 30 July, and the fact that the Cabinet did not meet on that day does not settle this matter one way or the other. More reliable is an undated note passed across the Cabinet table from Harcourt, the Colonial Secretary, to Lloyd George. The note reads: "You must now speak for us.

Grey wishes to go to war without any violation of Belgium."[4]

There is plenty of material which shows that Lloyd George responded to Harcourt's invitation, and that his attitude was very different from that of the Foreign Secretary. In a substantial series of Cabinet notes to Lloyd George, Churchill, the First Lord of the Admiralty, whose bellicosity is beyond dispute, tried to bring the Chancellor round to his own point of view:

> I am most profoundly anxious that our long co-operation may not be severed. Remember your part at Agadir. I implore you to come and bring your mighty aid to the discharge of our duty.

> All the rest of our lives we shall be opposed. I am deeply attached to you and have followed your instinct and guidance for nearly 10 years.

> Together we can carry a wide social policy . . . The naval war will be cheap . . . You *alone* can take the measures which will assure food being kept abundant and cheap to the people;[5]

> *Please* study the question before you make up your mind. There are all sorts of vital and precise facts – which you *cannot* have at your fingers' ends.[6]

The final note here is closely connected, in my view, with a six-page memorandum which Churchill told a member of his Naval War Staff to prepare on 1 August for Lloyd George. Entitled "A short survey of the present military situation in Europe", this concluded:

> Germany's chief object . . . lies in preventing the arrival of the British expeditionary army. Its absence from the battlefield will exercise an influence out of all proportion to its numerical strength . . . That the effect on the morale of the French army will be great is not doubtful . . . "Nous sommes trahis" are three ominous words, which have been the precursors of most French disasters. There is reason to suppose that the presence or absence of the British army will determine the action of the Belgian army. It will very probably decide the fate of France.[7]

177

Churchill was not alone in campaigning to bring Lloyd George round to an interventionist position. One note for Lloyd George from C. F. G. Masterman, Chancellor of the Duchy of Lancaster, reads: "I am with McKenna and Runciman in fighting for *time*, sooner than break up the Cabinet. Twelve hours might find us united. Our collapse would be unthinkable – what is to happen to the Empire if we break to pieces! Do *fight* for unity."[8] Lord Beaverbrook recalled Masterman "at a gathering which included several important members of both parties . . . pressing the case for intervention earnestly and vigorously, all the time watching carefully for the effect of his remarks on those of his Radical colleagues who were known to be hesitating . . . As he talked, his whole interest was concentrated on the effect his remarks were having on Lloyd George."[9]

This particular meeting is hard to date and place precisely, but that there was such a meeting is an indication of the lengths to which it was thought Lloyd George would go. On the afternoon of 2 August, between Cabinet meetings, Morley drove with Lloyd George and Simon, the Attorney-General, to the house of Beauchamp, the First Commissioner of Works. The talk as they drove, according to Morley, "was on the footing that we were all three for resignation".[10] By then, a list had been drawn up, by Churchill and A. J. Balfour, the former leader of the Conservative Party, of possible Conservative replacements for Lloyd George and those expected to resign with him in what would then have become a coalition Cabinet. The list, in the papers of the editor of *The Times*, Geoffrey Dawson, consisted of Lord Lansdowne, the Duke of Devonshire, Sir Edward Carson, and Mr A. Bonar Law.[11]

As we know, Lloyd George did not resign. In fact, on the morning of 3 August he made a strong appeal to the neutralists to remain in the Cabinet.[12] The turning point for Lloyd George seems to have come during the evening of 2 August. Walter Runciman, then President of the Board of Agriculture, said later:

> Right up to tea-time on Sunday, 2 August, Lloyd George told us that he was doubtful of the action he would take. In conversation with about one-half of our Ministerial colleagues on the afternoon of that day, he said he would not oppose the war but that he would take no part in it, and

would retire for the time being to Criccieth. He would not repeat his experience of 1899–1902 . . . he had had enough of standing out against a war-inflamed populace.[13]

Another Cabinet was held at 6.30pm. It received news of the German invasion of Luxemburg. In the later evening Lloyd George, Simon, Masterman and Ramsay MacDonald dined with Lord Riddell, of the Newspaper Proprietors' Association. After dinner, the telephone rang. General Sir John French was on the line. He asked Riddell, in MacDonald's hearing: "Can you tell me, old chap, whether we are going to be in this war? If so, are we going to put an army on the Continent, and, if we are, who is going to command it?" Riddell went back into the dining-room, came back to the telephone, and told Sir John French that we would be in the war, that we would send an army to the Continent, and that he would be in command. Of those in the dining room, only Lloyd George had the authority and seniority to make any such statement. Riddell recalls adding – to French: "Lloyd George says 'Be at Downing Street tomorrow at 10 o'clock sharp'."[14]

In October 1914 Lloyd George told Ramsay MacDonald that if Germany had not invaded Belgium he would have resigned. MacDonald, however, had made his own record of the night of 2 August, as follows:

Evening at Sir George Riddell's, Lloyd George, Simon, Masterman, Illingworth [Liberal Chief Whip], Riddell and myself. Discussed war. Masterman jingo, George ruffled, Simon broken. George harped on exposed French coasts and Belgium but I gathered that excuses were being searched for.[15]

Ramsay MacDonald, described by Lloyd George in his *War memoirs* as "a tramp", was right. Excuses *were* being searched for, both then (the Foreign Office only received news of the German ultimatum to Belgium at 10.55am the following day)[16] and subsequently, by Lloyd George, for his failure to resign, for his last-minute adoption of the foreign policy of Sir Edward Grey.

It is possible to identify some of the elements that went into Lloyd George's decision. Harcourt, who had organized much of the opposition to Grey, had defected at the morning Cabinet of 2 August, passing across the table, with regard to one of Grey's appeals, a note to J. A. Pease, President of the Board of Education, which read, "I can't decline this":[17] in Morley's words, Harcourt "ran away at the last moment not even having resigned for an hour or two".[18] By the evening of 2 August only John Burns, President of the Board of Trade, and hardly the most impressive of ministers, had resigned. Simon wrote his letter of resignation while at Riddell's, and showed it to Lloyd George, who handed it back to him without comment.[19] Morley's resignation was in Asquith's hands the following morning; and at the Cabinet held at 11am Beauchamp (known as "Sweetheart" to Asquith) announced that he too would resign. The seven or eight that Simon anticipated would join Burns in resigning had not materialized.[20]

There was also the known readiness of the Conservatives to participate in a war government. If only four ministers had to be replaced, this was not an impossible task facing Asquith, as Simon's resignation letter recognized.[21]

In addition there was the clear disposition of Grey and Asquith to resign if the Cabinet voted for neutrality. They would have taken with them, in the view of Samuel, President of the Local Government Board, at least three others.[22] The three others are most probably Crewe,[23] the Secretary of State for India, Churchill, and Masterman. To replace such senior figures (with the exception of Masterman) from the ranks of the Liberal and Labour Parties – and here must be brought into play the fact that Lloyd George had proposed a coalition with Labour to Ramsay MacDonald on 15 June 1914[24] – would have been a much harder task for Lloyd George, had he taken Asquith's place.

The press aspects have also to be taken into account. Hobhouse, the Postmaster-General, noted that, at the very beginning of the crisis, Lloyd George had been anti-German (which is consistent with a conversation he had on 27 July which thoroughly alarmed C. P. Scott, editor of the *Manchester Guardian*, and which may well be connected with Churchill's invitation to him of 29 July to keep free the night of Friday 31 July to receive the results of enquiries of the Conservatives regarding a coalition[25]) but had veered round and become "peaceful" because the Liberal newspapers had come out very strongly against any British participation in any war.[26] Riddell, having spoken on the morning of 3 August to Robertson Nicoll, editor of the *British Weekly*, whose own attitude had changed since 29 July, now said he thought the British had no alternative but to support France and must all stand together and sink differences of opinion, immediately wrote a note to Masterman repeating what Nicoll had said, and suggested that Masterman show it to Lloyd George, which he did. Riddell noted: "I think Lloyd George attached considerable importance to Nicoll's decision."[27] At 4pm on Saturday 1 August, Ramsay MacDonald had told Illingworth that no war was at first unpopular.[28] It is not at all unlikely that Lloyd George came to the same conclusion, even though he professed to regard the cheering crowds through which he was passing as "not my crowd",[29] and therefore decided to risk the wrath of C. P. Scott, who had told him during the crisis that any Liberal who supported the war would never be allowed to enter another Liberal Cabinet. For Lloyd George, as one minister reminded Margot Asquith, it was important to know how much backing he would have in the country.[30]

After the morning Cabinet of 3 August, Herbert Samuel wrote to his wife from 11 Downing Street, where he was having lunch with Lloyd George. Of those who had resigned, he wrote: "Those four men have no right to abandon us at this crisis – it is a failure of courage."[31] That there was a failure of courage on the part of Lloyd George might equally be said. Throughout the crisis he acted with an eye to the main chance, as he perceived it in terms of political possibilities and public opinion. He lacked the courage of his convictions because, in the end, this intriguer for a coalition with the Labour Party in 1914 and for one with the Tories in 1910, this opponent of high naval estimates who was nevertheless prepared to embrace conscription,[32] this Mansion House speaker of July 1911 who was deserting the Liberal Imperialist ground in being prepared in January 1912 to play off Russia against Germany in Asia Minor and the Persian Gulf[33] and in March 1912 to grant Germany a formula for British neutrality,[34] this voter with the Liberal Imperialists against Cabinet supremacy in November 1911, this declarer of January 1912 that if Grey was hounded out of office he would go too,[35] this advocate in the autumn of 1911 of an exploration of the option of sending the British Expeditionary Force to Belgium rather than to France,[36] this viewer with complacency in November 1912 of the prospects of rousing the British people to war over a Balkan issue,[37] had no convictions. Checkmated by Asquith's loyalty to Grey, and by the loyalty of the majority of the Cabinet, when it came to the crunch, to Asquith, he chose to remain in the government rather than to retire to Criccieth. His opportunism contrasts starkly with the resolution displayed by Grey, Asquith and Churchill.

## II

Prince Karl Max von Lichnowsky, the German ambassador to Britain, stopped in Berlin on 29 June and 5 July on his way to and from Silesia. On both occasions he met the German Chancellor, Bethmann Hollweg, and the acting Foreign Secretary, Zimmermann. On 6 July, immediately after his return from Germany, Lichnowsky went to see the British Foreign Secretary. On the following day Sir Arthur Nicolson, permanent under-secretary at the Foreign Office, added a postscript to a letter to Maurice de Bunsen, British ambassador in Vienna, written on the 6 July but not yet posted. The postscript, printed here for the first time, read as follows:

> July 7. I may tell you for your own private and personal information that we heard yesterday *privately* that Berlin is most anxious lest Vienna should take some measures against Servia of a rather strong character, owing to tone of Servian Press etc. and that though no territory would be annexed some "humiliation" would be inflicted on Servia. I have my doubts as to this though I know the anxiety exists among German high official circles who are nervous as to the consequences and the effect which might be produced in Russia.[38]

De Bunsen's interpretation of what he received, which was "that Berlin would be against strong measures against Servia being taken from Vienna",[39] was the interpretation that pervaded the Foreign Office, and this interpretation of Lichnowsky's "private information" is the key to British policy for almost the whole of July 1914. The German ambassador's "private information" cancelled out the rest of what he told Grey, some of which, as Grey recorded it, was of what would otherwise have been a distinctly alarming character.[40] In response to Lichnowsky's earnest hope "that, if trouble came, we would use our influence to mitigate feeling in St. Petersburg", Grey, in good faith and as a *quid pro quo* for the private information that Berlin would hold back Vienna, saw the Russian ambassador Benckendorff and advised that the Russian government disabuse the German government of any idea that a coup was being prepared.[41] Grey's confidence in Germany can only have been increased when, on 9 July, Lichnowsky "expressed himself as hopeful . . . that the German government might have succeeded in smoothing the Austrian intentions with regard to Servia".[42]

Grey was misinformed. In fact, he was *dis*informed. Lichnowsky, the conductor of the disinformation, had himself been disinformed.[43] Grey's misplaced confidence in Berlin enabled him to ignore increasingly alarmist reports from Vienna that an unacceptable ultimatum was being prepared.[44] On 20 July he viewed the Austro-Serbian quarrel "optimistically", believing that a peaceful solution would be reached.[45] On the evening of 22 July Lichnowsky telegraphed that in London they were expecting "that our influence at Vienna has been successful in suppressing demands that cannot be met":

> They are counting with certainty on the fact that we shall not identify ourselves with demands that are plainly intended to bring on war, and that we will not support any policy which makes use of the murder at Sarajevo merely as an excuse for carrying out Austrian desires in the Balkans, and for the annulment of the peace of Bucharest.[46]

Grey's confidence in Berlin survived the receipt of a long letter from Hoyos to Lord Haldane, the Lord Chancellor, justifying the action Austria proposed to take.[47] There was, after all, in Grey's view, still time for the German government to justify his placing of faith in Berlin, and for the situation to be retrieved on very much the same lines as had been employed in 1913, after the second Balkan War. Apprised by the Austrian ambassador, Mensdorff, on 23 July of the gist of the forthcoming Austrian note, Grey took the line that it would be a terrible thing if as many as four Great Powers—"let us say Austria, France, Russia, and Germany" – were engaged in war.[48] He adhered to this line with Lichnowsky on the evening of 24 July, and it is, arguably, most unfortunate that he spoke to the German ambassador in such a way as to permit him to report to Berlin:

The danger of a European war, should Austria invade Serbian territory, would become immediate. The results of such a war between four nations – he expressly emphasised the number four, and meant by it Russia, Austria-Hungary, Germany and France – would be absolutely incalculable.[49]

## III

From this point Grey was under great pressure, initially from the Russians, and later from the French, to announce that, if it came to a European war, Great Britain would be on their side. The Russian Minister for Foreign Affairs, Sazonov, told the British ambassador, Buchanan, on 24 July: "If war did break out, we would sooner or later be dragged into it, but if we did not make common cause with France and Russia from the outset we should have rendered war more likely, and should not have played a 'beau rôle'."[50] On 25 July, Benckendorff asked Grey to give some indication to Germany to make her think that Britain would not stand aside if there was a war. He was not satisfied with Grey's reply, that he "had given no indication that we would stand aside",[51] and rightly so, for this was not at all the same thing. At 10.30pm the same day another telegram arrived from Buchanan, who had seen Sazonov again. Buchanan's own argument, that "England could play rôle of mediator at Berlin and Vienna to better purpose as friend who, if her counsels of moderation were disregarded, might one day be converted into an ally, than if she were to declare herself Russia's ally at once", were brushed aside by Sazonov. Buchanan's no. 169 ended with his rendering of Sazonov's bleak blackmail:

> For ourselves position is a most serious one, and we shall have to choose between giving Russia our active support or renouncing her friendship. If we fail her now we cannot hope to maintain that friendly cooperation with her in Asia that is of such vital importance to us.[52]

Here, it has to be pointed out that a much-needed improvement in Anglo-Russian relations was the main item of business in the British

Foreign Office at this time. As Nicolson wrote to de Bunsen on 6 July, "We are . . . chiefly busying ourselves with endeavouring to arrange matters with Russia in regard to Persia, and, in a secondary degree, Tibet."[53] The commencement of negotiations for an Anglo-Russian naval convention, on which the Russians had insisted in the spring, and of which the Germans had learned through a spy in the Russian embassy in London, was intended to help improve Anglo-Russian relations. What most imperilled them, however, and what had given the Russians the leverage to insist successfully on an Anglo-Russian naval convention, was the deterioration of relations as a result of the operation of the 1907 Convention relating to Persia. On 8 July, Grey instructed Sir G. Clerk to prepare a memorandum on Anglo-Russian relations in Persia. Shortly afterwards, the Russians raised the prospect of a triple Russian–British–Japanese guarantee of their respective Asiatic possessions. Grey welcomed this overture, so different in tone from most recent communications from St Petersburg, and undertook to bring it to the attention of the Prime Minister and Cabinet as soon as the parliamentary and Irish situations allowed.[54] Clerk finished his memorandum on 21 July. It started with the statement:

> After seven years HM Government are faced with the urgent necessity of taking stock of their position in Persia, for the incapacity of the Persians and the steady advance of Russia have together created a situation which cannot be allowed to drift any longer without the most serious danger to those British interests whose maintenance constitutes one of the most cardinal principles of Imperial policy.

Having gone on to say that Russia was "the one Power with whom it is our paramount duty to cultivate the most cordial relations", the memorandum ended with a suggested list of concessions to Russia which added up, effectively, to a new Anglo-Russian convention. The list was based on the assumption:

> that the first principle of our foreign policy must be genuinely good relations with Russia, and founded on the belief that if we do not make relatively small sacrifices, and alter our policy, in Persia now, we shall both endanger our friend-

ship with Russia and find in a comparatively near future that we have sacrificed our whole position in the Persian Gulf, and are faced in consequence with a situation where our very existence as an Empire will be at stake.

Minuting the memorandum on 23 July, assistant under-secretary Sir E. A. Crowe accepted Clerk's "main contention that the principal thing we must keep before us is the necessity of placing our relations with Russia on a satisfactory and so far as possible lasting foundation"; Nicolson, who on 22 July had commented on an article in *Le Matin* about Russian military strength and German fear of it: "Russia is a formidable Power and will become increasingly strong. Let us hope our relations with her will continue to be friendly", agreed both with Crowe and with Clerk's recommended concessions. He regarded the matter as urgent and foresaw dangers "in paltering further with the question".[55] With respect to the editor of volume XI of *British documents on the origins of the war*, J. W. Headlam-Morley, MA, CBE, this material, these concerns and anxieties, these expressions of what for the British Foreign Office was clearly an imperial scale of priorities, most certainly did have an immediate connection with the outbreak of the First World War.[56] Grey's personal decision for war cannot be understood and appreciated fully if this background is not taken into account. Grey's appreciation of all the above considerations had already caused him to make it clear to Berlin that there were limits to what Britain could do in the way of putting pressure on Russia. As Lichnowsky reported on 15 July, Grey had said that "if a tremendously excited commotion should arise in Russia as the result of Austria's military measures, he would not in any way be in a position to keep the Russian policy in hand and, in view of the feeling of dislike toward England which is at the moment on top in Russia and of which Count Pourtalès can inform you, he would have to humour Russian sensibilities."[57]

Buchanan's no. 169, together with the news which Nicolson brought to Grey when having shown that telegram to Lichnowsky's cousin Benckendorff on 26 July he learned that the German ambassador was convinced that Britain could stand aside and remain neutral,[58] put an end to Grey's attempt to distinguish between an Austro-Serbian and an Austro-Russian quarrel. Nicolson and Sir W. Tyrrell, Grey's private secretary, saw Lichnowsky during the evening of 26 July. As Lichnowsky reported to Berlin:

> Tyrrell . . . pointed out to me repeatedly and with emphasis the immense importance of Serbia's territory remaining unviolated until the question of [a conference of ambassadors in London] had been settled, as otherwise every effort would have been in vain and the world war would be inevitable. The localisation of the conflict as hoped for in Berlin was wholly impossible, and must be dropped from the calculations of practical politics.[59]

On 27 July Grey personally disabused Lichnowsky of the possibility of British neutrality. "Irritated for the first time", Grey managed to convince Lichnowsky that "we [Germany] should no longer be able to count on British sympathy or British support"; Lichnowsky was certain that England "would place herself unconditionally by the side of France and of Russia, in order to show that she is not willing to permit a moral, or perhaps a military, defeat of her group. If it comes to war under these conditions, we shall have England against us"[60]. In Grey's version, the words he used to combat Lichnowsky's observation "that if Germany assisted Austria against Russia it would be because, without any reference to the merits of the dispute, Germany could not afford to see Austria crushed" were: "Just so other issues might be raised that would supersede the dispute between Austria and Servia, and would bring other Powers in, and the war would be the biggest ever known".[61] Translated into English, these words constituted the categorical warning that Lloyd George later accused Grey of not delivering. This and the keeping together of the First Fleet at Portland was Grey's response to the issues and British interests raised by Russian pressure, of which there was more in the course of that day.[62] It remained to counter what Prince Henry of Prussia had elicited in the course of a visit on 26 July from King George V – namely the King's statement "that England would maintain neutrality in case war should break out between Continental Powers". Asquith went to see the King-Emperor on 28 July to tell him the facts of imperial life: "Russia says to us, 'If you won't say you are ready to side with us now, your friendship is valueless, and we shall act on that assumption in the future'." Nicolson and Buchanan were far from being alone in appreciating that the present

187

crisis "might be taken by Russia as a test of our friendship, and that were we to disappoint her all hope of a friendly and permanent understanding with her would disappear".[63]

## IV

Convinced that an Austro-Serbian war could not be localized (news of the Austrian declaration of war on Serbia reached London at 6.45 pm on 28 July);[64] convinced that war would spread quickly to engulf all the members of the two blocs of powers, with the possible exception of Italy; and convinced that Germany would launch an attack on France through Belgium, Grey prepared carefully for the Cabinet meeting due to be held on the morning of 29 July. Under the heading "Belgian neutrality in 1870", he ordered to be printed for distribution to the members of the Cabinet a selection of extracts from despatches and speeches of the July and August of the year of the outbreak of the Franco-Prussian War. He also arranged for ministers to see copies of the report commissioned by Lord Granville in August 1870 from the Law Officers of the Crown, on the British obligation to Belgium under the Treaty of London of 1839. One minister retained in his mind "a picture of the unfolding of the original neutrality pact [the British treaties with Prussia and France of August 1870], old and yellowed, with notes by Gladstone".[65] Grey's determination to present the case as he saw it, and the way in which events would unfold, was only strengthened by the news which came in on the morning of 29 July, that Russia had ordered the mobilization of the military districts of Odessa, Kiev, Moscow and Kazan.[66]

It was at the Cabinet of 29 July that Grey discovered the force of the opposition to war, whatever the course of events might be, on the part of his ministerial colleagues. An overwhelming majority resisted every point he tried to make. The majority disagreed with his, and the 1870 Law Officers', interpretation of the 1839 treaty, to the effect that it was of a binding nature, with the result that Asquith had to report to the King that the Cabinet had decided "that the matter if it arises will be rather one of policy than of legal obligation". When Grey went on to say that "at any moment the French government might ask us whether we would support them, and if we said No, whether we would renew the 1870 treaty to prevent violation of Belgium", he was supported only by the Prime Minister, who said that "the Germans, if they attacked France would go through Belgium and hesitate in [*sic*] attack in any other way". The Cabinet refused to rise to the bait of a repetition of Gladstone's and Granville's 44-year-old solution to the problem. When Grey stated, as Harcourt recorded in marginalia on material in front of him, "We not deciding factor", the Cabinet took the opposite view, and Grey had to compromise to the extent of agreeing that he tell the French ambassador "Don't count upon our coming in", and the German ambassador "Don't count on our abstention".[67]

It had been, as John Burns recorded at the time, "a critical Cabinet". His final comment on it, "It was decided not to decide",[68] meant that Grey had failed to move his colleagues in the direction he wanted, despite support from the Prime Minister and from Churchill. Grey had prepared, but perhaps not too well, and perhaps, contradictorily, *too well*, in so far as one of the extracts from a Gladstone speech of 10 August 1870 contained the words: "I am not able to subscribe to the doctrine of those who have held in this House what plainly amounts to an assertion, that the simple fact of the existence of a guarantee is binding on every party to it irrespectively altogether of the particular position in which it may find itself at the time when the occasion for acting on the guarantee arises. The great authorities upon foreign policy to whom I have been accustomed to listen – such as Lord Aberdeen and Lord Palmerston – never, to my knowledge, took that rigid and, if I may say so, that impracticable view of a guarantee." Grey had also, perhaps, been premature, in that he had anticipated a French request that was never, in fact, to be made in those terms. It might have been better to wait until he could have produced such a request from his pocket. Grey and Asquith were fortunate to avoid what was from their point of view the "worst-case" scenario, of having "to announce to the world at the present moment that *in no circumstances* would we intervene". Churchill's immediate establishment of contact (whether with the connivance of Asquith and Grey is still not clear, but certainly with the knowledge of Lloyd George) with the Conservative leadership, through the medium of F. E. Smith, was an understandable product of desperation.[69]

Grey only partly executed his Cabinet brief. He saw Cambon, the French ambassador, and told him:

In the present case the dispute between Austria and Serbia was not one in which we felt called to take a hand. Even if the question became one between Austria and Russia we should not feel called upon to take a hand in it . . . If Germany became involved and France became involved, we had not made up our minds what we should do; it was a case that we should have to consider.

Cambon took this quite calmly. He did, however, make it clear that France could not be neutral in a German-Russian war: if Germany demanded French neutrality the French could give no such assurance.[70] Grey then saw Lichnowsky. Drawing on information from Rome to the effect that the Serbs might accept all the Austrian demands, he urged the Germans to call Austria off before it was too late, as it would be if Austro-Hungarian troops set foot on Serbian soil. He let fall the remark, "one could never tell whose house might remain unscorched in the midst of such a conflagration . . . even little Holland was now arming herself".[71] Evidently dissatisfied with the force of these representations, Grey called Lichnowsky back to the Foreign Office later in the afternoon, to say:

The British Government desired now as before to cultivate our previous friendship, and it could stand aside as long as the conflict remained confined to Austria and Russia. But if [Germany] and France should be involved, then the situation would immediately be altered, and the British Government would, under the circumstances, find itself forced to make up its mind quickly. In that event it would not be practicable to stand aside and wait for any length of time.[72]

Kaiser Wilhelm II was correct to regard this as "a threat combined with a bluff"[73] for, as already shown, the British Cabinet was determined, at this point, to keep its options open.

Before Bethmann Hollweg received Lichnowsky's account of this second interview with Grey, the German Chancellor had, as a result of a meeting at Potsdam during the evening of 29 July, approached the British ambassador with a bid for British neutrality at the expense of Belgian neutrality and no annexation of French territory except colonies. This overture, described by Asquith as "a rather shameless attempt on the part of Germany to buy our neutrality", drove Grey into what his parliamentary private secretary described as a "white heat of rage".[74] When it was presented to the Cabinet on 31 July (no Cabinet was held on 30 July) it made no difference. Pease drew a cartoon of a frog devouring a sausage.[75] This was the Cabinet during which, after an outbreak of bellicosity on the part of Churchill, Harcourt passed across to Pease a note which read, "It is now clear that *this* Cabinet will not join the war."[76] This was the Cabinet which, on being told that Austria and Russia were still talking, took the line, as Harcourt noted, that "if Russ [*sic*] unreasonable we wash our hands".[77] John Burns' diary entry for this day suggests that he at least thought Russia needed no help in order to beat Germany: "If war Germany is in an unenviable position."[78] All that Grey, who had already on the previous day rejected Bethmann Hollweg's overture without referring it to his colleagues, could extract from the Cabinet on this occasion was permission to ask the French and German governments whether they were prepared to engage to respect the neutrality of Belgium so long as no other Power violated it. The relevant telegrams were sent at 5.30pm.

The French reply, giving the assurance requested, arrived at 2.15am on 1 August. At 3.30am a telegram arrived from Goschen in Berlin: the German Foreign Minister, von Jagow, had taken the diplomatic equivalent of the Fifth Amendment, and refused to answer on the grounds that he might incriminate himself: any reply the German government might give "could not fail, in the event of war, to have the undesirable effect of disclosing to a certain extent part of their plan of campaign".[80] The Cabinet that lasted from 11am to 1.30pm on 1 August discussed these replies. Grey's colleagues were not impressed by the differences between the replies, but the following statement was agreed for communication to the German ambassador:

> The reply of the German Government with regard to the neutrality of Belgium is a matter of very great regret, because the neutrality of Belgium does affect feeling in this country. If Germany could see her way to give the same positive reply as that which has been given by France, it would materially contribute to relieve anxiety and tension here, while on the other hand, if there were a violation of

the neutrality of Belgium by one combatant while the other respected it, it would be extremely difficult to restrain public feeling in this country.[81]

Even for this, Grey had to fight very hard: Asquith was clearly referring to a declaration made during this Cabinet when recording it for Venetia Stanley's benefit: "Grey, of course, declares that if an out-and-out and uncompromising policy of non-intervention at all costs is adopted, he will go."[82] For both Grey and Asquith this Cabinet meeting came, as Asquith put it, "near to the parting of the ways", with Morley and Simon at one extreme, and himself and Grey at the other.[83] Moreover, as a *quid pro quo* for the statement about Belgium, the Cabinet decided against sending the British Expeditionary Force to help France. This decision was embodied in a note from Asquith to the CIGS saying that training was not to be suspended and ""putting on record" the fact that the Government had never promised the French the E[xpeditionary] F[orce]".[84]

In communicating this decision to the French ambassador, Grey tried to take the edge off it by saying that the decision taken was "that we could not propose to Parliament at this moment to send an expeditionary military force to the continent"[85] ("at this moment" and "to the continent" were the blunting words). On the other hand, when making to Lichnowsky earlier in the afternoon the communication authorized by the Cabinet, Grey evaded a direct answer to Lichnowsky's question – "whether he could give me a definite declaration on the neutrality of Great Britain on the condition that we respected Belgian neutrality". Grey replied, according to Lichnowsky, "that that would not be possible for him".[86] The majority of his colleagues would have had no such qualms.

In Cambon's account of his interview with Grey, an account which he started to telegraph to Paris at 6.24 in the evening, the efforts Grey made to blunt the effect of the Cabinet's stance, and to give the French something still to hope for, are more evident than in Grey's own record, which the Cabinet might demand to see. In Cambon's account, Grey disclosed that he had refused to give Lichnowsky the declaration asked for on British neutrality; Grey also said that, although the British government did not favour a landing of British troops on the Continent, there were *"d'autres points où l'intervention lui paraîtrait sans doute justifiée"*. In the first place, Grey undertook to take up again with the Cabinet the recent German non-reply about Belgium, and to seek authorization to declare in the House of Commons on Monday 3 August that Britain would not permit a violation of Belgian neutrality. In the second place, Grey would propose to his colleagues that they resist any attempt by units of the German fleet either to enter the Channel or, if they had already done so, to attack the French coast. Cambon's account ends:

> Ces deux questions seront traitées au Counseil qui se tiendra demain ou au plus tard lundi matin. J'ai fait observer que d'ici lundi de graves incidents pouvaient survenir et que l'opinion française serait surprise d'une intervention trop tardive; mais Sir Ed. Grey m'a affirmé que, pour le moment, il ne pouvait faire plus. J'attire l'attention de Votre Excellence sur la nécessité de garder secrètes les intentions de Sir Ed. Grey: si elles transpiraient et parvenaient à la connaissance de l'Allemagne, la flotte imperiale se hâterait de traverser le détroit.
>
> [These two questions will be addressed at the Cabinet to be held tomorrow or on Monday morning at the latest. I made the observation that between now and Monday serious incidents might take place and that French opinion would be surprised at too tardy an intervention; but Sir Ed. Grey insisted that, for the moment, he could do no more. I draw the attention of Your Excellency to the necessity of keeping secret the intentions of Sir Ed. Grey; if they were to leak out and come to the notice of Germany, the imperial fleet would hasten into the Channel.][87]

There is no indication here that Cambon had lost faith in Grey, whom the previous evening he had described, correctly, as "partisan de l'intervention immédiate". He may well, however, have lost faith in Grey's ability to achieve his expressed *intentions* and swing the Cabinet behind his interventionist policy. A little more pressure would not come amiss. Hence the scene which, on the authority of H. Nicolson, son of Sir. A. Nicolson, Cambon proceeded to make – *"Ils vont nous lâcher, ils vont nous lâcher"* – followed by the scene which, on the same authority, Nicolson himself proceeded to make:

Nicolson went upstairs to interview Sir Edward Grey. He found him pacing his room, biting at his lower lip. Nicolson asked whether it was indeed true that we had refused to support France at the moment of her greatest danger. Grey made no answer beyond a gesture of despair. "You will render us," Nicolson said angrily, "a by-word among nations."[89]

Grey *was* in despair, at the attitude of the Cabinet, at the fact that the majority of them was still at the opposite extreme from himself, and at the fact that he had to defer to the majority view. It would appear, however, from what Cambon telegraphed to Paris at 6.24 and 6.40pm, that Grey had already decided that, on the following day, he would have it out with the Cabinet once and for all and that, if they refused to follow his lead and support the French, he would implement his threat to resign. News from Paris received at 8pm, that the French War Minister had responded to German *Kriegszustand* measures but had left a zone of ten kilometres between French troops and the German frontier, that the French would not attack, and that he had told the British military attaché, "We rely on ourselves first and on you",[90] only strengthened Grey's resolve. That night Grey dined at Brooks's with his parliamentary private secretary, Arthur Murray. After dinner they played billiards. Grey told Murray that he would have his "tussle" with the Cabinet the following day.[91] He then went to see the Prime Minister.

## V

Grey spared Cambon two things on 1 August. He did not tell him that he had already threatened the Cabinet with his resignation. Nor did he tell him about another matter. Just before the Cabinet met at 11am Grey had telephoned Lichnowsky and asked him for an assurance that if France remained neutral in a Russo-German war, Germany would not attack France, and Lichnowsky had given Grey this assurance.[92] This telephone call was made as a result of a meeting between Asquith, Grey and Haldane at about 10.30am. Haldane, described by Asquith on 1 August as "diffuse and nebulous",[93] occupied an intermediate position between Grey and Asquith on the one hand and, say, Harcourt and Simon on the other, in respect of intervention. He wanted British intervention in any continental war to be delayed as long as possible. He wrote to his mother later that day: "I shall not give up hope till war breaks out. I trust that we shall not be dragged in"; on 2 August, before the first Cabinet of the day, he wrote to his sister: "The ideas that on the one hand we can wholly disinterest ourselves and on the other that we ought to rush in are both wrong. And the real course, that of being ready to intervene if at a decisive moment we are called on, is difficult to formulate in clear terms. Yet I think this is what we must attempt."[94] A founder member of the Liberal Imperialist faction and, as War Minister from December 1905 to June 1912, the architect of the Expeditionary Force, Haldane was a very close colleague of Grey and Asquith. A bachelor, he had always been on particularly intimate terms with the widowed Foreign Secretary, and had, indeed, spent most of the previous week living under the same roof.

It was with a view to winning over this most important and valued member of the Liberal Imperialist group that Grey raised with Lichnowsky the question of French neutrality. For Grey, the fate of Belgium was less important than the fate of France. If French obligations to Russia allowed her to be neutral in a German-Russian war, or if the French and German armies could, even after mobilization, remain in arms without crossing any frontiers, then Britain might be able to keep out of it. If French obligations to Russia did not permit any of this, and Cambon had already stated that they did not, then at least Grey would be able to prove to Haldane that he had gone as far as he possibly could in exploring every avenue of escape from involvement.

Although Grey had promised Lichnowsky that he would make use of his assurance at the Cabinet, he did not do so. Nor did Grey consult Cambon before seeing Lichnowsky at 3.30pm. At the interview with Lichnowsky, Grey did admit that "he had been wondering whether it would not be possible for [Germany] and France to remain facing each other under arms, without attacking each other, in the event of a Russian war". Grey also admitted, in reply to the direct question that Lichnowsky had to ask, as to whether he was in a position to say whether France would agree to a pact of that sort, that he had taken no steps to "inform himself", and Lichnowsky's view of this interview was that it cancelled the prospect about which he had telegrammed at 11.14am. As he returned to the German Embassy he met the editor of the *Daily Express* in St James's Park, and said to him: "I am afraid we can do no more. I have just seen Sir Edward Grey, and you are likely to take sides with the French."[95]

Grey claimed that he said to Cambon, at their later interview: "Now, the position was that Germany would agree not to attack France if France remained neutral in the event of war between Russia and Germany. If France could not take advantage of this position, it was because she was bound by an alliance to which we were not parties, and of which we did not know the terms."[96] If Grey did indeed say this, for it is not present in his later account of that day's transactions,[97] it was more of a statement than a question, and Cambon took it as such. Grey's telegram no. 297 to Bertie at 5.25pm,[98] was as far as he dared go in the direction of "informing himself", for Haldane's sake. Grey's heart was, after all, far more with Cambon and the French than even with Haldane. The course of the interview with Cambon, and the ammunition provided by it, and, shortly afterwards, by Nicolson, which could be used in Cabinet the following day, caused Grey not to pursue the matter beyond making the enquiry of Bertie which was really only a question of courtesy to Lichnowsky and of a consistency internal to that interview. Grey had finally emerged from Haldane's tutelage, and become his own man.

Grey's effort to please Haldane caught up with him in the mid-evening when he was summoned to Buckingham Palace to explain a telegram just received from the Kaiser. A form of words was devised to deny that any of this had taken place: "there must be some misunderstanding as to a suggestion that passed in friendly conversation between Prince Lichnowsky and Sir E. Grey this afternoon".[99] On receipt of Grey's no. 297, Bertie was aghast. He replied:

> Do you desire me to state to French Government that after mobilisation of French and German troops on Franco-German frontier we propose to remain neutral so long as German troops remain on the defensive and do not cross French frontier, and French abstain from crossing German frontier? I cannot imagine that in the event of Russia being at war with Austria and being attacked by Germany it would be consistent with French obligations towards Russia for France to remain quiescent. If France undertook to remain

so, the Germans would first attack Russians and, if they defeated them, they would then turn round on the French.
Am I to enquire precisely what are the obligations of the French under Franco-Russian Alliance?[100]

On the following morning Bertie received Grey's response: "No action required now on my telegram no. 297 of 1st August."[101]

## VI

The first Frenchman to raise the question of Anglo-French action based on arrangements made in 1912 was Paléologue, the ambassador in St Petersburg. His remark that France would want to know at once whether the British fleet was prepared to play the part assigned to it was embodied in Buchanan's telegram no. 169 of 25 July.[102] At this time the French representative in London was in Paris on a visit from which he returned only on 28 July. Early in the morning of 30 July, Viviani, the French Foreign Minister, instructed Cambon to remind Grey of the exchange of letters of November 1912, in which it had been agreed that in cases of extreme tension between the European Powers the two governments would discuss together how they might proceed.[103] Cambon did so, only to be told by Grey that the British government had decided that no pledge to support France could be given at that time.[104] On the afternoon of 1 August, Cambon declared that the French coasts were exposed to German naval action, which was all the more dangerous because, he claimed, France, in agreement with Britain, had concentrated the bulk of its navy in the Mediterranean. In conversation with Nicolson immediately afterwards, Cambon suggested that the time had come to make use of the texts of the letters exchanged in November 1912, possibly by incorporating them in an official note.[105] Nicolson on 31 July had urged Grey to press for the immediate mobilization of the army.[106] During the night of 31 July–1 August information reached him which so convinced him that the Germans were about to take the offensive on both their western and eastern frontiers that he not only wrote a note begging Grey to act but also took with him to see Grey at 8am on the morning of 1 August, General Sir Henry Wilson, the Director of Military Operations – a personal call thwarted because the Foreign Secretary was still in bed.[107] Nicolson dubbed Cambon's resurrection of the November 1912 letters "a happy inspiration", and proceeded to write to Grey as follows:

> M. Cambon pointed out to me this afternoon that it was at our request that France had moved her fleets to the Mediterranean, on the understanding that we undertook the protection of her northern and western coasts. As I understand you told him that you would submit to the Cabinet the question of a possible German naval attack on French northern and western ports it would be well to remind the Cabinet of the above fact.[108]

Nicolson's note, which Grey discussed with Asquith and Haldane later that night, provided the Foreign Secretary with the ammunition he needed. In the rather charged encounter which preceded the writing of the note, Nicolson had said to Grey, regarding the Cabinet's decision not to send the Expeditionary Force: "But this is impossible, you have over and over promised M. Cambon that if Germany was the aggressor, you would stand by France." In what must have been a tone of immense regret, Grey had replied, "Yes, but he has nothing in writing."[109] The Grey–Cambon letters did constitute something in writing, and although it was the case that, as Grey had had to tell Cambon, he had assured Parliament "again and again that our hands were free",[110] the letters had been overseen throughout the drafting stages and finally agreed by the Cabinet as a whole before the exchange took place in November 1912. They represented a possible solution, a possible escape for Grey from his dilemma. They allowed him to say, as he did say in response to a plea from Kühlmann, Lichnowsky's Counsellor of Embassy, that Britain remain neutral: "That's all very well, but we have obligations of honour to France."[111] If the Cabinet took his view of them, he would not have to resign. If they did not, the resignation card remained to be played. In what he saw as an honourable cause, Grey proceeded to do a dishonourable thing. Cambon's claim, that the French coasts were exposed because "*d'accord avec l'Angleterre, nous avons concentré le gros de nos forces navales dans la Méditerranée*", was not true. It was simply not the case, and in the autumn of 1912 the Cabinet, including Grey, had gone to considerable lengths to avoid the putting in the future of this construction on what they had communicated to the French.[112] Nevertheless, in the heat of the moment of 1 and 2 August neither Nicolson, nor Grey, nor Churchill, nor Asquith, saw fit to challenge Cambon's contention. They presented it to the Cabinet, and Grey presented it to Parliament on 3 August in a curious mélange of a speech which mixed up British honour and British interests, as a fact.

Grey's ploy, his and Cambon's and Nicolson's distortion, did not carry the day unaided on 2 August: the resignation card had to be played. Even to get permission only to assure the French that if the German fleet came into the Channel or through the North Sea to undertake hostile operations against French coasts or shipping the British fleet would give all the protection in its power, Grey had to threaten to resign.[113] John Burns maintained that any such assurance meant war, and did resign.[114] Simon's letter of resignation began: "The statement which Grey made to Cambon this afternoon, and which he does not propose to reveal to Germany until the announcement is made in the House of Commons tomorrow, will, I think, be regarded as tantamount to a declaration that we take part in this quarrel with France and against Germany."[115]

What did carry the day for a policy of intervention in the war between Germany and Austria-Hungary on the one hand and France and Russia on the other was a combination – of Grey's determination to resign if any other policy was adopted; of Asquith's determination to follow Grey; of, as Bernard Wasserstein has recently appreciated, Herbert Samuel's engineering of two formulas which split the majority and appeased some of the non-interventionists by making it appear that the onus fell on Germany (as Samuel put it to his wife: "it will be an action of Germany's, and not of ours, which will cause the failure and my conscience will be easy in embarking on the war");[116] of the support of the Conservative Party leaders Bonar Law and Lord Lansdowne for a policy of supporting France and Russia, unqualified by any mention of Belgium and no longer dependent on the word of Churchill or F. E. Smith (the ending of Simon's resignation letter, "It may be that a Coalition Government will be best (and one of your colleagues, I think, desires and intends it)"[117] was a reference to Churchill); of the slowness off the mark of the non-interventionists, who did not produce immediately the Cabinet resolutions regarding Cabinet supremacy of November 1911 to reinforce paragraph one of Grey's letter to Cambon of 22 November 1912; of the news which came in throughout the afternoon of 2 August that German forces had entered Luxemburg;[118] and of the reluctance of Liberal non-interventionists to vacate the corridors of power.[119]

## VII

At 5.45pm on 31 July Sir Eyre Crowe had brought to General Sir Henry Wilson a despatch from Buchanan in St Petersburg which had arrived at 5.20pm. The despatch said that the Russian government had decided to issue orders for a general mobilization. On his copy of this despatch Wilson minuted that Crowe told him:

> that he had had three quarters of an hour with E. G[rey] and he thought the case was hopeless. Grey spoke of the ruin of commerce etc. and in spite of all Crowe's arguments appeared determined to act the coward. Crowe begged me to see Asquith or Grey, but of course they would not see me. Crowe was in despair.[120]

(Crowe's despair produced his memorandum of the same day, putting on paper his arguments that British interests required the country to stand by France in France's hour of need, and rebutting the commercial arguments for peace.)[121] Thirteen months after the war ended Crowe was still furious with Grey. In December 1919 he spoke again with Wilson, now CIGS. Wilson's diary entry reads:

> Crowe gave me some of his reminiscences at the FO in July and August 1914, showing the hopelessness and timidity of Grey. His stories showed what a futile useless weak fool the man was – and is. In 1914 he was determined *not* to go to war if by any conceivable means he could shirk his duties.[122]

As demonstrated above, this particular Foreign Office view of Grey could not have been more wrong. It was as wrong as that expressed by Lloyd George in his *War memoirs*. Crowe, himself unencumbered by colleagues of the calibre of Lloyd George and also of another persuasion, simply made no allowance for the extent to which Grey was thus encumbered. A judgement expressed by Lord Lansdowne to Lord Loreburn, an assiduous critic of Grey's foreign policy as a whole, is much fairer. Commenting on the proofs of Loreburn's book *How the war came* (London, 1919), Lansdowne wrote:

> I have always believed that the war might have been avoided if Grey had been in a position to make a perfectly explicit statement as to our conduct in certain eventualities. I am under the impression that he would himself have been ready enough to make such a statement, but that he could not venture to do so, and could not have got the support of the Cabinet if he had asked for it.[123]

Another judgement sounder than Crowe's is to be found in a memorandum by Sir Walford Selby, who in 1914 was Grey's assistant private secretary; writing to Tyrrell in 1934 that the policy of Grey must be reverted to, he said:

> I speak of Algeciras and Grey's magnificent retort to the German Ambassador when he complained of Sir A. Nicolson's attitude at the Algeciras Conference, a retort which resulted shortly afterwards in the signature of the Act of Algeciras; of Agadir and Mr Lloyd George's intervention at the Mansion House undertaken with the full approval of Grey; not of the last days of July 1914, when Grey was presented with the terrific dilemma, knowing what was at stake, desiring to bring in a united country, desiring to avoid an internal crisis lest the Germans should slip into Paris before Great Britain had made up her mind.[124]

Grey's personal decision for war was made as soon as the Russian government made it clear that they would not tolerate a forcible Austro-Hungarian solution of the Serbian problem. The Cabinet, as such, never did make a decision for war. The measures which converted the Anglo-French *entente* into a functioning alliance were not Cabinet decisions. The keeping together of the fleet, the sending of it to its war stations, the implementation of naval dispositions for the Channel, the eventual sending of most of the Expeditionary Force, were no more Cabinet decisions than was the drafting and sending of the ultimatum to Germany to stop the invasion of Belgium within 24 hours which was produced by Grey and Asquith after Grey's speech in the House of Commons on the afternoon of Monday 3 August. They were actions taken by the remaining functioning Liberal Imperialists, together with their most zealous recruit,[125] whose energy and application completely eclipsed that of that very temporary associate of the Liberal Imperialist group, the Chancellor of the Exchequer. The only decisions taken by the remainder of the Cabinet were decisions either to resign (two), or to resign and retract (two) or to remain in office (the rest). The price to be paid was the implementation and realization of the policy of the *entente* on which Grey and Asquith insisted. The rest, as they say, is history.

## Notes

1. D. Lloyd George, *War memoirs*, I (London, 1933), pp. 57–60. Among the counter-blasts from the Grey camp was an article, "Lord Grey of Fallodon", by Arthur Murray, in *Quarterly Review* **262**, 1934, pp. 12–16.
2. R. MacDonald MSS, Memorandum by MacDonald, p. 14.
3. Ibid., p. 13.
4. Harcourt to Lloyd George, undated, (?)2 August 1914, printed in F. Owen, *Tempestuous journey* (London, 1954), p. 264.
5. Undated notes from Churchill to Lloyd George, ibid., pp. 264–5; Churchill's italics.
6. Undated note from Churchill to Lloyd George, in R. S. Churchill, *Winston S. Churchill*, Companion vol. 2, part 3 (London, 1969), p. 1999; Churchill's italics.
7. Memorandum by A. H. Ollivant, 1 August 1914, printed in C. Hazlehurst, *Politicians at war* (London, 1971), pp. 321–6; H. H. Wilson, Diary, 1 August 1914.
8. Masterman to Lloyd George, (?)2 August 1914, in Owen, *Tempestuous journey*, p. 265.
9. L. Masterman, *C. F. G. Masterman* (London, 1939), p. 267. As Max Aitken, Beaverbrook had been approached by F. E. Smith regarding participating in a coalition government: M. Gilbert, *Winston S. Churchill*, vol. 3 (London, 1971), pp. 12–13.
10. Morley of Blackburn, *Memorandum on resignation* (London, 1928), p. 14.

11. Dawson MSS 64, ff. 68–74, Notes on some critical Sundays, July and August 1914.
12. Asquith to Venetia Stanley 3 August 1914, in *H. H. Asquith, letters to Venetia Stanley*, M. Brock & E. Brock (eds) (Oxford, 1985), p. 148.
13. Owen, *Tempestuous journey*, p. 267.
14. Riddell, *Lord Riddell's war diary* (London, 1933), p. 6.
15. MacDonald Memorandum, pp. 8 and 14.
16. Villiers to Grey, 3 August 1914, BD, xi, no. 521.
17. See K. M. Wilson (ed.), "The Cabinet diary of J. A. Pease, 24 July to 5 August 1914", *Proceedings of the Leeds Philosophical and Literary Society*, xix, part III (1983), p. 8.
18. MacDonald Memorandum, p. 13.
19. Riddell, *War diary*, p. 4.
20. Simon to Burns, 2 August 1914, MS Simon 50, f. 96.
21. Simon to Asquith, 2 August 1914, MS Simon 2.
22. Samuel to his wife, 2 August 1914, printed in C. J. Lowe & M. Dockrill, *The mirage of power*, vol. iii (London, 1972), pp. 489–91.
23. Re Crewe: on 30 July Asquith said that it did not matter to him if certain ministers resigned, "so long as Crewe and Grey are there": see M. Asquith, *Autobiography* (London, 1962), p. 281; see also J. Pope-Hennessy, *Lord Crewe* (London, 1955), p. 144; Crewe had known of the military conversations with France longer than anyone in the Cabinet except Grey, Haldane and Asquith, having been a member of a sub-committee of the Committee of Imperial Defence set up in October 1908 in the course of whose proceedings they were mentioned: CAB 16/5, proceedings of 23 March 1909.
24. MacDonald Memorandum, p. 1.
25. C. P. Scott to Bryce 30 July 1914, Bryce MSS 131; C. P. Scott diary, 27 July 1914, Add. MSS 50901.
26. E. David (ed.), *Inside Asquith's Cabinet: the diaries of Charles Hobhouse* (London, 1977), p.179.
27. Riddell, *War diary*, pp. 6–7. The French Ambassador wrote to a friend three weeks later: "Il y a ici un fort parti de financiers judéo-allemands qui possède les journaux libéraux, qui a des accointances dans le Cabinet et qui a fait des pieds et des mains pour empêcher l'Angleterre d'intervenir", P. Cambon to Xavier Charles, 20 August 1914, in *Paul Cambon: Correspondence*, H. Cambon (ed.)(Paris, 1940–46), vol. iii p. 72.
28. MacDonald Memorandum, p. 8.
29. B. Wasserstein, *Herbert Samuel* (Oxford, 1992), p. 164.
30. Asquith, *Autobiography*, p. 287.
31. Wasserstein, *Herbert Samuel*, p. 164.
32. The editor of the *Morning Post*, H. A. Gwynne, wrote to his proprie-

tor, Lady Bathurst, on 27 February 1912, of an overture from Lloyd George to the Conservatives about putting defence outside the arena of party and imposing conscription if necessary. Gwynne remarked: "If it is true and *if Lloyd George is sincere*, it is the biggest thing going." Glenesk–Bathurst MSS.

33. A. Murray diary, 7 January 1912, Elibank MSS 8814.

34. J. A. Pease diary, 29 March 1912: "Lloyd George and I pressed Grey to alter our words and introduce neutrality to please Germans and play up to Bethmann Hollweg . . . Grey and Churchill wanted no further weakening of our words." Gainford MSS.

35. Murray diary, 17 January 1912, Elibank MSS 8814.

36. K. M. Wilson, *Empire and continent* (London, 1987), pp. 126–40.

37. Dawson diary, 20 November 1912, MS Dawson 18, f. 167.

38. Nicolson to de Bunsen, 6 and 7 July 1914, de Bunsen MSS, box 15, Nicolson's italics.

39. De Bunsen to Nicolson, 17 July 1914, BD, xi, no. 56.

40. Grey to Rumbold, 6 July 1914, ibid., no. 32.

41. Grey to Buchanan, 8 July 1914, ibid., no. 39.

42. Grey to Rumbold, 9 July 1914, ibid., no. 41.

43. See H. F. Young, *Prince Lichnowsky and the Great War* (Athens, Georgia, 1977), pp. 97–9; F. Fischer, *War of illusions* (New York, 1975), pp. 470–73.

44. De Bunsen to Grey, 16 July 1914, BD, xi, no. 50; see also C. H. D. Howard (ed.), "The Vienna diary of Berta de Bunsen 28 June to 17 August 1914", *Bulletin of the Institute of Historical Research*, LI(124), 1978, p. 215.

45. Lichnowsky to German Foreign Office, 20 July 1914: K. Kautsky (ed.), *Outbreak of the World War: German documents* (New York, 1924), no. 92.

46. Ibid., nos 118, 121; see also Cambon to his son, 22 July 1914, *Paul Cambon*, p. 68.

47. Hoyos to Haldane, 20 July 1914, printed in Sir F. Maurice, *Haldane 1856–1915* (London, 1937), pp. 349–52. Haldane was less sanguine, noting: "This is very serious. Berchtold is apparently ready to plunge Europe into war to settle the Serbian question. He would not take this attitude unless he was assured of German support. Hoyos' letter is clearly intended to prepare us for the ultimatum and is an attempt to scare us into neutrality with the Russian bogy. The one hope is that Bethmann Hollweg's influence in Berlin will prevail."

48. Grey to de Bunsen, 23 July 1914, BD, xi, no. 86; Mensdorff to Berchtold, 24 July 1914, OD 10600.

49. Lichnowsky to German Foreign Office, 24 July 1914, Kautsky no. 157. The Germans picked up the emphasis on four. The Kaiser, for his

part, merely noted: "He forgets Italy."

50. Buchanan to Grey 24 July 1914, BD, xi, no. 101. The passage quoted is underlined in red on a copy of this telegram in Montagu's papers. Which minister did the underlining or gave Montagu the telegram is not clear. The words "efface ourselves" and "general European question" are underlined in an earlier sentence: "[Sazonov] replied that the Serbian question was but a part of general European question and that we could not efface ourselves"; the words "HM Govt. would proclaim their solidarity with France and Russia" are underlined in a still earlier sentence which begins: "[Sazonov] expressed the hope that", Montagu MSS AS6/10/4.

51. Grey to Buchanan, 25 July 1914, BD, xi, no. 132.

52. Buchanan to Grey, 25 July 1914, ibid., no. 125.

53. Ibid., no.33, p. 26.

54. Ibid., p. xi.

55. Memo by Clerk, 21 July 1914; and Minutes by Crowe and Nicolson, FO 371/2076/33484; Minute by Nicolson, 22 July 1914, ibid., 2094/32813. See K. M. Wilson, "The struggle for Persia: Sir G. Clerk's memorandum of 21 July 1914 on Anglo-Russian relations in Persia", in *Proceedings of the 1988 Brismes International Conference on Middle Eastern Studies* (Leeds, 1988), pp. 290–334.

56. BD, xi, p. xi, lines 4 and 5. It is as well never to forget what Harold Nicolson wrote in CID paper 251B of 10 July 1920: "For the last century the policy of His Majesty's Government has been inductive, intuitive and quite deliberately opportunist, but through it all has run the dominant impulse of the defence of India", CAB 4/7.

57. Lichnowsky to German Foreign Office, 15 July 1914, Kautsky no. 52.

58. Nicolson to Grey, 26 July 1914, BD, xi, no. 144.

59. Lichnowsky to German Foreign Office, 26 July 1914, Kautsky no. 236. Tyrrell went to speak to the Austrian Ambassador in the same vein on 29 July; as Mensdorff reported: "Tyrrell wholly confirms the view I hold gained of the attitude here, which I would sum up as follows: Great Britain seems to be trying by all means possible to keep out of a European complication; Russian interests leave England cool; but should it affect a vital interest of France's or what is more a question of France as a Power, no English Government would be capable of preventing a participation of Great Britain on the side of France." OD 10973.

60. Lichnowsky to German Foreign Office, 27 July 1914, Kautsky nos. 258, 265.

61. Grey to Goschen, 27 July 1914, BD, xi, no. 176.

62. Buchanan to Grey, 27 July 1914; Grey to Buchanan, 27 July, ibid., nos. 170, 177.

63. German Naval Attaché, London, to Imperial Naval Office, Berlin, 26 July 1914, Kautsky no. 207; J. A. Spender & C. Asquith, *Life of Lord Oxford and Asquith*, vol. ii (London, 1932), p. 81; Nicolson to Buchanan, 28 July 1914, BD, xi, no. 239.

64. Crackanthorpe to Grey, 28 July 1914, ibid., no. 225.

65. "Belgian neutrality in 1870", July 1914, CAB 37/120/95; for Law Officers' Report, see BD, viii, pp. 378–9; Pease diary, 29 July 1914; notes by Harcourt on FO telegrams 11662, Harcourt MSS 552; Masterman *C. F. G. Masterman*, p. 265.

66. BD, xi, nos. 247, 258.

67. Pease diary, 29 July 1914: marginalia by Harcourt on telegrams 11662, Harcourt MSS 552; Asquith to the King, 30 July 1914, in Spender and Asquith *Life of Lord Asquith*, ii, p. 81.

68. Burns diary, 29 July 1914, Add. MSS 46336.

69. CAB 37/120/95; Asquith to Venetia Stanley, 29 July 1914, in Brock *H. H. Asquith*, pp. 132–3, Asquith's italics; Churchill to Lloyd George 29 July 1914 in Owen, *Tempestuous journey*, p. 264; F. E. Smith to Churchill, 31 July 1914, in M. Gilbert, *Winston S. Churchill*, Companion vol. 2, part 3, p. 1990.

70. Grey to Bertie, 29 July 1914, BD, xi, no. 283.

71. Lichnowsky to German Foreign Office, 29 July 1914, Kautsky no. 357.

72. As Note 71, 29 July 1914, no.368.

73. Ibid., p. 322.

74. Asquith to Venetia Stanley, 30 July 1914, Brock *H. H. Asquith*, p. 136; K. Robbins, *Sir Edward Grey: a biography of Lord Grey of Fallodon* (London, 1971), pp. 293–4. The German Chancellor's overture finally convinced Grey that Nicolson, who had told him on 26 July, "Germany is playing with us", was right: BD, xi, no.144.

75. Pease diary, f.104, Gainford MSS.

76. See my edition of the Pease diary, p. 7.

77. Note by Harcourt on telegrams 11663, Harcourt MSS 552.

78. Burns diary, 31 July 1914, Burns MSS Add. MSS 46308; at lunch with Grey on 1 August, Burns told him of his "fears as to Germany beaten allying herself with Russia and Japan": Burns diary, 1 August 1914, Add. MSS 46336.

79. Cambon to Viviani, 31 July 1914, DDF 3rd series, xi, no. 459; BD, xi, nos 303, 348.

80. BD, xi, nos 382, 383.

81. Lichnowsky to German Foreign Office, 1 August 1914, Kautsky no. 596.

82. Asquith to Venetia Stanley, 1 August 1914, Brock, *H. H. Asquith*, p. 140.

83. Ibid.
84. H. H. Wilson diary, 1, 2 August 1914.
85. Grey to Bertie, 1 August 1914, BD, xi, no. 426.
86. Kautsky no. 596; Grey to Goschen, 1 August 1914, BD, xi, no. 448.
87. Cambon to Viviani, 1 August 1914, DDF 3rd series, xi, no. 532.
88. Ibid., 31 July 1914, no. 445.
89. H. Nicolson, *Lord Carnock: a study in the old diplomacy* (London, 1930), p. 419.
90. Bertie to Grey, 1 August 1914, BD, xi, no. 425.
91. Murray diary, 1 August 1914, Elibank MSS 8814.
92. Lichnowsky to Jagow, 1 August 1914, 11.14am, Kautsky no. 562.
93. Asquith to Venetia Stanley, 1 August 1914, Brock, *H. H. Asquith*, p. 140.
94. Haldane to his mother, 1 August; to his sister 2 August 1914, Haldane MSS 5992, 6012.
95. Lichnowsky to German Foreign Office, 1, 2 August 1914, Kautsky nos. 596, 603, 631; R. D. Blumenfeld, *R.D.B.'s diary 1887–1914* (London, 1930), p. 248.
96. Grey to Bertie, 1 August 1914, BD, xi, no. 426.
97. Ibid., no. 447; see also A. Thierry, *L'Angleterre au temps de Paul Cambon* (Paris, 1961), p. 202.
98. Grey to Bertie, 1 August 1914, BD, xi, no. 419.
99. George V to Wilhelm II, 1 August; Wilhelm II to George V, 1 August 1914, Kautsky nos 612, 575.
100. Bertie to Grey, 1 August 1914, BD, xi, no. 453.
101. Grey to Bertie, 2 August 1914, ibid., no. 460. The existing writing on this particular question consists of H. F. Young, "The misunderstanding of August 1, 1914", *Journal of Modern History* 48, 1976, pp. 644–65; and S. J. Valone, "'There must be some misunderstanding': Sir Edward Grey's diplomacy of August 1, 1914", *Journal of British Studies* 27, 1988, pp. 405–24. The real, and only, misunderstanding was Lichnowsky's, of whatever Tyrrell said to him about 2pm, which he interpreted as British neutrality even if Germany was at war with both France and Russia: see Kautsky no. 570.
102. BD, xi, no. 125.
103. DDF 3rd series, xi, no. 305, p. 263; BD, xi, no. 319.
104. Grey to Bertie, 31 July 1914, BD, xi, no. 367.
105. Nicolson, *Lord Carnock*, pp. 419–20.
106. BD, xi, no. 368.
107. H. H. Wilson diary, 1 August 1914.
108. Nicolson, *Lord Carnock*, pp. 419–20; Nicolson to Hardinge, 5 September 1914, Hardinge MSS, vol. 93. Nicolson kept up his pressure on Grey during 2 August, mentioning his confidence in the leaders of

the Conservative Opposition, at least one of whom he had tried to stir into action: BD, xi, no. 466; Nicolson to Balfour, 2 August 1914, Balfour MSS Add. MSS 49748. Balfour had spent Saturday 1 August "conveying to the French and Russian Ambassadors that the rumour of Unionist reluctance to take our share in defending France and Belgium was totally unfounded" and in mobilizing Bonar Law and Lansdowne: Balfour to Alice Balfour, 8 August 1914, ibid., 49832.

109. H. H. Wilson diary, 2 August 1914.
110. BD, xi, no. 447.
111. Walford Selby, *Diplomatic twilight* (London, 1953), p. 181.
112. BD, x (ii), nos. 381–417.
113. Pease diary, 2 August 1914.
114. Ibid.
115. Simon to Asquith, 2 August 1914, MS Simon 2.
116. Wasserstein, *Herbert Samuel*, p. 163. For a different view of Samuel, see B. B. Gilbert, "Pacifist to Interventionist: D. Lloyd George in 1911 and 1914. Was Belgium an issue?", *Historical Journal*, 28(4), 1985, pp. 881–2.
117. Bonar Law's and Lord Lansdowne's letter is printed in R. Blake, *The unknown Prime Minister* (London, 1955), p. 212. It was read out at the morning Cabinet of 2 August. It constituted one of several reasons why W. A. S. Hewins wrote on 3 August that "But for our support, the Government would have had to run": Hewins MSS box 96/23.
118. A. Murray diary, 2 August 1914, Elibank MSS 8814; BD, xi, nos. 465–8, 476.
119. See K. M. Wilson, *The policy of the Entente* (Cambridge, 1985), pp. 135–47.
120. Minute by Wilson, 31 July 1914, H. H. Wilson MSS 3/8/4. On the timing of the sending of Buchanan's despatch, see J. Stengers, "1914: safety of ciphers", in *Intelligence and international relations 1900–1945*, C. Andrew & J. Noakes (eds), (Exeter, 1987), p. 48, fn.74.
121. BD, xi, no. 369. See also Crowe to his wife, 31 July 1914, cited in Sibyl Crowe and Edward Corp, *Our ablest public servant: Sir Eyre Crowe 1864–1925* (Braunton, 1993), p. 265.
122. H. H. Wilson diary, 4 December 1919.
123. Lansdowne to Loreburn, 28 April 1919, Lansdowne MSS L(5)30. I must thank the Trustees of the Bowood Estate for permission to quote from this letter.
124. Selby, *Diplomatic Twilight*, p. 152.
125. See Gilbert, *Winston Churchill*, vol. 3, pp. 23, 25–8; and his *Churchill – a life* (London, 1991), pp. 266–8.

# Chapter Eight

# *Japan*

## Ian Nish

Japan's decision to make war on Germany on 23 August 1914 arose out of a simple, almost naïve, request from Britain for its naval assistance. Its consequences were to extend the wartime grand alliance by including a Pacific partner and increase its scope to take in the territory of China and the waters of the Pacific Ocean, though this was scarcely the intention of Sir Edward Grey when he made the request.[1]

Like all the other powers involved in the war, Japan considered the prospect in terms of thinking about its own defence. Although it had mastery of the Pacific Ocean and had a proven army, it was worried about security. Unlike other countries, Japan had had experience of what a major modern war was like. Following its victory in the Russo-Japanese war, Japan had formulated a defence policy (*kokubo hoshin*) in 1907 which envisaged the "enemy" of its army as Russia and the "enemy" of its navy as the United States. While it was a success that this had been worked out, it did in fact conceal much jealousy and recrimination between the two services.[2]

In general, the higher echelons of the army were filled from members of the Choshu clan and had been trained either in Germany or in the German tradition. The most prominent soldier-politician, General Katsura Taro, had been Minister-President on three occasions (1901–6, 1908–9 and 1912–13). Unquestionably this gave the army leaders a special rôle in Japanese decision-making. Behind Katsura stood the four remaining Elder Statesmen (*genro*) who were strongly under army influence: General Yamagata was the most senior of these, and General Oyama, who had acquired a high reputation during the war of 1904. The army's position had become complicated by Japan's annexation of Korea in 1910, which brought its right up against the frontier of its "contemplated enemy", Russia. The army leaders therefore asked for two extra divisions for the purpose of Korean defence. This was disputed by the navy and by the political parties which had power over financial matters in the Diet (Parliament). It was true that there had been two agreements with Russia, in 1910 and 1912, seeking a *modus vivendi* over frontiers in Manchuria. But the army did not rate these too highly.[3]

The personnel of the navy was based on the Satsuma clan in Kagoshima. The navy felt that its needs for defence funding had been underestimated over the previous 50 years and it was in a mood to claim more. To that end it opposed the army's claim for two extra divisions. During 1914 there were still rumours of an impending American–Japanese war, the truth of which had to be contradicted by the government on several occasions.[4] Whether these rumours were encouraged by the navy in order to give prominence to its rôle in national defence (in the manner of Admiral Sir John Fisher) is hard to say.

This army–navy rivalry led to instability in the political field. The coming to the throne of the Emperor Taisho coincided with a series of political crises, sometimes known as the Taisho crises. The third Cabinet of General Katsura (1912–13) was hounded out of office by the main opposition political party, the Seiyukai, which opposed the demand for two extra divisions. It was the Seiyukai which gave political support in the Diet to the successor Cabinet of Admiral Yamamoto Gombei (1913–14) formed in February 1913. This had not been in office for a year when a major international scandal arose concerning bribery of Japanese admirals over shipbuilding contracts. This was the Siemens affair, which surfaced in January 1914. A motion of no confidence was tabled in February. The government survived, but it encountered determined opposition in the House of Peers over its budget, which called for increased naval estimates. Following a vote of censure in the Lower House the Cabinet resigned on 24 March. The scandal injured the reputation of the navy in the eyes of the people. In May, Admiral Yamamoto, the former Prime Minister, was placed on the reserve list of officers along with Admirals Saito and Takarabe, the other senior office-bearers who had to assume token responsibility.[5] For Yamamoto this was an unprecedented disgrace, since he was held to be the "father" of the Japanese navy. His political rivals claimed that he had "disgraced the honour of Japan abroad".[6]

Clearly, there was great instability in the Japanese body politic. The four remaining Elder Statesmen, who were entrusted with the task of finding the next Prime Minister, were determined that the Cabinet should not be Seiyukai-dominated. Fortunately a new political grouping, the Doshikai, had been formed by Kato Takaaki, a former diplomat and Foreign Minister. But Kato had gone out of his way to antagonize the *genro* in the past, and they were opposed to his heading the forthcoming administration. Instead they called (after a few abortive attempts and a long delay) on Okuma Shigenobu to form the next ministry. He was able to announce his new coalition Cabinet, which combined most of the anti-Seiyukai parties, on 13 April. Kato became Foreign Minister and managed to ensure that members of his Doshikai party obtained the most prestigious offices. But there were serious elements of instability in that the various constituent groups who were united solely by jealousy of the burgeoning political power of the Seiyukai needed some spectacular successes if they were to remain in power for long. The paradox was that Okuma, who had been chosen by the *genro*, had because of the realities of the political world to seek alliance with the Doshikai Party, which was highly suspicious of *genro* politics. After three Cabinets in as many years, there would have to be a general election soon if Japanese party politics were not to become a laughing stock. The new Cabinet had half an eye on that election, which did, in fact, take place in March 1915.

It was a parliamentary Cabinet without any connection with the clans. But the old issues were still unresolved. General Oka, the war minister, was a strong advocate of the two extra divisions, while the navy minister, Admiral Yashiro Rokuro, favoured a programme for expansion of the fleet. Okuma was independent-minded, and Kato, who held the key post as foreign minister, was rather high-handed and abrasive with Japanese, though by all accounts fairly suave towards foreigners.

How, then, did this insecure government view the deteriorating situation in Europe? It should first be said that Japan was following events in the Balkans fairly closely. It had maintained an embassy in

Vienna since 1906 (following on from the earlier legation). It was the embassy's task to report fully on the critical situation in the Balkans – what the Japanese oddly described as *"Kinto mondai"* – "the Near Eastern question".[7] So the Japanese Cabinet and press were not ignorant of events, even if they did not see themselves as being particularly concerned.

The political parties, which felt that Japan was groaning under the weight of taxes since the Russian war, had no sense of the need for involvement in a global war. The navy, which was anxious to erase the ill-reputation it had acquired as the result of the Siemens scandal, was by contrast anxious to get involved in the war, to the extent of expanding Japan's operational sphere in the Pacific. The strategists of the army were preoccupied with the defensive needs of Korea and had little interest in Europe.

But there was one positive outcome of this world crisis. Following a special session of the Diet on 20–29 June to discuss the naval estimates, Okuma announced that the matter would be studied by the Council of National Defence, a mechanism by which the views of the army and navy could be harmonized with considerations of foreign policy and finance. He did not consider, he went on, that the presence of the chiefs of staff in the Council would constitute interference in the processes of civilian government. The Council, which met with the Prime Minister in the chair, bears some resemblance to the Committee of Imperial Defence in Britain. Though it was designed to deal primarily with army–navy antagonism, especially over the share of the budget, it probably also handled international issues. But not much is known about the rôle it played in the August crisis to which we must now turn.[8]

## The diplomacy of Japan's entry

On 1 August 1914, Foreign Secretary Grey told Japan that, "if we do intervene, it would be on the side of France and Russia and I therefore do not see we were likely to have to apply to Japan under the alliance". Two days later, Grey warned the Japanese that war between Britain and Germany was a distinct possibility and, "if the fighting should extend to the Far East, and an assault on Hong Kong and Weihaiwei were to occur, HM government would rely on the support of the Japanese government".[9] This did indeed reflect the terms of the various Anglo-Japanese treaties. This message was received during a Cabinet meeting which had assembled at 9.30am on 4 August in order to discuss the war in faraway Europe. The meeting broke up at 2.30pm and the Foreign Ministry issued a statement saying that Japan hoped to observe an attitude of strict neutrality but would be ready to take the necessary steps in accordance with its obligations under the British alliance. This sudden and unexpected decision confirmed the line which Kato had proposed to lay before his colleagues.

When the British ambassador called he was given a fuller account. While Japan would maintain a strict neutrality towards a European war, it would, in the event of an attack on Hong Kong or Weihaiwei, or a similar act of aggression, be prepared at once to support Britain, if called upon. The inclusion of the phrase "if called upon" gave London the impression that Japan would only act at Britain's behest. Grey, therefore, replied that, just as Japan had not requested British intervention during the Russo-Japanese war, so Britain in turn would, if possible, avoid drawing Japan into any trouble: "but, should a case arise in which we needed her help, we would gladly ask for it and be grateful for it".[10]

There is here a discrepancy between the British and Japanese records. What Japan had intended was that, in the case of a clear act of aggression (say) on Hong Kong or Weihaiwei, the alliance would come into effect straight away; but only in cases such as attacks on British ships on the high seas (where the terms of the alliance were not explicitly relevant) would there be the need for consultation. There was evidence that the Japanese already meant business. Kato in addition revealed that the second squadron, containing four warships, had been mobilized and was ready for action; that Japan's latest battleship, the *Kongo*, would shortly join the squadron; and that other craft had been stationed at the ports of Nagasaki, Hakodate and Pusan (Korea).[11] The discrepancy, though a small one, may have given the London authorities the impression that Japan's involvement would only come as the result of a positive initiative from them.

It was Britain's uncertainty about its naval and commercial position in the China seas which brought a change in the British attitude. On 5 August the Foreign Office, after consultation with the Admi-

ralty, prepared a memorandum which was passed over by Sir
Conyngham Greene two days later:

> HM Government would gladly avail themselves of the prof-
> fered assistance of Japanese Government in the direction of
> protecting British trading vessels from German armed mer-
> chant cruisers, while British warships are locating and en-
> gaging German warships in Chinese waters . . . it would be of
> the very greatest assistance to HM Government if they would
> be good enough to employ some of their warships in hunting
> out and destroying German armed merchantmen in China.
> British Government realize that such action on the part of
> Japan will constitute declaration of war with Germany, but it
> is difficult to see how such a step is to be avoided.[12]

While the naval rôle expected of Japan was secondary, in so far as it
was aimed against armed merchantmen, and not the German Pacific
fleet, the political implications of asking for Japan to declare war
were, of course, enormous. Kato, whose response was again positive,
claims to have told Greene that he did not see how Japan's assistance
could be limited to armed merchantmen only.

Britain's request raised new considerations and Kato called on the
Prime Minister at his official residence. He put forward three proposals about Japan's entry into the war: Japan should enter the war;
its entry should not be limited to pursuing armed merchant vessels;
and Japan should negotiate with Britain about the form which its
declaration of war should take. Okuma agreed to these points and
called an emergency Cabinet meeting at 10pm on 7 August at his
personal residence at Waseda. This was presumably to keep the
newspapermen, who were greatly excited at the prospect of Japan
going to war, off the scent. Kato deployed the arguments in favour of
entering the war. The only opposing argument came from the Minister of Education, Ichiki Tokuro, who asked whether an attack on
Tsingtao would infringe China's neutrality. Ichiki had been a professor of law at Tokyo Imperial University in the 1890s before becom-
ing a bureaucrat and politician.[13] But Kato eventually persuaded his
colleagues that to enter the war on the broad basis of the British alliance would not only comply with the basic intention (*honshitsu*) of
that alliance but also build up Japan's peace-keeping rôle in East

Asia. The meeting adjourned after 2am.[14] A national decision of great consequence had been reached at breakneck speed.

At 5.30am, Kato left Ueno station for Nikko to report on the decision to the Emperor. Returning to Tokyo in the evening, he attended a joint meeting between the Cabinet and the *genro*: Yamagata, Matsukata and Oyama. The Elder Statesmen, more cautious than the Cabinet, raised the possibilities of Japan sustaining substantial losses and of Germany emerging victorious in Europe. *Genro* Inoue Kaoru, who was unable to attend, wrote in a memorandum: "this is the divine aid (*tenyu*) of the new Taisho era for the development of Japan's national destiny (*kokuun*)".[15] Kato's enthusiasm carried the day and the decision was ratified. Japan's decision-making process was complete. For a nation normally slow in deliberation, it was a record-breaking decision: it had all been resolved within 36 hours of Britain's request.

Japan proceeded to discuss with Britain the nature of an ultimatum to Germany. In a message to London on 9 August, Japan made it clear that it wanted to go beyond hunting merchantmen and to incorporate in any declaration of war the statement that peace in East Asia had been imperilled as a result of Germany's aggressive actions there and that Japan was declaring war at the request of Britain. Kato's message concluded as follows:

In order to avoid possible misapprehension, the Japanese Government wish to know as soon as possible if the British Government concur in the aforesaid statement of the grounds upon which the Declaration of War will be based. If they have no objection to this, the Imperial Government also wish that Britain will . . . make a statement which will not conflict with that of the Imperial Government.[16]

Japan had agreed to declare war but not to accept limitations on the scope of her naval activities: its participation was to be "total" (*zemmenteki*).

Meanwhile, the German ambassador in Tokyo, Graf von Rex, who had been annoyed by Japan's intentions, which had leaked out in the press, gave the *Gaimusho* (Foreign Ministry) a none-too-subtle warning that, if Japan was foolhardy enough to attack the German-leased territory at Tsingtao, it would encounter tough resistance and sustain many casualties. This helped Kato to sell his policy among sceptics in Japan.

Britain was taken aback by the Japanese enthusiasm for action. Sir John Jordan, British minister in Peking, and Sir Martyn Jerram, commander-in-chief, China Station, were contacted for their views, and Japan was asked to delay any action.

Kato responded immediately on 10 August, to the effect that Japan failed to understand why Jordan was apprehensive "lest a declaration of war on the part of Japan may give rise to the impression that extensive operations affecting China may take place, which would have a serious effect on the stability of that country". He could assure Britain that Japan's action would be limited to "the ultimate destruction of German power in these regions for which no extensive operations are required".[17]

Britain's position was undercut by new reports from Jordan that crews of British and German gunboats had been withdrawn from the Yangtse river; and from the commander-in-chief, China Station, that it was not true that British merchantmen were being attacked by German armed ships. Apparently Whitehall, which clearly wanted to preserve the status quo in China, had panicked unnecessarily five days earlier.

## Britain's reverse course

On 11 August Britain took a most serious step, telling Tokyo that it believed that acts of war in the Far East would for the present be restricted to operations at sea and that it was thought desirable to maintain this position as long as possible; Britain therefore refrained for the present from invoking action under the alliance treaty. The British view was that their request for intervention had been positively withdrawn.[18]

In Japan's view, the new development was little short of a disaster. For the Japanese government to stop its war preparations at this stage was out of the question; riots were likely to result unless something were done. Japan's decision to take military action had been reported to, and approved by, the Emperor. Under his authority, military preparations were almost complete and only the issue of the official declaration of war was outstanding. This information was in the public domain. Therefore if it became generally known that Britain had once invited Japan to take part and then retracted the invitation, it would rebound to the discredit of the alliance. Britain was therefore asked to reconsider its decision and agree to Japan's form of words.

Grey was reluctant. He explained his understanding of the whole business: Japan had undertaken to enter the war if Britain were to make such a request, "leaving the extent and mode of such assistance to the discretion of the British government". This was a fundamental difference of view. Grey claimed that the situation had in any case changed in so far as Germany had now made threats and the interests of Japan itself were at stake. He could quite understand Japan wanting to declare war and had no objection to Japan justifying her action in opening hostilities by referring to the alliance, but preferred the public declaration to say that Japan and Britain, after close consultation, had decided to take measures to defend their respective interests under the alliance. He further urged Japan to announce that she would restrict the range of its operations and not proceed as far as occupying German territories in the Pacific or the south and west China seas. Japan's ambassador in London, Inoue Katsunosuke, who was the son of *Genro* Inoue Kaoru, replied that Japan had already made clear that it had no territorial ambitions and that it could not limit the range of its activities because its merchant marine operating in the Pacific was also at risk and had to be defended.

While the tone of these communications was cordial enough, the substance was damaging. The retraction of the invitation, and now the request for limiting the range of Japan's operations, indicated Britain's suspicions of Japan. But the Japanese were not prepared to be browbeaten by Britain, which was evidently acting under some pressure from the United States, the Netherlands, its own territories in Australia and New Zealand, and China itself. Moreover, the underlying note of British suspicion was confirmed in the diplomatic exchanges. The two partners were not prepared to withdraw from their firmly-held positions so they had no choice but to go their separate ways with as good a grace as was possible. Kato told ambassador Greene that it was completely impossible to include any territorial limits in the declaration of war but that Japan was prepared to give other countries individual assurances. On this basis, Grey responded affirmatively.

217

The preamble to Japan's ultimatum, which was handed over to Germany by various routes on 15 August, read as follows:

> Considering it highly important and necessary in the present situation to take measures to remove all causes of disturbance to the peace of the Far East and to safeguard the general interests contemplated by the Agreement of Alliance between Japan and Great Britain, in order to secure a firm and enduring peace in Eastern Asia, establishment of which is the aim of the said Agreement, [the Japanese] sincerely believe it their duty to give advice to [Germany].[19]

The advice was twofold: to withdraw or disarm German vessels in eastern waters; and to deliver to Japan by 15 September the German-leased territory of Kiaochou. The main copies were passed to Graf von Rex in Tokyo and to Baron Funakoshi Mitsunojo, the chargé d'affaires in Berlin.

The ultimatum made no mention of limiting Japan's area of operation. But, true to his word, Kato assured the representatives in Tokyo of Russia, France, the United States and the Netherlands – the so-called colonial powers – that Japan had no thought of territorial aggrandizement and would not infringe their interests. It would appear that assurances of a similar kind were not given to China. In a speech to a conference on 17 August, the Prime Minister, Count Okuma, further clarified the position:

> Japan's object is to eliminate from the Continent of China the root of the German influence, which forms a constant menace to the peace of the Far East, and thus to secure the aim of the alliance with Great Britain . . . Japan's warlike operations will not, therefore, extend beyond the limits necessary for the attainment of that object and for the defence of her own legitimate interests.[20]

This statement was conveyed to Britain two days later.

Before Okuma had spoken, the British Foreign Office, without consulting Japan, issued a unilateral statement that kept up the tension. It read:

> It is understood that the action of Japan will not extend to the Pacific Ocean beyond the China Seas except in so far as it may be necessary to protect Japanese shipping lines in the Pacific nor beyond Asiatic waters westward of the China Seas, nor to any foreign territory except territory in German occupation on the Continent of Eastern Asia.[21]

Britain's worry was clearly over naval action in the Pacific rather than military action in China itself. Not unnaturally, Japan protested forcefully; but Grey defended his position by saying that he was only articulating Britain's version of Japanese intentions. Hence the use of the phrase "it is understood". Foreign Minister Kato, for his part, disclosed to the press that there was no advance understanding with Britain over the geographical limits of Japan's military action, thereby making clear that Britain's "understanding" of Japan was purely speculative.

On 23 August, the deadline stipulated in Japan's ultimatum, Germany declined to reply. Journalists waiting outside the German embassy in Tokyo came away empty-handed. It has to be said that Germany made no attempt at horse-trading with Japan over Tsingtao. Since Japan in its "advice" was asking for unconditional surrender, there was perhaps little room for manoeuvre. Germany was hardly in the mood to negotiate on such a basis. But it does not seem even to have tried. It would appear that Germany was preoccupied with central issues in Europe and uninterested in peripheral issues elsewhere in the world. But remarkably little seems to have been done to prevent an all-out invasion by Japan of Germany's leased territory in China.

Japan made the official declaration of war by a rescript issued in the Emperor's name:

> the action of Germany has at length compelled Great Britain, Our Ally, to open hostilities against that country, and Germany is, at Kiaochow, its leased territory in China, busy with warlike preparations, while its armed vessels cruising the seas of Eastern Asia are threatening Our commerce and that of Our Ally. The peace of the Far East is thus in jeopardy. Accordingly Our Government and that of His Britannic Majesty, after a full and frank communication with each

other, have agreed to take such measures as may be necessary for the protection of the general interests contemplated in the Agreement of Alliance, and We, on Our part, being desirous to attain that object by peaceful means, have commanded Our Government, to offer, with sincerity, an advice to the Imperial German Government.[22]

The terms of the imperial proclamation make clear the ambiguous nature of Japan's involvement. While it had declared war against Germany on the occasion of the outbreak in Europe, Japan's concern was purely with the East Asian and Pacific aspects of the war, not with issues connected with European aspects of the conflict. It was not unexpected, therefore, that Japan should respond negatively to requests to send troops either for the western or the eastern fronts in Europe.

The references to the "general interests contemplated in the Agreement of Alliance" were included partly as justification for Japan's action. It was as though the Japanese Cabinet would derive extra support for its action if the alliance were dragged in. It did not say that the terms of the *casus belli* under the alliance, namely a German attack on Weihaiwei or Hong Kong, were likely to apply. Nor were the terms in which the alliance was mentioned objectionable to London.

What the Japanese call the German–Japanese war had begun. The blockade of Tsingtao port began without delay on 24 August. At the opening of the Diet on 4 September, a war budget was presented which took account of Japan's new strategic situation.

The Austro-Hungarian ambassador left Japan on 27 August, as did ambassador Sato Aimaro from Vienna. Diplomatic ties were therefore broken, though the two parties did not declare war on each other. It is uncertain whether they were technically at war, though many, such as Winston Churchill in Britain, considered them to be at war. But it was not until later that Japan, in view of the anomalies that arose, eventually decided to bring the issue to the boil by treating Austro-Hungary as an enemy state on 19 January 1917.[23]

## Domestic aspects

It is easier to describe the preliminary diplomatic stages of Japan's decision to go to war than the domestic background. Certainly there had been wide-ranging consultations, taking in the Emperor, the full Cabinet, the Elder Statesmen and the Council for Defence. Among the Elder Statesmen, there was some scepticism from the most senior, General Yamagata. He was politically and personally hostile to Kato and was probably by 1914 less committed to the British alliance than he had earlier been. It cannot be said that he was overruled at the meetings; he must not have raised his voice too strongly. His daughter was in Berlin, married to Baron Funakoshi, who did not like the way matters were handled with Germany; and this may have affected Yamagata in the later months of 1914. On the other hand, *Genro* Inoue Kaoru, who had not been present at some of the meetings, clearly regarded it as a moment of great opportunity. As one Japanese scholar concludes:

> Certainly the Japanese political leaders' diplomacy of entering the war was based on the opportunism of the "one chance in a thousand years" which had opened up with the absence of the European powers who were preoccupied with the war there.[24]

Among the army, there was remarkable silence, neither interposing difficulties nor being wildly enthusiastic for the struggle. It must have been hard for the upper echelons of the army, who had mainly been trained in Germany, to contemplate a European war with that country. Moreover, they were perhaps self-conscious that the standard of their army had since 1905 fallen behind that of European armies. At the same time, the possibility of acquiring the German base at Tsingtao must have been a considerable temptation which weighed heavily on the other side. By contrast, the navy seems to have been relatively enthusiastic over seeing action both at Tsingtao and in the Pacific area. As Professor Ikeda writes:

> There is no disputing the fact that, within naval circles (*Kaigunbu*) generally, pro-British sentiments were strong in contrast to the Germanophil attitudes of the army; and those who positively welcomed entry into the war with a

view to saying thank you for the favourable assistance given
by the Royal Navy during the Russo-Japanese war were very
numerous. At the same time, the activities of the Japanese
fleet in the war were to save the navy which had lost the
confidence of the people through the Siemens affair and to
revive the plans for an 8–8 fleet which were being held in
abeyance for the time being.[25]

It does not appear that Foreign Minister Kato was being dragged
along by the navy. On the contrary, there is evidence to suggest that
Kato (at the age of 54) was in the saddle and was leading the elderly
Prime Minister, Count Okuma (aged 76). Also, the sheer advantages
of a modest intervention were so obvious to those outside military
circles that there was remarkably little opposition. Press opinion, still
supportive at this stage of the Okuma Cabinet, then in its honeymoon period, was generally in favour of the war. The sole exception
was the *Toyo Keizai Shimpo*, which wanted Japan to remain at peace.
Public opinion (in so far as it can be assessed) appears to have been
similarly enthusiastic.

What were the motives behind Japan's decision? At the outset it
should be made clear that the Balkan issues and Germany's violation
of Belgium's neutrality were of little concern. We should consider
three factors which may have affected Japan's decision-making: the
China factor; the German factor; and the alliance factor.

### The China factor

It is commonly argued in Western books that Japan saw that the outbreak of war in Europe would give it a free hand in China and that it
would be of advantage to it to become a belligerent from the start
and capture the German-leased territory of Tsingtao. The rhetoric of
the Japanese ran against this. They had no territorial ambitions, they
argued. Obviously there is considerable retrospective support for the
contrary view from the Twenty-one Demands which were presented
to China in January 1915. But this is not necessarily reliable evidence. We know that, as soon as the declaration of war had been issued, the Japanese minister to China reported that this would offer a
good occasion to clear up outstanding disagreements with the Chi-
nese; and Kato responded that it was still premature. It was only fol-

lowed up systematically later in the year. It could be that the possibility of sorting out China issues followed the declaration of war. None the less there is a strong presumption that China was much in the thoughts of the decision-makers. As Kato had confessed to Grey during his last months as ambassador in London in 1913, this was a time of great opportunity in China.[26]

## The German factor

Both in the ultimatum and in the Imperial Proclamation of War, Japan had used a phrase about giving sincere advice to Germany. This was similar to, but not identical with, the phraseology used by Germany to Japan in May 1895, at the time of the Dreibund crisis. One should not infer that the motive for Japan's actions and intentions in 1914 was merely some sort of belated revenge for the insult done to that country twenty years earlier. But the choice of language used suggests that it was more than a diplomatic coincidence. There was much anti-German feeling among Japanese and in the Okuma Cabinet; and they may have nursed this grievance and unearthed it in 1914 to Germany's detriment. The language used was widely discussed in the newspapers of the day, both Japanese and foreign. It has also been emphasized by a later generation of historians.[27]

It has to be said that the Germans who claimed that they had been stabbed in the back by Japan did not handle the Japanese very sensitively during the crisis leading up to the declaration of war. The abusive language used by Graf von Rex has already been mentioned. But Count von Dernburg, in a public speech in Washington, made a point of condemning Britain for "seeking help from yellow men". It rather appeared as if Germany was reverting to the language of the "Yellow Peril" which had so outraged Japan in the 1900s.[28] There was therefore resentment against Germany, which may explain the choice of words and the style of the approach, but that was hardly enough to persuade Japan to become a belligerent against Germany if its national self-interest did not point so strongly in that direction.

## The Alliance factor

In 1914 all countries sought to explain and justify their participation in the war in terms of their political commitments. We should distinguish here between the actual diplomacy and the way that the Japanese politicians depicted these actions to their electorates and media. In the actual diplomacy, I do not find anything difficult about Kato's approach. He never claimed that Japan was required to enter the war under the specific terms of the alliance (Article II of the 1911 agreement). His claim was to support Britain under the *spirit* rather than the letter, of the alliance. The problem was complicated by Britain's request for assistance in dealing with armed merchantmen, and the subsequent withdrawal of that request. But Japan had its own agenda; and Sir Edward Grey evidently did not like the idea of Japan entering the war to attain its own objectives and blaming it on the alliance. Kato's insistence on including references to the alliance in any published documents indicated that he wanted to present the issue to his electorate as favourably as possible and to meet objections by stressing Japan's obligations under the British alliance. It has to be remembered that Japan had had recent experience of a punishing war and that, in so far as it envisaged a land campaign in China, it was to be directed against a German fortress and was a daunting task. Japan could well have adopted the posture that Britain had adopted towards its ally during the Russo-Japanese war in 1904, and maintained an attitude of benevolent neutrality.

All three of these factors have some substance and contributed something to Japan's decision for war. But there were also issues driving Japan in the other direction. Though there was a reasonable presumption that the European countries would leave the east because of the European war, there was no guarantee that the United States would act in a similar way. The Wilson administration had shown itself to be protective of China and suspicious of the Anglo-Japanese alliance; and the Japanophobe press in the United States was showing itself hostile to any idea that Japan would have a free hand in East Asia by virtue of declaring itself a belligerent. This restraint on Japan's actions was lessened when Washington declared on 21 August:

> [The US] notes with satisfaction that Japan, in demanding the surrender by Germany of the entire Leased Territory of Kiaochow, does so with the purpose of restoring that territory to China . . . Should disturbances in the interior of China seem to the Japanese Government to require meas-

ures to be taken by Japan or other Powers to restore order, the Imperial Japanese Government no doubt desire to consult with the American Government before deciding on a course of action [in accordance with the Root–Takahira pact of 1908].[29]

This communication was enough to indicate to Japan that, while Washington did not favour Japan's entry, it was not prepared to get involved.

Thus Japan had entered the war with Germany with vigilance and a complex balance sheet of national advantage. Vigilance was understandable. Like all their contemporaries, the professionals in Japan's army and navy could hardly predict the length of the war or the likely victor. There were voices for caution in both services; but those who saw Japan's entry into the war as a positive advantage to Japan as a nation were in the majority and won the day.[30]

Japan, where the decision had to be made after the war in Europe was already under way, was not concerned with preventing the spread of war to the east. Indeed, its entry ensured that the war *would* extend to East Asia and the Pacific. It had the consequence of drawing Japan into the wartime grand alliance, and specifically into the *Entente*, at the cost of extending the range of hostilities to China and the Pacific.

It has also to be said that there were substantial disagreements within the British leadership about how to deal with the Japanese. Since the alliance was largely a naval alliance, it was natural to expect that the Admiralty should hold out high hopes of Japanese naval assistance. Grey and the Foreign Office, who were on the receiving end of much opposition from other powers suspicious of Japan's involvement, had to be more guarded. When Grey sent his memorandum of 11 August to Japan, he sent copies to the Cabinet, and Winston Churchill lost no time in commenting:

I think you are chilling to these people. I can't see any halfway house myself between having them in and keeping them out. If they are to come in, they may as well be welcomed as comrades. This last telegram is almost hostile. I am afraid I do not understand what is in yr mind on this aspect – tho I followed it so closely till today . . . The telegram gives me a shiver. We are all in this together & I only wish to give the fullest effect & support to your main policy. But I am altogether perplexed by the line opened up by these Japanese interchanges . . . You may easily give mortal offence – wh will not be forgiven – we are not safe yet – by a long chalk. The storm has yet to burst.[31]

Grey replied with an expletive, though (typically) he followed it up with a gentlemanly apology that he "was being awfully knotted at the time and felt I must swear". Churchill wrote independently to Admiral Yashiro on 13 August.

After Japan's entry to the war, Churchill was still beating the same drum: "It would seem only fitting", he wrote on 29 August, "that the Japanese Govt should be sounded as to their readiness to send a battleship squadron to co-operate with the allied powers in the Meditn or elsewhere. The influence & value of this powerful aid could not be over-rated. It would steady & encourage Italy, & would bring nearer the situation so greatly desired of our being able to obtain command of the Baltic. There is reason to believe that the Japanese would take such an invitation as a compliment."[32] One has the feeling that the naval attaché's staff at the London embassy had been making optimistic noises about the Japanese navy's enthusiasm for playing a large rôle in the war on a global basis. Churchill's enthusiasm was understood; but other leaders were all too well aware of the risks entailed. Thus Lord Esher, a member of the Committee of Imperial Defence, mentioned only one consideration:

[The Japanese] will take anything else that they can get hold of. This would mean Samoa, and possibly other islands, that have already been offered to the Dominions. If Japan were to seize these places, it would probably lead to very serious trouble with the Colonies.[33]

If Britain's leaders differed widely over the future shape of the war, so too did the Japanese. They were, however, united in one respect: they both saw it as likely to be a short war. While the countries of Europe held that the war would be over by Christmas, the Japanese leaders saw it as a limited war: limited in time and limited in range. The campaign against Tsingtao, while it was assumed that it would be strategically and diplomatically difficult, was not likely to be protracted; and, because of the early mobilization of the fleet, the campaigns against the German Pacific squadron and the German Pacific islands were quickly under way. Because of the expectation of a speedy conclusion, swift participation in the action was essential for Japan. This was not merely desirable on strategic grounds but also necessary to bolster a shaky ministry.

## Notes

(Japanese names throughout this paper are rendered with the family name first and the personal given name following.)

I tender my thanks for help with this chapter to Professor Ian Gow of Sheffield University and Mr Kaneko Yuzuru of the National Institute for Defence Studies, Tokyo, two experts in the field.

1. The main sources used in this chapter were *Nihon Gaiko Bunsho*, Taisho 3-nen, vol. 3 (Tokyo, 1966) (hereafter cited as *NGBT*); and *British documents on foreign affairs*, part I, series E, Asia, vol. 10 (Bethesda, Maryland, 1989) (hereafter cited as *BDOFA*). There are two biographies fundamental to the story of Japan's entry into the war, those of the Foreign Minister: Ito Masanori, *Kato Takaaki*, 2 vols (Tokyo, 1929); and the ambassador to London, Inoue Katsunosuke, whose brief biography (Koshaku Inoue Katsunosuke kun ryakuden) is found in *Segai Inoue-ko den*, vol. 5 (Tokyo, 1934). The secondary literature includes War Ministry, *Nichi-doku Senshi*, 3 vols (Tokyo, 1918); Kajima Morinosuke, *Nihon Gaikoshi*, vol. 10 (Tokyo, 1971) dealing with the First World War; Hora Tomio, *Dai-1 Sekai Taisen* (Tokyo, 1966); Muneta Hiroshi, *Heitai Nihonshi: Dai-1 Sekai Taisen* (Tokyo, 1975); Ikeda Kiyoshi, *Nihon no Kaigun*, 2 vols (Toyko, 1987). I. H. Nish, *Alliance in decline* (London, 1972) devotes ch. 7 to this subject.
2. J. B. Crowley, in J. W. Morley, *Japan's foreign policy, 1868–1941* (New York, 1968), pp. 21–30.
3. I. H. Nish, "Japan, 1914–18", in *Military effectiveness,* vol. 1, *First World War,* A. R. Millett & W. Murray (eds) (Boston, 1988), pp. 229–48; *BDOFA*, vol. 10, docs 86–7.
4. *BDOFA*, vol. 10, docs 94–8; 130–2.
5. Ikeda, *Kaigun*, vol. II, pp. 37ff; and *BDOFA*, vol. 10, docs 102–21 *passim*.
6. Ikeda, *Kaigun*, vol. II, p. 41.
7. *NGBT*, vol. 3, pp. 1–32.
8. *BDOFA*, vol. 10, doc. 148.

9. *NGBT*, vol. 3, no. 91.
10. *NGBT*, vol. 3, no. 95.
11. *Nichi-Doku Senso*, vol. 1.
12. *NGBT*, vol. 3, no. 104.
13. *Kato*, vol. II, p. 78.
14. Ibid., pp. 78–81.
15. *Segai Inoue ko den*, vol. 5, pp. 366–71.
16. *NGBT*, vol. 3, no. 108.
17. Ibid., no. 112; Kajima, *Nihon Gaikoshi*, vol. 10, pp. 16–20.
18. *NGBT*, vol. 3, no. 114.
19. Ibid., no. 154.
20. Ibid., no. 206.
21. Ibid., no. 196.
22. Ibid., no. 240.
23. Kajima, *Nihon Gaikoshi*, vol. 10, pp. 29–30.
24. Ikeda, *Kaigun*, vol. II, p. 43.
25. Ibid.
26. Hioki to Kato, 26 and 29 August 1914, in *NGBT*, vol. 3, nos 562–3; Nish, *Alliance in decline*, pp. 88–91; *Kato*, vol. II, pp. 137ff.
27. For example, F. S. G. Piggott, *Broken thread* (Aldershot, 1950), p. 88.
28. Kajima, *Nihon Gaikoshi*, vol. 10, pp. 20–23.
29. *NGBT*, vol. 3, no. 228.
30. The best accounts of discordant views within the army and navy establishments are to be found in Hirama Yoichi, "Dai 1-ji sekai taisen e no sanka to kaigun", *Gunji Shigaku* 22, 1986, pp. 27–36; and Nagaoka Shinjiro, "Oshu taisen sanka mondai", *Kokusai Seiji* (1958), pp. 26–37.
31. Churchill to Grey, 11 August 1914, in M. Gilbert, *W. S. Churchill*, Companion vol. 3, part I (London, 1972), p. 30.
32. Churchill to Grey, 29 August 1914, ibid., p. 65.
33. Diary of Lord Esher, 11 August 1914, ibid., p. 31.

# Chapter Nine
# *Ottoman Empire*

F. A. K. Yasamee

## I

The importance of the Ottoman Empire's decision to enter the First World War on the side of the Central Powers has not been underestimated. Lloyd George and Ludendorff were at one in claiming that it enabled Germany to prolong her military struggle with the Entente Powers by two years.[1] For the Central Powers, the Ottoman war was a massive diversion, achieved at little cost to themselves, which forced the Entente to squander considerable resources which might otherwise have been deployed in the crucial European theatre. As important, it cut Russia's lifeline from the Black Sea into the Mediterranean, making a significant, if unquantifiable, contribution to the collapse of the Tsarist Empire in 1917. And, of course, it also led, in the end, to the destruction of the Ottoman Empire, and to the creation of a new political order in the Middle East.

For all its importance, the Ottoman decision for war has not so far been fully explained, and conceivably may never be. The problem is lack of evidence. The archives of the Ottoman government have yielded little to historians, which is not surprising, for other sources indicate that the planning and execution of the Empire's decision for war were conducted outside official channels, with scant regard for the formalities of documentation. The archives of the Unionist Party, which controlled the Ottoman government in 1914, disappeared at the end of the war, and may have been destroyed. Nor have any significant private papers come to light, with the single exception of the

229

diary kept by Cavid Bey, the Finance Minister.[2] Some of the Empire's wartime leaders wrote memoirs, and some made statements to a post-war parliamentary enquiry; but the evidence these sources offer is neither comprehensive nor always reliable.[3] Much useful information may be gleaned from the correspondence and writings of foreign diplomats and military officers who were active in the Ottoman Empire in 1914, and also from accounts left by lesser Ottoman officials, both civil and military; but in the nature of things, such testimony can shed no more than an indirect light upon the behaviour of the inner circle of Ottoman decision-makers.[4]

Not surprisingly, historical discussion of the Empire's decision for war has sometimes been controversial, and frequently confused. The decision has been presented as an "accident" or "stroke of fate", and as the product of "drift"; it has been blamed on the machinations of the Germans, or the Entente Powers.[5] Part of this confusion, it may be suggested, stems from a failure to acknowledge that the Empire took not one, but *two* decisions for war in 1914. The first decision was taken in July, but not implemented; the second was taken in October, and led to the naval attack on Russia which provoked the Entente Powers into declaring war on the Ottoman Empire in November. The two decisions envisaged different kinds of war. The first envisaged an essentially Balkan war, to be fought as an adjunct to the larger European war between the Great Powers; the second envisaged a direct assault upon the Entente Powers, on the widest possible geographical scale. Both decisions were taken in conspiratorial fashion, by small groups within the Ottoman government, acting behind the backs of their colleagues, and seeking to create *faits accomplis*. Behind the two conspiracies lay a protracted power struggle within the Ottoman leadership. The mechanics of this power struggle seem reasonably clear. Much less clear are the details of the conflicting foreign policy agendas, and also of the personal ambitions and rivalries, which drove the struggle; it is in these respects, chiefly, that the Ottoman decisions for war remain something of a mystery.

## II

As obscure as the Ottoman Empire's decisions for war is the background from which they sprang. The nature of the Ottoman government in 1914, and of that government's foreign policy, remain imperfectly understood. None the less, some attempt must be made to consider these issues, in however conjectural a fashion, if the decisions for war are to be placed in an explanatory context, and treated as more than strokes of fate or *actes gratuits*.

In theory, the Ottoman Empire was a constitutional monarchy, in which the reigning Sultan-Caliph and his ministers were controlled by an elected parliament. In reality, it was a one-party state, controlled by the party (or "committee") of Union and Progress. The Unionists had played a leading rôle in Ottoman politics since the constitutional revolution of 1908, but not until January 1913 did they achieve supreme and exclusive power, as the result of a military *putsch*. Thereafter they had consolidated their authority, suppressing all organized opposition, installing a Unionist Cabinet (with minor portfolios for token independents), placing their own men in key positions in the armed forces and civil administration, and securing the election of a packed Parliament with an overwhelming Unionist majority. The regime's real power bases were the officer corps of the army, and the Unionist organization, a network of branches and committees spread across the Empire, and incorporating army officers, civil officials, members of the professions, and provincial men of property and influence. The regime's programme was defined by an assertive Turkish nationalism, not devoid of Pan-Turanian and Pan-Islamic elements; by ambitious hopes of modernization, particularly in the military and economic fields; and by a loose anti-imperialism expressed in a determination to assert the Empire's sovereign independence and equality in the face of the European Great Powers.[6]

Within this regime, ultimate authority lay neither with the Cabinet, nor with the Unionist Party's central committee, but with an "inner circle" of some half-dozen Unionist bosses, each of whom held high governmental office, and each of whom possessed a significant personal following within the officer corps or the party organization. Talat Bey, the Interior Minister, was generally considered to be *primus inter pares*, chiefly on account of his influence within the party organization; Halil Bey, the president of the lower house of Parliament, had influence among Unionist MPs; Cavid Bey, the Finance Minister, possessed a financial expertise that rendered him indispensable to a regime which harboured considerable economic ambitions, and which depended upon foreign loans to achieve them;

Enver Paşa and Cemal Bey, respectively Minister of War and Minister of the Navy, had followings in the all-important officer corps. The odd man out was Said Halim Paşa, the Egyptian prince who presided over the Cabinet as Grand Vizier, and also held the office of Foreign Minister: though nobody's puppet, he lacked a strong personal following, and in Unionist terms was something of a lightweight.[7] The inner circle reserved all major issues of policy for itself, frequently ignoring the formal Cabinet altogether. Its own inner processes of consultation and decision-making were highly informal – an affair of private meetings, *ad hoc* decisions, and verbal understandings. Such a system gave great scope for individual initiative, and also for mutual intrigue; not surprisingly, outside observers found the processes of Ottoman government baffling.[8]

The rôles of the Minister of War and Minister of the Navy call for particular comment. The Unionists' reliance upon military backing to achieve supreme power inevitably had increased the influence of the Unionists' own "military wing", whose most prominent spokesmen were Enver Paşa and Cemal Bey. Both were energetic and ambitious army officers, and both had risen fast. A mere lieutenant-colonel in 1913, Enver was by 1914 – at the age of 34 – a major-general and Minister of War, and had married into the Imperial family. As War Minister, he had quickly tightened his personal grip on the army, installing himself as Chief of Staff, conducting a purge of senior ranks, sidelining rivals, and promoting his own partisans. He had also made astute use of the arrival of a German military mission, headed by General Liman von Sanders. The mission's task was to reform the Ottoman army, and in order to ensure the success of the reforms, its members were installed in key positions of operational command, thereby incidentally safeguarding Enver against the emergence of Ottoman rivals. Some mistakenly believed that this placed the Ottoman army under German control; the truth was that it reinforced Enver's personal control.[9] The one potential threat to Enver's position came from Cemal, who had similarly risen from lieutenant-colonel to major-general, who similarly enjoyed a following in the officer corps, and who served as the natural focus for officers who resented Enver's swift rise, and his appointment of Germans to key commands.[10]

The Unionists had originally entertained considerable foreign policy ambitions. After 1908, they had set out to develop an army and navy strong enough to hold all the Balkan states in check, and also strong enough to increase the Empire's diplomatic standing with the European Great Powers. They had made plain their intention of reducing the Powers' rights of interference in the Empire's internal affairs. In particular, they were anxious to remove the capitulations – fiscal, judicial and economic privileges traditionally enjoyed by the Powers' subjects within the Empire – seeing in these privileges not only an affront to national independence, but also a major obstacle to the Empire's economic and industrial development. Ultimately, they hoped to revive the Empire, if not as a Great Power, at least as a major regional power in the Near and Middle East, capable of exercising influence beyond its own borders, and of bargaining with the Great Powers on terms approaching equality. All these ambitions were thrown into question by the catastrophic defeat the Empire suffered in the First Balkan War in 1912, a defeat whose consequences had been no more than partially assuaged by the recovery of Eastern Thrace in the Second Balkan War in 1913.[11] Not only had the Empire lost the bulk of its European territories. Its new frontiers were vulnerable to Bulgaria and to Greece. Its political and military prestige had been shattered, increasing its traditional vulnerability to the European Great Powers, and encouraging them to think in terms of eventual partition. Above all, the Empire had been left vulnerable to Russia, a Power believed to have designs upon the Straits and the Ottoman capital, and strongly suspected of harbouring designs upon eastern Anatolia. The victories gained by Serbia and Montenegro in the two Balkan Wars had strengthened Russia's regional influence, and weakened that of her traditional rival, Austria-Hungary: by 1914, there were clear signs that Romania was abandoning her long-standing reliance upon Vienna, and speculation that Russia might embrace all the Balkan states within a new Balkan League, which the Ottoman Empire itself would have little option but to join. In Asia, too, Russia was advancing: since 1909 her forces had been in effective occupation of much of northern Iran, including regions bordering on the Ottoman Empire, and since early 1913 Russia had been pressing openly for a privileged voice in the affairs of the Armenian-inhabited regions of eastern Anatolia.

All available evidence suggests that the Unionist leadership's response to these dangers was hesitant and divided. One view, espoused by Said Halim, and to some degree by Talat, argued that the

Empire was too weak to stand alone, and must seek the protection of an alliance with one of the Great Power blocs; Said Halim and Talat clearly preferred an arrangement with the Triple Alliance, but were prepared, if necessary, to accept an accommodation with the Triple Entente. Their view was strongly opposed by Cavid, who argued that security lay in avoiding involvement in the Powers' mutual rivalries: the safest course, in his view, was to settle outstanding disputes with each of the Powers, and thus achieve a period of tranquillity abroad, which would enable the Empire to concentrate upon development at home, particularly in the economic sphere. Finally, there was a view which may be termed "revisionist", which held that the external situation resulting from the Balkan Wars was so fundamentally threatening that it must be overthrown by force, through a third Balkan war, whose consequence, it was foreseen, might well be a European or world war, in which the Empire's interests would lie on the side of a victory for Germany and Austria-Hungary over Russia. The principal exponent of the revisionist view was Enver.

During the ten months which elapsed between the end of the Second Balkan War and the outbreak of the First World War, the Unionist leadership pursued all three of these policies, more or less simultaneously. Agreements for the resolution of outstanding disputes with the various Powers were pursued, and concluded with Britain, France and Russia.[12] Meanwhile, however, the revisionists set out to woo Bulgaria, the state which had been defeated in the Second Balkan War, and which possessed similarly revisionist ambitions: during the autumn of 1913, the Empire pursued a military alliance with Bulgaria, with a view to preparing for a third Balkan war. It did not conceal the fact that its own ambitions included the recovery of Western Thrace, Bulgaria's one substantial gain from the wars of 1912–13; none the less, it indicated that it would assist Bulgaria in gaining compensation in Macedonia, at the expense of Greece and Serbia.[13] At the same time, working through party and army channels, the revisionists set out to develop a subversive network in Greek and Serbian Macedonia, and also in the newly-established Albanian state.[14] The revisionists also placed their faith in an early revival of the Empire's military strength. As noted, a much-strengthened German military mission was brought in at the beginning of 1914, and considerable hopes were placed on the development of the navy, where a British naval mission had been active since 1908, and which had two large battleships, the *Sultan Osman* and the *Reşadiye*, being built in British yards.[15]

By early 1914, however, the revisionists' plans appeared to be running out of steam. The Bulgarians proved evasive on the subject of an alliance, prompting fears that they might turn to the Entente.[16] More important, Germany was disappointingly reluctant to support the notion of an Ottoman alliance with Bulgaria, and indicated that the Empire would do better to reach an understanding with Greece. Since the Balkan Wars, the Germans had grown sceptical of the Empire's value as a potential military ally, and did not conceal their scepticism.[17] The consequence was a seeming tilt in Ottoman policy towards the Entente Powers, facilitated by an agreement with Russia, concluded in February 1914, on the subject of reforms in eastern Anatolia, and by the conclusion of a French loan for 26 million francs in April. In the following month, Talat paid a well-publicized visit to the Tsar at Livadia and, in conversation with Sazonov, touched on the possibility of a Russo-Ottoman alliance; in June, Cemal paid a similar visit to France.[18]

These overtures to the Entente, the seriousness of which remains difficult to assess, took place against the background of an increasingly bitter dispute with Greece over the possession of certain Aegean islands off the western coast of Anatolia.[19] The islands had been occupied by Greece during the First Balkan War, but their ultimate ownership had been left to the arbitration of the Great Powers. In February 1914 the Powers ruled in favour of Greece, a decision which the Ottoman government refused to accept. Its refusal was prompted partly by considerations of domestic prestige, but also by security concerns: if controlled by Greece, it was feared, the islands would serve as a base for the subversion of the Greek population of the western Anatolian seaboard. The Ottoman government began pressing Greece for an agreement for an exchange of populations. The Germans offered to mediate, and expressed support for an Ottoman–Greek alliance; the Romanians and the Serbs also offered their good offices. By June, however, the dispute had taken a sharp turn for the worse, as the Unionists, working through party rather than governmental channels, embarked upon an alternative solution of their security problem, by expelling the Greek population of the coastal regions. Greece responded with an ultimatum: war was widely anticipated.

## III

The Ottoman government reacted to the Sarajevo assassination with outward calm, and for the first half of the ensuing "July crisis" it maintained a low profile. Its more pressing preoccupation appeared to be the state of its relations with Greece. An attempted mediation by a British journalist had produced no progress towards a solution of the Aegean islands dispute, but it had helped to reduce tension: there was serious discussion of a proposal that the Grand Vizier and the Greek Prime Minister, Venizelos, should arrange a personal meeting somewhere in Europe, and even some suggestion that the Empire might offer Greece a formal alliance, should a satisfactory settlement of the islands question be achieved.[20] Not until the middle of the month did Ottoman policy change. Between 19 and 22 July, the Grand Vizier, Enver and Talat made a series of approaches to the Bulgarian minister, Toshev, the Austro-Hungarian ambassador, Pallavicini, and the German ambassador, Wangenheim, expressing their desire to conclude an alliance with Bulgaria, under the auspices of the Triple Alliance; if refused, they warned, the Empire would conclude an alliance with Greece, under the patronage of the Triple Entente.[21] Clearly, these overtures were an attempt to revive the revisionist programme of preparation for an early Balkan war, and were presumably prompted by the following considerations: a growing realization that the Austro-Serbian crisis might end in a war which would afford an opportunity to open other Balkan questions; the news that Bulgaria had just concluded a large loan in Germany, thus tying her more closely to the Triple Alliance; and the knowledge that the *Sultan Osman* would be delivered by its British builders in early August, thus enabling the Empire to achieve naval supremacy over Greece in the Aegean, and, potentially, a similar supremacy over Russia in the Black Sea.[22]

The initial responses from Wangenheim and Pallavicini were discouraging, though the Bulgarians did indicate that, in the event of an Austro-Serbian war, they would consult with the Empire before taking any military action.[23] On 24 July, however, the German government decided that with a major Balkan crisis in prospect it could not risk driving the Empire into the arms of the Entente.[24] This sudden change of attitude enabled the Grand Vizier to develop a proposal for an offensive–defensive alliance between the Empire and Ger-

236

many, directed against Russia: he submitted the proposal to Wangenheim on 28 July, the day Austria-Hungary declared war on Serbia.[25] The ensuing negotiations, like the overtures which had preceded them, were conducted in the strictest secrecy. On the Ottoman side, only Said Halim, Enver, Talat and Halil knew: the Cabinet was at no stage informed, and nor, in view of their likely opposition, were Cemal and Cavid.[26] The Germans at once indicated that they would wish the Empire to intervene on their side should they become involved in a war with Russia as a result of the current Austro-Serbian conflict; that the German military mission would remain in the Empire in the event of war, though it should then exercise actual command over the Ottoman army; that Germany would guarantee the Empire's territorial integrity against Russia; and that the alliance should be valid only for the duration of the present Austro-Serbian conflict, and of any international complications which might arise from it.[27] The Grand Vizier objected that this last provision would expose the Empire to a future revenge attack by Russia, and proposed that the alliance should remain valid until 1918. The Germans accepted this point, and also agreed that their military mission should exercise "an effective influence", rather than actual command, over the direction of the Ottoman army. On this basis, final agreement was reached on 1 August, the day Germany declared war upon Russia, thus entailing the *casus foederis* for the Empire.[28] The agreement was embodied in a secret treaty of alliance, signed by Said Halim and Wangenheim the next day; the Ottoman government immediately prorogued Parliament, imposed martial law, and decreed a general mobilization.[29]

## IV

The alliance of 2 August was a political coup of the first order: concluded with the knowledge of no more than four members of the Unionist inner circle, it formally committed the Empire to join Germany in the war which had been launched against Russia one day previously. However, the alliance's Ottoman authors had made two fundamental miscalculations: they had assumed that the Central Powers would win the war in short order, and they had assumed that the Bulgarians, and perhaps the Romanians, would fight alongside the Central Powers. The first of these miscalculations did not become apparent until September, following the Central Powers' reverses in Galicia and at the Marne; the second, however, became apparent almost immediately. Although Wangenheim and Pallavicini had indicated that the Central Powers would conclude an alliance with Bulgaria, and had also encouraged a direct Ottoman–Bulgarian understanding, their superiors in Berlin and Vienna had proceeded more cautiously, and not until the outbreak of war did they take up the question of a Bulgarian alliance as a matter of urgency. The Bulgarians, however, proved wary, expressing concern lest intervention against Serbia expose them to invasion by Romania, and to naval attack by Russia. They also expressed concern lest the Ottoman government demand passage for its forces through Western Thrace, in order to attack Greece.[30] As the extent of Bulgaria's hesitations grew obvious, doubts and dissensions began to emerge within the Ottoman leadership, to a point where the Empire's decision for war was thrown into question.

From the start, the authors of the German alliance took somewhat different views of the war to which they had committed themselves. The Grand Vizier assumed that the Empire would fight a Balkan War, in partnership with Bulgaria, against Serbia and Greece, the prizes bring the Aegean islands and Western Thrace, with Bulgaria being compensated in Macedonia. He was reluctant to try military conclusions with the Russians, and apprehensive lest they launch a pre-emptive attack upon the Straits and the capital; for this reason, he preferred to postpone the opening of hostilities until the Central Powers were within sight of final victory. He viewed the German alliance as, primarily, a guarantee of the Empire's post-war security: hence his insistence that the alliance should run until 1918.[31] On 3 August he warned Wangenheim not to expect an immediate declaration of war: the Empire must first complete its mobilization, take delivery of the *Sultan Osman*, and conclude an alliance with Bulgaria. On the same day, Said Halim informed the Entente Powers that the Empire's policy was armed neutrality.[32]

In contrast, Enver Paşa was anxious to enter the war as soon as was practically possible, and willing to attack Russia directly. He was convinced that the Central Powers would win quickly, and anxious to claim a share of the spoils. Furthermore, he envisaged something more than a Balkan war: he also wished to fight a "Pan-Turanian" war, with the aim of ejecting Russia from the Caucasus, and perhaps from territories beyond. Even so, Enver's military plans assumed that the Empire would make its principal effort in the Balkan peninsula, where he hoped to join forces with the Bulgarians and the Romanians, in an offensive against Russia's southern flank, or, alternatively, to join Bulgaria in an attack upon Serbia and Greece; in the Caucasus, he proposed to rely upon the methods of revolutionary warfare, by stimulating uprisings among the Muslim population. He considered that it would take a full month to mobilize sufficient forces for a trans-Balkan offensive against Russia, and a further month to mobilize forces for an offensive against Greece. He was also anxious that the Germans should make good the armed forces' acute shortages of munitions and other supplies.[33]

Already, however, Enver had placed the Empire's public neutrality at risk, for even before the treaty of 2 August was signed, he had invited Germany to send warships to the Straits – a clear violation of the international rule which forbade neutrals to harbour the warships of belligerents. He subsequently extended the invitation to Austria-Hungary as well. Enver's reasoning was straightforward: the achievement of naval supremacy in the Black Sea was vital to the success of land operations against Russia, and might also encourage Bulgaria and Romania to join the Central Powers. It is certain that the Grand Vizier knew of this invitation, though less certain that he approved of it; but it is unclear who else knew.[34] Austria-Hungary proved unable to comply, but on 3 August the German admiralty instructed Rear Admiral Souchon, the commander of their Mediterranean squadron, to proceed at once to the Dardanelles with his ships, the battle-cruiser *Goeben*, and the light cruiser *Breslau*.[35]

The Germans were increasingly anxious to secure an early Ottoman declaration of war. France entered the war on 3 August, and Britain a day later. The Germans feared that Britain's entry, in particular, might frighten the Ottoman government into permanent neutrality; but at the same time, they had hopes that the religious influence of the Ottoman Caliphate might be used to stimulate Muslim uprisings in Egypt and India, thus diverting British troops away from the vital European theatre.[36] This new suggestion of a "Pan-Islamic" war was at once endorsed by Enver, who had considerable faith in the possibilities of revolutionary warfare, and was already taking steps to organize Muslim risings in the Caucasus and Serbian Macedonia, through a newly-created department of the War Ministry, the Special Organization.[37] On 6 August he indicated that he was ready to organize uprisings in Egypt, Tripolitania, Tunis, Iran, Afghanistan and India. He also proposed to induce the Amir of Afghanistan to invade India, and asked the Germans to assist him in sending a military mission to Kabul.[38]

Enver's colleagues were more cautious. They faced the prospect of hostilities with Britain and France, as well as with Russia; Italy and Romania remained conspicuously neutral, despite their long-standing alliances with the Central Powers; and on 3 August the British government had sequestered the *Sultan Osman* and the *Reşadiye*, along with all other foreign warships being built in British yards, thereby depriving the Empire of its anticipated naval supremacy over Greece, and aggravating its vulnerability to Russia.[39] Above all, they remained anxious to know Bulgaria's intentions. The Grand Vizier had informed Toshev of the Empire's alliance with Germany and, together with Enver, had pressed him to open negotiations for an Ottoman–Bulgarian treaty of alliance, stressing that the Empire could do nothing without Bulgaria, and that active intervention in the war should be postponed until the "final liquidation". The Bulgarians, however, were manifestly reluctant to commit themselves – even to talks – and objected that intervention against Serbia or Greece would expose them to the risk of attack by Romania. The Grand Vizier took the point, and told Toshev that he would favour a tripartite understanding between the Empire, Bulgaria and Romania, but he stressed that he remained anxious for a direct Ottoman–Bulgarian understanding, irrespective of other combinations.[40] The Bulgarians, however, remained silent, prompting Said Halim to fear that they might be playing a double game, and waiting for the Empire to engage the Entente Powers directly, so that they might attack it in the rear. On 4 August, in consequence, he warned Wangenheim that the *Goeben* and the *Breslau* would not be admitted to the Straits until the Empire had concluded an alliance with Bulgaria.[41]

It had also become clear that there would be difficulties with Cemal and Cavid, the two members of the Unionist inner circle who had been excluded from the alliance negotiations with Germany. They had belatedly been informed of the German alliance on 2 August, and promptly raised strong objections. Cemal had threatened to resign; there is some suggestion that he may have had hopes of an alliance with the Entente Powers.[42] Cavid, a neutralist, had objected that the Germans might lose the war, that they could not protect the Empire against Russian attack, and that the alliance treaty promised no territorial or other gains.[43] The Grand Vizier and Talat conceded that the treaty might be revised, and on 4 August a supplementary programme was agreed: the Empire must not intervene in the war until Bulgaria had done so, and until Romania's neutrality was assured; the Empire's eastern frontiers must be extended to establish a link with the Muslims of the Caucasus, and its Balkan frontiers must be extended to Turkish-inhabited regions; the judicial and economic capitulations must be abolished, and Germany must pledge herself to secure the other Powers' assent to this at the war's end; Germany must not conclude peace until any Ottoman territories which might fall under enemy occupation in the course of the war had been evacuated; and the Empire must receive a share of any war indemnity.[44]

In the event, these terms were not presented to the Germans, and instead, Said Halim approached Wangenheim on 6 August with a more modestly-phrased programme: Germany was asked to assist in securing the abolition of the capitulations; to support the Empire's efforts to secure "the indispensable understandings" with Romania and Bulgaria, including an agreement with Bulgaria on the division of any territorial spoils in the Balkans; to secure the restitution of the Aegean islands, should Greece enter the war and be defeated; and to secure a frontier correction which would bring the Empire into contact with the Muslims of Russia. The provisions concerning the conclusion of peace and a future war indemnity were left as originally formulated. At the same time, the Grand Vizier indicated that the Empire would, after all, admit warships of the Central Powers to the Straits, though it would none the less maintain its formal neutrality.[45] To the Germans, this was the essential point: they were confident that the arrival of the *Goeben* and the *Breslau* would publicly discredit the Empire's pretensions to neutrality, and force it into the war. Not surprisingly, Wangenheim accepted the Grand Vizier's programme on the spot, an action immediately endorsed by his superiors in Berlin.[46]

The Germans' confidence was misplaced. Enver pressed Wangenheim to bring the *Goeben* and the *Breslau* to the Straits as soon as possible, and undertook to send them directly into the Black Sea; he also renewed his request for Austro-Hungarian ships, proposing that they be used to disrupt Russian troop transports in the Black Sea.[47] But his colleagues insisted that the Empire could not intervene in the war without Bulgaria. On 7 August the Bulgarian government finally agreed to discuss a treaty of friendship, and the Grand Vizier instructed Talat and Cemal to hold talks with Toshev. Cemal proposed a military convention, to provide for the passage of Ottoman forces through Western Thrace, and an agreement on the division of future territorial spoils; at the same time, however, he and Talat assured Toshev that they regarded their talks as a means of countering Germany's pressure for early intervention, and would wish to draw them out until the outcome of the war became clearer. They even suggested that the Empire might join the Entente, if the Central Powers looked like losing the war.[48]

The Grand Vizier had more ambitious plans. The Romanians had approached him with a proposal for a neutral Balkan bloc, to be formed by Romania, the Empire and Greece. Said Halim preferred a four-power bloc, to include Bulgaria; he also saw an opportunity to invoke Romania's mediation in the Aegean islands question, and invited Greece to open negotiations.[49] At the very least, these new diplomatic possibilities furnished Said Halim and his colleagues with further arguments for delay. On 9 August the leading Unionist members of the Cabinet met as a ministerial committee to formally consider "the form and degree of our observance" of the treaty with Germany, and took three major decisions. First, "the course of action to be followed as of now will consist of gaining time until the war situation becomes to some extent clear. The hastening of events will be avoided. The Germans will not be given to sense this." Second, "the door will be opened to talks with Rumania and Bulgaria, on the one hand, and with Greece, on the other. Until these talks achieve a definite result, there will be no material steps taken." Finally, approaches would be made to the Russian and French ambassadors, "in order to give the Entente Powers confidence in our neutrality".[50] That day the Grand Vizier gave Wangenheim a clear warning that the Empire intended to remain neutral for the time being, and to pursue the idea of a four-power Balkan bloc, which, he claimed, would isolate Serbia, and amount to a "new Balkan league" under the auspices of the Central Powers. However, he added that in order to safeguard the Empire's neutrality, it would be necessary to carry out a *pro forma* disarmament of the *Goeben* and the *Breslau* upon their arrival, and to transfer them to the Ottoman navy by means of a fictitious sale.[51]

The *Goeben* and the *Breslau* reached the Dardanelles late on the afternoon of 10 August. Acting on his own military authority, Enver had them admitted to the Straits. That evening, the inner circle met to consider the implications for the Empire's neutrality. Discussion was heated, with Cavid and Cemal accusing the Germans of seeking to force the Empire into hostilities against its will – evidence, it appears, that these two ministers were unaware of the Grand Vizier's previous dealings with Wangenheim. Wangenheim was summoned, but refused to consider disarming the cruisers, or sending them away, though by Cavid's account, he did agree to consider the possibility of a fictitious sale. In the event, it was decided to present the Germans with a *fait accompli*, and to announce the cruisers' purchase in the next day's newspapers.[52] The inevitable protests from the ambassadors of the Entente Powers were met with assurances that the Empire remained neutral, that the *Goeben* and the *Breslau* were now Ottoman property, and that their German crews would be removed as soon as suitable Ottoman replacements were found. The last two assurances were moonshine: no genuine purchase having taken place, the warships remained German, as did their crews. None the less, the Entente Powers were prepared to give the Empire the benefit of the doubt for the time being, though they warned that the cruisers must remain within the Straits. As a precaution, British warships took up watch outside the Dardanelles.[53]

Temporarily, at least, the crisis provoked by the arrival of the German warships had been surmounted, and the Ottoman leadership could revert to its strategy of procrastination, and negotiation with its Balkan neighbours. Wangenheim was warned that the *Goeben* and the *Breslau* must remain within the Straits until the Empire had concluded an alliance with Bulgaria, and Greece was invited to consider a new formula for the settlement of the Aegean islands dispute: the islands should be restored to the Ottoman Empire, but should be granted substantial administrative autonomy under a Christian governor-general.[54] But otherwise, the Empire's leaders were in some disarray. Enver accepted that Romania's attitude ruled out a trans-Balkan offensive against Russia, but remained determined to commit the Bulgarians against Serbia, and so free the Empire to attack Russia elsewhere.[55] Talat and Cemal were for delay, and for exploring the possibilities of understandings with the Balkan states: together with Toshev, they drafted a proposal for a defensive alliance between the Empire, Bulgaria and Romania.[56] The Grand Vizier preferred a four-power bloc, with Greece included, and suggested to Toshev that this might create opportunities for gains, "even without war": possibly he had territorial compensations in mind. He confidentially advised the Bulgarians not to attack Serbia, and hinted that the Empire might eventually demobilize.[57]

Said Halim could not carry his colleagues this far: only Cavid was ready immediately to advocate a policy of neutrality.[50] On 14 August it was agreed that Germany and Austria-Hungary should be told that the Empire would not intervene until Bulgaria did so, and until the Romanians offered some guarantees. It was decided to send Talat and Halil to Sofia and Bucharest for talks with the Bulgarian and Romanian governments; it was also decided to ask Greece to send a plenipotentiary to Bucharest, for separate talks on the islands question. Talat and Halil were instructed to explore four options. In the first instance, they were to persuade the Bulgarians to mobilize, and to "secure their action"; once this was achieved, the Greeks should be offered a defensive alliance, on condition of their acceptance of the Empire's latest proposal on the islands. In the event that this first option was not secured, however, the two Ottoman envoys were to seek a defensive alliance between the Empire, Romania and Bulgaria. The third option envisaged a four-power Balkan bloc, though not, as the Grand Vizier had proposed, one based upon neutrality. Instead, it proposed an offensive alliance, directed against the Entente Powers, between Greece, Bulgaria, Romania and the Empire, on the basis of an agreed revision of Balkan frontiers, with Greece securing the islands and a share of Serbian Macedonia, Bulgaria gaining a share of Serbian Macedonia, Romania gaining Bessarabia from Russia, and the Ottoman Empire recovering a portion of Western Thrace. This option, however, was not to be pursued unless the Germans or the Austrians were willing to support it. Finally, should all these options fail, the Greeks should be offered a defensive convention, in return for a settlement of the islands question on the Empire's latest terms. Talat and Halil left for Sofia next day.[58]

Germany and Austria-Hungary were asked to assist Talat and Halil. The Central Powers had already warned that they would accept no arrangements based upon neutrality, but agreed to support an understanding between the Empire, Bulgaria and Romania. The Germans had been disappointed by the Entente Powers' mild response to the arrival of the *Goeben* and the *Breslau*, and faced a further disappointment in Bulgaria, where King Ferdinand was refusing to sign a treaty of alliance with the Central Powers which his ministers had approved on 10 August. The proposed Ottoman–Bulgarian–Romanian arrangement, Wangenheim argued, would at least "hold Bulgaria firm". He also accepted that it was desirable that the Ottoman Empire should have some assurance as to Bulgaria's attitude, before it entered the war.[59] None the less, it was already clear that a failure at Sofia and Bucharest would not affect Germany's demand for early Ottoman intervention against the Entente. For the Germans, the possibility of Ottoman military action in the Balkans was a matter of secondary interest: their hopes were focused on a world-wide "Islamic movement" against the Entente Powers, and they were anxious that the Ottoman government should concentrate its efforts in this area.[60]

## V

The opening of talks with the Balkan states did at least give the Empire a temporary respite from German pressure. The Grand Vizier had little faith in the talks' success. Like Cavid, he now favoured a policy of strict neutrality, and claimed that the Germans had tricked him into signing the alliance of 2 August, by misrepresenting Bulgaria's attitude. Cemal, too, seemed to favour a policy of neutrality.[61] Yet all three men were uneasily aware that the arrival of the *Goeben* and the *Breslau* had provided Enver with a means of forcing the Empire into the war, regardless of their own wishes: he could order a naval attack upon Russia in the Black Sea.[62] With news arriving of spectacular German advances on the western front, Enver was more than ever convinced that the Central Powers would win, and that early action was worth the risk.[63] The mobilization had significantly increased Enver's independent powers. He had assumed the functions of Deputy Commander-in-Chief of the armed forces, with direct authority over the navy as well as the army. He had established his own general headquarters, and staffed it with German officers, drawn from the military mission, and he liaised directly with German general headquarters, bypassing his colleagues.[64] He was already making provocative use of his martial law powers, commandeering cargoes and equipment from Entente merchant vessels in Ottoman ports, and employing military censorship to bias press reporting in favour of the Central Powers.[65]

In spite of his colleagues' fears, however, Enver was not ready to embark upon an "adventure". His German advisers were divided over strategy. Liman believed that the arrival of the *Goeben* and the *Breslau* would facilitate an amphibious operation at Odessa, in the Russians' rear, but Souchon was doubtful of success, and preferred to send a land expedition against the British in Egypt. As important, the fleet could not be sent into the Black Sea, for fear that British warships would force the Dardanelles, whose existing shore and minefield defences were seriously deficient.[66] Enver and Souchon asked Germany to send coastal defence experts, and 200 additional sea-mines; pending their arrival, the defence of the Dardanelles would depend upon the fleet, which would have to remain within the Straits.[67] Enver was condemned to wait. He used the time to continue his military preparations, requesting munitions, supplies and military personnel from Germany; these began to arrive towards the end of the month.[68] He also took steps to consolidate his personal hold over the navy, appointing Souchon commander-in-chief of the fleet, installing German officers on Ottoman warships, and securing the transfer of the members of the British naval mission to meaningless desk jobs. Interestingly, Cemal appears to have acquiesced in these measures – a first indication that the Navy Minister was keeping his options open.[69] These persistent violations of neutrality did not escape the attention of the Entente Powers, who were increasingly exercised by the Empire's failure to remove the German crews from the *Goeben* and the *Breslau*; but their protests to the Grand Vizier were to no avail: in military matters, Enver's authority was unchallengeable.[70]

The Entente Powers had already guessed that the Empire had concluded some alliance with Germany.[71] None the less, they remained anxious to pursue any opportunity of keeping the Empire neutral, or at least, non-belligerent, and began to hint that Ottoman neutrality might be rewarded. The Russians suggested that the Empire might resume Germany's substantial economic concessions in Asia Minor, while the British offered assurances that the *Sultan Osman* and the *Reşadiye* would be returned at the end of the war, and appropriate compensation paid for their temporary detention.[72] On 17 August, the Russian ambassador, Giers, the French ambassador, Bompard, and the British ambassador, Mallet, made a joint approach to Said Halim, and gave him a verbal assurance that if the Ottoman Empire would observe "scrupulous neutrality", Britain, France and Russia would uphold the Empire's independence and integrity against any threat which might arise during the course of the war.[73] The Grand Vizier and Cavid were quick to seize the opportunity: if neutrality could be shown to pay, they believed, there would be a good chance of gaining the support of Talat and others, and of isolating Enver.[74] On 19 August, Cavid offered the three ambassadors terms: the Entente Powers must offer the Empire written, individual guarantees of its long-term independence and integrity – above all, against Russia; and they must agree to the full abrogation of the financial, economic and judicial capitulations. In return, Cavid hinted, the Entente Powers should demand the dismissal of the German military mission, as well as assurances of Ottoman neutrality.[75] Cemal went further, telling Mallet that the *Sultan Osman* and the *Reşadiye* must be returned forthwith; that the Entente Powers must renounce all rights of interference in the Empire's internal affairs; that they must secure the return of the Aegean islands to the Empire; and that they must guarantee the Empire possession of Western Thrace, should Bulgaria join the Central Powers.[76] The Entente Powers replied that they were ready to negotiate a reduction of the existing capitulations, subject, in particular, to safeguards in judicial matters; and that they would consider a joint written guarantee of the Empire's independence and integrity, to be valid for the duration of the war, and also binding upon the subsequent peace settlement.[77]

Meanwhile Talat and Halil had made no worthwhile progress in their talks with the Balkan states. On 19 August, Talat signed a treaty of alliance and friendship with Bulgaria, but the treaty's terms did not oblige the Bulgarians to enter the war: the Bulgarian government insisted that it must first obtain written guarantees that Romania would remain neutral.[78] The Romanians, however, declined to give such guarantees, despite repeated appeals from Talat and Halil, supported by the Central Powers' representatives at Bucharest. The most the Romanians would offer was a personal assurance from

King Carol to King Ferdinand, which the Bulgarians dismissed as inadequate.[79] To make matters worse, it became known that the Bulgarians were negotiating simultaneously with the Entente Powers, and that the Russians had offered them Ottoman territory in Thrace.[80] Talks with Greek representatives on the islands question were similarly deadlocked: the Greek side declined the Empire's offer of limited autonomy for the islands, and countered with a proposal for a leasing arrangement, which would leave the islands in Greece's *de facto* possession.[81] On 31 August, Talat returned to the Ottoman capital for consultations, leaving Halil to continue discussions with the Greeks and the Romanians.[82]

## VI

The failure of the Bucharest negotiations coincided with an adverse turn in the Central Powers' military fortunes. At the beginning of September, the Austro-Hungarian army suffered a major reverse in Galicia, losing Lemberg to the Russians; within days, the German advance across France was thrown back at the Marne. The consequence was an intensification of the Central Powers' pressure for immediate Ottoman intervention. The Austrians, hard-pressed by the Russians in Galicia, and increasingly fearful of a hostile Romanian intervention at their rear, appealed for an Ottoman expedition to Odessa as a matter of urgency.[83] The Germans doubted that this was feasible, and advised Enver to give priority to a land expedition against Egypt, and to the stimulation of a revolutionary "Islamic movement" in the Caucasus, Egypt and India. Preparations for an Egyptian expedition had already begun, but it was clear that they would take at least a month to complete. In the meantime, the Germans urged, the Empire should take immediate steps to establish its naval supremacy in the Black Sea, by authorizing Souchon to attack the Russian fleet.[84]

Increasingly, however, the Ottoman leadership was divided. Only Cemal remained undecided. Said Halim and Cavid were resolute for neutrality. Talat, in contrast, joined Enver in advocating early intervention on the side of the Central Powers: on 8 September he told Toshev that the Empire could wait a month at most.[85] The grounds of Talat's conversion are not entirely clear, though there is some evidence that he was fearful of jeopardizing the German alliance, and of forcing the Empire back into diplomatic and military isolation.[86] Practically, however, the interventionists faced the problem of the Empire's complete lack of diplomatic and military security with regard to Bulgaria and Greece. It was symptomatic that Enver began to speak of threatening the Bulgarians with attack if they failed to intervene against Serbia. It was also symptomatic that both he and Talat were now ready to settle the Aegean islands dispute on Greece's terms, evidently in the hope that this would remove an objection to intervention against Russia.[87] The anti-interventionists saw the trap: they preferred to leave the islands question open, and on 11 September the Grand Vizier instructed Halil to adjourn his discussions at Bucharest and return.[88]

Enver was ready to risk intervention without the Bulgarians, but warned Wangenheim that this would limit the Empire's strategic options: an attack upon the Russian fleet would be possible, as would be an expedition against Egypt, but the bulk of the Ottoman army would have to be retained in Thrace, as a precaution against Bulgarian attack.[89] Talat, however, continued to insist that the Empire could not intervene without Bulgaria, and the first half of September saw two fresh attempts to reach an acceptable accord with Sofia. Genadiev, a former Bulgarian foreign minister well known to the Unionist leaders, paid a private visit to the Ottoman capital; meanwhile, Enver despatched two of his staff officers, Lieutenant-Colonel Hafız Hakkı Bey and Major Refik Bey, to Sofia, with instructions to negotiate a military convention that would provide for Bulgaria's intervention in the war.[90] Neither initiative bore fruit. Genadiev was given a clear picture of the Ottoman leadership's divisions: while Enver and Talat pressed him for intervention, Said Halim and Cavid urged him to keep Bulgaria neutral. The two Ottoman staff officers were given a cool reception in Sofia, where they were told firmly that Bulgaria must remain neutral until Romania's position became clear; they returned empty-handed on 14 September.[91]

The anti-interventionists, meanwhile, were increasingly confident that they could obtain major concessions from the Entente Powers in the matter of the capitulations. Enver and Talat could scarcely oppose them in this question, and on 9 September, as a bargaining ploy, the Ottoman government announced its abrogation of all the existing capitulations, with effect from 1 October.[92]

Mallet, Giers and Bompard immediately protested against the unilateral form of this step, but indicated that they were ready to discuss the substance of the issue. The ambassadors of the Central Powers were less accommodating. Pallavicini condemned the timing of the announcement, and alleged that Britain and France would declare war; but much to Cavid's satisfaction, the most violent reaction came from Wangenheim, who subjected him to two solid hours of abuse and threats, complaining, with some justice, that the abrogation of the capitulations was simply a manoeuvre to forestall the Empire's entry into the war.[93] In the circumstances, however, Berlin and Vienna had little option but to withdraw their opposition, and by 13 September the Ottoman leadership was confident that it could persuade the Powers to accept a compromise: immediate abolition of the financial and economic capitulations, in return for special arrangements to take the place of the judicial capitulations.[94] The ambassadors of the Entente Powers indicated that these terms were acceptable for discussion; Halil was appointed to negotiate with them.[95]

The anti-interventionists' deeper game was to play for time. Their success over the capitulations, they believed, had given them a temporary advantage; in the longer term, they calculated, growing financial difficulties would force the Empire to demobilize. The Treasury was in poor shape. The outbreak of the war in Europe had caused serious disruption to the Empire's commerce; government revenues were falling sharply, and the armed forces were already short of funds.[96] As Finance Minister, Cavid Bey exploited the Treasury's difficulties to the maximum, repeatedly warning Enver that all revenues were spoken for, refusing to impose new taxes, or to raid the funds set aside for the service of the Empire's foreign debt, and predicting that the abrogation of the capitulations would bring in no additional revenue in the short term. Eventually, on 13 September, he offered the War Ministry an extra Ltq500,000 (Turkish pounds) per month – a quarter of the sum that Enver had demanded.[97] Three days later, Cavid told Giers that the Entente Powers should insist upon an Ottoman demobilization as the price for their assent to the abolition of capitulations.[98]

In addition, the armed forces faced a serious shortage of supplies. As noted, the Germans had begun shipping munitions and equipment in the second half of August. However, the only available route passed through Romania, whose government, under Entente pressure, grew steadily more obstructive, reducing the flow of supplies to a trickle, and periodically interrupting it altogether. By mid-September, Enver had received a mere fraction of the supplies he had requested from Berlin, and prospects for further deliveries remained problematical; crucially, however, the 200 sea-mines which Enver had requested for the Dardanelles had got through.[99]

Faced with apparent deadlock within the Ottoman leadership, the Germans attempted to force a decision. The arrival of the requested sea-mines, and of a team of German coastal defence experts, enabled them to argue that the Dardanelles could be defended against any attempt to force them, and that it was safe to send the Ottoman fleet into the Black Sea. As a first step, they urged the Empire to close the Dardanelles to all shipping, and to mine the passages.[100] Wangenheim and Pallavicini suggested that the fleet should cruise to Varna and Constanza, as a means of reassuring the Bulgarians and intimidating the Romanians. Souchon, for his part, urged that the fleet be sent into the Black Sea for essential training. These were excuses: the Germans' real aim was to give Souchon an opportunity to attack the Russian fleet, and thereby force the Empire into the war. They were confident that Enver would assist them, and that his colleagues would bow to a *fait accompli*.[101] Enver was less sure. As Deputy Commander-in-Chief, he controlled the armed forces, and could order the fleet to attack the Russians; but he did not control the government, and he was wary of provoking a leadership crisis from which he might not emerge victorious. On 14 September he gave Souchon permission to take the fleet to Varna and Constanza, adding confidentially that any Russian warships which might be encountered on the way should be attacked; evidently, Enver was hoping to provoke an incident which might be blamed on Russia. The Grand Vizier and Talat saw through this, however, and forced him to retract the permission.[102]

The Germans increased their pressure. On 19 September, Souchon threatened to send the *Goeben* and the *Breslau* into the Black Sea without Ottoman permission, but after consultations with the Ottoman leadership he was told that the ban on the egress of the fleet still stood, though he might send two torpedo-boats into the Black Sea.[103] Next day, on Wangenheim's orders, Souchon sent the *Breslau* into the Black Sea for a few hours. This demonstration failed to

impress the anti-interventionists, despite a characteristically bluster-
ing statement from Wangenheim, who warned the Grand Vizier that
Germany was entitled to deploy her own ships as she saw fit, without
recourse to the Ottoman Navy Ministry, though he added that
Souchon would do nothing without Enver's approval.[104] At meetings
that day, Enver and Talat proposed that the fleet be sent into the
Black Sea, as a means of deterring Romania from joining the Entente. Their colleagues objected that a naval demonstration would
not influence the Romanians, and did not conceal their suspicion
that the real aim was to provoke a naval incident with Russia. Enver
warned that Souchon might take the *Goeben* and the *Breslau* into the
Black Sea without authorization, but his colleagues replied that in
that case, the two cruisers must be refused re-admission to the
Straits. Cavid and Cemal even suggested that the Bosphorus forts
should be instructed to open fire on the German vessels if they attempted to enter the Black Sea without permission.[105]

Their bluff was quickly called, for next day Souchon took the
*Goeben* into the Black Sea.[106] This produced near-panic among the
anti-interventionists, fuelled by reports that Souchon had summoned
the entire fleet to follow, and was preparing to attack the Russians.[107]
The *Goeben* returned within a few hours, but Enver informed
Wangenheim that his colleagues were at last ready to make concessions: they were prepared to acknowledge Souchon's right to pursue
German interests, even when these collided with Ottoman interests;
they could not permit Souchon to take the Ottoman fleet into the
Black Sea, for fear that he would provoke an incident with Russia;
they would not prevent him from taking the *Goeben* and the *Breslau*
into the Black Sea, though they would disavow him if he provoked
an incident; they were anxious, however, that Souchon should be
formally installed in the Ottoman navy as the head of a German
naval mission; once Souchon accepted this proposed status, they
would permit him to take the entire fleet into the Black Sea.[108] This
last concession seems surprising, and may not have been authorized;
none the less, the Germans accepted the offer with alacrity, and on
24 September Souchon was formally installed in the Ottoman navy
with the rank of Vice-Admiral.[109] Events soon appeared to play further into the Germans' hands: faced with the manifest "Germaniz-
ation" of the Ottoman fleet, the British government had already
withdrawn its naval mission, and on 26 September the commander

of the British warships stationed outside the Dardanelles announced that he would henceforth treat any Ottoman warship which ventured outside the Straits as hostile. Without consulting his colleagues, Enver promptly ordered the closure of the Dardanelles to all shipping; by 29 September the passages had been mined, seemingly freeing the fleet for action in the Black Sea.[110]

Yet it was already apparent that the Germans had not obtained a free hand with the Ottoman fleet. Though Enver was ready to absolve Souchon of any responsibility to a higher Ottoman authority, Cemal was not: the Navy Minister insisted, successfully, that Souchon must give an undertaking not to attack the Russians, or even to take the fleet into the Black Sea, without Enver's approval.[111] Enver, however, was still blocked by his colleagues, who on 27 September unanimously reaffirmed their refusal to allow Souchon to take the fleet into the Black Sea.[112] In the end, it was the Germans whose bluff had been called. They could not attempt decisive action without Enver, and Enver could not take decisive action without firmer support from his colleagues within the Unionist leadership. The result was deadlock. By 30 September, Souchon had faced reality: he advised his superiors that he would concentrate upon training for the time being.[113]

Time still appeared to favour the anti-interventionists. The threat of an enforced demobilization remained real. The troops were already on half pay, and there were insufficient funds to support the planned expedition to Egypt. The supply position was worsening: the Entente Powers were taking steps to restrict the Empire's coal imports, vital for the navy, and on 2 October the Romanians definitively closed their borders to shipments of military supplies from Germany.[114] Meanwhile, discussions with the Entente ambassadors on the subject of the capitulations were continuing.[115] The Entente was also maintaining its policy of restraint in the face of Enver's provocations, which by now included blatant efforts at subversion in Egypt, and an attempt to stimulate a tribal uprising in the Russian-occupied region of Iranian Azerbayjan.[116] Finally, there were signs that opinion within the armed forces was turning against the idea of early entry into the war. Following his abortive mission to Sofia earlier in September, Hafız Hakkı Bey had given the War Minister a detailed report in which he stressed the utter uncertainty of Bulgaria's intentions; the approach of winter, which ruled out early operations

in the Caucasus; and the army's growing supply and funding difficulties. He proposed that the Empire demobilize, conserve its resources, and postpone a decision on entry into the war until the
spring of 1915.[117] It appears that these arguments, reinforced by the
Germans' failure at the Marne, won the support of other officers on
Enver's staff, and in face of this pressure Enver issued orders on 4
October for certain token measures of demobilization. To Wangenheim, Enver professed optimism, assuring him that the Empire
would no longer insist upon Bulgarian intervention as a precondition
for its own entry into the war; he added, however, that the Central
Powers must first secure a decisive victory, in France or in Galicia.[118]

## VII

Sometime in early October, Enver and Talat decided to break the
deadlock. They agreed that the Empire's defences were strong
enough to risk immediate intervention, regardless of the attitude of
Bulgaria, and regardless of the Central Powers' failure to secure a
decision on any European front. They also gained the support of
Halil.[119] With remarkable speed, they succeeded in overcoming the
major obstacles to intervention: they solved the problem of financ-
ing a war; they won over Cemal; and they managed to lift the anti-
interventionists' ban on the deployment of the fleet in the Black Sea,
thus opening the way to the naval attack upon Russia which Enver
had long contemplated. The only remaining problem was the attitude of the Grand Vizier and Cavid; this was resolved by arranging
the intervention behind their backs, and presenting them with a *fait
accompli*.

Best explained is the interventionists' success in resolving their financial problems. On 27 September, Enver had suggested that the
Germans should be approached for a loan. The anti-interventionists
did not object: Cavid, for one, was convinced that the Germans
would refuse any financial assistance until the Empire had entered
the war.[120] He proved to be mistaken, for the Germans quickly announced their readiness to consider a government-to-government
loan, and on 6 October they made a definite offer of a 6 per cent
loan of Ltq5,000,000, with an advance of Ltq250,000 payable before the Empire entered the war. Cavid remained sceptical, and the

Finance Ministry made no attempt to pursue the offer.[121] The interventionists, however, were prepared to go behind the Finance Ministry's back, and to leave the formalities of a loan agreement until later. As Enver explained to Wangenheim on 9 October, all that was required was a guarantee that the German embassy had adequate funds in its possession; no disbursements need be made until the Empire had opened hostilities.[122]

Less well explained is the interventionists' success in winning over Cemal. Ever since the beginning of August, the Navy Minister had played a baffling double game, alternately aligning himself with the proponents and the opponents of intervention, but never finally committing himself. There was a strong suspicion, which still remains, that his attitude was fundamentally opportunistic, being governed by his personal ambitions, and by his underlying rivalry with Enver. On one point alone had he shown any consistency: namely, his growing preoccupation with the fate of Egypt, the nominal Ottoman dependency that had been under British military occupation since 1882. Cemal had reacted with striking belligerence when the British declared a state of war in Egypt at the beginning of September, speaking of their action as a *casus belli*; he told Mallet subsequently that the British should give a pledge to evacuate Egypt at the end of the war; and in conversation with Bompard, he described Egypt as the Ottoman Empire's "Alsace-Lorraine". The secret of this preoccupation is difficult to fathom, for Cemal had no personal connections with Egypt. There are, however, suggestions that he may have seen himself as Egypt's future ruler.[123] Be that as it may, his military following meant that he could not be ignored by the interventionists. On 9 October, Enver informed Wangenheim that he, Talat and Halil had decided to confront Cemal next day, and force him into line. The confrontation proved to be successful, though it remains unclear whether Cemal was intimidated by threats, or whether, as seems possible, he was bought off with promises of a big rôle in Syria and command of the expedition against Egypt.[124] On 11 October, Cemal joined Enver, Talat and Halil at a secret meeting with Wangenheim, to discuss financial arrangements: they indicated that they would attack Russia as soon as the German embassy could show that it had Ltq2,000,000 in gold in its possession. The only remaining doubt concerned the willingness of the Romanians to permit the transport of the gold across their territory.[125]

Least well explained is the interventionists' success in lifting their colleagues' ban on fleet manoeuvres in the Black Sea. Since late September, Souchon had been permitted to send warships into the Black Sea for training, but only in small numbers and for a few hours at a time; the prohibition on the egress of the full fleet still stood, and the *Goeben* and the *Breslau* remained within the Straits.[126] However, on 12 October Souchon took the entire fleet, with the two German cruisers, into the Black Sea on manoeuvres, not returning until two days later.[127] Doubtless Cemal's conversion to the interventionist cause had helped, but what is striking is the apparent absence of any protest on the part of Said Halim and Cavid. It is possible that they were unaware of Cemal's conversion, and almost certain that they were ignorant of the interventionists' financial deal with Germany. None the less, their willingness to surrender a vital card remains perplexing: evidently, an important part of the story is missing.[128]

The requested German gold arrived in two shipments, on 16 and 21 October, the Romanians having created no difficulties.[129] This finally cleared the path for action, and on 22 October Enver despatched his war plan to German headquarters. The plan envisaged an immediate attack upon the Russian fleet, without a prior declaration of war; the proclamation by the Sultan-Caliph of a Holy War against the Entente Powers; the use of Ottoman land forces to pin down Russia's armies in Transcaucasia; and the despatch, after a further six weeks' preparation, of an expedition against Egypt. Otherwise, the plan was vague: there was an allusion to the future possibility of joint operations in the Balkans with Bulgaria, and also with Romania, should these states decide to join the Central Powers; allusion was also made to the future possibility of an expedition to Odessa, should military circumstances favour it. There was, however, a clear warning that the Empire would be obliged to retain the bulk of its forces in Thrace and the Marmara region for as long as the attitude of the Balkan states remained uncertain. For the Germans, this plan was good enough: their primary concern was to get the Empire into the war, and they promptly signalled their approval.[130]

Also on 22 October, Enver gave Souchon sealed orders to attack the Russian fleet and secure naval supremacy in the Black Sea. At Wangenheim's insistence, these orders were repeated in an open form, and a copy deposited at the German embassy. Cemal, in his capacity as Navy Minister, obliged with an order of the day to the fleet, instructing all officers and ratings to obey Souchon's orders as if they were his own.[131] Almost at the last moment, Talat and Halil indicated that they would prefer to postpone intervention until the spring of 1915.[132] Enver and Cemal were determined to press on, but on 25 October they conceded, *pro forma*, that Halil should proceed to Germany to plead the case for delay. Nothing came of this: Talat was quickly talked round, and Halil postponed his departure.[133] As far as can be judged, Said Halim and Cavid were still unaware of the interventionists' plans, and not until 26 and 27 October did Cavid receive urgent warnings from Giers and Bompard, who had divined what was afoot from intercepted Austro-Hungarian telegrams. He responded with professions of disbelief.[134]

Souchon took the fleet out on 27 September. Once at sea, he disregarded his instructions to seek out the Russian fleet, and instead ordered a series of raids on the Russian coast. The raids were carried out successfully on the morning of 29 September: the ports of Sebastopol, Novorossiysk, Feodosia and Odessa were bombarded, and a quantity of merchant shipping was sunk. The provocation was blatant.[135] Immediately after the raids, Souchon sent a wireless message to Enver's headquarters, claiming that his ships had been attacked by the Russian fleet while on peaceful manoeuvres, and had fired in self-defence. This fiction was designed to assist the interventionists in any difficulties with their colleagues, and had presumably been pre-arranged with Enver.[136] Said Halim and Cavid were not deceived, but the interventionists' firm denials of any foreknowledge or responsibility were not without effect upon other members of the Cabinet, which met the next day to review the situation – as far as can be traced, the only occasion when this body discussed the issue of peace or war. Even while the ministers were assembling, the ambassadors of the Entente Powers called to request their passports; they warned that nothing short of the immediate dismissal of all German personnel in the Ottoman armed forces could avert war. Cavid attempted to pursue this suggestion in the Cabinet, but was blocked by Enver and Cemal, who insisted that the armed forces could not function without German specialists. Instead, it was decided to send the Russian government a note, firmly denying all responsibility for the Black Sea "incident", but expressing the hope that a peaceful way out might be found.[137] That evening, at a meeting with members of the Unionist Central Committee, the Grand Vizier made a strong defence of his pacific policy, and dismissed notions of territorial conquest in Egypt and the Caucasus as idle dreams; both he and Cavid indicated that they would resign.[138]

Time was now on the interventionists' side, and they managed to postpone delivery of the note to the Russian government until 1 November, by which time Russian forces had opened hostilities in the Caucasus, and British warships had bombarded Akaba.[139] The Russians rejected the note, warning that nothing short of the expulsion of all German military personnel would satisfy them.[140] The interventionists' more pressing concern was to forestall a major leadership crisis, and while they permitted three non-Unionist ministers to resign, they insisted that Said Halim and Cavid must stay.[141] By 2 November the Grand Vizier had been talked round, but Cavid remained deaf to all entreaties and threats: his resignation was finally accepted on 5 November.[142] By then there was no going back: Russia had formally declared war on 2 November, and Britain and France followed suit three days later. The Empire replied with a counter-declaration of war on 11 November, and on the same day the Sultan proclaimed a Holy War against the Entente Powers.[143]

## VIII

The October decision for war can scarcely be presented as an "accident": the naval attack upon Russia was a deliberate provocation, whose consequences were clearly foreseen by its perpetrators. Nor can the decision be portrayed as a product of "drift": since mid-August, the drift in Ottoman policy had been away from war, as the diplomatic, military and financial obstacles became steadily more apparent; it took a determined effort by the interventionists to reverse the drift. No more credible is the suggestion that the decision sprang from German dictation and control. The Germans undoubtedly facilitated the Empire's decision, but they depended throughout upon the co-operation and resourcefulness of the Ottoman interventionists; they were never masters of the situation. Finally, there appears to be no convincing reason to blame the decision on the Entente Powers, who had shown considerable restraint in the face of numerous provocations, and conciliatoriness in the matter of the capitulations; it is not obvious that greater concessions would have changed the Empire's decision.

The October decision is better viewed as the outcome of a power struggle within the inner circle of Ottoman leaders, which broke out in the aftermath of the failure of the July decision for war. Each of these leaders pursued a personal agenda. As far as can be judged, Enver was solid for war throughout; Cavid was equally determined upon neutrality; Said Halim had favoured a Balkan war initially, but quickly moved towards Cavid's position; Talat was at first for delay, but eventually gave his support to Enver; Halil followed a course similar to Talat's; Cemal played an obscure double game, before finally throwing in his lot with the interventionists. It seems clear that these various policy agendas also reflected personal rivalries, and calculations of personal advantage, though the details largely remain obscure.

That the interventionists eventually won was due to the fact that, by virtue of Enver and Cemal's offices and personal influence, they exercised direct control over the armed forces; to the fact that the Germans were ready to supply the necessary ships, munitions and money; and to the fact that the anti-interventionists were an unstable coalition of genuine neutralists, procrastinators and plain opportunists. That the interventionists took so long to triumph was due to the determination of their opponents; to the Entente Powers' refusal to rise to any provocation short of open military attack; and to the disappointment of the interventionists' initial hopes of an early German victory and a Bulgarian intervention against Serbia. In the end, three factors tipped the balance in favour of intervention: the German alliance, which Talat in particular was reluctant to betray; the presence of the *Goeben* and the *Breslau*, which gave the Empire naval security against Russia, as well as an easy route into the war; and the Germans' offer to subsidize the Ottoman war effort.

The struggle between the interventionists and their opponents did not take place in a vacuum. It reflected not only the peculiar "polycracy" within the Unionist leadership, and the hybrid civilian and military nature of the Unionist regime, but also doubts and divisions over foreign policy which had emerged in the aftermath of the Balkan Wars, and which were far from resolved in June 1914. Behind these doubts over foreign policy, it is possible to discern a deeper uncertainty over the future the Ottoman Empire should pursue, an uncertainty reflected in the growing intensity of Unionist ideological debate, with its various Pan-Islamic, Pan-Turanian and Westernizing strands. These larger issues remain to be explored. Such, at least, are the conclusions suggested by the limited evidence available. It is to be hoped that more and better evidence, perhaps in the shape of Ottoman private papers, may eventually turn up; it is also to be hoped that thorough studies of the Unionist regime and its leading personalities, and also of its foreign and military policies, of which almost none have been produced to date, may eventually place the decision for war in its proper context.

## Notes

1. Dan van der Vat, *The ship that changed the world* (London, 1985), p. 15; Moukhtar Pacha, *La Turquie, l'Allemagne et l'Europe* (Paris, 1924), p. 265.

2. Cavid's diary is kept in the library of the Turkish Historical Society, Ankara. It is extensively quoted in Yusuf Hikmet Bayur, *Türk İnkılabı Tarihi*, II:iv (Ankara, 1952), and III:i (Ankara, 1953).

3. Halil Menteşe, *Halil Menteşe'nin Anıları* (Istanbul, 1986); Talat Paşa, *Talat Paşa'nın Hatıraları* (Istanbul, 1946); Djemal Pasha, *Memories of a Turkish Statesman 1913–1919* (New York, 1922). The proceedings of the 1918 parliamentary enquiry were published as *Said Halim ve Mehmed Talat Paşalar kabinelerinin Divan-ı Ali'ye sevkleri hakkında Divaniye Mebusu Fuat Bey (merhum) tarafından verilen takrir üzerine bera-ı tahkikat kura isabet eden Beşinci Şube tarafından icra olunan tahkikat ve zaptedilen ifadatı muhtevidir* (Istanbul, 1334/1919); the title is henceforth given in abbreviated form as *Beşinci Şube*.

4. See, for example, Ali Ihsan Sabis, *Harp Hatıralarım*, I (Ankara, 1943); Galip Kemali Söylemezoğlu, *Hatıralar* (Istanbul, 1940); Liman von Sanders, *Fünf Jahre in der Türkei* (Berlin, 1920); Friedrich Freiherr Kress von Kressenstein, *Mit den Türken zum Suezkanal* (Berlin, 1938); Joseph Pomiankowski, *Das Zusammenbruch des Ottomanischen Reiches* (Leipzig, Zürich, Vienna, 1928); Maurice Bompard, "L'entrée en guerre de la Turquie", *La Revue de Paris*, 1 and 15 July 1921.

5. For discussion see Bayur, *Türk İnkılabı*, III:i, pp. 267–4; Y. T. Kurat, "How Turkey drifted into World War I", in *Studies in International History*, K. Bourne & D. C. Watt (eds) (London, 1967); Sina Akşin, *Jön Türkler ve İttihat ve Terakki* (Istanbul, 1987), pp. 268–76; and the

various Ottoman memoirs cited above.

6. For general accounts of the Unionist regime, see the works by Akşin and Bayur, cited above, and also Tarık Zafer Tunaya, *Türkiye'de Siyasal Partiler*, 3 vols (Istanbul, 1984–6).

7. Alone among the Unionist leaders, Enver has been the subject of a substantial biography: Şevket Süreyya Aydemir, *Makedonya'dan Ortaasya'ya Enver Paşa*, 3 vols (Istanbul, 1970–72).

8. See the interesting comments by Wangenheim in GFO, *Deutschland 128 nr. 5 secreta*, Wangenheim to FO, no. 995, 8 October 1914.

9. Jehuda L. Wallach, *Anatomie einer Militärhilfe: die preussisch-deutschen Militärmissionen in der Türkei 1839–1919* (Düsseldorf, 1976), pp. 126ff.

10. Sabis, a member of Enver's headquarters staff, describes the relationship between Enver and Cemal as one of mutual hatred; Sabis, *Harp Hatıralarım*, p. 91; cf. Bompard, *La Revue de Paris*, 1 July 1921, p. 80.

11. There is no comprehensive study of Ottoman foreign policy between September 1913 and July 1914. The following account is based upon the information contained in Bayur, *Türk İnkılabı*, II:i and II:iv, and upon the statements made by Said Halim and Cavid to the post-war parliamentary enquiry: *Beşinci Şube*, pp. 9ff. and pp. 193ff.

12. These agreements are examined in detail in Bayur, *Türk İnkılabı*, II:i.

13. Information on the negotiations with Bulgaria is provided in Tevfik Bıyıklıoğlu, *Trakya'da Milli Mücadele*, I (Ankara, 1955), pp. 88ff.; Djemal Pasha, *Memories*, pp. 52–6; and in numerous documents in DDNB.

14. Bıyıklıoğlu, *Trakya*, I, pp. 89–92; Dimitär G. Gotsev, *Natsionalno-osvoboditelnata borba v Makedoniya 1912–1915* (Sofia, 1981), pp. 133–5; Basil Kondis, *Greece and Albania 1908–1914* (Thessaloniki, 1976), pp. 121–3.

15. Background in Paul G. Halpern, *The Mediterranean naval situation, 1908–1914* (Cambridge, Mass., 1971), pp. 314ff.; cf. K. F. Shatsillo, *Russkiy imperializm i razvitiye flota* (Moscow, 1968).

16. *Beşinci Şube*, pp. 193–5 (testimony of Cavid Bey).

17. Ulrich Trumpener, *Germany and the Ottoman Empire 1914–1918* (Princeton, New Jersey, 1968), pp. 14–15; Gerard E. Silberstein, *The troubled alliance. German–Austrian relations 1914 to 1917* (Lexington, Kentucky, 1970), pp. 8–9.

18. Bayur, *Türk İnkılabı*, II:iii, pp. 183–5; II:iv, pp. 549–58; ÖUA, VIII, no. 10410, Pallavicini to Berchtold, 20 July 1914.

19. Bayur, *Türk İnkılabı*, II:iii, pp. 245–63.

20. Ibid., pp. 265–70.

21. DD, I, no. 81, Wangenheim to FO, 19 July; no. 117, 22 July; ÖUA, VIII, no. 10409, Pallavicini to Berchtold, 20 July; DDNB, no. 193, Toshev

to Radoslavov, 7/20 July; no. 196, 9/22 July.

22. Wolfgang-Uwe Friedrich, *Bulgarien und die Mächte 1913–1915* (Stuttgart, 1985), ch. 2, *passim*; Silberstein, *The troubled alliance*, pp. 22–3; Bayur, *Türk İnkılabı*, III:i, pp. 68–70.

23. *DD*. I, no. 117, Wangenheim to FO, 22 July; no. 149, 23 July; *DDNB*, no. 199, Radoslavov to Toshev, 10/23 July.

24. *DD*, I, no. 144, Jagow to Wangenheim, 24 July.

25. Ibid., II, no. 285, Wangenheim to FO, 28 July.

26. Bayur, *Türk İnkılabı*, II:iv, p. 629.

27. *DD*. II, no. 320, Bethmann Hollweg to Wangenheim, 28 July.

28. Ibid., II, no. 411, Wangenheim to FO, 30 July; III, no. 508, Bethmann Hollweg to Wangenheim, 31 July.

29. Ibid., III, no. 733, Wangenheim to FO, 2 August; Bayur, *Türk İnkılabı*, III:i, pp. 63–4.

30. Friedrich, *Bulgarien*, pp. 114–17; Silberstein, *The troubled alliance*, pp. 24–30; *DDNB*, no. 213, Toshev to Radoslavov, 13/26 July.

31. *DDNB*, no. 223, Toshev to Radoslavov, 15/28 July; no. 233, 17/30 July; no. 263, 20 July/2 August; Bayur, *Türk İnkılabı*, III:i, pp. 147–9; *Beşinci Şube*, pp. 41–3 (testimony of Said Halim Paşa).

32. *DD*, III, no. 795, Wangenheim to FO, 3 August; Trumpener, *Germany and the Ottoman Empire*, p. 23.

33. GFO, *Deutschland 128 nr. 5 secreta*, Wangenheim to FO, nos. 406, 407, 2 August; Ulrich Trumpener, "German military aid to Turkey in 1914: an historical reinterpretation", *Journal of Modern History* **xxxii**, June 1960, pp. 145–6.

34. GFO, see Note 33.

35. Trumpener, *Germany and the Ottoman Empire*, pp. 25–6.

36. *DD*, IV, no. 751, Jagow to Wangenheim, 3 August; no. 836, 4 August.

37. GFO, *Deutschland 128 nr. 5 secreta*, Wangenheim to FO, no. 438, 6 August; Bıyıklıoğlu, *Trakya*, I, p. 88.

38. GFO, *Weltkrieg*, Wangenheim to FO, no. 443, 6 August; Ulrich Gierke, *Persien in der deutschen Orientpolitik*, 2 vols (Stuttgart, 1960), I, pp. 22–4; II, pp. 10–11.

39. E. W. R. Lumby (ed.), *Policy and operations in the Mediterranean, 1912–14* (London, 1970), p. 427.

40. *DDNB*, no. 267, Toshev to Radoslavov, 21 July/3 August; no. 277, 23 July/4 August; no. 289, 23 July/4 August; no. 294, 24 July/6 August.

41. GFO, *Weltkrieg*, Wangenheim to FO, no. 426, 4 August; *Deutschland 128 nr. 5 secreta*, Wangenheim to FO, no. 429, 4 August.

42. Izzet Pascha, *Denkwürdigkeiten* (Leipzig, 1927), pp. 269–70.

43. Aydemir, *Makedonya'dan*, II, pp. 514–17; *Beşinci Şube*, pp. 196–7 (testimony of Cavid Bey).

44. Aydemir, *Makedonya'dan*, II, p. 518; *Beşinci Şube*, pp. 197–8 (testi-

mony of Cavid Bey).

45. GFO, *Deutschland 128 nr. 5 secreta*, Wangenheim to FO, no. 438, 6 August; Bayur, *Türk İnkılabı*, pp. 98–9.

46. GFO, *Deutschland 128 nr. 5 secreta*, Wangenheim to FO, no. 437, 6 August; FO to Wangenheim, no. 330, 7 August; *Weltkrieg*, FO to Wangenheim, no. 350, 10 August.

47. GFO, *Weltkrieg*, Wangenheim to FO, no. 443, 6 August. It was at this point that Enver began a short-lived series of confidential overtures to the Russian embassy, hinting at his willingness to conclude an alliance with Russia in return for territorial and other concessions. It seems almost certain that these overtures were insincere, and designed to cover the impending arrival of the German cruisers. See Harry N. Howard, *The partition of Turkey: a diplomatic history 1913–1923* (Norman, 1931), pp. 96ff.; Trumpener, *Germany and the Ottoman Empire*, pp. 24–5.

48. *DDNB*, nos 303, 311, Toshev to Radoslavov, 25 July/7 August; no. 322, 27 July/9 August.

49. Ibid., no. 334, 29 August/11 September; GFO, *Deutschland 128 nr. 2 secreta*, Wangenheim to FO, no. 457, 8 August; Bayur, *Türk İnkılabı*, III:i, p. 122.

50. Bıyıklıoğlu, *Trakya*, I, pp. 97–8.

51. GFO, *Deutschland 128 nr. 2*, Wangenheim to FO, no. 469, 9 August.

52. Bayur, *Türk İnkılabı*, III:i, pp. 79–84; GFO, *Weltkrieg*, Wangenheim to FO, no. 473, 11 August.

53. Bayur, *Türk İnkılabı*, III:i, pp. 35–6; Lumby, *Policy and operations*, pp. 247–8.

54. Bayur, *Türk İnkılabı*, III:i, p. 123; GFO, *Weltkrieg*, Wangenheim to FO, no. 473, 11 August.

55. GFO, *Weltkrieg*, Wangenheim to FO, no. 471, 10 August.

56. GFO, *Deutschland 128 nr. 8 secreta*, Wangenheim to FO, no. 505, 15 August; *DDNB*, no. 324, Toshev to Radoslavov, 27 July/9 August; no. 342, 31 July/13 August; no. 353, 2/15 August.

57. *DDNB*, no. 327, Toshev to Radoslavov, 28 July/10 August; no. 334, 29 July/11 August.

58. Bayur, *Türk İnkılabı*, III:i, pp. 102–3; Bıyıklıoglu, *Trakya*, I, pp. 99–100.

59. GFO, *Deutschland 128 no. 8 secreta*, Wangenheim to FO, no. 505, 15 August; FO to Wangenheim, no. 407, 15 August.

60. GFO, *Deutschland 128 nr. 5 secreta*, Bethmann Hollweg to FO, no. 17, 20 August; no. 29, 1 September; Wangenheim to FO, 13 September; *Weltkrieg*; Wangenheim to FO, no. 728, 6 September.

61. Bayur *Türk İnkılabı*, III:i, pp. 112, 147–9; *DDNB*, no. 356, Toshev to Radoslavov, 3/16 August.

62. GFO, *Deutschland 128 nr. 8 secreta*, Wangenheim to FO, no. 490, 18 August; *DDNB*, as Note 61.
63. Bayur, *Türk İnkılabı*, III:i, pp. 102–3.
64. Sabis, *Harp Hatıralarım*, I, pp. 101, 155. Sabis states that Enver assumed the post of deputy commander-in-chief on 3 August, simultaneously with the general mobilization. This is confirmed by Enver's official service record, reproduced in Aydemir, *Makedonya'dan*, III, pp. 693–4. The "deputy" in Enver's title reflected the constitutional fiction that the Sultan remained commander-in-chief of the armed forces.
65. Bayur, *Türk İnkılabı*, III:i, pp. 97–8, 186; Sabis, *Harp Hatıralarım*, I, pp. 136–7.
66. Trumpener, *Germany and the Ottoman Empire*, p. 35; GFO, *Weltkrieg*, Wangenheim to FO, no. 499, 14 August.
67. Trumpener, "Military aid", pp. 146–7.
68. Ibid., pp. 147–8.
69. The *Goeben* and the *Breslau* were ceremonially transferred to the Ottoman navy on 16 August, and given the Turkish names *Yavuz Sultan Selim* and *Midilli*. Djemal Pasha, *Memories*, pp. 120–2; Kurat, "How Turkey drifted", pp. 303–4. But see the letter sent by Cemal to Enver on 20 August quoted in Aydemir, *Makedonya'dan*, III, pp. 424–5.
70. *Correspondence respecting events leading to the rupture of relations with Turkey. Presented to both Houses of Parliament by Command of His Majesty. November 1914* [Cd. 7628], no. 23, Mallet to Grey, 19 August; no. 30, 22 August; no. 32, 24 August; no. 39, 26 August; nos. 42, 43, 27 August; no. 48, 30 August; nos. 49, 50, 1 September; Martin Gilbert, *Winston S. Churchill*, Companion vol. 3, part 1 (London, 1972), pp. 56–60, 102–3.
71. Silberstein, *The troubled alliance*, p. 78.
72. *Correspondence*, no. 34, Grey to Mallet, 25 August; Howard, *The partition of Turkey*, pp. 98–9; Gilbert, *Winston S. Churchill*, Companion vol. 3, part 1, pp. 38–41.
73. *Correspondence*, no. 17, Grey to Beaumont, 16 August; no. 20, Mallet to Grey, 18 August.
74. Bayur, *Türk İnkılabı*, III:i, pp. 152–3.
75. Ibid., pp. 152–5; Friedrich Stieve, *Das russische Orangebuch über den Kriegsausbruch mit der Türkei: Seine Fälschungen über das Garantie-Angebot der Ententemächte an die Ottomanische Regierung* (Berlin, 1926), no. 48, Giers to Sazonov, 6/19 August.
76. *Correspondence*, no. 24, Mallet to Grey, 20 August.
77. Ibid., no. 28, Grey to Mallet, 22 August; Bayur, *Türk İnkilabi*, III:i, pp. 156–7.
78. Bayur, *Türk İnkılabı*, III:i, p. 112; Biyiklioglu, *Trakya*, I, pp. 101–277.

79. Bayur, *Türk İnkılabı*, I:i, pp. 159–60; Silberstein, *The troubled alliance*, pp. 85–6; Friedrich, *Bulgarien*, p. 124.
80. Bayur, *Türk İnkılabı*, III:i, pp. 157–8. It may also be noted that Mallet attempted to sound out Cavid on the possibility of opening the Straits to British and Russian warships: ibid., p. 177.
81. Ibid., pp. 127–8.
82. Ibid., pp. 113–14, 159–61.
83. Silberstein, *The troubled alliance*, p. 86; Pomiankowski, *Das Zusammenbruch*, pp. 81–2.
84. GFO, *Deutschland 128 nr. 5 secreta*, Wangenheim to FO, no. 725, 6 September; no. 779, 11 September; no. 795, 13 September; Jagow to Wangenheim, no. 117, 9 September.
85. *DDNB*, no. 413, Toshev to Radoslavov, 27 August/9 September.
86. Such is the tenor of a number of Talat's reported remarks. See, for example, Menteşe, *Halil Menteşe*, pp. 204–5.
87. Bayur, *Türk İnkılabı*, III:i, pp. 113, 159–61.
88. Ibid., pp. 132–3.
89. GFO, *Deutschland 128 nr. 5 secreta*, Wangenheim to FO no. 762, 8 September.
90. Sabis, *Harp Hatıralarım*, I. p. 187; Bayur, *Türk İnkılabı*, III:i, p. 204.
91. *DDNB*, no. 407, Toshev to Radoslavov, 24 August/6 September; no. 413, 27 August/9 September; GFO, *Deutschland 128 nr. 5 secreta*, Michahelles to FO, no. 140, 15 September.
92. Bayur, *Türk İnkılabı*, III:i, pp. 161–4.
93. Ibid., pp. 165–71.
94. Ibid., pp. 171–2.
95. Stieve, *Das russische Orangebuch*, no. 85, Giers to Sazonov, 2/15 September; no. 87, Sazonov to Giers, 6/19 September; *Correspondence*, no. 77, Grey to Mallet, 16 September.
96. Bayur, *Türk İnkılabı*, III:i, pp. 182–8; *Beşinci Şube*, pp. 223–4 (testimony of Cavid Bey).
97. Ibid., pp. 187–9.
98. Stieve, *Das russische Orangebuch*, no. 86, Giers to Sazonov, 4/17 September.
99. Trumpener, "Military aid", pp. 147–8.
100. Trumpener, *Germany and the Ottoman Empire*, pp. 36–8.
101. GFO, *Deutschland 128 nr. 5 secreta*, Wangenheim to FO, no. 762, 8 September; no. 779, 11 September; no. 795, 13 September; Jagow to Wangenheim, no. 117, 9 September; Bethmann Hollweg to FO, no. 43, 14 September; Carl Mühlmann, *Das deutsch–türkische Waffenbündnis im Weltkrieg* (Leipzig, 1940), pp. 20–21.
102. GFO, *Deutschland 128 nr. 5*, Wangenheim to FO, no. 836, 19 September; Trumpener, *Germany and the Ottoman Empire*, p. 39.

103. GFO, *Deutschland 128 nr. 5*, Wangenheim to FO, no. 836, 19 September; Ulrich Trumpener, "Turkey's entry into World War I: an assessment of responsibilities", *Journal of Modern History* **xxxiv**, December 1962, pp. 371–2.

104. GFO, *Deutschland 128 nr. 5*, Wangenheim to FO, no. 848, 20 September; Trumpener, "Responsibilities", p. 372.

105. Bayur, *Türk İnkılabı*, III:i, pp. 90, 197, 206.

106. GFO, *Weltkrieg*, Wangenheim to FO, no. 857, 21 September; Sabis, *Harp Hatıralarım*, I, pp. 192–3, states that Souchon sent the *Goeben* into the Black Sea with Enver's permission.

107. Cavid drafted his resignation. Bayur, *Türk İnkılabı*, III:i, p. 92; *Beşinci Şube*, pp. 199–202 (testimony of Cavid Bey).

108. However, Enver added that it was also proposed to send Halil to Berlin, to explain the difficult situation in which it was placed by the uncertain attitudes of Romania and Bulgaria. In the event, this proposal was not followed up. GFO, *Deutschland 128 nr. 5 secreta*, Wangenheim to FO, no. 847, 21 September.

109. GFO, *Tuerkei 139*, FO to GHQ, no. 533, 23 September; Note verbale from Ottoman Embassy, Berlin, 24 September; *Deutschland 128 nr. 5 secreta*, FO to Wangenheim, nos 191, 194, 24 September; Trumpener, *Germany and the Ottoman Empire*, pp. 42–3.

110. Trumpener, *Germany and the Ottoman Empire*, pp. 46–7; Gilbert, *Winston S. Churchill*, Companion vol. 3, part 1, p. 105; Bayur, *Türk İnkilabi*, III:i, pp. 93–4.

111. GFO *Tuerkei 139*, Besprechung mit Djemal Pascha an 24.9.14.

112. Bayur, *Türk İnkılabı*, III:i, pp. 92–3.

113. GFO, *Deutschland 128 nr. 5 secreta*, Wangenheim to FO, no. 940, 30 September.

114. Trumpener, "Military aid", pp. 148–9; Kurat, "How Turkey drifted", pp. 309–10; GFO, *Deutschland 128 nr. 5 secreta*, Besprechung mit Enver Pascha an 3 Oktober 1914.

115. Stieve, *Das russische Orangebuch*, no. 94, Giers to Sazonov, 12/25 September; no. 105, 18 September/1 October; Bayur, *Türk İnkılabı*, III:i, pp. 172–3.

116. Bayur, *Türk İnkılabı*, III:i. pp. 220–7; *Correspondence*, no. 51, Mallet to Grey, 1 September; no. 85, Cheetham to Grey, 21 September; nos. 89, 90, 91, Mallet to Grey, 24 September; no. 96, 26 September; no. 97, 27 September; no. 104, 2 October; no. 114, 7 October; no. 125, Cheetham to Grey, 30 September; no. 143, Mallet to Grey, 4 October; *Beşinci Şube*, p. 203 (testimony of Mahmud Paşa).

117. Sabis, *Harp Hatıralarım*, I, pp. 187–9.

118. Bayur, *Türk İnkılabı*, III:i, p. 212; GFO.

119. GFO, *Deutschland 128 nr. 5 secreta*, Wagenheim to FO, no. 1010, 9 October.

120. Bayur, *Türk İnkılabı*, III:i, p. 191.

121. Ibid., pp. 191–2; *Beşinci Şube*, p. 229 (testimony of Cavid Bey); Trumpener, "Responsibilities", pp. 374–6.

122. GFO, *Deutschland 128 nr. 5 secreta*, Wangenheim to FO, no. 1010, 9 October.

123. Bayur, *Türk İnkılabı*, III:i. pp. 196–7; *Correspondence*, no. 164, Grey to Mallet, 23 October; Bompard, *Revue de Paris*, 15 July 1921, pp. 274–5.

124. GFO, *Deutschland 128 nr. 5 secreta*, Wangenheim to FO, no. 1010, 9 October.

125. Ibid., no. 1022, 11 October.

126. *Beşinci Şube*, pp. 9–10 (testimony of Said Halim Paşa).

127. *Correspondence*, no. 119, Mallet to Grey, 12 October; no. 126, 14 October.

128. In conversation with Toshev, Said Halim hinted that the fleet had been sent into the Black Sea as a means of impressing the Romanians, whose policy had been thrown into doubt by the recent death of King Carol. *DDNB*, no. 471, Toshev to Radoslavov, 29 September/12 October.

129. Trumpener, "Responsibilities", p. 377.

130. GFO, *Deutschland 128 nr. 5 secreta*, Wangenheim to FO, no. 1087, 22 October; Carl Mühlmann, *Deutschland und die Türkei 1913–1914* (Berlin, 1929), pp. 101–2; Trumpener, *Germany and the Ottoman Empire*, pp. 51–3.

131. Trumpener, *Germany and the Ottoman Empire*, pp. 53–4; Bayur, *Türk İnkılabı*, III:i, pp. 229–31, 235.

132. Menteşe, *Halil Menteşe*, p. 205; Djemal Pasha, *Memories*, pp. 129–30; GFO, *Deutschland 128 nr. 8 secreta*, Wangenheim to FO, no. 1094, 24 October; *Deutschland 128 nr. 5 secreta*, no. 1107, 25 October.

133. However, Hafız Hakkı Bey and Bronsart Paşa, both members of Enver's staff, were sent ahead to Berlin. Bayur, *Türk İnkilabı*, III:i, p. 230.

134. Ibid., pp. 235–6.

135. Hermann Lorey (ed.), *Der Kreig zur See 1914–1918: Der Kreig in den türkischen Gewässern*, 2 vols (Berlin, 1928–38), I, pp. 46–56.

136. Trumpener, *Germany and the Ottoman Empire*, p. 55.

137. Bayur, *Türk İnkılabı*, III:i, pp. 242–9; *Beşinci Şube*, pp. 56–7 (testimony of Mahmud Paşa), pp. 215–6 (testimony of Cavid Bey).

138. Bayur, *Türk İnkılabı*, III:i, pp. 250–53; *Beşinci Şube*, pp. 216–17 (testimony of Cavid Bey).

139. Bayur, *Türk İnkılabı*, III:i, pp. 254–7.
140. Stieve, *Das russische Orangebuch*, no. 129, Sazonov to Benckendorff and Izvolskii, 19 October/1 November.
141. Bayur, *Türk İnkılabı*, III:i, p. 258–9; *Beşinci Şube*, p. 43 (testimony of Said Halim), pp. 58–9 (testimony of Mahmud Paşa), pp. 67–8 (testimony of İbrahim Bey), p. 218 (testimony of Cavid Bey), p. 349 (testimony of Hayri Efendi).
142. *Beşinci Şube*, p. 219 (testimony of Cavid Bey).
143. Bayur, *Türk İnkılabı*, III:i, pp. 259–60, 317–25.

# Index

Adriatic Sea 88–9n, 108

Aegean Islands 235, 236, 238, 242, 243, 244, 247–8

Aehrenthal, Alois Count Lexa von, Austro-Hungarian foreign minister 11–13

Afghanistan 240

Africa 152

Albania 42, 59, 88n, 234

Albert, King of the Belgians 44, 140, 151, 154
   and public opinion 161–2, 163, 165
   rôle of 158, 160–1, 174n

Albertini, Luigi 60, 68, 73, 77

Alexander, Crown Prince of Serbia 55, 57, 58, 73–4
   appeal to Tsar Nicholas II 75–6
   orders mobilization 82

Anatolia 233, 235

Andrian-Werburg, Leopold, Baron von 10, 11, 13–14

Anglo-Russian Convention (1907) 101, 102, 107

Antwerp, defences 152

"Apis" see Dimitrijević

Asquith, H. H., British Prime Minister 180, 182, 186, 199
   and Belgian neutrality 188, 189, 192
   and Haldane 194–5

Austria-Hungary,
   alliance with Germany 17–18, 21, 22–3
   annexation crisis (1907–11) 12
   armed forces 16, 105
   Council of Ministers (7 July 1914) 15, 51n, 68
   decision to make war on Serbia 9, 15, 16–17
   declaration of war on Serbia (28 July) 83
   defeats in Galicia 248
   effect of Balkan Wars on 233
   expansionist group of diplomats 11–13, 14
   and Japan 220
   not responsible for escalation of war 9, 19–20, 23
   and Ottoman Empire 239, 242
   perception of Russian support for Serbia 16, 17, 18, 60, 68
   perception of threat from Serbia 13, 14–15, 62, 67, 85n
   and Sarajevo murders 56, 59–63, 64–6, 67, 90n
   ultimatum to Serbia (23 July) 15, 51n, 62, 66, 72–3

Auswärtiges Amt, Germany 29, 32, 36, 51n

Avarna, Count G. d', Italian ambassador in Vienna 69

Baernreither, Josef Maria 12

balance of power, shifts in 6–7

Balfour, A. J. 208n

Balkan alliance, proposed 242–3, 245–6

Balkan Wars (1912–13) 13, 57, 86n, 108, 109, 233

Ballin, Albert, German shipping magnate 28, 32, 33

Baltic Sea 107

Balugdžić, Zivojin, Serbian minister in Athens 58, 86n

Bark, P. L., Russian Minister of Finance 111, 112

Barrès, Maurice, French nationalist 131

Basily, N. de, Russian Foreign ministry 125, 126, 146n

Beauchamp, 7th Earl, Lord President of the Council 178

Beaverbrook, Lord 178, 202n

Belgium 157, 166–7
   Catholic party 154, 155, 157
   German invasion of 142, 151, 163, 165
   and German threat of war with France 44, 151
   German ultimatum to 139–40, 158–60

Belgian reply 160–2
Grey Books (official records) 166–7
and Italy 167
military policy 152–3, 155, 166
mobilization 158, 166
national character 164–5
neutrality 151–3, 154–5, 157
  British consideration of 139, 165,
  173n, 188–9
patriotic fervour in 161–3
political sympathies 155–6
press 152, 157
reaction to Sarajevo 157
relations with France 152, 153–4, 155,
  166–7
relations with Germany 153–4, 155, 166,
  172n
and Romania 167
and Russia 166–7
and Serbia 167
Belgrade 55–6, 60, 77, 81
Below-Saleske, Klaus von, German
  ambassador in Brussels 160, 161, 172n
Bénazet, Paul, French War Ministry 148n
Benckendorff, Count A. K., Russian
  ambassador to Britain 183, 184
Berchtold, Leopold Count, Austro-Hungarian
  foreign minister 11–12, 13, 14, 61, 204n
  and ultimatum to Serbia 15, 16, 71, 82
Berlin 32, 48n
Bertie, Sir Francis, British ambassador to
  Paris 124, 196–7
Bertrab, Count, German
  Oberquartermaster 17–18
Bethmann Hollweg, Theobald von,
  Chancellor of Germany 31, 34, 39, 42–3,
  52n, 109, 182
  responsibility for war 28, 29, 30, 32
  view of war as inevitable 5, 35, 37–8
  wants British neutrality 190–1, 204n
Beyens, Baron, Belgian envoy in Berlin 157–
  8, 166–7
Bienerth, Freiherr Karl von, Austrian military
  attaché Berlin 42
Bienvenu-Martin, M., French Minister of
  Justice 122, 123
Bilinski, Ritter von, Austro-Hungarian
  finance minister 13, 14–15
Black Sea, German access to 239, 241–2,
  245, 246, 248, 251–4, 256–7
Bompard, H., French ambassador to
  Turkey 247, 250, 257
Bonaparte, Prince Roland 138
Bonar Law, A. 178, 199
Boppe, Jules, French minister in

Belgrade 93n
Bošković, Serbian minister in London 74, 75,
  78
Bosnia 55–7, 66
Bosnian crisis (1908–9) 107, 108
Brockdorff-Rantzau, Ulrich Count von,
  German ambassador in Copenhagen 44
Broqueville, Count Charles de, Belgian Prime
  Minister 160–1
Buchanan, Sir George, British ambassador to
  Russia 43, 184, 186, 187, 197, 200, 205n
Bucharest, Treaty of (August 1913) 59, 76
Buchholz, Dr, German historian 37
Bulgaria,
  neutrality 83, 87n, 95n, 249
  and proposed Balkan bloc 242, 243, 244–
  5, 247–8
  relations with Ottoman Empire 233, 234–
  5, 236, 238, 239, 240
  relations with Serbia 59, 61, 76, 244
Bülow, Bernhard Prince von 28–31, 39
Burns, John, British Cabinet minister 180,
  189, 191, 199
Butterfield, Herbert 2, 3

Cambon, Jules, French ambassador in
  Berlin 158, 160, 166
Cambon, Paul, French ambassador in
  London 155, 189–90, 195–6, 203n
  request for British support 132, 192–3
Capelle, Admiral von 52n
capitalism, as cause of war 6
Carol, King of Romania 248, 267n
Carson, Sir Edward 178
Cavid Bey, Ottoman Finance Minister 230,
  231, 237, 250, 254–5
  neutralist 234, 241, 244, 245, 247, 248,
  259
  opposition to German alliance 240–1,
  242
  resignation 257–8
Cemal Bey, Ottoman Navy Minister 232,
  235, 237, 248, 252, 253
  joins Enver 254, 255, 256–7, 259
  opposition to German alliance 240–1,
  242, 244, 245
Chambrun, Comte de, French First Secretary
  in Russia 125–6, 146n
China 214, 216
  German-leased territory in 214, 215, 218,
  219
Choshu clan, and Japanese army 209
Churchill, Winston, British First Lord of the
  Admiralty 178, 180, 191, 199
  on Belgium 156, 170n

and F. E. Smith 189
  on France 177
  on Germany 177
  on Japan 225–6
ciphers, safety of 126, 128, 146n
Claparède, Alfred de, Swiss ambassador to
  Berlin 41
Clémentel, Etienne 130, 132, 148n
Clerk, Sir G. R., British Foreign Office 185–
  6
Colloredo-Mannsfeld, Heironymus Count,
  Austro-Hungarian naval attaché Berlin 41
communications,
  radio 122, 123
  telegraph 129
Conrad von Hötzendorff, Baron Franz,
  Austrian Chief of Staff 16, 44
Cora, Giuliano, Italian *chargé d'affaires* 87n
Coulard-Descos, Leon, French minister in
  Belgrade 93n
Couyba, Senator, French Minister of Work
  and Social Affairs 134, 136
Crackanthorpe, D., British *chargé d'affaires* in
  Belgrade 75, 78, 81, 92n
Crewe, Marquess of, Secretary of State for
  India 180, 203n
*Crna Ruka see Ujedinjenje ili Smrt*
Crowe, Sir Eyre, British Foreign Office 186,
  200–1
Czernin, Otto Count 11

Dardanelles,
  closed 251–3, 265n
  German warships in 239, 240, 241–3,
    246
Davignon, M., Belgian Foreign Minister 160
de Bunsen, Sir Maurice, British ambassador in
  Vienna 182, 185
Dedijer, Vladimir, on Sarajevo 56
Delcassé, Théophile, French ambassador to St
  Petersburg 43
Denmark, neutrality of 44
Dernburg, Count von, German ambassador
  in Washington 223
Devonshire, 9th Duke of 178
d'Hestroy, Baron Gaiffier, Belgian Foreign
  Ministry 156
Dimitrijević, Colonel Dragutin ("Apis"),
  Serbian Military Intelligence 57, 58, 59, 60
disease, in Russia 113n
Djordje, Prince, of Serbia 63, 73
Djordjevic, Milan, Serbian minister 61, 66,
  89n
Doumergue, Gaston, French foreign
  minister 138, 141

Draškić, General Panta, adjutant to Crown
  Prince Alexander of Serbia 55
Dreibund crisis (1895) 223
Duruy, French military attaché to Bel-
  gium 155, 156

Egypt 239, 240, 246, 253, 255
Enver Paşa, Ottoman Minister of War 232,
  236, 259, 264n
  and Bulgaria 249
  and closure of Dardanelles 251–3
  and German alliance 237, 238–40, 241–2,
    243
  independent power of 245–6, 253
  invitation to German warships 239, 240,
    241–2, 243, 245–6
  overtures to Russia 263n
  war plans 256–7
Esher, Viscount 226

Falkenhayn, Erich von, Prussian war
  minister 32, 38
Ferdinand, King of Bulgaria 245, 248
Ferry, Abel, French under-secretary of
  State 47n, 127
Flotow, Hans von, German ambassador to
  Italy 32
Forgách, János Count, Austro-Hungarian
  minister in Belgrade 11, 12, 17
France,
  and Austrian ultimatum 74–5, 79, 93n,
    122
  and Belgian neutrality 139–40, 142, 190–
    3
  and Belgium 155–6
  decision-makers isolated 122–3
  *entente cordiale* with Britain 107
  fear of German dominance 47n, 145
  German demand for neutrality 135, 189
  Germany declares war on 140
  loan to Turkey 235
  military preparations 45, 54n, 105, 132–
    4, 143
  need for British support 121, 131–2, 133,
    137
  need for unity (*union sacrée*) 121, 123–4,
    130–1, 134–5, 136–8, 141–4
  popular opposition to war 123–4, 131,
    143
  relations with Serbia 20–1, 61, 70, 72
  Russian alliance 101, 107, 115n, 121–2,
    135–6
    cost of 144–5, 158, 166–7, 195–7
  and Russian mobilization orders 125–30,
    132

socialist party 123, 130–1, 136
view of German mobilization 132, 137
war must be defensive 121, 124, 132–3,
135–7, 140, 144–5
Yellow Book 167
Franckenstein, Georg Baron von 11
Franco-Prussian War (1870–1) 124
Franz Ferdinand, Archduke,
assassinated at Sarajevo 9, 48n, 55–7
character 61
plots against 56, 85n, 89n
Franz Joseph, Emperor of Austria-Hungary 21
French, General Sir John 179
Freycinet, de 167
Frobenius, Colonel 37
Funakoshi Mitsunojo, Baron, Japanese chargé
d'affaires in Berlin 218, 221

Gauthier, French Navy Minister 137–8
Genadiev, Bulgarian politician 249
Génie, French military attaché 155
George V, King of England 43, 71, 132, 187
Germany 6–8, 27
access to Black Sea 239, 241–2, 245, 246,
248, 251–4, 256–7
admission of responsibility 27–9
alliance with Austria-Hungary 18–19, 20,
21–3, 33, 109
alliance with Ottoman Empire 232, 234,
235, 236–45, 250–8
Bülow's criticism of 29–31
declares war on France 140
deliberate policy for European war 18–
19, 20–1, 35–6, 187
disregard for Austro-Hungarian
interests 21–3
domination of military leaders in 38–9,
48–9n
fear of Russian rearmament 33–4, 35, 36–
7, 45–6, 107, 186
leased territory in China 214, 215, 218,
219
military superiority 43, 44–5, 53–4n, 105
preparations for general war 19–20, 40–
1, 42, 197
pressure on Austria-Hungary 32–3, 36,
39, 40
and proposed Balkan bloc 244–5
prospect of war with Russia 33, 34–5, 36–
7, 40, 112
relations with Great Britain 34, 39, 40,
52n, 186–7
relations with Japan 215–16, 218, 219–
20, 223

supports Austria-Hungary against
Serbia 17–18, 37–8, 39, 40
timing of war 32, 33, 37, 40, 44–5, 158–9
ultimatum to Belgium 158–9, 163–5
view of Belgium 155, 156, 158, 172n,
191–2
view of Serbia's rôle 22, 23
view of war with France 32, 33, 35, 36,
37, 44, 194
Waldersee's view of timing 44–5
"war council" (1912) 40–1
warships to Dardanelles 239, 240, 241–3,
246
Gerschenkron, Alexander 98
Giers, M. M. N., Russian ambassador to
Turkey 247, 250, 257
Giesl, Baron Vladimir von, Austro-Hungarian
minister in Belgrade 15, 51n, 60, 67–8, 71
presents ultimatum 72–3, 81
Goltz, Field Marshal Baron Colmar von
der 27
on Turkey 42–3
Goremykin, I. L., Russian finance minister 111
Goschen, Sir Edward, British ambassador to
Berlin 31, 191
Great Britain 19, 20–1, 141, 200
alliance with Japan 213, 220
and Anglo-French entente 107, 197–200,
201–2, 205n
armed forces 105
and Belgian neutrality 139, 165, 173n,
188–9, 190–2
and Cabinet unity 141, 180, 188, 191,
192, 201–2
resignation threats 198–9
Conservative party 178, 180, 189, 208n
effect of German invasion of Belgium
on 165, 175–6
fear of German dominance 34, 41, 145
and French request for support 132, 176,
189–94, 195–7
and German demand for neutrality 31,
181, 186–7, 190–1, 204n, 206n
Labour party 180
and limits to Japanese intervention 216–
17, 219, 225–6
naval mission to Turkey 234–5, 252–3
naval superiority 41–2, 52n, 105
neutrality suggested 176
proposes international mediation 19, 39,
83, 187
reaction to Sarajevo 61, 87n
relations with Russia 101, 102, 115n,
184–8

request for Japanese naval assistance 213–15, 216–17
and Serbian request for support 75, 78, 83
ultimatum to Germany 202
warships for Turkey 234–5, 236, 240, 247
Greece,
  and Ottoman Empire 233, 234, 235
    alliance contemplated 235–6, 242
    threat of attack by 234, 238, 239, 240
  and proposed Balkan bloc 242, 243, 244, 248
  support for Serbia 59, 76, 78, 94$n$
Greene, Sir Conyngham, British ambassador to Japan 214, 217
Grenfell, Commander H. G., British naval attaché in Russia 117–18$n$
Grey, Sir Edward (British Foreign Secretary) 5, 175–7, 186, 201–2
  asks for Japanese naval assistance 209, 212–13, 217, 224, 225–6
    retracts 216–18
  and Austrian policy 183–4
  and Cabinet unity 141, 180, 188–9, 191, 194, 201–2
  French request for support 132, 141, 189–94, 198–9
  and German policy on Austria-Hungary 182–3, 187
  rejects German bid for British neutrality 191
  and Serbian request for support 75, 78
  and suggestion of French neutrality 194–7
Grigorovich, I. K., Russian Minister of the Marine 111
Gruić, Slavko, Serbian foreign ministry 64, 70–1, 81, 92$n$
Guchkov, Alexander, Russian Commission for State Defence 103
Guchkov family 100
Gwynne, H. A., *Morning Post* 203–4$n$

Habsburg Empire 7, 13
  *see also* Austria-Hungary
Hafiz Hakki Bey, Lt Col, Turkish staff officer 249, 253–4
Haldane mission (1912) 34
Haldane, Viscount, British Lord Chancellor 183, 194–5, 196, 204$n$
Halil Bey, Ottoman politician 231, 237, 250, 254, 257, 259, 266$n$
  and proposed Balkan bloc 244–5, 247, 248, 249
Harcourt, L., British Colonial Secretary 176–

7, 179–80, 189, 191
Hardinge, Sir Charles, British ambassador to Russia 109
Hartwig, Nikolai, Russian minister in Serbia 57, 60, 67–8, 87$n$
Hatzfeldt, German diplomat 32
Haymerle, Franz Freiherr von, Austro-Hungarian legation in Berlin 51$n$
Headlam-Morley, J. W. 186
Heinrich, Prince, brother of Kaiser 41
Heligoland 41, 42, 52$n$
Hennion, French Prefect of Police 131, 137
Henry, Prince of Prussia 187
Hewins, W. A. S. 208$n$
historiography 2–3
Hobhouse, C., British Postmaster-General 180
Holtzendorff, Admiral H. von 52$n$
Hoyos, Alexander Count 11, 12, 14, 36
  letter to Haldane 183, 204$n$
  mission (5 July 1914) 9, 17–18, 37
Hymans, Paul, Belgian Foreign Minister 174$n$

Ichiki Tokuro, Japanese Minister of Education 214
Ikeda, Professor K. 221–2
India 205$n$, 239–40
industrialization 6
Inoue Kaoru, Japanese Elder Statesman 217, 221
Inoue Katsunosuke, Japanese ambassador in London 217
intentionalist analysis of causes of war 2, 97–8
International Court at The Hague 82
Iran 233, 253
Islamic movement 239–40, 245, 248
Isvolsky, A. P., Russian ambassador to Paris 126, 135–6; Russian Foreign Minister (1906–10) 107–8
Italy 61
  neutrality 83, 132, 240
  and Serbian request for support 71, 75, 78, 79, 82

Jagow, Gottlieb von, German foreign secretary 36–7, 46, 191
  Bülow's view of 29, 30, 31
  responsibility for war 28, 29, 32
  support for Austria against Serbia 33, 67, 71
Japan 6
  and Austria-Hungary 220
  and British alliance 213, 220, 221, 224

China factor 222–3
declaration of war 215–17, 219–20
defence policy 209
Doshikai political party 211
and Germany 215–16, 218, 219–20, 221, 223
Grey's request for naval assistance 209, 212–13, 217, 224, 225–6
interest in Balkans 211–12
naval-military rivalry 209–11, 212, 221–2
no territorial limits to intervention 217, 218
perception of Russia as enemy 209–10
political instability 210–11
press and public opinion in 222
relations with United States 224–5
Seiyukai opposition party 210, 211
ultimatum to Germany 218, 219
view of war as limited 226–7
Jaurès, Jean, French Socialist leader 124–5, 130–1
Jeftanović, Gligorije, Bosnian Serb politician 62, 66, 89$n$
Jerram, Sir Martyn, British commander in chief, China Station 216
Joffre, General J. J. C., French Chief of Staff 133, 136, 139–40, 144
Joll, James 3–4, 10
Jordan, Sir John, British minister in Peking 216
Jovanović, Jovan, Serbian minister in Vienna 58, 61, 63–4, 71, 76
and Berchtold 65
on rejection of ultimatum 81
warning of dangers to Archduke 89$n$
Jovanović, Milutin, Serbian embassy in Berlin 65, 86$n$, 91$n$

Kanner, Heinrich, journalist 13
Kato Takaaki, Japanese Foreign Minister 211, 213, 219, 221
favours entry into war 214–15, 222
Katsura Taro, General, Japanese Minister-President 209, 210
Kiaochou, German-leased territory 218, 219
Kiel Canal, widening of 41–2, 51–2$n$
Klobukowski, A., French minister in Brussels 156, 157, 161, 164, 173$n$
Kokovtsov, V. N., Russian Finance Minister 104, 108, 110–11
Korea, annexed by Japan 210
Kosovo 55
Krivoshein, Alexander, Russian Minister of Agriculture 110–11
Kühlmann, Richard von, German diplomat in

London 47$n$, 156, 198

Laguiche, General Pierre Marquis de, French military attaché in Russia 125–6
Laguiche, Marchioness de 125, 126
Lalaing, Comte de, Belgian envoy in London 167
Lansdowne, 5th Marquis of 178, 199, 201
Lazarevic, Vasil, Belgrade chief of police 64–5
Le Peuple, Belgian socialist newspaper 162–3
Leopold III, King of the Belgians 151
Lerchenfeld, Count H. von, Bavarian envoy to Berlin 53
Leslie, John 10–11
Lichnowsky, Prince Karl Max von, German ambassador to Britain 28, 32, 49$n$, 186–7, 190, 192
British neutrality 196, 207$n$
and French neutrality 194–6
on Russian threat 182–4
Liège 152, 159, 163, 171$n$
Liman vin Sanders, General Otto, German military mission to Turkey 232, 246
Lloyd George, David, Chancellor of the Exchequer 175–7, 181–2, 200
and Cabinet unity 177–80, 181
proposal for coalition 180, 181, 204$n$
London, Treaty of (1839) 188
Loreburn, Lord 201
Lützow, Heinrich Graf von 12
Luxemburg, German invasion of 137, 156, 163, 179, 200
Lyncker, Moritz Freiherr von, head of German Military Cabinet 38

Macchio, Baron Karl von, Austro-Hungarian government 12, 65
MacDonald, J. Ramsay, British Labour Party leader 137, 176, 179
Macedonia 234
McKenna, R., British Home Secretary 178
Maggi company, Paris, attacks on 137
Magrini, Luciano, Italian journalist 73, 92$n$
Maklakov, N. A., Russian Minister of the Interior 111
Mallet, Sir Louis, British ambassador to Turkey 116$n$, 247, 250, 255, 265$n$
Margerie, Pierre de, French foreign office 122
Masterman, C. F. G., British Cabinet minister 178, 179, 180
Matsukata, Japanese Elder Statesman 215
Mensdorff, Count Albert von, Austrian ambassador to Britain 183, 205$n$

Messimy, Adolphe, French Minister of War 125, 133, 134

Metternich, Count Paul von, German ambassador to London 34

Mihajlović, Serbian *chargé d'affaires* in Rome 82

Mijusković, Lazar, Montenegrin minister in Belgrade 76, 78

Moltke, Helmuth Count von, Chief of German General Staff 17–18, 27, 29, 32, 40, 46, 155
  and King Albert of Belgium 44
  on timing of war 53n, 159, 160, 171n

Montagu, Edwin, British Financial Secretary 176

Montenegro 233
  relations with Serbia 59, 65–6, 76, 77–8

Morley, John (Lord Morley of Blackburn), Lord President of the Council 176, 178, 180, 192

Moroccan Crises,
  First (1905) 107
  Second (1911) 40, 108, 109

Müller, Admiral Georg A. von, head of German Naval Cabinet 38, 39

Murray, Arthur, parliamentary private secretary to Grey 194

Musulin, Alexander Baron von 11, 12, 14

*Narodna Odbrana*, Serbian propaganda society 77

Naumann, Viktor, German publicist 17, 36

Nicholas II, Tsar of Russia 47n, 84, 108, 112
  autocracy of 104, 109–11

Nicholas Nicholaevich, Grand Duke 103

Nicoll, Robertson, *British Weekly* 181

Nicolson, Sir Arthur, British Foreign Office 78, 182, 185, 186, 187, 207–8n
  and French request for support 193–4, 197–8

Nicolson, Harold 205n

Nikita, King of Montenegro 59, 76, 89n

Niš, Serbian government move to 77, 81, 83

Oka, General, Japanese war minister 211

Okuma Shigenobu, Count, Japanese prime minister 211, 214, 218, 222

Ottoman Empire 7, 61
  and Aegean Islands dispute 235, 236, 238, 242, 243, 244, 247–8
  alliance with Germany 235, 236–45, 259
  alliance with Greece contemplated 235–6, 242
  armed neutrality 238, 239, 241, 242–3, 247

  attempted alliance with Bulgaria 233, 234–5, 236, 237–8, 240, 241, 242, 249
  British naval mission 234–5, 252–3
  British-built warships 236, 240, 247
  decision for war 229, 258–60
  declaration of war (November 1914) 230, 258
  foreign policy 232–5, 259–60
  German loan to 254–5, 256
  German pressure for intervention 245, 250–8
  German warships
    in Black Sea 251–3, 256–7
    in Dardanelles 239, 240, 241–3, 246, 259
  lack of records of 229–30, 260
  leadership divided 248–51, 259
  nature of government 230–2, 259
  overtures to Entente Powers 235, 246–7, 249–50, 253–4, 258–9
  Pan-Islamic elements 231, 239
  plays for time 240, 241, 242–3, 250
  relations with Russia 233, 235, 237, 246
  relations with Serbia 59, 61, 70
  revisionist view of Balkans 234–5, 236
  Turkish nationalism 231
  Unionist party 229, 231, 232–4, 259–60

Oyama, General, Japanese army 210, 215

Paču, Lazar, Serbian minister of finance 72, 73, 82, 92n

Pakrac theological college 64, 67

Paléologue, Maurice, French ambassador to Russia 124, 167
  and Anglo-French accord (1912) 197–200
  and Russian mobilization orders 125–6, 127–30, 147n

Pallavicini, Count J., Austro-Hungarian ambassador to Turkey 61, 236, 238, 250

Pašić, Nikola, Serbian Prime Minister 57–9
  and Austrian ultimatum 74–6, 77–9, 81, 84
  and Austro-Hungarian *démarche* 63, 69–70, 71
  conciliatory conduct 63–4, 66–8, 83
  and press 62–3, 66, 67, 68
  reaction to Sarajevo murders 56–7, 59–60, 61

Pavlović, Colonel Živko 92

Pease, J. A., British Cabinet minister 180, 191, 204n

Persia 185

Petar Karadjordjević, King of Serbia 57–8

*Pijemont*, Serbian newspaper 55
Pirenne, Henri 161, 162
Poincaré, Raymond, French President,
  and assassination of Jaurès 130–1
  assessment of 144–5
  and French unity 121, 123–4, 130–1,
    134–5, 136–8, 141–2
  and military preparations 132–3
  need for British support 121, 132, 139–
    42
  and popular opposition to war 123–4
  relations with Russia 108, 124, 127, 144
  state visit to Russia (July 1914) 47*n*, 72,
    121–3
  on Viviani 123, 138
Pourtalès, Freidrich Graf von, German
  ambassador to St Petersburg 47*n*, 186
press,
  Austrian 62–3, 65
  Belgian 152, 157
  British 180–1
  French 131, 152
  influence of 62–3, 65, 88*n*
  Serbian 60, 62–3, 65
Princip, Gavrilo, assassin (Sarajevo) 62
Protić, Stojan, Serbian minister of the
  Interior 56, 60, 77

Rathenau, Walter 28
Rauchensteiner, Manfried 20–1
Rediger, A. F., Russian Minister of War 102,
  103–4
Refik Bey, Major, Turkish staff officer 249
Rex, Graf von, German ambassador to
  Japan 215, 218, 223
Ribot, A. F. J., and Franco-Russian alli-
  ance 167
Riddell, Lord, Newspaper Proprietors'
  Association 179, 180–1
Riezler, Kurt, personal assistant to Bethman
  Hollweg 33–4, 35
Ritter, von, Bavarian minister in Paris 122
Romania 61, 167, 233, 237
  blockade by 251, 253, 267*n*
  neutrality 240, 241, 242, 251
  and proposed Balkan bloc 242, 243, 244–
    5, 247–8
  support for Serbia 59, 70, 76, 78
Runciman, Walter, President of Board of
  Agriculture 178–9
Russia 19, 20–1, 47*n*, 111–12
  alliance with France 101, 107, 115*n*,
    121–2, 135–6, 144–5, 158, 196–7
  armed forces modernization 45, 102–6,
    115–16*n*, 117–18*n*

Black Sea ports attacked 230, 257–8
  economy 6, 98–102
  foreign policy 107–9
  industry 100, 103
  mobilization orders 112, 126–30, 146*n*,
    188, 200
  nature of Tsarist state 109–11
  negotiations with Bulgaria 248
  and Ottoman Empire 229, 233, 235, 237,
    246–7, 251
  relations with Britain 184–6
  relations with Germany 107–8, 112
  rôle of foreigners in 99, 100–1
  rôle of merchant class 99–100
  support for Serbs 40, 60–1, 68, 70, 83, 84
    advises concessions to Austria-
      Hungary 79–81
    in Balkan Wars 108, 110–11
    uncertain 59, 72, 75–6, 78–9
Russo-Japanese War (1904-5) 102, 209, 213
  effect on Russian military 102, 104, 105,
    106

Said Halim Paşa, Ottoman Grand Vizier and
  Foreign Minister 232, 233–4, 236, 257–8
  German alliance 237, 238, 240, 241–5
  neutral Balkan bloc 242–3, 244, 245
  and neutrality 245, 247, 248, 259
Salisbury, Robert Cecil, 3rd Marquess of 5
Samuel, Herbert (Viscount Samuel) 180,
  181, 199
San Giuliano, Aidi, Italian Foreign Minister 70, 71, 82
Sarajevo crisis 4, 5
  inquiry into murders 59–60, 64–5, 68–9,
    85*n*
Sato Aimaro, Japanese ambassador in
  Vienna 220
Satsuma clan, and Japanese navy 210
Sazonov, Sergei, Russian foreign
  minister 47*n*, 60–1, 66, 70, 87*n*
  need for British support 184–5, 205*n*
  reaction to Austrian ultimatum 79–80
  and relations with France 108, 128, 147*n*
  and relations with Germany 108
  suggests British mediation 83
  and visit of Poincaré 72
Schlieffen Plan 112, 158, 160
Schoen, Wilhelm von, German ambassador to
  Paris 47*n*, 122, 128, 135, 140
Scott, C. P., *Manchester Guardian* 180, 181
Selby, Sir Walford 201
Sembat, Marcel, French socialist 137
Serbia,
  appeal for international arbitration 82–3

defence of sovereignty 59, 66, 67, 73, 76
election campaign 58, 70, 72
fear of Austro-Hungarian interference 66, 67
military weakness 58–9, 60, 74
mobilization 74, 76–7, 82
nationalist activity in 55, 57, 64
official reaction to Sarajevo 60–1
Pakrac theological students 64, 67
Pan-Serbian aspirations 13, 58, 65–6, 70, 84
press reaction to Sarajevo 60, 61
relations with Austria-Hungary 57, 58, 60, 65
relations with Russia 57, 59, 60, 68, 233
request for Russian support 72, 73–4
support from Great Powers 71–2, 73, 75–6, 78–9, 81–3
tactlessness of diplomats 65–6, 90n
ultimatum from Austria-Hungary 73–81
and rejection 77, 79–80, 81, 83–4
*Vidovdan* celebrations 55, 60
Siemens scandal in Japan 210, 212
Simon, Sir John (Lord Simon) 178, 179, 180, 192, 199
Smith, F. E. (later Lord Birkenhead) 189, 199, 202n
Social Darwinism, German interpretation of 14
Solf, Wilhelm, German colonial secretary 47n
Souchon, Rear Admiral,
German fleet commander 239, 246, 251–3, 256–7
joins Ottoman navy 252, 264n
Spalajković, Miroslav, Serbian minister in Russia 60–1, 66, 70, 72, 84
anonymous statements 89n
and Russian advice to Serbia 79–81
Squitti, Baron N., Italian minister in Belgrade 94n
Stamfordham, Lord, private secretary to George V 43
states, sovereign, and inevitability of war 5
Steed, Henry Wickham, *Times* 70, 71, 91n
Stefanović, Dusan, Serbian minister of War 56, 59, 74, 76
Steiner, Zara 10
Stolypin, P. A., Russian Prime Minister 1906–1911 109, 110
Stone, Norman 10
Storck, von, Austrian *chargé d'affaires* in Belgrade 64, 67
Strandtmann, V. N., Russian *chargé d'affaires* in Belgrade 68, 73, 83

structural causes of war 2, 5–6, 97–8
Stumm, Wilhelm von,
responsibility for war 29, 31, 32
and ultimatum to Belgium 159
on war with Russia 33, 36, 37
Stürgkh, Count Karl, Austrian Prime Minister 14, 15
Sukhomlinov, General V. A., Russian Minister of War 104, 108, 110, 111
Szápáry, Friedrich Count, Austro-Hungarian ambassador in St Petersburg 11, 14
Szögyény-Marich, Count L., Austro-Hungarian ambassador to Berlin 17, 18
Taisho, Emperor of Japan 210
Talat Bey, Ottoman Interior Minister 231, 233–4, 235, 236, 247
and German alliance 237, 241, 242, 244
joins Enver 248–9, 254, 259
and proposed Balkan bloc 244–5, 247–8
Tangier incident (1905) 107
Tankosić, Major Vojin, Serbian nationalist 86n
Taylor, A. J. P. 2
*The Times* 70, 87n
Tirpitz, Admiral Alfred von 34, 35, 40–1, 52n, 159
Tisza, Count Istvan, Hungarian Prime Minister 13, 15, 67, 68, 69, 90n
Tittoni, T., Italian ambassador to France 123
Toshev, A., Bulgarian minister to Ottoman Empire 236, 240, 242, 244
Triple Alliance 153
see also Austria-Hungary; Germany; Italy
Triple Entente 153
see also France; Great Britain; Russia
Tschirschky und Bögendorff, Heinrich von, German ambassador to Vienna 13, 15, 17, 32, 33
Tsingtao, German-leased territory 214, 215, 219, 221, 222
Turkey see Ottoman Empire
Tyrrell, Sir William, private secretary to Grey 186–7, 201, 205n

*Ujedinjenje ili Smrt*, Serbian nationalist movement 55, 57, 58
United States of America 6, 209, 224–5
Urbas, Emanuel 11, 12

Venizelos, Eleutherios, Greek prime minister 78, 236
Vesnić, Serbian minister in Paris 74–5
Villiers, Sir Francis, British envoy in Brussels 162

Viviani, René, French Prime Minister 123, 134, 135, 138
    and Anglo-French co-operation 197
    on French reaction to Sarajevo 61
    and Russian mobilization 126–7, 128, 129
    state visit to Russia (July 1914) 47n, 122

Wagner, Hermenegild, German journalist 89n
Waldersee, Count Alfred von, German Quartermaster-General 44–5, 46
Wangenheim, H. von, German ambassador to Ottoman Empire 236–7, 238, 241–2, 243, 256
    and German loan 255
    and Ottoman procrastination 250, 251–2
    and proposed Balkan bloc 245
wars,
    general, causes 1–4
    inevitability of 4–5
Wedekind, Frank, German playwright 47n
Wedel, Count Botho von, German ambassador to Vienna (from 1916) 34–5
Wenninger, General von 39
Whitlock, Brand, American minister in Brussels 163–4

Wight, Martin 4
William, Crown Prince of Germany 29, 32, 33, 37, 43
William II, Emperor of Germany 29, 32, 38, 190
    and Belgian reaction 165
    chauvinism of 34, 35
    Potsdam meeting (1910) 108
    on prospect of war (1913) 42, 43, 44, 151
    telegram (31 July) 21–2
    "war council" (1912) 40–1
Williamson, Samuel 10, 69
Wilson, General Sir Henry 156, 197, 200
Wilson, Woodrow, US President 224
Wolff, Theodor 28, 32–4, 36–7

Yamagata, General, senior Japanese officer 209–10, 215, 221
Yamamoto Gombei, Admiral, Japanese prime minister 210–11
Yashiro Rokuro, Admiral, Japanese naval minister 211, 226
Yugoslavia, Serbian plans for unification 58

Zimmermann, Arthur, German foreign ministry 29, 37, 49n, 59, 87n, 182